Praise for *End Your Story, B* W9-CCS-821

"There are no fancy poses or intricate breathing techniques in
here, but this is the real deal. Such a beautiful teaching. So lucid
and clear. Let go of your imaginations about who you are and
what the world is, your 'story,' and discover your true nature. I
have known Jim for over 25 years now. We struggled together
toward clarity. He has done an excellent job of clearly stating
both the practice and the teaching, making it relevant to life
as we know it, and making it a fun, interesting read. I have no
hesitation in wholeheartedly recommending this work."

—ERICH SCHIFFMANN, yoga master and author of *Yoga:
The Spirit and Practice of Moving into Stillness*

"A powerful and wisdom-rich book that will help you reclaim
your greatest life."

—ROBIN SHARMA, author of the national bestsellers *The
Monk Who Sold His Ferrari* and *The Saint, the Surfer and the CEO*

"This is the book all seekers of spiritual awakening have been
waiting for. Jim takes the ageless spiritual truths from the East
and presents them in a practical, easily understood manner
from a Western perspective. This book will get you onto the
right path to spiritual fulfillment; it changed my life and will
change yours as well."

—BOB NOZIK, MD, professor emeritus,
University of California San Francisco Medical
Center, author of *Happy 4 Life: Here's How to Do It*

CH

"I love this book! It is for anyone who is serious about enlightenment and the freedom it brings. Through his own experience and wisdom, Jim Dreaver demystifies awakening and—using the simple tools he calls the practice and the teaching—makes its realization more tangible and reachable with every page. Profound and comprehensive, easily understandable, and down-to-earth practical, this manual may literally shorten a seeker's path by decades."

—MADHUKAR THOMPSON, author of
The Odyssey of Enlightenment

"Written in a simple, straightforward style, this book is a real gift to the world. I'd call it a primer for living."

—SUSAN CAMPBELL, PhD, author of
Getting Real and *Truth in Dating*

"Jim Dreaver is a brilliant thinker and writer. Steeped in rich personal experience, *End Your Story, Begin Your Life* makes complex and confusing Eastern concepts accessible to the Western mind. With extraordinary clarity and simplicity, this book takes us on a journey that leads to the fulfillment of our deepest hopes and longings."

—JOHN AMODEO, PhD, author of *The Authentic Heart*
and *Love and Betrayal*; coauthor of *Being Intimate*

"For many, life can feel like a skipping record—the same patterns repeating themselves over and over again, creating a narrative that limits our ability to truly live. *End Your Story, Begin Your Life* is overflowing with wisdom. Jim Dreaver's words are both inspiring and life-changing. This book offers a powerful yet simple path that leads from the prison of the mind to the expanded freedom that is possible in everyone."

—DARREN MAIN, author of
Yoga and the Path of the Urban Mystic

END
YOUR
STORY

BEGIN
YOUR
LIFE

WAKE UP, LET GO, LIVE FREE

JIM DREAVER

HAMPTON ROADS

This edition first published in 2011 by
Hampton Roads Publishing Company, Inc.
Charlottesville, VA 22906
www.hamptonroadspub.com

ISBN: 978-1-57174-659-7
Library of Congress Cataloging-in-Publication Data
is available on request.

Cover design by Jim Warner
Interior design by Frame25 Productions
Typeset in Goudy Old Style

Printed in the United States of America
QG
10 9 8 7 6 5 4 3 2 1

The paper used in this publication meets the minimum
requirements of the American National Standard for Information Sciences—Permanence of Paper for Printed Library
Materials Z39.48-1992 (R1997).

For Adam, with love.

And for his generation
and all the generations to come . . .

Whoever enters the Way without a guide will take a hundred years to travel a two-day journey.
—Rumi

Contents

A Vision

I have a vision: the world is at peace, at last. It is a dynamic, vibrant, and creative peace. All the countries of the world are like one big, happy family. Sure, they continue to bicker and squabble with one another, as families do, and they still have their own internal problems stemming from their economies, environmental challenges, and different social issues.

However, there is enough real consciousness throughout humanity to ensure cooperation and harmony between nations. Wars and terrorism have ended. Wealth is more evenly distributed, which means extreme poverty and hunger are now rare. Very few are oppressed or downtrodden.

People throughout the world have each other's best interests at heart. They care about, support, and cheer each other on. Competition takes the form of everyone encouraging others to be their best, and to excel at whatever they do. With so much love and goodwill in the air, peace really does prevail on earth.

So how did this happen? It is simple. Enough of us looked inward long enough to wake up to the wisdom, love, and freedom inside. We realized that the entire conceptual realm between our ears—all our personal, cultural, national, religious, and ethnic stories—was not fundamentally real.

We saw that the stories we tell ourselves and others appear and disappear, shift and change, and yet we, as the awareness or consciousness that notices and creates them, are ever-present, always here. We came to the realization, in other words, that there are no enemies, except those we fabricate in our own minds. This knowledge frees us from psychological and emotional suffering and is the source of our individual and collective peace, joy, and meaning.

This, then, is my vision. The book you hold in your hands is my plan for helping make it a reality. If the vision resonates with you, share it with others. Awakening to the truth of who and what we are is the most important task facing us. It always has been, only more so now than ever. Working together, we can change the world.

Introduction

The teaching and practice making up the heart of this book come directly out of my own experience as a seeker of truth. I was on a spiritual journey for twenty years, seeking enlightenment, or inner freedom.

Then, in the spring of 1995, my seeking came to an end when I finally realized my true nature. I have been at peace, free from conflict and suffering, ever since. The main elements of my own story, that of how I came to understand that I am not my story, are in this book.

However, I will relate one key anecdote now. Between September 2003 and the end of January 2004, I experienced a health crisis that literally turned my life upside down. I had three strokes, each worse than the last. The third landed me in the hospital for six days, spending four in intensive care. When I came out, I couldn't move the right side of my face, my right arm and hand were severely impaired, I walked with a limp on the right side, and I had difficulty thinking and speaking. It took me almost two years to recover.

Soon after the strokes, a few people who didn't know me well said things like, "Gosh, it must have been really scary for you," or "You must have been terrified." But the truth was, I wasn't afraid. After all, I had already realized my true nature. I knew myself as pure consciousness, that which was not born and does not die. When you live knowingly as the awareness you are, fear and other negative emotions cannot touch you for more than a moment. You just flow with whatever is happening.

As I see it, this is the litmus test of our freedom: how we deal with life's changes and challenges. The more unconscious and unaware we are, the more such challenges will cause us to spiral down into fear, unhappiness, depression, despair, suffering, and misery. The more conscious and aware we are, the more we discern the difference between real and imaginary challenges.

From this place of clarity and awareness of the present, we deal with whatever actual challenge may be confronting us, meeting it calmly and confidently, with wisdom and love. Whether we must deal with a relationship issue, a work problem, a financial struggle, a health crisis, an unfolding natural disaster, or a terrorist act in the making, we draw upon all the creative powers at our disposal to address it. We stay with it and respond to its call for as long we need to.

This is why I have written this book. If you absorb the teaching in these pages and learn to do these practices every time you experience emotional conflict, upset, or suffering, you will awaken to freedom, to the inner peace that does not depend on circumstances, much, much more quickly than I did. As an example of how this can happen, read Juliana Dahl's story at the beginning of chapter 1. A mother of four, she awakened to her true nature just three short years after we met.

The teaching itself is simple: while we are a storytelling people, the stories we tell come and go—they change— but we, in our essences, are always *here*. We, as the pure awareness that sees and knows, are still here, still looking through our eyes, sensing with our bodies, feeling with our hearts and guts. To realize we are that which is always present, and *not* the ever-changing thoughts or stories, is to be awake and free.

The practice, which is also simple, helps you embody the teaching and make it your own lived experience. I will describe the practice at the end of this introduction. The first time I witnessed it working for people was when I was teaching a workshop at the famed Esalen Institute. Esalen is an alternative education and retreat center devoted to the exploration of human potential, situated on California's rugged Big Sur coast.

On the third morning of a five-day workshop, one of the female participants came in and reported she had been to Esalen many times during the past few years, and she talked about a man on the staff with whom she had some personal issues. She had been trying to figure out a way to avoid him, but when she saw the man that morning, she suddenly remembered the practice I taught.

As soon as she became aware of her discomfort, she stopped and did something she had never tried before: she became very present with her experience of conflict. Then she looked inwardly at the story she was telling herself about this man, basically, "How can I avoid him?" She noticed it was just a *story*, a thought. In almost the same breath, she saw she was not the story, not any story. Rather, she was what *looked* at the story. She was the lucid, ever-present awareness *behind* the story.

When she saw this, a magical thing happened. As the story dissolved before her eyes, the emotional tension created by identifying with the story and wanting to avoid a confrontation also dissipated, and she felt freer, clearer, more *here*. She then went up to the man and had a totally fresh, new interaction with him.

Of course, she didn't become completely free after one moment of insight, but it was a beginning. It cracked an opening in the shell of her ego and all the stories holding it together. She experienced a glimpse, a taste, of the inner freedom which is her true nature.

Freedom is a powerful word. It is perhaps one of the most cherished words in the English language. Certainly it is so here in the United States, where we value our freedom more than anything. Yet what does it mean to be free?

On the level most people relate to the notion of freedom, they mean the ability to express themselves in whatever way they wish: to choose their work or careers, their friends, their politics, their religions, and where they live.

However, based on my life experience, I have a very different understanding of freedom. At its most vital level, it means being allowed to *be*, to be the beautiful, conscious person you are. It is to be *inwardly* free, not restricted or bound by any mental or emotional limitation, not subject to emotional reactivity. Being free means feeling relaxed, at peace, and open in each and every moment. This was the woman at Esalen's experience during her moment of awakening.

So, how do you get to this state of inner freedom, the freedom simply to *be*? The quickest path I know, and the subject of this book, is to undergo a shift in perception that leads directly to inner freedom. It is seeing, like the woman at Esalen, that you are *not* your story. You are not any story. You are not your psychological and emotional history, nor are you your self-image. You are not your cultural, ethnic, national, social, or religious story.

And what is a story? It is anything we think or tell ourselves or others to describe what has happened, is happening, or is going to happen. Some stories are true and some are fictional, but either way they are still just *stories*, a collection of words inside our heads.

Problems arise and our freedom is hindered when a story defines us, when we derive our identities, our senses of meaning from it, as in: *Things shouldn't be this way; That person is a bad person; I am totally alone, loved by no one; I was abandoned/abused as a child;* or *I fear God's judgment.*

All your stories, memories, and experiences have shaped your personality, but they are still only that: your *stories*. They may have been real once, or seemed real, but are definitely not real now. They are an illusory world existing between your ears, in the form of fleeting thoughts, beliefs, pictures, and ideas of "self," with corresponding feelings and emotions in your body.

When conflict or suffering arises or your buttons are pushed, it is because a person or an event, real or imagined, contradicts your views or expectations—your story—about the way things ought to be. You experience the conflict in your body as a disturbing feeling or emotion, whether anxiety, anger, fear, or something else.

However, the upsetting feelings and emotions only exist because of the stories feeding them, keeping them alive. And the stories, thoughts, and beliefs are always changing. They come and they go. When you are not holding onto any story in your mind, but are simply very aware and relaxed in the present, your emotional state is always one of ease, harmony, and flow. This is a very important point to understand if you are interested in finding true inner peace.

This is true freedom: to know this, to find your identity not in stories, not in your body, mind, or personality, but in the moment-by-moment flow of *being* itself. Then we feel inspired to write new, *conscious* stories for ourselves, stories that work by supporting our own and others' well-being. We begin to literally infuse our lives, relationships, and work with ever-new consciousness and the positive, creative stories flowing from it. As a result, our power to manifest what we truly need and want is greatly magnified, and living itself becomes a lot more fun.

This is an instructional manual on what may be the simplest and shortest way to the most liberating transformation we can undergo. Why do I say simplest and shortest? Because there is nothing you have to *do*, other than the practice, which involves simply being very alert and noticing when you are getting caught up in a story.

While other, more traditional practices like meditation, prayer, yoga, and emotional release work can all be beneficial to body, mind, and spirit (and I have done them all myself), you don't actually have to do any of them in order to find freedom. You don't even have to do good works to get free, although you will certainly do them as freedom becomes a reality for you.

All that is required for awakening to your true nature is to undergo this shift in perception, in the way you see and experience reality. You will make a shift from experiencing life from the limited point of view of me, myself, and my story, to seeing it from your wholeness. You will awaken to the expanded view of universal consciousness itself, the consciousness that is being expressed through you right now, in your uniquely individual personality.

Many people are still confused about awakening or enlightenment. They have many stories about it. One of the most common misconceptions is thinking of it as some kind of salvation or magical state of being, freeing one forever from life's problems and challenges. However, this is an idealized, mountaintop view. (For instance, there was nothing ideal about the strokes I had, although there were certainly gifts in the experience, as you will read at the end of the last chapter.)

Awakening needs to be brought down from the detached perspective of the mountaintop into the real world of the marketplace. It needs to work in the nitty-gritty of our relationships, work, and daily lives. After all, if the truth can't flourish here, where we all live, what good is it?

The world is in crisis, suffering the constant presence of terrorism, war, injustice, oppression, poverty, hunger, and disease. All this conflict exists because people's inner unease and insecurities are projected outwardly. Struggling for some sense of meaning and purpose in their lives, they identify with and cling to particular stories—whether cultural, religious, political, or personal—which are continually re-created by their minds.

Each story, of course, is shored up by a whole set of beliefs, judgments, and assumptions. The problem is that beliefs, by their nature, are divisive. When taken to extremes, they can result in a willingness to fight for, even kill and die for, what is so fervently believed.

More than ever, the world needs the healing that awakening brings. The key to embodying awakening lies in understanding that it is very much an inner, personal journey. You must be willing to face yourself honestly, to examine closely who and what you think you are. If you're not prepared to look deeply into this self you have imagined yourself to be, inner freedom will continue to elude you. You'll carry on believing whatever it is you are looking for—happiness, validation, approval, success, or freedom from self-doubt—lies somewhere outside yourself.

However, something else can help accelerate your quest for self-realization: guidance. This is why I chose the Rumi quote at the beginning of this book: "Whoever enters the Way without a guide will take a hundred years to travel a two-day journey."

You can awaken on your own, without a guide, but this is not so common and usually takes a long time. Clear, objective guidance from someone already awake speeds up your journey. It also ensures you receive accurate directions for beginning the process of self-inquiry and how to go deep with it when blocks or obstacles arise, as they will.

Throughout this book, I will be your guide. I will walk with you every step of the way and show you what you must both *do* and *know* in order to set yourself free in the shortest time possible.

I have already spoken of the *doing*. It is the practice. You must stop and pay attention to what is happening inside you whenever you are in conflict or are upset. Then you must be present with whatever you are experiencing, be it a feeling, an emotion, or an event, *without* any story. This is the key to the practice: learning to face your fears, your conflicts, your demons, without a story, without judgment, resistance, or mind games.

The practice requires openness and emotional vulnerability. It does not mean you become a doormat and allow people to walk over you. By all means, you will make changes where change is needed or desired. You retain the ability to say "No" to unwanted experiences. But inwardly, you resist nothing. Awakening is, above all, a state of psychological and emotional freedom. It is manifested as a nonresistance to life, an all-embracing ability to flow with life's ever-changing conditions and circumstances.

But to really unlock the secret of awakening (and to understand why it persists in remaining a secret in the minds of those who have not yet figured it out), there is something you have to *know*. This is the teaching.

Behind every negative emotion, every form of personal angst, there is some kind of story you are telling yourself. You have to see and recognize the story as just a *story*. It may or may not have some basis in reality, but it is only one way of seeing things, and it is not who or what you *are*.

Any story you hold on to in your mind, consciously or unconsciously, gets in the way of your ability to be present, to fully show up. Freedom lies in understanding what produces the story, what maintains resistance and perpetuates conflict, fear, and suffering within you. You need to see, from the perspective of the consciousness, the wholeness that is your true nature, through the very me itself. You need to see through the I, the ego, the *storyteller* who is forming the basis of your self-identity, the person you think you are.

The teaching is based on nondual wisdom. It is called nondual because ultimately, there is no difference between the spiritual and the material. It is all one reality. The nondual approach is also known as the direct path to awakening. It confronts the one obstacle to true inner freedom—the belief in the sense of I or me as having a real, separate existence apart from consciousness—and reveals it to be the illusion that it is.

The world between our ears—in other words, the world of I, me, and mine—is not real. It is a fabrication, a story we have spent a lifetime making up and believing. By inwardly examining our thoughts, beliefs, reactions, and ideas about ourselves, we begin to realize our personal stories are always changing.

The more we see this, the more the internal drama falls away. When we are simply present with our breathing, our bodies' sensations and feelings, and our immediate environment, the stories let go of *us*. We start to know ourselves *as* the pure, luminous awareness that sees and experiences reality here and now, including the stories we tell ourselves.

This knowledge may be somewhat intellectual at first, but gradually it becomes embodied. More and more frequently it becomes our lived experience, and manifests itself as a feeling of ease, flow, and relaxed yet alert presence. As our heads clear and our hearts open further, we awaken to the true beauty and meaning of life. The mind is then no longer a distraction, but a powerful ally. Our life purposes become clear, and love ultimately guides us in everything we do.

The following pages will support you in making the shift toward inner freedom. Much of the content is drawn from actual dialogues I've had with countless truth seekers, both privately and in workshops, over many years. In addition, I tell many stories to clarify my meaning, as well as offering short mini-meditations in each chapter.

Woven into each chapter is the entire, seamless, nondual approach to awakening, which states that realization is a matter of seeing you are neither your story nor your thoughts. You are the clear, ever-present consciousness that is aware of *everything*, including the contents of your mind. Throughout this book, I will emphasize this teaching and repeat it in many different ways, from many different angles, again and again. This is the way to have it sink into your mind and consciousness.

As you read these pages, it should become very clear what is involved in seeing through your own story and letting go of whatever beliefs, ideas, or concepts of self you may still be holding onto. The more you are able to simply be present and release all you inwardly hold on to (by seeing it is not real), the more you will find yourself relaxing into the awakened awareness that is your true nature.

Then, inner peace and freedom will occur more and more often, and periods of conflict, stress, and suffering will be fewer and shorter in duration. Increasingly, a heartfelt sense of love and gratitude for life will be your predominant emotional reality. Then, you can share the gift of awakening with others. You can share the new story you are creating for your life. In this way, our world will gradually be made whole.

Eventually, the day will come when you will pass through the final door of self-knowing. A profound and unshakeable sense of ease, presence, and beauty will then be yours.

The Practice of Freedom

The essence of this practice is learning to see and experience life as it is, in this very moment, free of any thoughts, concepts, beliefs, or stories. You are not projecting your own ideas or values upon what is. You are not trying to make it into what you wish or want it to be. You are not resisting it or wanting it to be different. You are just accepting it, flowing with it, and, if need be, dancing with the situation at hand, be it an internal feeling or an outer circumstance.

However, most people so heavily identify with their core stories that they really believe they are their stories, and when things are going well in their lives, they tend to become complacent. They usually show little interest in awakening to deeper levels of freedom. Hence the practice, below. Whether it is minor suffering, like irritation, boredom, or annoyance, or major, like the death of a loved one, a health crisis, or a financial loss, we use the suffering to initiate the practice. Personal suffering of any degree becomes our doorway to freedom.

Step 1: Be Present with Your Experience

Whenever upset, conflict, or struggle arises, something pushes your emotional buttons, or you find yourself challenged in some way, learn to be present with it, to allow it to be. Learn to pay attention to any disturbance in your body, in your energy field. Be with it. Don't avoid, deny, or resist it through rationalization or analysis.

Ask yourself: "What am I experiencing right now?" Then just be aware of whatever the contraction or disturbance is. Breathe, and feel it out, attune to the sensations. Eventually, you will learn to welcome such reactions. After all, they are showing you where you are not yet free.

If the experience of suffering is especially intense and proves too difficult to be with, then just handle it in the way you've always done, knowing that eventually, you will have to face it if you ever want to be free.

In the meantime, breathing deeply, slowly, and consciously is the best way to remain present in the face of intense emotion…

Step 2: Notice the Story

Behind every reactive emotion, whether it is stress, self-doubt, guilt, anger, envy, jealousy, loneliness, anxiety, depression, shame, or fear, there is almost always a story, belief, or thought. Notice the story you are telling yourself, keeping the emotion alive. It may be a story from the past triggering the reaction, or a fear of something in the future. Don't go into any new story, rationalization, or analysis. Just notice.

If it helps, you can say to yourself: "Oh, I'm getting caught up in a story again."

Step 3: See the Truth

Now take a deep, slow breath, and relax. Continue to be present with the feeling or sensation. Notice how the story, thought, or bodily sensation is always changing, shifting. It comes and it goes, appears and disappears, but you, as an aware being, are still very much here. Your thoughts are ever-changing, but you, as the background awareness, are ever-present.

Seeing this truth from the perspective of the clear, present-time awareness you are produces a shift in your energy. The emotional contraction will unwind, and you will feel more relaxed and at ease. You will feel more truly present, more centered and grounded. Then you see everything anew, and you can deal with what's in front of you from a place of confidence and strength. You use the power of thought consciously. You are able to communicate clearly, and create what you are passionate about.

As you master this practice, you will become freer, more present, and more in the flow more of the time. You will begin to know yourself as the awareness behind the story, the awareness that watches your body, mind, and personality. At some level, you begin to realize your true, fundamental nature is clear, vibrant, present-time consciousness itself.

Eventually, if you are really curious about your true nature, you will take the fourth and final step to awakening, the one that will completely and, for all intents and purposes, permanently free you.

What is the fourth step? It is to question this very me, this I you take yourself to be. With deep self-inquiry you will discover it is just a story, too—the storyteller. The I telling the story is no more real than any other thought. Even though it occupies center stage in your personal life, you cannot actually find the I or me thought anywhere in your mind.

At some point, it will dawn on you that your true nature is the beautiful, timeless consciousness behind everything. As consciousness, you are the source of everything you experience in your life, including the I thought, the ego itself, and the many stories you tell. To know this, and then to embody the knowledge, is to be free.

Step 1: Be Present with Your Experience

THE FIRST PERSON TO ASK me to be her teacher was Juliana Dahl, the mother of four children, the youngest of whom was still in high school when we met. For the next year, we spoke twice a month on the phone, as she lived in Boulder, Colorado, and I was in Northern California. Then, in 2006, I started traveling to Boulder to teach a series of workshops in her home. Here, in her words, is her story:

> I first got a taste of enlightenment in November of 1991 while living in Saudi Arabia. During a healing session, my Kundalini energy uncoiled at the base of my spine. It shot through my crown chakra and united me with all things as oneness. It was definitely a unitive experience. I felt everything surrounding me as part of me, and I, part of it. It was very blissful and ecstatic, and because the energy shot through my sexual chakra on its way up to the crown, I also had huge waves of sexual

energy running through me. It is how I would imagine making love with the divine would be. I was in a euphoric state for days, and for six months after this opening, I would swoon in ecstasy when I gazed in the eyes of the person I was with whenever this occurred.

This experience changed my life, because from that moment on, anything in my life that was not in total integrity would fall away. After about a year, I returned to my ordinary way of being, with suffering and hardships meeting me daily, but this Kundalini awakening definitely put me on my spiritual journey. I wanted to discover as much as I could about regaining the feeling of unity consciousness and the freedom I had experienced.

It was not until January of 2004, while I was presenting a workshop on female sexuality at the Sacred Sexuality, Enlightenment, and Shamanism Conference in Santa Fe, that I met Jim. The subject of his talk was "Why Enlightenment Matters." I was drawn to attend his presentation and sat right in the front row, and knew immediately I wanted him to be my teacher. I also understood for the first time that it was not necessary to wait lifetimes to wake up. He let me know we just needed a burning desire for freedom and a fundamental shift in perception, and liberation could be ours.

During the year I studied with him, I could gradually feel the veils of illusion dropping away. Every time I experienced suffering, I would use the simple practice he taught me, the practice that is the foundation of his work. My energy would shift, and I would feel freer and more present.

I loved the clarity and depth of his teaching style, and we soon became good friends. I gathered a group of friends in Boulder to hear Jim's teaching. He returned several different times to teach in Boulder, where I hosted him. As my relationship with Jim continued over the next two years, I realized I was getting closer and closer to the freedom I wanted to live.

During the summer of 2008, Jim was teaching a workshop at my home. That Saturday evening, he and I were driving out to dinner. On the way, he said to me, "I'm really happy with your progress of the path of awakening, Juliana. You really do see that everything between your ears is an illusion . . . well, almost everything. You're still identified with one story."

I actually pulled the car over to the side of the road when he said that. I knew exactly what he was talking about. I'd been holding onto a judgment about a former roommate. I felt she had interfered in my relationship with my then-boyfriend, so I had asked her to move out, and I hadn't forgiven her. I said to Jim, "My God, you are right . . . I see now that that, too, is just a story!"

This realization just hastened my resolve to awaken fully, and I decided I did not want to wait any longer. I could feel that I was ready to make the permanent shift. The actual moment of awakening happened the very next day, June 1.

What happened was that he invited me to sit in presence with him. He asked me to go deep inside and see what there was that was keeping me from being totally free. As I shut my eyes, I saw several different stories I had bought into as reality for so many years, and which had caused me many hours, days, and weeks of pain and suffering. Each one I was able to release as I knew these scenarios were not who I was.

Then Jim asked, "Is there anything else which is keeping you from being fully awake and free?" I closed my eyes. This time I saw pure black void. I heard the words, "You are empty, there is nothing else . . . You are free."

When I opened my eyes, I knew I had fully awakened to my true nature as pure consciousness, and knew I could experience the bliss and freedom I had only tasted seventeen years ago all the time. Studying with Jim for these three years really focused my burning desire to have freedom, and his clarity, wisdom, and strong presence—and unwavering love and support—helped launch me back into what I have always been: "pure awareness, expressing through this body, mind, and personality known as Juliana."

I spoke on the phone with Juliana recently, almost a year after she awakened. She is living in Aspen now, enjoying the timeless peace, bliss, and fun of being free, working with her sacred sexuality clients, doing massage, teaching yoga, and sharing the message of awakening with those who are open to it.

Awakening to What We Are

Our true nature cannot be expressed in words. However, consciousness, awareness, beingness, and presence are some words that come closest to defining what we are, here, right now. We always start from this moment now, from the present.

So, what can be said to be real right now is that you are alive, present, and reading this book. What is real now is your existence. You are *conscious* of existing, of being alive. Your true nature *is* consciousness itself. It is the one thing always present, whether you are asleep or awake, and whether you are aware of it or not.

What you are in your essence is the lucid, unchanging consciousness giving birth to everything in the world of the senses, including all your thoughts, stories, and memories, and to your body, mind, and this unique personality called "you." To understand this is to grasp the literal meaning of the words attributed to St. Francis: "What we are looking for is what is looking." You become aware of yourself, your true nature, *as* consciousness, awareness, or presence itself.

Now, most people are not aware of this. They tend to live as if in a dream—a dream which sometimes turns into a nightmare. They take their ego and their thoughts—the personal self and its many stories—to be real; are caught in habitual patterns of conflict, self-doubt, and worry; and have only occasional glimpses of the timeless beauty and mystery of existence.

The goal of spiritual or transformational work is to wake up from the dream. It is to break free of the internal dialogue. It is to see through the mind-created illusion of me, myself, and my story, the imaginary world you have created between your ears, making you feel separate and apart from others.

These stories, memories, and experiences have shaped your personality, but they are still only your *stories*. They may have been real once, but are definitely not real now. They are an imaginary world existing inside your head, in the form of fleeting thoughts, beliefs, pictures, and ideas of self, with corresponding feelings and emotions in your body. And they are always changing, always coming and going; yet *you*, as the awareness that sees them and experiences them, are always here.

Every time you see the truth of this, your head clears, your body relaxes, your heart opens, and you experience a release from inner conflict, stress, and suffering. You become, in a word, *present*.

Awakening itself is realizing you are not your stories, not your thoughts, but the consciousness in which stories and thoughts—in which all existence—arises. You are not an object, a human being in space and time who has only intermittent glimpses of consciousness, the source of creation. You are not a wave, occasionally remembering your connection to the ocean. Rather, you are consciousness itself, viewing all of creation through the eyes of this human being called you. You are the ocean itself, manifested in this individual human wave form.

As this realization occurs, you find yourself connected to an inexhaustible source of wisdom, love, and inner joy. Instead of living out of some myth or story about who you are and what life means, you live in awareness in the present. Meaning and identity no longer depend on beliefs, stories, or circumstances, but flow directly out of the beauty and dynamism of the life force itself. They arise from the sense of oneness, from the intimacy you feel with life—from the fullness and fragrance of *being* itself. You live in a state of openness, of welcoming everything that comes into your awareness.

With this awakening to the truth of being, the incessant chatter of the mind no longer dominates your consciousness. Your inner state becomes one of clarity and ease—at times, radiantly so. You become aware of a deep, vast silence, a universal spaciousness without center and without borders. You feel yourself to be one with that silence.

From within this inner silence you use thinking—including the I thought—for the extraordinary creative tool it is, but there is no attachment to thinking itself, nor to the concepts I, me, and mine.

Whenever you use these personal pronouns, you are clear you are speaking as impersonal consciousness expressed through your personal form. You use them in a functional way, free of personal ownership, pride, or emotional reactivity. Because of this openness and freedom from ego, from attachment to the personal perspective, living becomes much more effortless. Regardless of what is occurring, each day has a quality of magic and adventure to it.

Contrast this with your experience when you have not yet awakened to truth. Whenever you say "I" or "me," there is a very definite identification with the personal, with the ego self—with some kind of story, judgment, expectation, assumption, or agenda. You often feel divided, as in: "A part of me feels *this* way, and yet another part of me feels *that* way."

There may be glimpses, but there is no abiding awareness of being one with the totality of consciousness. Instead, separation, isolation, and a feeling of aloneness, even meaninglessness, is the prevailing experience. This personal identification with your story, with who you think you are, triggers self-doubt, stress, worry, and fear. It perpetuates the experience of conflict and suffering.

Awakening, as will become clear, means freedom from conflict and suffering. This is the promise of the inner quest. It doesn't matter what your circumstances are, or where in this world you live—inner freedom can be yours, simply because it *is* your true nature.

The feeling-tone associated with being established in pure consciousness is one of relaxed ease, harmony, and presence, of openness and welcoming, of gratitude and appreciation. It is one of feeling the energy of being alive in your body. Thoughts may or may not be present, but you are not identified with them. There is no you in the way. There is just the flow of being, that which in Zen is called the "suchness" of life, and you are one with the suchness. Everything then happens out of oneness.

Truly, to know yourself as consciousness, and then to embody the knowing, is the greatest blessing.

See if you can feel it, your true nature, right now. Just be very present, very aware of all that is . . . Then let the awareness that you are permeate your body . . . Notice how your breath flows in and flows out in the awareness you are . . . Then notice how sensations arise and fall in your body . . . How thoughts, images, and stories come and go in your mind . . . Be aware of yourself as the awareness, the consciousness, which is aware of all this . . .

Getting Our Stories in Perspective

Many people have a problem and go into resistance when I say that they are not their stories. After all, they so identify with their stories. In fact, the history of humanity is one vast interwoven story. The theologian Anne Foerst described us as a storytelling people—*Homo narrandus*. There are as many stories as there are people, and it is natural and human to share our stories with each other.

A story is simply anything we think or believe or tell to others to explain what has happened, is happening, or is going to happen in our lives. This is how we derive a sense of meaning and purpose in our lives, until we tap into a deeper level of being and no longer depend on any story for our identity.

There are stories of need and desire, abundance and lack, contentment and dissatisfaction, success and failure, justice and chaos, wealth and poverty, health and disease, hope and despair. Sometimes our stories are mundane and ordinary, sometimes they are fun and even exciting or inspiring, and sometimes they are painful or sad. Stories or parables also serve as teaching devices. We learn from them. We use them as teaching tools to illustrate certain lessons. But whatever emotions they evoke or lessons they teach us, our stories are not who or what we are. They are only *expressions* of who we are.

Those who are in the process of awakening to truth and inner freedom understand this at some level. They learn from the story, but they don't get lost in the drama of it. Instead, they derive their identities from simply being alert and present in each moment, from the flow of energy and fullness being felt right now.

However, most people still identify with some kind of story at the personal, self-defining level. The attachment to these stories creates the emotional experience of either heaven or hell, or something in between the two, in our bodies, minds, and hearts. Strong emotions are always the result of being identified by a story. When we are simply present as the awareness we are, not identified with any story, our emotional state is always one of ease, harmony, and flow.

Until we go through this shift in identity, and as long as we don't know ourselves at the level of pure, primordial consciousness, we are doomed to a life of uncertainty, anxiety, and suffering.

Suffering is the personal response, through the creation of a story in one's mind, to pain or unwanted experience. For suffering to arise, there has to be someone—a person, an I or a me—who suffers. People always have a story around their suffering. To put it another way, pain plus a story equals suffering.

However, as you become inwardly freer, pain or unwanted experiences are just that—pain or unwanted experiences. You may initially get upset about an event, but you remember who and what you are—pure consciousness, being expressed in this body, mind, and personality called you—and you just deal with it. You do not create a story around it—or, if you do, it is a functional, factual story. It is a story that describes what actually happened or is happening.

Almost all the human suffering in the world is due to identification with a story of some kind—from people taking their stories to be reality. It may be a personal story of abandonment, loneliness, guilt, or fear. It may be a story of power and control. It may be due to a state-imposed religious story with its own harsh or restrictive edicts and subsequent denial of human rights. It may be a self-imposed religious story with a whole set of beliefs and dogmas, which you then feel compelled to embrace.

The more entrenched you are in your own story, your own version of truth, the more you will likely resist what I am sharing. Whether it's some personal story of insecurity, pride, or fear, a cultural story causing you to be identified by a particular ethnic group or custom, or one of the many religious stories that have always been promoted as the truth and the way to humankind, you will tend to cling even more tightly to it. A lot of fear can come up as you contemplate letting go of a story, any story, by which you have previously been identified.

In my work, people sometimes ask me, "But who or what am I *without* my story?" When you know the answer to that question, know it in the depths of your being, then you will be free, and your search for yourself will be over. It is my intention to guide you gently and skillfully toward the answer, but I can tell you this right now: you will find it on virtually every page of this book.

Welcome Your Experience

A lot of people have trouble welcoming very unpleasant experiences. That is natural; yet if you are truly committed to awakening, eventually you will learn the subtle art of welcoming.

For now, it is enough to simply be present with what you are feeling or experiencing. In time, as you become freer from all that binds you, welcoming will be easier. In fact, you begin to develop an attitude of "Bring it on!" You want to see where you still get caught in suffering or reaction, because you want to be free of those demons.

You have to accept, and ultimately welcome, whatever arises within your experience. After all, it is what *is*. It is reality, and as the spiritual teacher Byron Katie says, when you argue with reality, you always lose. But when you accept what is, then you are in harmony with it, and you can work to change it, heal it, or fix it.

Until awakening begins to become a reality, most people have difficulty being fully present, especially without an agenda. They invariably require an agenda, which may be a shared interest, a personal or business meeting with a particular focus, or some kind of gathering for a specific purpose.

In this work, you are using your own suffering as an agenda for being present. You are not denying it, you are not trying to avoid it or escape it. You are not trying to rationalize it or understand it through some form of analysis. You are facing it head-on by accepting it, and even, as I said, welcoming it.

Now, you may immediately realize the totality of the situation. You may notice the story you are telling yourself that is triggering the upset, and you may grasp, even affirm to yourself, "I am *not* my story." This may produce a shift. Suddenly you are fully present, no longer caught up in any self-identifying story. You may have a glimpse of your true nature, of what you *are*. You are the consciousness that is aware.

But for many of you, the shift in identity will be brief and you will revert again to getting caught up in your story. But at least now you know. You've had an "Ah-ha!" moment. You've tasted the truth of your being.

Keep persisting with the practice of alert presence, and I promise you it will get easier. You'll have more and more awakened or enlightened moments. The body has a cellular memory of wholeness and ease. It remembers its natural state. When you are in the state of wholeness, it's almost like the cells are saying, "Ah, this is how I'm *supposed* to feel." Then life itself will feel smoother, more harmonious, more flowing.

The idea of welcoming as being true acceptance played a vital role in my own awakening. The more I was willing to acknowledge I *wasn't* free, I was still in conflict or suffering, the closer I found myself moving toward true freedom. And the single most powerful mantra (a word or phrase which leads to freedom) precipitating my awakening, and which I used whenever I was conflicted, was this: "Ah, I welcome this experience. It is showing me where I am not yet free."

In other words, you've got to befriend your upsets, demons, and negative emotions. You have to stop running from them and turn to face them. This contradicts our learned tendency, which is to live in resistance and denial. The power of adopting a truly welcoming attitude indicates your acceptance of where you are right now. You may not like it, but you accept it. Acceptance, in turn, brings an immediate relaxation, an ease of being, and an allowing, which may then open the door for the shift in perception called awakening.

Jean Klein, the man who played the role of my spiritual guide or teacher, and whom I first met in 1984, talked about the importance of welcoming. "Welcome your experience," he used to say.

After all, openness, acceptance, and surrender to what is create a surer path to freedom than resistance and struggle. You must sink deep within yourself to find out who and what you are, and you cannot do so if you are fighting with what is or are struggling against your situation in any way.

Born in Europe, Jean studied music in Vienna, fought in the French resistance during the Second World War, and became a naturopathic physician. But he always had a passionate interest in truth, in a way of living free of the materialistic addiction sweeping Europe after the war. As a result, he spent a number of years in India studying with several spiritual masters.

In time, he became a master in his own right, a skilled exponent of Advaita Vedanta. This is the enlightenment tradition known as the direct path or the nondual path, because it points directly to consciousness, to the one energy that is our true nature.

Jean was an urbane, cultured, and intellectually sophisticated man. Even though he was in some ways detached from the normal hurly-burly of the marketplace and had more of a mountaintop teacher's style about him, he was still in the world. He wasn't a white-robed, celibate, ascetic teacher completely withdrawn from everyday life. He enjoyed the finer things in life. While he could sometimes be aloof, he remained one of us, and he always emphasized the simple but profound truth of awakening: the terms "teacher" and "student" are only a device. When you realize you are, in your essence, the same beautiful person you took your teacher to be, you will be free.

Soon after I met him, I had a private session with him. With all the eagerness of a true seeker, I told him that I felt I needed to divorce my wife, who didn't support my spiritual practice, leave my son, close my chiropractic practice, and go live in a retreat somewhere where I could meditate for long hours every day, and really focus my energy on the quest for enlightenment.

He looked at me for a few moments, his clear blue eyes sparkling and twinkling. (He probably thought to himself, "What on earth is this poor man thinking?") Then he smiled, and said in his thick European accent, "Don't change anything in your life. Just be who you are. You are beautiful as you are."

Instantly, I relaxed. Later, I realized I had received a transmission, an infusion of energy from the light and warmth in his eyes. Nobody had ever told me I was beautiful as I was. I always thought I wasn't good enough. That was the moment when I began to accept myself, warts and all.

Another contribution Jean made to my understanding was the practice of stepping back with my awareness and experiencing myself as the space in which my body appears, in which breathing happens, in which my personality, with its sensations, feelings, and thoughts arise.

Doing this practice whenever I was anxious or stressed gave me a sense of detached presence. By "detached presence," I mean I would still feel the upsetting emotion, and yet I would at the same time have a sense of freedom from it, and the glimmerings of the realization that my true nature *was* this freedom, this spacious awareness, and not the emotion, or the story which was fueling it.

The focus on awakening to freedom is integral to the whole nondual approach. Become established in the openness of your true nature and then live your understanding every day. Continue with the lifelong work of becoming a more compassionate and loving human being. But if you have a story about awakening as being a living exemplar of selfless love—as many people are wont to—then you are unlikely to ever get there. You will forever fall short of your own unrealistic standards.

Awakening is waiting for every single one of us, precisely because it *is* our true, inner nature. Being awake doesn't make you better or smarter than anyone else. It doesn't make you superior. All it does is set you free. It frees you from conflict, worry, and fear, and brings you back to the deep inner peace and fulfillment, the innocence and openness of mind and heart, that you once knew when you were very, very young. Except now, you have the wisdom, maturity, and life experience of adulthood to serve as a protective container for this new way of seeing and being in the world.

The more of us who find the inner peace which comes with awakening to who and what we are underneath all our beliefs, myths, and stories, the more we will see peace in our world. Then our children can grow up in an atmosphere of love and caring, rather than fear and uncertainty. Then we can come together as a global community to solve the many social and economic problems facing us.

What better or more selfless motive for awakening, for enlightenment, could there be than this?

No Resistance, No Suffering

You have to be particularly alert when your story is active, or when the I thought is occupying center stage in your consciousness. The quality of witnessing presence may be enough to stop the thoughts in their tracks.

You will begin seeing that the I thought is not who you are. After all, you can observe the I thought; you can witness the machinations of your own mind. You can watch the story you tell yourself, watch it unfold. Therefore, you can't *be* the story. You can't be the I. You are whatever is watching. You are whatever is looking, witnessing. This is the teaching in action, seeing you are *not* your story. This in itself can bring the moment of realization.

Awakening is coming to the same realization the Buddha did: there is no independent self. This psychological and emotional entity we take ourselves to be doesn't actually exist, except as an idea, a story, a fictional creation between our ears.

Due to our conditioning, the cultural and social myths we were raised with, we grow up convinced there is, indeed, a separate, special us living inside these bodies of ours. There is a me inside this body that came from somewhere prior to birth, and that will go somewhere after death. We believe this so firmly that this me, this ego, actually feels real. The idea of letting go of it feels scary, indeed. When loneliness, depression, or unhappiness in any form strikes us, we certainly feel it—which just reinforces the idea there is someone inside this body/ mind suffering.

Awakening reveals that the suffering only happens precisely because we are so *identified* with our body, mind, and senses. We identify with our ego, with the concept of me, and with all the stories that shore it up.

When we see that this me we have taken ourselves to be is just an idea we have been buying into, a story we have been telling ourselves repeatedly all these years, all thoughts about being a unique, separate, special someone dissolve, and suffering drops away. There is literally no person to suffer.

We return to our natural state, to our true identity as pure consciousness. We are no longer holding onto any image of ourselves or of the way things should be, so there is nothing in us to resist the flow of life.

The teaching and the practice are the tools you will use whenever you find yourself in a state of conflict, upset, worry, or suffering. They will help you get clear. They will enable you to move your energy quickly and efficiently whenever you feel uncomfortable, stressed, or anxious. They will empower you to shift your state of consciousness from one of contraction into one of expansion and ease.

Eventually, as you work with the teaching and the practice, they will become one. They will become second nature, like breathing, moving, sensing, and feeling. When the teaching and the practice become one, you will find yourself at the doorway to true inner freedom. You may not be completely free, but you will realize you are free enough, and that most of your worry and fear stories have left you. The inner dialogue will wind itself down, and you will simply be more present. You will be a person pretty much at peace with yourself.

Self-doubt, personal conflict, and suffering will rarely visit you anymore. When they do, you will quickly notice yourself getting caught up in conflict, in some story you are telling yourself. Then you do the practice. Use the welcoming mantra: "Ah, I welcome this situation. It is showing me where I am not yet free." Notice the story, and the very noticing will be your key to come back to a heightened awareness, to alertness and openness in the present moment.

To Be Present Is to Live in the Now

How do you know when you are present? When there are no stories or thoughts distracting you, so that your mind is clear and your attention is fully, alertly here—right here, right now—then you are present. Your body feels relaxed. You're like a perfectly spinning top, humming in place without the slightest wobble, but with a consciousness very attuned to what is going on within and around you. You're totally in the flow of the moment, awake and sensitive to all that is . . .

Be like that top now. Try stepping back behind yourself with your awareness . . . Step back out of the story, away from the contents of your mind . . . Then visualize yourself as empty space on the inside . . . Vast, empty space, yet containing whole worlds, including the world of your body, mind, and personality, as well as all thoughts, your stories . . . You are this very clear awareness, simply present with it all . . . Get the sense of being this, this humming presence, this all-knowing consciousness . . . Then open your eyes, and be the awareness which you are . . .

I remember taking a hike in the hills above Santa Rosa one day, many years ago, with my friend, Erich Schiffmann, a yoga master from whom I first heard the spinning top analogy. We were talking about yoga and other approaches to transformation, and what the real goal was when a teacher worked with students.

He said, "I think whatever gets them into the now moment is what it's about."

Erich's words were right on. They were a pithy yet potent Zen—or in his case, yogic teaching. The path of awakening is all about being in the now moment. It is about discovering that only the now exists, that time is an arbitrary mental construct. While functional time is the natural evolution and expansion of creation, it is still arbitrary. After all, we devised the clock. We made the decision to divide a day into twenty-four hours, an hour into sixty minutes, and so on.

Then there is psychological time, the ego, the me living in its story, in its memories of the past and its thoughts about the future. The me struggles to be present, but it is haunted by the past and either lives in fear of the future or clings to the hope of the future providing the happiness and fulfillment lacking in the now. Underneath hope, lurking somewhere deep within the psyche, is the fear of the future not turning out well after all.

People often ask me, "But what about making plans?" Planning is a function of the mind, and when you need to make plans, you make plans. But then when you have finished planning, you always come back to being aware in the present.

So long as we take ourselves to be a separate psychological/emotional entity, so long as we remain identified with and attached to this world between our ears called me, myself, and my story, we live in constant insecurity. Underneath all insecurity is fear. We are afraid of unwanted outcomes, of being alone, of becoming sick and helpless, and ultimately, of dying. The fear of death is not even so much a fear of the body dying, but of what happens to me—the person I think I am inside my body—when the body dies.

In Advaita Vedanta, this identification with self and story is called *avidya*, or ignorance. Ignorance is the fundamental error, the first mistake, the original sin. It is the equivalent of the Biblical story of the fall from grace, where Adam and Eve ate of the fruit of the tree of knowledge of good and evil—knowledge being a metaphor for self knowledge. When Adam and Eve started identifying with their personal sense of self and judging themselves, all their troubles began.

In the same way, we, through ignorance of our essential nature, are the creators of our own insecurity, fear, and suffering. For example, most people are afraid of death and of what happens to *them*, the me, when they die.

None of us can know for sure, but we can get a clear, intuitive sense of what happens. However, in order to do so, you must first find out who this person is that you take yourself to be. It means asking one of the most profound and liberating questions you can ever ask yourself: "If I can observe a thought, even the I or me thought, then I cannot be the thought. Who or what is observing, then? Who or what am I?" In time, if it is not becoming clear to you already, you will realize the inner voice asking these questions is itself another thought, another concept. You will realize that who and what you are is the awareness that notices and witnesses everything, including the arising of the I thought. In other words, your true fundamental nature is pure, silent awareness, expressing itself through this body/mind/self called "you."

To realize your true nature is to step through the door marked "Enlightenment." It is to liberate yourself from the thought-based world inside your head. It is to discover there is only the present, this moment now. The past is a memory, and the future is simply the present expanding. And the key to discovering this is awareness or presence itself. Being supremely present and open to all of existence brings you fully into this moment, where all of creation is happening. Everything is taking place right here, right now. This moment now is reality.

Understanding this is the secret of time management. People who worry about time, who feel stressed because they feel they are running out of time, tend to live in their heads. Most of their thoughts are about the future and how they have so much to do and so little time.

But when you see you are not your story, not your thoughts, but are the awareness behind them, then you live in the present, in the timeless zone, as I call it. Then you have an abundance of time. No matter what your watch or the clock says, the time is always *now*. You come to realize every moment is new. It is very liberating.

A seeker once asked this question of me: "I remember when I was in high school, I had a job working in a salad factory, where it was freezing. It was a windowless room with fluorescent lighting. It felt like a true hell to me. The only thing keeping me going was watching the clock and wishing my day away, knowing at four thirty I could get out of there. Isn't it only natural to hate such an environment and be glad when you can get out of it? How can you be focused on the now when you are trying to cope with a horrible now, and daydreams and fantasy are able to take you away from it?"

It is natural to dislike where we are presently when we are not yet free. This is the unawakened human conditioning, and it is called suffering. The problem is not the now. It is this I, this me, this person you take yourself to be who is unhappy, who fondly remembers the good old days, can't stand what's currently happening, and watches the clock or the calendar, dreaming of a better time in the future.

Enlightenment is seeing that the self you have been building since about age two inside your head is totally unreal. Once you see this, once you get it, you will be awake. You will live fully and effortlessly in the present, because you will understand that the present is all that exists. You will always be at peace. You will always flow cheerfully with whatever is happening. Sure, there may be more fun awaiting you tomorrow evening, when you have a hot date or some other exciting activity planned, but you don't dwell on that.

After all, there is only now, there is only ever the now, and even working in a freezing, windowless salad factory is okay when you are inwardly free. As I advised the questioner, you may certainly form a plan from a place of clarity and presence, to move on from the salad factory as soon as you realistically can—and, in the meantime, maybe wear an extra sweater!

Whenever you find yourself doing something you don't really want to do, it helps if you ask yourself, "If I were an enlightened Zen master (or Sufi, or Christian mystic, or whatever inspires you) how would I approach this?" Then act accordingly.

Remember, awakened people are not defined by their personal history or any other story about reality. If they are defined by anything at all, it is the timeless beauty, vibrancy, and creative energy of this moment, *now*. They honor the past, they keep an eye on the future, but they are always right here, fully appreciating and flowing with whatever is happening now.

I often get asked some version of this question: "How can I remember to be present, to be here now? It seems like I forget so easily, and then I find myself being stressed out."

This is why we do the practice. Whenever you are upset or suffering, the first thing to do is to be present with it. Then look for the story you're telling yourself, and notice you are not the story. You are the awareness *looking* at the story. Then just be present with the feeling or emotion without trying to change it, without going into your head and creating a new story around it.

But short of living with your own personal guru or having a partner who is highly aware and will remind you on a regular basis (which many people would probably find, at first, very annoying!), you will need to use inattention itself to bring you back to attention. J. Krishnamurti was the first teacher I actually heard describe this phenomenon.

What I have since found is that it works this way: you hear the truth about being present often enough, and you begin to associate presence with the clarity, ease, and deep well-being characteristic of the awakened state. Then it becomes easy. Suffering becomes the trigger.

Whenever you feel yourself suffering, unhappy, caught in conflict, or worrying in some way, it is your reminder to breathe, be present with whatever is happening, and look for the story running you and causing your upset. Then realize you are *not* your story; you are the awareness that is here right now. So come back to being very aware in this moment now.

A person I was working with said to me once: "When I am present, there is no problem."

Interestingly, we are often the most present when facing danger or experiencing an actual crisis. The situation demands our presence. This is why people seek out adventurous activities like mountain or rock climbing, or certain sports like surfing or snowboarding. These activities force them to be present in such a way as to make them feel really alive.

But if you take the path of awakening, you'll always feel alive, present, and engaged by the moment, no matter what you are doing. And you can still climb mountains, surf, or snowboard.

Now, what about when the emotional contraction—anger, say, or fear—happens so quickly it just overtakes you, and there isn't any obvious story? When this happens, simply experience the emotion. Feel angry, feel the fear. You breathe and somehow get through it. It is important to not go into your head about it, not to try to figure out why you feel the way you do. Don't create a new story around it. When the emotion subsides, then you can go into your head and look for the story that triggered your reaction. You may have to look deeply into your past to find it.

But know this: there's *always* a story behind your anger or your fear, telling you the ways you were wronged, or how you got scared.

Meditation

Just as enlightenment is a fancy word for knowing who you are and being inwardly free, so is meditation a fancy word for being very present and watching the thoughts, sensations, and feelings arise and subside without getting caught up in them.

In the introduction, I said you don't actually need to meditate or do anything else in particular to find the freedom of enlightenment. It is totally the result of a shift in perception, through realizing that you are not your ever-changing story, not this I or me you have taken yourself to be, but that you are pure, ever-present awareness itself. There are people who have never formally meditated, yet have experienced this sudden awakening to the truth of their being, and their lives have been transformed by it.

However, if you're not yet fully awake, if you are still identifying with some story or notion of self, meditation can be a useful practice to help you quiet the mind and begin to take a closer look at this person you imagine yourself to be. It certainly was a vital practice for me.

The essence of meditation is to sit and just be very aware of everything going on within and around you. You can meditate for a formal period of five minutes, fifteen minutes, or an hour or longer. Meditation helps train your mind, so that you become the master of it rather than having your thoughts—the stories inside your head—control you. It helps you develop the witnessing consciousness or presence. It enables you to become the supreme watcher of your mind, emotions, and body processes. This is a very important step.

When you can slip easily into the role of the detached observer of your own internal processes, you are close to freedom. I say "close," because as long as you still identify with some concept or image of yourself as the witness or observer, you are caught in duality—"me" and "other"—and are not yet truly free. True freedom exists when you do not identify with any image or concept in your mind, and are just fully aware, present, and responsive in each unfolding moment.

When you meditate, you may sit with your eyes open, or they may be closed. There are really no rules. The main thing is the quality of awareness you cultivate. When you are truly present, it doesn't matter whether your eyes are open or closed. The experience of timelessness and of alert beingness is the same.

If you take the time to sit and meditate for awhile in the morning, you will find it a lovely way to start the day. Of course, it won't always be so lovely in the beginning stages. Sometimes you will struggle with tension, anxiety, or other uncomfortable states. But part of meditation is dealing with all of it. In order to be free, you must willingly face and welcome everything that comes up. You must be a spiritual warrior.

When you sit to meditate, or when you are driving in your car on the freeway, if you just step back with your awareness and watch your mind, your thoughts will eventually settle. Of course, while you are being aware of your mind as you drive on the freeway, you are simultaneously remaining aware of the freeway and the traffic! If you are new to meditation, getting some detachment from your mind can be difficult at first. But it will come with practice. I give a specific practice for this at the end of this chapter.

The more detachment you develop, the clearer, calmer, and more spacious your mind will feel. Then you will be able to tap into even deeper layers of consciousness. When the surface noise dies down, the deeper sounds can be heard.

Albert Einstein supposedly said we use only 5 or 10 percent of our brain power. That's because we get caught up in the same old patterns of thought. Deepak Chopra once said we have something like 65,000 thoughts a day, and 90 percent of them are the same as the thoughts we had yesterday. Certainly not very original or creative thinking!

As space opens up in your mind, new thinking can come in. That means insight, imagination, creativity, wisdom, and even psychic abilities, such as the ability to see the future or to tune in to levels of reality not obvious to the ordinary senses. The mind itself is nonlocal, which means you can't really find it anywhere in particular. Analytical thinking, however, does have a locus or point of origination. It comes from in back of the forehead, just behind the point between the eyes known as the "third eye."

A noisy, overactive mind is one of the main barriers to freedom. Meditation is about learning to dwell in present-time awareness and to *use* thinking as a tool, rather than living out of your head, your thoughts, with only occasional glimpses of clear awareness. Then, your mind no longer controls you, but rather you, as consciousness, control it.

The more you embody the quality of relaxed yet alert presence, the more you come to the place where your mind is consistently quiet, clear, and spacious. This spaciousness allows thoughts to come and go. They are no longer a problem. You no longer allow yourself to identify with them or get caught up in them. You are then able to focus your intention in a powerful way when needed, and to use your rational and intuitive modes of thinking with creativity and ingenuity.

"Do you still meditate?" is a question I am asked frequently. When I was on the path to discovering my true nature, meditation was an important daily practice for me. Initially, meditation helped me tame my wild mind, and then to dip deeper into the clarity I eventually began to experience. But once you know who and what you are, in a very real way you are always meditating. You are always aware and always present, so there is no need to formally meditate anymore. However, I still like to sit occasionally, especially in the mornings. It is good to just sit and *be*—to be quiet, alert, and very aware of all that is. It is a good time to review your intentions, what you want to manifest in your life.

D. T. Suzuki, the famous Zen master, said: "Even after enlightenment, practice must continue so as to deepen and expand the experience."

In Zen meditation, the basic practice is *zazen*, which is sitting and being present for long periods of time. The more you practice being consciously aware in this way, the more you embody the consciousness that you are and the more you express your true, enlightened nature in every word, action, and deed.

Let's experience true meditation, a meditation on pure being, right now . . .

Simply be present with what is . . . Now take a deep, slow breath, and relax . . . Notice the thoughts, beliefs, or stories passing through your mind, like "I'm uncomfortable," or "This moment isn't it, there has to be something more . . . " Then observe how everything that can be seen appears and disappears, including these thoughts, but you, as pure awareness, are always here . . . Every thought, sensation, and feeling shifts and changes . . . But you are the ever-present awareness behind everything . . . So feel the energy of your true nature . . . Be the awareness you are . . .

Use Your Meditation as a Tool for Exploration

Someone once said to me, "I had many questions I wanted to ask my teachers, both in school and college, as well as spiritual teachers I have sat with. But most of the time I have been too nervous, too afraid to speak up, or when I finally did summon up the courage, it was too late, and I missed my opportunity. How can I deal with this—even better, be done with it once and for all?"

I advised this person this way: "When looking for the story you are telling yourself, you may have to ask, 'So, what is it about the nervousness I feel whenever I go to ask a question? Where does it come from? What is the fear about?'"

This is self-inquiry in action. You have to bring real awareness, presence, to the inquiry. In fact, your presence is the most powerful transforming agent available to you. When you practice the power of presence throughout the day, day in and day out, eventually it becomes second nature. Bring this presence into your meditation, face your fears—those painful memories from the past—in this alert, open way and they begin to lose their power over you.

More and more you realize that what you actually are is the clear, present-time awareness, or consciousness, that looks at the story or at the memory. Then the memories and stories lose their emotional charge. They cease being a button or trigger for you. No one can push that button anymore, or at least not in any significant way.

You are human, and there will still be residue. You may still have the tendency to get nervous when asking a question, but you will just get very present, breathe, be totally in the moment, and you'll put up your hand and ask the question anyway. Maybe there will be a slight catch, a hint of nervousness in your voice, but it won't matter. It's no big deal. It won't stop you. You will no longer be blocked by the fear.

Many of our past memories are unconscious, so they may not surface right away. You may not see the story immediately. So, you simply live with the question. Every day when you sit to meditate, you bring it up and look at it anew. You keep it at the back of your mind during the day.

So long as you define the question clearly—"What is going on with me in this particular instance? Why am I being triggered so?"—I assure you, the answer will eventually come, and usually it will come sooner rather than later. We always get what we ask for. It is a law of the universe.

Perhaps it will come in a dream, when you are washing your hair in the shower, or when you are getting a massage or bodywork. It can even happen when you are making love. When you live with the question, you can be doing anything, and then suddenly, at the most unexpected moment, the forgotten memory or image will pop into your mind. Once you have seen it, you won't forget it.

Then, as soon as you get some alone time, sit down in meditation, or take a meditative walk out in nature, and face it. Shine the light of awareness on the memory, the story, the button that was pushed.

Remember, this work of self-inquiry is not about denying or rejecting your feelings and emotions. But you must understand that the unresolved memories, especially the memories associated with shame, betrayal, abandonment, rejection, or failure, keep the negative feelings alive. These negative feelings are experienced as guilt, envy, jealousy, resentment, loneliness, depression, meaninglessness, and despair. All of these feelings have some kind of a story behind them. The story is what fuels them.

So, when the feelings and emotions arise, be present with them, even welcome them from the perspective of them showing you where you are not yet free. Then look at the story you are telling yourself. The story is what keeps the negative feelings and emotions alive. The more you let go of the past, the story, the freer you are of those feelings. And you let go of the story by seeing that it isn't real.

But as you let go of the story, if you feel you are having difficulty with the disturbing emotion, then face the upset directly. Locate it in your body. Be very present with it. Don't try to analyze or understand it. Don't go into your head. Don't create more story around it. Just be very alert and watch it. If you don't interfere with the story-making mind, with the I or me, the energy will soon shift. You will feel more relaxed, whole, and present.

The great teaching of Advaita, the nondual path, is that these stories and memories have no reality in the present. They are illusions that appear real when we cling to them, when we identify with them. This must be seen again and again. You must bring a powerful presence to the seeing so that it comes alive, is dynamic.

When you actually see this, your mind clears, your emotions become stable and harmonious, and you feel good inside. You feel relaxed and at ease in the present. Then your emotional energy flows much more spontaneously and authentically. You may cry when something sad happens; you may get angry when you see injustice being perpetrated; you may laugh when you hear something funny. But it all happens naturally, and there is no holding onto anything. You are just here in the present, dancing with the ever-changing, ever-new, ever-interesting drama of creation.

In a very real way, it is like being a child again. Young children live very much in the moment. They feel things deeply, and then they let them go as their eyes open with fresh wonder at something new happening. To be free is having this childlike quality of innocence and newness, except you also have all the wisdom from decades of living.

Suzuki Roshi, the Zen master who inspired so many Americans to take up Zen, called it "beginner's mind." He said: "In the beginner's mind there are many possibilities, but in the expert's mind there are few."

In the meditation practice at the end of this chapter, I show you how to apply the practice of freedom to any situation that is causing upset, conflict, or suffering in your life. It brings a wonderfully liberating dimension to your daily meditations. Instead of just meditating to find a degree of inner peace and renewal (which is fine in and of itself), you are using it to as a tool for awakening, for self-realization or enlightenment. You are using it as your ticket to ultimate freedom.

Dive into the Well of Your Own Being

There are many physical practices and disciplines available to help you awaken to the energy of your true nature.

Yoga is one such practice. I discovered it in my late twenties, and it taught me to be supremely present in my body and supremely present with my awareness. And even though the health benefits of doing yoga, such as stretching and relaxing muscles, increasing flexibility, and enhancing health and vitality are significant, there is another, more vital benefit, as well.

Patanjali, the ancient philosopher of yoga, in the opening verses of his *Yoga Sutras*, stated, "Yoga is the stilling of the thought waves of the mind." When the thought waves of the mind become calm and still, there is no longer any disturbance, conflict, or fear present in the psyche. Then we can see reality with startling clarity, and we feel connected to the awesome power and energy behind creation itself—the energy of our true nature.

Yoga brings about an integration of body, mind, and spirit. Doing the yoga postures, or asanas, is a moving meditation. The pauses and periods of stillness in between them can be profoundly blissful and healing. Whenever you bring a heightened awareness to your body, inhabiting your body more consciously, you feel its aliveness more acutely. Tuning in to sensation and feeling at a somatic level takes you out of your mind. Releasing the problems associated with thinking gives you a direct experience of the fullness and power of *now*. Bringing a heightened consciousness to your body is one of the keys to awakening.

I first discovered this when I was studying yoga with Erich Schiffmann. Not long after our friendship began, I was hanging out with him one weekend afternoon at his house in Santa Rosa. We did some yoga together and then decided to sit in meditation. As we closed our eyes and sat, I noted the usual tension in my body, and the restless noise and chatter in my mind. The longer I sat, and the more I slowed my breathing, the more my mind quieted down.

Yet the real peace and serenity, which I had tasted in brief moments of yoga and meditation, eluded me. I had only been on my spiritual path a few years. The whole journey of awakening was still fairly new to me. I was grateful to have Erich as a friend, a fellow traveler, and a guide on the path.

After sitting for perhaps fifteen or twenty minutes, I started to get restless again. I opened my eyes to sneak a look at Erich. His eyes were closed, and he had a peaceful smile on his face. Whatever his inner experience was, it obviously felt good to him. Clearly, he was deeply connected to some source of inner joy, and the realization caused a pang of envy within me. I almost wanted to say to him, "Hey, what have you found in there? I want some, too."

Then I heard myself saying, "Well, Jim, why don't you go within? Why don't you dive inside yourself and see if you can find the same place within you?"

And I did. I closed my eyes again, breathed slowly and consciously. I got very present and let my awareness drop deep into my body. As I allowed every muscle, every single cell of my body to relax and open up, I began to feel the most exquisite energy start to move and to bubble up inside me.

It was as if every cell was being quickened, as if each cell was being gently massaged from within. It felt very blissful. As I continued to breathe consciously and allowed myself to surrender more deeply to the feeling inside me, I began to smile myself. In fact, it felt like my whole being was smiling on the inside.

Some time later, I opened my eyes, and—as these things would have it—Erich opened his at precisely the same time. We looked at each other in a knowing way, both of us smiling, and then we threw our heads back and laughed out loud. Then I put my hands together and bowed my head, saying "Namaste," a Sanskrit word which means, "I honor the God in you . . . the same God that is in me." Silently, I thanked my friend for his transmission.

That was one of the most important lessons I received. By getting still and going inside, you literally dive into the well of your own being, and in this way discover the source of true well-being. You discover the healing energy of bliss—what the yogis call the shakti energy, the divine vibration, or feeling—that lives within us. To connect with that bliss for even a few minutes is very healing. It allows you to move through the rest of the day with clarity, ease, and presence.

The Practice of Meditation

The more you practice being present, the more presence becomes second nature for you. By consciously meditating—slowing down your breathing, relaxing and sensing your body, and being fully alert and awake in the here and now—you begin to free yourself from the stories, thoughts, and images generating conflict, worry, and self-doubt.

(Note: In the following meditation practice, you close your eyes for a period of time. Either read it through first to make sure you understand it or have a friend read it for you and guide you through it; then you can do the same for them.)

Sit in a comfortable position. Take in your surroundings for a moment or two, and then close your eyes. Breathe slowly and consciously down into your belly, pelvis, and legs.

Now let your awareness expand until it feels as if you, as a localized field of awareness, are slightly behind and above your head. From this vantage point, scan the length and breadth of your body. Make your body an object of observation, just as you would a tree, a house, a car, or a person. Get the sense of yourself, your real being, as the awareness in which your body lives. You have a body, but you are not fundamentally your body. Rather, your body is an expression, or extension of the awareness that you are.

Now let your hearing expand, and listen to the sounds in your environment, whether of your own breathing or a bird, a car, a person's voice, or the hum of an appliance. Notice how all sounds come out of silent awareness, and dissolve back into it; yet you, the aware being who notices the sounds, are always here.

Then pay attention to the sensations and feelings shifting and changing inside your body. Notice that you are the ever-present, changeless awareness observing the coming and going of the sensations and the feelings.

Now watch the stories, thoughts, beliefs, and images passing through your mind. Notice the I thought, the me thought. Notice how you have all these thoughts, but they are not who you really are. Thoughts, even judgmental or negative thoughts, simply come and go within the larger field of the awareness that you are . . .

Notice how you can make thought an object of observation in the same way you can observe your body, your breath, or anything else. Watch your thoughts as if they were birds flying across the sky of your mind. In simply observing them and not getting caught up in any particular thought, stillness and peace unfold.

Now, use the peace you may be experiencing to explore a situation or issue that you've been struggling with recently. Use it to catapult you into a deeper state of presence. Apply the steps in the practice of freedom . . .

Step 1: Be present with the situation, whatever it is. If it's particularly intense, bringing up a whirlwind of emotions and thoughts, you may have to breathe more deeply and consciously to stay present with it. If the intensity is too much, deal with it in the best way you can, maybe even taking a break and coming back to it the next time you meditate. Eventually though, you want to embrace it, welcome it, because it is showing you where you are not yet free.

Step 2: Notice the thought or story you are telling yourself. For example: Why is this happening to me? I'll never get it right, I can't trust anyone, I must have this to be happy, I'm not worthy, etc. Just notice it without getting lost in analysis or rationalization. You can say to yourself: Oh, I'm getting caught up in that story again.

Step 3: See the truth . . . and the truth is that the thought or story comes and goes, just like the suffering comes and goes, but you are the spacious, aware being who is always here. So breathe, relax, and be the beautiful, aware being you are . . .

Then, when you are ready, slowly and consciously rise from your chair or meditation cushion and proceed with your day.

⪦ 2 ⪧

Step 2: Notice the Story

UNTIL ABOUT THE AGE of two, you were pure con-sciousness, shining through the little toddler's body known as you. You were very aware of sensation and feel-ing, of sensory stimulation, but the idea of being a self with a personal history was unknown to you. You lived in the present. Only your experience of now was real for you.

However, somewhere around age two, the thinking faculty developed enough to discriminate between "self" and "other." You gradually began to perceive a difference between yourself and other people. You began to believe there was a unique person living inside you; this idea was reinforced by your family, not to mention the whole social and cultural milieu.

Thus began the fall from grace. You ate from the tree of self-knowledge, and entered the world of duality, of black and white, of good and evil. You began to identify with ideas of right and wrong, of good and bad. You began to take yourself to be a separate person, a person who found joy in many activities and experiences, but who also went through a lot of conflict and suffering whenever things didn't go the way you wanted.

Now, as an adult, you are firmly entrenched in the belief that a distinct you lives inside your body, which is separate from everybody else. You have forgotten your true, original nature: the ocean of pure consciousness, manifested in the unique wave form of your particular body/mind/personality. You have made your happiness dependent on events outside yourself. You live in the past or the future, rarely in the now. The conditions of your life, to a greater or lesser degree, control you. You are emotionally reactive. Your buttons can easily be pushed.

At times, you feel like a victim of the circumstances in your life. A victim can be defined as someone who is totally identified by and at the mercy of his or her story. For example, most victims are eager to tell their tale of woe to anyone who will listen. People who are caught in the trap of victimhood are completely out of touch with their true natures.

In its simplest definition, enlightenment or awakening is rediscovering the truth of who and what you are. It is turning your gaze back in upon yourself, and waking up to the fact that the person you have been taking yourself to be since about age two is, in fact, an illusion. It is not real.

All the beliefs, judgments, memories, opinions, labels, and experiences you have accumulated in your mind, and which make up the story of your life and support the idea of being a person with a history, are just that—a story. The story has deep roots and has molded and shaped your personality. It has contributed to the face you now display toward the world. But in actuality, your psychological and emotional history has little to do with the reality of now, with what is actually happening right now.

All your thoughts and beliefs about who and what you are keep you from being open and available in the present. The agendas and considerations you hold inside your head, and which generate emotional tension in your body, act as a barrier between yourself and other people. They block you from truly connecting with others. They prevent the possibility of true intimacy. Ultimately, they stop the flow of love.

Whenever you find yourself in the presence of authentic love, the negative beliefs about yourself will be triggered, your buttons will be pushed, and you will tell yourself you are unworthy or undeserving. Or, you may tell yourself you *are* deserving, but then think you have to play certain games or act in a particular way in order to keep the love alive.

Whether it is love or just life, as long as you take yourself to be a person with a history, you are not really present. So long as you live with an image or story about self, there will always be a problem with self-esteem. There will always be some agenda, some consideration in your mind. You will always second-guess yourself. You will often judge yourself, and by extension, judge others.

To be awake is to know who and what you truly are at the deepest level of your being, beyond all your thoughts, beliefs, concepts, and stories *about* who you are. It is to know and feel yourself as being one with, and an expression of, universal consciousness, manifested in this body/mind/self called you.

This knowing brings a tremendous sense of inner freedom, a freedom from personal conflict and suffering. It brings the experience of true inner peace, the peace which passes all understanding. Once you have awakened to that peace, once you know yourself as nothing—no thing—and everything at the same time, you can then share your knowledge with the world. You can share your peace with the world.

Envision yourself at peace, and the world at peace. That alone should be all the motivation you need to discover the truth of who and what you are. Interestingly, I had someone say to me once, "The world at peace . . . Wouldn't that be kind of boring?" I responded with, "If you were truly at peace, you wouldn't ask such a question."

After all, boredom is itself a state of mind that is restless, weary, seeking some form of stimulation or excitement. True inner peace is a mind that is clear, calm, and spacious. It is a mind that is awake and alert in the present. It is a mind that is loving and fearless. It is a mind free of any thought of self, and thus interested in and open to all possibilities.

Residue

A man once asked Jean Klein, "What if everybody in the world became enlightened?" Jean looked at the man, and then smiled. "Why," he said, "Then there would only be dancing!"

By dancing, he meant, of course, celebration, play, and creativity. But it doesn't mean the normal human problems and challenges would go away. With awakening, we don't just then abide in some kind of effortless perfection.

As Jean said on another occasion, enlightenment doesn't mean problems go away, it just means they are no longer problematic. You just deal with the challenges before you. You deal with them from a very clear, present, and responsive place.

Nisargadatta Maharaj, a guru from Mumbai, was visited by many seekers from the West. Once, one of them asked him if he still had any fears. He replied, "Occasionally an old reaction, emotional or mental, happens in the mind, but it is at once noticed and discarded. After all, as long as one is burdened with a person, one is still exposed to its idiosyncrasies and habits."[1]

When I read this statement by Nisargadatta, whose name means "one who abides in the natural state," it was very liberating for me. It took a great weight off my mind. It was okay to still be human, even to experience occasional moments of fear.

Even great sages, established in truth for decades, are human, I realized. Their bodies fail them; they have their moments when the instrument, the body/mind, is not clear at all. They get indigestion; they may get irritated at times. They are not always so sweet and loving. They can be abrupt, aloof, or withdrawn. Their ordinary humanity gives us permission to be less than perfect ourselves, which takes a lot of pressure off us. This means we can relax more easily into the clarity and presence which is our true nature.

Jean spoke of these reactions from the past. He called them "residues," which is where I got the term. Liberation is seeing through the story called me, myself, and I, so that you no longer derive your identity or meaning from your thinking processes or your personal history. Instead, it comes from being itself, from the fullness and vibrancy of the life force, the energy of creation felt right here, right now. You know yourself as consciousness, the changeless awareness in which the flux and flow of creation happens.

Once awakening happens, you are free. But elements of your personal history, those residues from the past, are still locked away in the musculature of your body. Any healer or body worker understands this

---

1   I Am That, 31.

phenomenon. It is similar to what the spiritual teacher Eckhart Tolle, a master of the art of presence, refers to as the "pain body." These residues can get activated from time to time.

For instance, if you were impatient by nature before self-realization, you will still have residual tendencies toward impatience after you wake up, although much less often. If before awakening you were afraid of confrontation, most of your fear will leave after you realize the truth of who you are. But should you get into a confrontational situation, an echo from the past may be triggered. In other words, there may be a brief flaring up of fear.

The difference is, when you are awake, you notice it and it falls away. You don't buy into it any more. You don't give it energy, and so it dissolves. Such upsets are like waves, momentary disturbances in the vast, clear ocean that is your natural consciousness, your natural state of being. To use the lake analogy, the surface waters of your being may get upset when there is a strong wind, but deep down you remain still, clear, calm . . .

Pause right now and be present with whatever you are experiencing . . . Notice if you are feeling any tension or discomfort anywhere, whether mental, emotional, or physical . . . Accept it, let it be there . . . Notice the story you may be telling yourself . . . Then breathe, relax, and see the truth . . . The stories, thoughts, sensations, and feelings are always changing, coming and going . . . but you, as the awareness witnessing it all, are still here . . . You don't need, in this moment, any story to define who you are . . . You don't need any concept, image, or idea of being somebody . . . You are aware of yourself in reality right now, and that is enough . . . From this place, everything happens . . .

Beyond Duality

When I teach, I get variations of this statement a lot: "I know awakening is often spoken of as nondual awareness, a freedom from the normal duality of everyday life. However, I don't understand how you can transcend duality. It seems to me that duality—night/day, good/bad, happy times/sad times—is reality. We live in a world of opposites, and you can't have the one without the other. You can't have the ups without the downs."

Obviously there is night and day, there is pleasure and pain, there is hot and cold, and there is wealth and poverty in the world, but even these distinctions are not clear-cut, not strictly black or white.

One person's pleasure is another person's pain, or at least discontent. Day gradually darkens into night, and in the morning, the dawning light heralds daytime once again. But in some parts of the world, in the polar regions, day lasts for twenty hours or more in the summer. Wealth and poverty are also a matter of perception. What we consider poverty here in the United States would be great wealth in some of the poorest third world countries.

The main point of the above statement is that we can't have the ups without the downs. That is true only when our happiness is based on events and circumstances outside ourselves. If you look to your partner for fulfillment, when your partner is happy and treating you well, you feel good. When your partner is unhappy and taking it out on you, or treating you badly, you feel bad. You don't like the situation and it affects you adversely.

The same principle applies to everything else. When money is flowing in, it brings happiness. When more is going out than coming in, the result, in the words of Dickens's Mr. Micawber, is misery. Or maybe you are enjoying deep, blissful experiences of meditation, which you label your spiritual life, but your material life—your relationship, or your work—produces a lot of conflict and suffering.

So again, let me be very clear: If you are going to rely on external factors for your happiness and well-being, you will inevitably fluctuate between periods of feeling good and periods of feeling bad. You will be caught in duality. You will be a victim of duality. It can't be any other way.

Indeed, the more you depend on outer circumstances for your happiness, the more likely you are to live with a chronic, underlying feeling of insecurity, never being quite sure when your good fortune will change or be taken from you. This is the lot of most people, yet it need not be this way.

When you live in the awareness, openness, and freedom of your true nature, your essential well-being no longer depends on outer events and circumstances or on what others think, say, or do. It comes from within. It shines through you as a direct expression of the beauty, fullness, and joy of being itself. Peace, in other words, is your true nature.

When awakening becomes real, you are always at peace within yourself, no matter what is happening outside. At the same time, you live in the world, in the dualistic reality. You are obviously going to make choices and act in such a way as to create the most optimal circumstances for your own survival, comfort, and well-being. The more smoothly your life works at a material, physical level, the freer you are to devote your energies to serving others and fulfilling your destiny.

You create positive karma. Karma is simply any action having reverberations, which results in a chain reaction. Positive karma is conscious action and generates feelings of love, compassion, and goodwill. Negative karma is caused by unconscious actions and always results in suffering.

But, again, the beauty of awakening, and why it is so important, is that your basic peace and well-being do not depend on whether outer conditions are favorable or not. It really does free you from being attached to and thus at the mercy of outer events, and from the inevitable insecurity and suffering such attachment brings. It frees you from suffering because it frees you from the idea of being a someone who gets attached and who suffers.

I remember clearly the first taste of enlightenment, or awakening, I had. It was a truly life-changing event. Like all such awakenings, it came completely unbidden. It happened a year after I graduated from Palmer College of Chiropractic, in Davenport, Iowa, and was living in Santa Rosa, in Northern California. I had come to the United States to study chiropractic. I really wanted to be a writer, a novelist, but I liked the idea of helping people, too, and thought chiropractic would be a good interim career. My plan after graduating was to return to New Zealand, establish a practice, write novels, and maybe get involved in politics, following in the footsteps of my paternal grandmother, who was the third woman elected to the parliament in New Zealand.

During my last year at chiropractic school, I had a health crisis. I began getting tightness in my chest along with difficulty breathing. I was doing a series of breathing exercises, and had somehow gotten it into my head that if I didn't continue to consciously control the flow of my breath, I would stop breathing altogether and die.

This resulted in all kinds of anxious feelings. It got to the point where I was afraid to go to sleep at night. I'd sometimes make a feeble attempt at prayer, but I no longer really believed in God. I'd finally fall asleep from sheer exhaustion, and when I woke up the next morning, I'd give thanks for still being alive.

For me, it was a very unsettling time, a time of great personal distress. However, it takes this kind of suffering to cause us to look deeply within ourselves. I didn't realize it at the time, but my spiritual journey, my quest for inner freedom, had begun.

To deal with this situation, I started practicing yoga. When I went for my morning run, I stopped timing myself to see how fast I was going, and made a conscious effort to appreciate nature more, to actually stop and notice things like the blue jay squawking in the apple tree, or the bees buzzing around the honeysuckle. I let go of trying to control my breath, and just started to trust more, to be more in the moment.

I took a course in Transcendental Meditation, and that made a big difference, stopping and sitting twenty minutes twice a day to just be. After a few months, the anxiety began to fade and I started to sleep well again.

As part of my quest for understanding, I read the books of Hermann Hesse and Alan Watts, and especially those of the spiritual philosopher, J. Krishnamurti. As I dove into Krishnamurti's writings, I soon discarded whatever belief I still had in God. Krishnamurti was, in many ways, the ultimate spiritual iconoclast. He said the prison of beliefs and concepts keeps us in bondage and causes all our suffering. Freedom, he said, lay in being free of the net of thoughts, of all concepts about God. Only then would we discover what was meant by the word "God."

It was a summer's morning when I had my taste of enlightenment. I woke up early and noticed a shaft of sunlight coming through a chink in the Venetian blinds. My gaze was transfixed by the dust motes dancing in the sunlight. Then I heard the soft, haunting call of a mourning dove, and suddenly everything in my mind fell away. Every thought, the residue of the night's dreams, it all just vanished, and I lay there in the most extraordinary state of clarity, stillness, and oneness I had ever known. There wasn't even a sense of a me having the experience. There was just a feeling of timeless presence, and no tension or conflict whatsoever.

After a while, a thought entered my mind: "So, this is what Krishnamurti and all these other teachers are talking about. There is nothing to seek. It is all right here. Life is beautiful and perfect as it is."

As the day wore on, the amazing feeling of oneness faded and I gradually reverted to my normal, cerebral, somewhat uptight self. But something changed in me forever. It was as if a hole was punctured in my ego-bound consciousness. I tasted the Reality behind reality. At some level I realized I *was* that Reality. I glimpsed the divine perfection of creation, the beauty that is always here, underneath the surface noise and conflict.

Now I knew what I was looking for. I wanted to live with that clarity, that sense of ease and oneness with life, all the time. I was totally committed and knew instinctively I was going to do whatever it took, to make whatever sacrifice was needed.

As a result of my inner commitment, I devoted the next eighteen years of my life to the pursuit of self-realization, to becoming fully established in the freedom I now knew was my true nature. Even as I outwardly lived a normal, worldly life, this became the central theme of my existence.

The Powerful Grip of Personal Stories

Until we see them for what they are, the personal stories running us are many, and they are very deep-rooted. It takes time to ferret out our stories so we can see them for what they are: just stories, with corresponding emotional fallout in the body, but no substantial reality other than that.

There are stories of ambition and deprivation, need and want, desire and lust, greed and hunger, guilt and resentment, sadness and despair, hope and longing, friendship and betrayal, and so on. These often have their origin in some form of personal trauma or abuse. It may have been a psychological or emotional event that happened one or many times, or it may have been a physical occurrence, such as an illness, accident, or some other calamity. Sometimes a psychological or emotional event also involves physical trauma.

Either way, we fabricate a story (and a related persona, the personality we project) about what happened to us, and we gradually shut down. Over many years, the story and the persona become us, literally become who we think we are. The intense feelings created by the story feel very real to us, and that just reinforces the importance of the story in our lives.

Let's take a closer look at some of the stories we tell ourselves, keeping us separate from the flow of life, making us feel, to some degree, like victims of circumstance or of life itself. Here they are, the bare bones, stripped-down versions without all the rationalization, justification, or personal narrative (just more story) that usually accompanies them:

I'm not worthy, I feel guilty, I feel ashamed.

I am/was an abandoned, abused, wounded child.

Nobody would want to be with me.

Life is tough, unfair.

This shouldn't be happening.

The only way you can get ahead is by ripping people off.

You can't trust anyone.

I don't manage money well.

I'd love to do such and such, but I won't because I'm not sure I would succeed.

He/she is my one chance for happiness.

I need/must have this or that in order to be happy.

I'm too busy to take time for self-reflection/meditation.

I can't seem to get my mind to shut up.

I'm getting old. It sucks.

I really screwed up.

I'm confused/lonely/depressed/miserable.

I'm bored. I need something new and interesting to stimulate me.

The persona I spoke about above often becomes part of what psychologists call our "shadow self," because we have no conscious awareness of it. Only later, when we are triggered by something that reminds us of the original event, do we experience the drama associated with mental and emotional reactivity. We take offense, become angry, or feel any of the other sorts of human emotions: sadness, loneliness, depression, shame, guilt, and so on.

The shadow, in Jungian terminology, represents the unconscious aspects of your behavior, the things driving you of which you are not even aware. The shadow rears its head in what are sometimes referred to as "demons." Personal demons can manifest themselves in many forms and guises, as I indicated above: fear, envy, jealousy, addiction, guilt, self-doubt, self-judgment, resentment, anger, depression, despair, and phobias.

The shadow is your disowned self. The more strongly you desire freedom, and the more closely you pay attention to your own thoughts, feelings, motives, and drives, the more you bring the shadow aspects into the light of awareness where you can see them. And it's in the seeing, the perceptual shift, that the healing happens.

You see the shadow—your anger, for example—and you look for the story you are telling yourself, such as, "How dare this person say or do this to me!" Then you breathe into the feeling. You stay very present, intensely alert. The stories, and the emotional reactions they trigger, are always changing, but you remember that you are the pure, changeless consciousness that is looking at the story. Remain in this place of awareness, and you'll find that the images and feelings associated with anger dissolve, and a new energy of wholeness unfolds.

As another example of this perceptual shift: many, many years ago a friend pointed out to me how judgmental I was about certain people. Perhaps it was because of the kind way in which she said it, but I had an epiphany: "My God, I am judgmental, aren't I?" Her observation literally stopped me in my tracks, and from that moment on, I became a lot less judgmental. In seeing the truth about myself, I allowed my judgmental tendencies toward others to begin to fall away.

Psychotherapy or some form of counseling or guidance is one way to get help in uncovering your shadow and coming to terms with the stories underlying your personal demons. Meditation, whether in the form of actual sitting or just a very conscious, ongoing self-awareness or self-inquiry, works well if you are highly motivated to find the truth within yourself. It requires a certain emotional maturity to do it on your own. You must have a passion for the truth, for freedom. You must be willing to confront your shadow, your demons, and find out just how real—or unreal—they are.

You must be patient, compassionate, and forgiving with yourself. Jean Klein always said the conditioning to be somebody—entrenched in your ego, with its obvious personal reactivity and its less obvious shadow self—is deep-rooted. You must break free of the identification with the sense of I, with the idea of a me living inside this body/mind, which is the major hurdle to awakening.

We are convinced there is really someone in here, when in fact there is nobody. There is just consciousness, luminous, self-aware presence, expressed through these body/minds and appearing as us.

Awakening, or enlightenment, is a figure/ground shift, quite literally. You no longer take yourself to be an object, a figure amongst countless others. Instead, you know yourself as the ground—as the ground of being, as consciousness. You know yourself as the ocean, manifested as a wave, whereas before you just thought of yourself as one more wave, another separate human being, in the vast sea of consciousness. Once you really see that, you are free.

Occasionally I meet people who are trying to free themselves from suffering through the direct, nondual approach, but who seem stuck in their heads. I feel they would have been better off spending a year or two working with a hands-on teacher, who could actually reconnect them with their feelings and emotions. Sometimes catharsis, the actual expression of intense emotion, is necessary to get free of it.

Just before I met Jean Klein, I spent a year doing a series of intensive workshops with a transformational therapist named Stephano Sabetti. He was a master at working with emotional energy and at connecting people with their vulnerability. He got people to access their deeper, unexpressed emotions—their grief, anger, or fear—and invited them to release it, usually through catharsis or through acting it out in some way.

It was good work, what I call the blood and guts work of transformation. It made me much more emotionally available to hear Jean Klein's teachings on inner freedom.

If you become a teacher or guide, you can only take people as far as you have traveled yourself. If you have not dealt with your own anger, for example, you won't know how to be at ease with other people's anger when it comes up. You'll inadvertently draw angry students or clients to you and be at a loss as to how to work with them.

The main thing here is intention. If you have the clear intention to be open to whatever unresolved emotional energy still lives within you, then life will bring you what you need. That could be just the right guide or therapist, or maybe, because of what is happening in your relationships, you will experience it and release it on your own.

Just by inviting these inner demons to come up and encouraging them to show themselves, you initiate the process. The invitation, the welcoming, is the critical step in getting free of them. This is the ongoing daily meditation—this inner awareness of all that is taking place within you, of your own judgments, fears, unhappiness, resentments—your shadow side.

People who are still caught up in their stories always have shadows of some kind. Maybe it is the priest with his unresolved sexual longing for women or boys. Or maybe it is the woman who appears to be so kind and so well-mannered, yet turns vicious when she is crossed in any way. Maybe it is the husband who pretends to his spouse that everything is hunky-dory, yet whose dissatisfaction and resentment come out in passive aggressive behavior, in snide remarks and hurtful acts, which only sabotage the relationship.

The way to be free of the shadow and its demons is to be very present. Begin to notice your behavior, your reactions, and the effect you have on people. This requires a commitment to self-honesty and to growth. You have to be willing to listen to the feedback your universe gives you, whether in the form of direct communication from others, or from the way people react to you. Looking at these deeper, darker aspects of ourselves is often not very pretty, but that's the gift of this work of welcoming. It is work that invites us to be easy on ourselves, to be forgiving. We cannot become free if we keep beating ourselves up.

The unconscious elements of your story, your beliefs and motivations, control you. The more conscious you become of what lives inside you, the less power these forces have over you. Under the clear light of awareness, directed within, guided by a loving and compassionate heart—and by a strong, warriorlike presence when necessary—the shadow's stuff is revealed. Because you are not giving it energy, it begins to fall away on its own. This is the transforming power of consciousness at work.

Residues of the shadow and those old demons may rear their head once in a while, but now you notice them, and you don't buy into them. You just don't go there anymore, because it doesn't serve you. Your awareness is right here, in the present.

Now, I am often asked about lessons, and why we have to keep learning the same old lessons. In every situation where there is suffering, there is a lesson to be learned. The work is to uncover the lesson and find out what you are supposed to learn. Then, instead of being stuck in the same old story, the same old predicament, over and over again, you are able to profit from each lesson that comes along, and move on smoothly and easily to the next.

The quicker you let go of the attachment to your own story, and just listen and pay attention to what is so, the sooner you will be able to identify the lesson you are supposed to learn, and the closer you'll be to the freedom you seek. You'll then be more of a creative force in your life.

And if there isn't any story going on inside your head, but you are feeling emotionally contracted or stuck anyway, then you just do the practice. Let's do it right now . . .

Be present with the emotional contraction, whatever it is . . . It is showing you where you are not yet free . . . Maybe you aren't in touch with the story behind it, but you can be sure it is there, somewhere in your unconscious mind . . . Then breathe, relax, and notice how the sensations of the contraction subtly shift and change . . . But you, as the awareness watching them, experiencing them, are always here . . . So, remain as the clear, radiant, ever-present awareness you are . . .

At some level, you will realize you are the clear, unchanging consciousness that looks at everything. You are the timeless awareness watching everything—your body, mind, and personality—come into being, including the ever-changing flow of your feelings and emotions.

Again, I want to emphasize that there is always a story behind your suffering, though it may be unconscious. If you can find the story and see you are not the story, but rather what is looking at the story, then the shift can happen even more quickly. After all, thought forms, which are ephemeral, dissolve virtually instantaneously when you, as the ultimate witness, just observe them. Contracted feelings and emotions, on the other hand, take longer to unwind.

Many people wonder about thoughts or stories that make them feel good, which don't cause emotional pain and suffering. For example, thinking about the new home you are going to move into, or the joy of graduating from college soon, or anticipating a new relationship, or something else great coming into your life—this is all pretty natural. These feel-good stories certainly do work to put a song in our heart and a smile on our face.

The thing is, to what extent are we identifying with these stories? To what extent do we depend upon their outcomes for our well-being? If the story becomes reality, then that is proof of the joy of anticipation. But sometimes anticipation is also expectation, and if our expectations are not met, we can be disappointed, sometimes bitterly so.

Remember, the essential message of this book is inner freedom. The freer you get inwardly, the less identified you are by any story, whether it's a suffering story or a feel-good story. Instead, you are more and more identified by *being* itself, with being here now. Feeling fully awake and alive in the present always feels very, very good. It feels the best. Moreover, the more you know you are not your story, the more fun it is to tell it. The freer you are of your story, the better a storyteller you become.

In the meantime, it is perfectly okay to indulge in a little feel-good storytelling, even a fantasy about something now and then. This is a perfectly normal and human thing to do. Just don't mistake it for reality. To discover reality, be right here, right now, open to the fullness of this moment.

Compelling Religious Stories

The early stages of life are marked by the development of and identification with our egos, with our stories, with the sense of self. Most of us start out here. Ego development and the discovery of personal freedom, which includes boundaries and limits, is an important stage of learning in early life.

This stage is characterized by a dependence on—or a grasping at—beliefs. Our well-being is very much tied to what we think and believe. Our thoughts, our stories, define who and what we take ourselves to be. Religion and fundamentalist, black-or-white thinking in general are a part of this developmental process. In Zen, they say of this black-or-white stage, "Mountains are mountains, rivers are rivers."

Everything is just what it seems to be. The mountains are over there, and we are over here, just trying to make some logical sense of our existence. We are trying to find something to hold on to, some belief or concept or ideal—whether religious or otherwise—to give us a feeling of meaning, purpose, and security.

However, what drives us is precisely this need for meaning and security. Doubt, fear, and the quest for some kind of certainty are common themes in our lives. We realize we don't know who we are or what is going to happen to us when we die, or we find ourselves suffering in some way: an illness, financial misfortune, the loss of a job, the death of a loved one, or a betrayal of some kind, followed by broken trust and shattered confidence.

Our fear and suffering cause us to look for something to believe in, something we can cling to for our psychological, emotional, and spiritual well-being. We want to know the mountains and rivers are going to stay the same and will always be there. We want to know what is going to happen to us, both in the near future and at the very end of our lives when we die.

This stage of the journey is very dualistic—us and them, me and it (the thing we idolize or fear). It is very much a journey of faith as we hope or trust there is, indeed, some greater power or benign energy—whether we call it God, spirit, Tao, or Buddha-nature—behind creation. So strong is this need that many of us develop a personal relationship with God, or whatever we call that power. We look to God—or our idea of God—whenever we are in need.

Some of us attribute the miracles in our lives to God's grace; yet we may wonder about disasters or times of extreme human suffering. What about when an airliner with three hundred people aboard crashes, killing everyone? Many of the dead probably had some form of "personal relationship" with God. How do we make sense of that? Can it be rationalized? Or do we accept it as a mystery? At this time in our journey through life, the last thing we want to be confronted with is that, in the end, we are just a random event in a cold and meaningless universe.

I grew up in New Zealand believing in God. When I was six years old, my mother taught me about God and Jesus. Although I was raised nominally as a Christian, I didn't particularly connect with the story of Jesus, but for me God became very real. There were times growing up when I would frequently stop and be still, look up at the sky, breathe into the beauty of the day, and feel the presence of God, of a supreme and utterly benign power behind creation.

As I got older, though, the whole idea of God became much less real for me. By the time I joined the army and arrived in Vietnam as a twenty-year-old second lieutenant, serving with the Royal New Zealand Artillery, I was cocky enough to rarely think about God. But then I saw combat for the first time. Our unit came under attack from the Viet Cong. I found myself hugging the ground as bullets and rocket-propelled grenades flew overhead. Suddenly, fearing for my life, I was grateful to remember—and to call upon—the God I once knew so intimately.

Most people seek meaning in their lives, of course, and religion is there to provide it. The function of religion, at least in its outer, mass appeal aspect, is to address our existential fears and provide answers to these soul-searching questions of ours. Throughout history, man has created many religions, and they all have their own story, their own explanation of the nature of God, creation, and what happens to us when we die. Some religions even try to claim God as their own, as if theirs is the one true religion and all the others are false.

Religion still has a role to play, even in an awakened world, but religion in and of itself cannot give us the experience of authentic inner peace. After all, the main limitation of identifying with a particular religious story is our inner well-being becomes very much dependent on what we think and believe.

We may adopt a particular set of beliefs, a neatly ordered worldview such as those offered by many religions, which are designed to give us the inner security we seek. But should someone (or something) challenge our beliefs or present a different or opposing perspective—and in a world as diverse as ours, this is always happening—it can throw us into confusion. It can, and inevitably does, throw us back into fear as the very belief system we have become dependent upon is now being called into question.

Beliefs, by their very nature, are divisive. They keep us in a state of resistance and fear. You can't cling to a belief *and* be in a state of welcoming. Holding onto a set of beliefs is the exact opposite of the all-embracing openness represented by awakening.

Not only do beliefs stir up conflict and doubt within us—"Which belief should I hold on to, which should I reject?"—they invariably create separation and rifts between one set of believers and another.

Most of the trouble in the world today is caused by the attachment to fundamentalist belief systems, whether religious, cultural, ethnic, or political. The more we see that all beliefs, including the most hallowed and emotionally charged ones, are just mental constructs—*assumptions* of truth, but not truth itself—the more we find ourselves wanting something deeper and more real than mere words and ideas.

The problem with religions is that, regardless of how long they have been around, how many adherents they have, or how noble or sacred their traditions, they are basically just stories about the origin, meaning, and purpose of life. And, as you are seeing, you are not your story, not any story.

Once you have seen through the illusion of the world inside your head, you can no longer cling to any story about reality, including a religious story. Instead, you find yourself equally honoring the core of truth and goodness in all religions.

However, the path to freedom is not incompatible with attending church or going to the mosque or temple. In fact, the freer you get of your own story and of attachment to ideas and images of self, the more clearly you'll understand and relate to the heart of the great spiritual and religious teachings. You just won't get lost in all the dogma, rules, restrictions, and guilt-tripping.

Meister Eckhart, the fifteenth-century German mystic, had clearly realized his true nature, but he continued to be a Christian preacher. The Dalai Lama is a contemporary example of an awakened human being who, because of destiny, finds himself speaking on behalf of Buddhism, Tibetan Buddhism in particular.

For a growing number of us throughout the world, however, the deeper our own inquiry into the true nature of God and creation, and the greater our own hunger for true inner peace and freedom, the less satisfied we are with attachment to any form of belief or story. We want the experience of freedom, of enlightenment, *now*.

For this to happen, we must be present in this moment now, see all our stories and beliefs for what they are—mere objects in consciousness—and realize what we *are* is the consciousness which sees . . .

Do it now . . . Be the consciousness you are. . . If it helps, step back with your awareness, out of any stories going on in your mind . . . Or, simply be present as the awake awareness you are . . . Then, notice how you, as this aware being, are still here, shining through your eyes, feeling with your heart . . . Yet, there is no need, in this moment, to define yourself by any story, whether religious, cultural, personal, or otherwise . . . There is no need to define yourself by any thought or concept . . . To realize this is to taste freedom, the freedom simply to be the beautiful, conscious person you are . . .

The Consciousness Story

If there is a story that explains the true nature of reality, we could call it the consciousness story. This story is one of consciousness evolving through us, actually wanting to flower, to be born, through us. And the full flowering of consciousness happens when we realize that we are consciousness itself in human form. Then peace and wholeness become the reality within, and as more and more people awaken to the truth within, so peace and wholeness will eventually be the reality without.

Now, if you are able to put whatever beliefs and concepts you are still holding onto aside, and look at the way physical reality is put together, you will come to a remarkable discovery. You will come to the same insights arrived at by many leading-edge scientists in our own time.

This discovery is that reality is a unified field of energy and consciousness. It is not the universe of separate objects and things, of us in here, and the rest of the world out there, as Newton believed. It is a participatory universe, where every particle and every atom are interconnected. Physical reality is so interconnected that just by observing or looking into a system, you affect and change the system—and are, in turn, affected and changed by it.

This perspective brings an entirely new and astonishingly contemporary—and yet timeless—meaning to the Buddha's statements: "Form is emptiness, and emptiness is form," and "All the ten thousand things are created by a single thought."

It allows us to hear Jesus' words, "I and the Father are one," in a new way, if you see "Father" as representing the consciousness we are. It makes it easier for us to understand Jesus when he said to his disciples (and I am paraphrasing his words here), "This applies to you, too. You are just as much a part of the Oneness as I am."

We are not separate from the rest of creation, but are one with it. Ramesh Balsekar, a contemporary Indian sage, reminds us that in Hindu mythology, the universe was perceived thousands of years ago as a multidimensional net of jewels, each a reflection of, and profoundly related to, the others. He quotes an ancient Chinese saying: "Pick a blade of grass and you shake the universe." The fundamental quality connecting everything is consciousness itself.

Let me give you an example. Imagine you are sitting with a group of people by a lake. You come from different countries, are different ethnicities, and speak different languages. But the one thing you have in common is that you have all awakened to your true natures. Each of you knows yourself at the deepest level of your being.

So, it's a beautiful day, the sky is clear, and you are all sitting in total silence, in harmony with all existence. And what you become aware of is what you have always been aware of ever since first awakening to the truth within. You become aware there is only one consciousness present, being expressed through each person—and all life—in unique and different ways.

Kunihiro Yamate, a contemporary Japanese social scientist and philosopher, says in *The Way of No Thinking*, a book describing his perspective on life:

When we awaken to the fact that instead of being humans or earthlings we are universarians, we will have that indescribable realization that we are the thinker-uppers of the entire universe. The people we look at now are not others. They are mirror image reflections of our own self . . .

Since we are mutually the whole universe, we can and should truly say: I am you, you are me. We have a holographic relationship. We are holographic beings and our dealings with each other are no longer individual-based. All us phenomena in the universe overlap. This is natural because we are all characters and props in a dream or play we are playing in our consciousness.[2]

One thinks of the brilliant playwright Shakespeare, in his own way a metaphysician, writing over five hundred years ago, "All the world's a stage, and all the men and women merely players."[3]

---

2   269.

3   *As You Like It*, Act 2, scene 7.

What becomes clear with the universal or holographic view is we are scripting the whole thing. Nothing happens without our thinking or dreaming it into being. The personal proof of this is deep, dreamless sleep, where there is no awareness and no world. Yet when you start dreaming, the dream world is very much there because you are aware of it. Then, when you wake up, the real world is here, because you are aware of *that*.

The more deeply you grasp this perspective, the more it transforms your understanding of who you are, what God is, how you have come to be here, and what happens to you when your body dies.

As you open to these deeper levels of reality, it dawns on you that consciousness itself—pure, radiant awareness—*is* your true and abiding nature. And if consciousness is your true nature, if consciousness is the primary force behind creation, then consciousness—the clear, undifferentiated consciousness expressed not just through the human brain or mind, but through all of creation—must be God.

In other words, the universe is God. God is the whole thing. God is consciousness itself and you, as this body/mind/self, are an individualized, unique expression of the one divine consciousness.

Understanding this, not just at an intellectual level, but with the whole of your being, so there is no longer any feeling of being separate from the flow of consciousness and creation, is the essence of what it means to be awake or free.

In this freedom, you use the power of stories and thoughts *consciously*, because you know how powerful the mind is. You use thoughts intentionally to create the reality that best supports you and the people you love—and best supports the environment.

With this freedom you experience a natural sense of oneness and unity, and this gives rise to a heightened sensitivity and compassion toward all of life. Above all, you experience a deep inner peace and silence.

This is the secret realized by all who venture beyond their identification with the I thought. They discover the vast realm of being lying beyond the mind, and yet which is the source of the whole of creation, including the mind and the I thought.

Releasing Stories about Fear

One of the traditional definitions of awakening, or enlightenment, is it is a state of fearlessness.

The journey of awakening is above all a process of uncovering and facing your different fears. As you see with more and more clarity that they are not real, they begin to fall away. Then you are naturally more loving and more connected to consciousness, God, spirit, or whatever you choose to call the mysterious Power behind creation.

Together, the teaching and the practice equip you to face and move through your fears, eventually leaving them all behind. Instead of shrinking from fear and turning it into some kind of monster, you meet it head on, like a warrior, and discover its real face. There's an old Irish saying: "If you run away from a ghost, it will chase you and haunt you for the rest of your life. But if you stop and turn and face it, it will disappear, because ghosts aren't real."

On the path of awakening, you are learning to face not just fear, but every moment in this alert and relaxed way. Years ago on my own journey, whenever I had a breakthrough, I found myself coming to the same realization every time. It involved letting go of some aspect of my past, my story—some pattern in my thinking or behavior which no longer worked for me.

Suddenly, I'd feel more relaxed, more *here*. I would say to myself, "Wow, my spiritual journey is all about getting here. It's about being more present."

You can probably relate to what I am saying. As you grow up and get caught up in your personal story, the account you inwardly write of your life, of your history of failures and successes, doubts and fears, hopes and dreams, you tend to start dwelling in this internal reality. You are not alone. We all do this until we learn differently. Yet it is the very attachment to this inner world of concepts, beliefs, memories, and images that keeps us from being present.

The deeper your awakening, the freer you get of psychological and emotional fear. You no longer worry about what *might* happen to you. You know now that you, as consciousness, will always be okay.

But even with awakening, biological fear, the fear of actual physical harm, still arises when danger threatens. It is a necessary survival mechanism. If someone moves as if to strike you, you are going to flinch or jump back. If you take up skydiving, even if your realization is deep and mature, chances are your stomach will feel nervous and queasy as you are about to step out of the airplane at ten thousand feet.

But even survival fear loses its edge as you awaken to the consciousness you are and connect with the astonishing creative energy that is always here, underneath the surface drama of life.

The more conscious and free you become, the more you find even in the face of danger, hardship, or loss, you remain clearheaded and supremely aware as you deal with the situation at hand. When you stop resisting and fighting it, life has its own surprising way of coming into balance and harmony. This is how miracles occur. It all happens not in some promised future or some imagined afterlife, but right now, in this present moment.

Rather than obsessing over what it takes to become enlightened, why you still suffer, or why you are not yet free, let go of the attachment to all your ideas and stories about enlightenment and suffering, and just focus on being fully aware, conscious, and present *now*. Then the experience of freedom will become more and more frequent, and the times of conflict and suffering will be fewer and briefer.

Eventually, as your internal gaze penetrates more deeply through the illusion of the world between your ears, the world you have for so long referred to as me, myself, and my story, all fear of life and death will leave you. Then the liberation you have been seeking will be yours.

The Practice of Looking for the Story

Step 1: Sit in meditation for a few minutes and observe your body, your breathing, sensations, thoughts, and feelings within the awareness you are . . . Now recall the most recent incident during which you were shaken or rattled, when your buttons were pushed, when you found yourself stewing over something or suffering in some way.

Simply be present with the memory. You can even welcome it, and affirm to yourself, "Ah, this is showing me where I am not yet free."

Step 2: Look for the story you told yourself immediately prior to the upset. Something happened, or someone said or did something, or you thought about something, and it triggered a reaction in you. It violated some deep-rooted belief or idea—your story—about the way things should be or ought to be. The consequence was upset and suffering.

From this more relaxed, meditative place, see how it was simply the story that caused the emotional reaction in you. Maybe the story arose from some rejection or hurt that happened to you far back in your past. You made up a story about it, and it's been running you ever since. This process may bring up other stories, other emotions, fears, and insecurities. Be present with them, too . . .

Notice how the story, thought, or belief you tell yourself shifts and changes, and the feelings and sensations you experience also shift and change.

Step 3: Then see the truth . . . You, as the awareness or witness watching it all, are always here. You don't change. Only the contents of your mind and the feelings in your body change . . .

If the situation triggering the upset is liable to happen again, you can visualize it in your mind. Imagine the worst-case scenario. See it happening. Then say to yourself, "What if this were to happen to me again? How would I respond to it if I were already free?" Then gently come back to being the clear, vibrant awareness you are.

This is an especially powerful way to work through your fear of death. What if you were about to die? What else can you do but be supremely present, face it with open eyes, so to speak? This is how a true warrior faces his or her last living moment—without any story—and you are learning to do the same.

You are developing the presence that will allow you to face all your fears and see their fundamental unreality. Your fears are just stories and pictures inside your head, with corresponding reactive feelings in your body. Who and what you really are is far, far bigger than anything you are experiencing.

As you illuminate these stories, beliefs, and images with the power of presence, with the clear light of your consciousness, they will dissolve. The contracted feelings will expand, and you will open up to the boundless clarity and freedom of your true nature.

3

Step 3: See the Truth

THE HEART OF THE teaching is seeing you are not your story. Rather, you are what is looking at the story—clear, vibrant, present-time consciousness. To make this real, you must practice being very present, very vigilant as you go through your day.

Eventually, you will come to realize you are the ultimate witness of everything you observe. You are the awareness, or consciousness, that notices your body, mind, personality, and the stories you tell yourself.

Such vigilance has vast rewards. When you truly see you are not your story, not any story, a shift will happen. You will find that stories lose their power over you and emotional upset and conflict dissolve, thereby freeing up your energy. You feel more centered and grounded in your true being, in pure consciousness itself. You see everything with new eyes. You can deal with what's before you with clarity and strength.

Now, a statement I sometimes hear is this: "I see the power of the shift you are talking about, yet I feel reluctant to let go of the religious story I grew up with. I guess I have lingering fears from my Catholic (or Protestant, or

Jewish, etc.) upbringing. I am afraid of God's judgment and of falling short of pleasing Him."

Our inner, spiritual journey only truly begins when we start the process of questioning the personal, cultural, and religious stories we have become so identified by, including our concepts of God and our fear of judgment.

The journey is a process of letting go of attachment to our inner conceptual reality as we seek, through silence and stillness, to find something beyond words and ideas, beyond our concepts and beliefs about God. It can be an unsettling time in our lives, because we are calling into question everything we've held most dear. Everything upon which we have built our personal senses of identity begins to come undone.

With deep self-examination, doubt and skepticism enter the picture, and we are no longer sure what to believe. We are no longer sure of who or what we are. In Zen, they say of this questioning phase: "Suddenly mountains are no longer mountains, rivers are no longer rivers."

This stage of our spiritual unfolding is a time of learning to be comfortable with *not* knowing, the necessary precursor to the attainment of true knowledge or insight. This phase can involve a lot of "dark night of the soul" experiences. These occur when all our inner fears, demons, and doubts build in intensity, and we feel as if there is absolutely nowhere to turn, least of all to a God in whom we have lost faith. Yet it is a perfect opportunity to develop our skill in the practice, in our ability to stay present and open to all of existence, in the face of self-doubt and uncertainty.

Here, our religious yearnings deepen and flower into true spirituality. Spirituality is religion made personal and experiential. Religion emphasizes beliefs, codes, doctrines, and the need for intermediaries—the priest, the pastor, the rabbi, the mullah—between us and the divine. Spirituality is characterized by letting go of beliefs and concepts, and opening to a more direct *experience* of the unity and joy which religion talks about.

This, of course, is after we have confronted, through the power of our own presence and unwavering awareness, whatever demons or dark nights may be assailing us. It requires us to be vulnerable, open to whatever is arising. At some point, most of us have to walk through our own personal fire, sometimes even a raging inferno of emotion, fear, or self-doubt, before we come to stillness and peace. It is perhaps no wonder someone once said, "Religion is for people afraid of going to hell; spirituality is for people who have already been there!"

If the religious stage of the journey is based on believing (or trying to believe) in some version of truth, or in whatever story about God and creation most appeals to us, this phase is where we start to actually know the truth for ourselves. Letting go of what we think we know, our awareness expands, and we begin to really *know*—to sense, in a deep and discernable way—the immensity and timelessness of the consciousness that is our true nature.

In moments of stillness, we can feel this consciousness as an actual energy, a flow, a powerful sense of mystery and presence. And this is where we find our faith: in the palpable nature of existence, rather than in stories, beliefs, and ideologies.

When you find yourself caught up in your head, in some story you are telling yourself, this is your signal to take a deep, slow breath, relax, and be present. Do the practice. Become very aware of what you sense and feel within and around you. Welcome, allow, whatever is arising in your experience. This is what it means to be a conscious human being.

Remind yourself of this often: you are *not* your story about who you are or what is happening. You are the ever-present consciousness, the timeless awareness witnessing, experiencing, and participating in the unfolding of creation.

The more you look within, the more you dive into the well of your own being—and here, in the depths of your own heart and soul, you discover the true source of well-being. The deeper you go into the present moment, the more likely you are to touch the bliss all spiritually awake people have discovered, regardless of religion, tradition, or lineage . . .

Do it now. Pause and be present for a few moments . . . Notice any thoughts or stories going on in your mind, and affirm: "I am not my story . . . " Then breathe, relax, and be present . . . Drop into the now . . . Then, from this place of clarity, visualize internally the vastness that is your true nature . . . The vastness manifested, when you are one with it, as bliss in every cell of your being . . . Breathe into this bliss . . . Relax into it . . . Then open your eyes and be fully present, here, now . . .

Bliss arises with knowing, through direct experience, that you really are a manifestation of the one divine energy or consciousness. You are a part of the loving force that births, nourishes, sustains, and guides the universe. This power is the source of all creation. When you know yourself as this power, the names we have traditionally given it don't really matter. As the *Tao Te Ching* says, "The Tao which can be named is not the Tao. If names be needed, wonder names it."

You may not be deeply established in this knowing yet. Maybe you often lose the sense of connectedness and unity. Maybe you still feel somewhat separate from the underlying flow of life. Maybe you hold to the idea of the witness, of being the dispassionate observer of the arising thoughts, feelings, and emotions, and this produces a certain dryness within you. This is inevitable.

Attaching to any concept or story, especially if it goes on for many years, always results in squeezing out the juice or extinguishing the passion from the moment-by-moment experience. Or maybe you go back and forth between peaceful, blissful meditative states and personal conflict, self-doubt, and resistance to what is.

Now, for many, many people, just to touch the divine in this way is enough, and they go no further. They find a home in their chosen religion or practice. They live in relative peace and harmony.

But for those seekers who hunger for full realization—as I did, and as you, reading this, probably do as well—relative peace and harmony are not enough. We want nothing less than for consciousness to awaken fully within us. By the time we get deeply into our inner journey, the barrier separating us from the realization of our true nature—our attachment to our story, to our beliefs, judgments, assumptions, prejudices, expectations, and desires—is becoming thinner and more transparent.

What takes us into the final phase of the journey is what fueled the hunger driving us to embark upon this questioning and seeking: the longing for true freedom.

Desire

Many people assume that awakening is synonymous with freedom from desire, but it actually means not being attached to desire. People who are awake are still living, breathing, feeling human beings. They still have desires and preferences, but the difference is that they are not attached to them. Consequently, they don't suffer. They don't experience disappointment, frustration, or anger when the desire is not fulfilled—or, if they do, it is only momentary, and they come back to their normal way of being, flowing with what is, very quickly.

Thomas Merton, the 20th century Trappist monk who was also keenly interested in Eastern wisdom, said, "The only desire not a sin is the desire for God."

Knowing that God is synonymous with awakening, or true inner freedom, you must want it more than you want anything else. That's the deal. You must want it more than you want money, power, fame, sex, relationships, or any of the seemingly infinite number of things human beings seek in order to find security, happiness, and fulfillment in their lives.

To desire these other things is not wrong in any moral sense, but it is a sin, as Merton points out. The original Greek word for sin meant "to miss the mark." A sin, then, is any action or behavior taking us away from the only place where authentic, lasting peace and happiness can be found: within the depths of our very own being, within our God-nature.

This is precisely why awakening continues to elude most people. They have been seduced by the media, movies, television, and popular magazines into thinking happiness lies out there somewhere. We are programmed to believe happiness lies in having more money, a bigger house, a more expensive car, a whiter smile, a thinner body, a prettier girlfriend, a more successful boyfriend, and so on.

There is nothing wrong with having any of these things in and of themselves. It's the attachment to them which creates all the suffering. If you make these things the sole focus of your life, you'll never find the deep happiness and freedom of your inner nature.

In this regard, Nisargadatta Maharaj said of enlightenment that it may seem arduous, but it is easy if you are earnest, and quite impossible if you are not. "Everything," he said, "yields to earnestness."[4]

Intention, which is earnestness with a focus, is fundamental to attaining anything worthwhile in life. Look at people who are successful in the world in every other sense, whether it's in politics, business, sports, entertainment, or just making money for its own sake. Such people are strongly motivated by their desires and have very clear goals. They pursue their goals with their whole heart and mind. They want to achieve their objectives more than they want anything else, and they are willing to make whatever sacrifice is necessary.

Awakening or enlightenment is no different. You must want it with your whole heart and mind. Yet there's a paradox here, too, because you must let go of the wanting at the same time. If you become too obsessed with getting enlightened, in the sense that you are always thinking about it, it gets in the way of your ordinary, daily life. You develop an unrealistic view of what enlightenment is. You develop a story about it. You can get so caught up in the pursuit of whatever you imagine enlightenment to be, you end up not dealing with such real-world issues as working, paying the rent, taking care of business. You end up not being present.

---

4   *I Am That*, 320

How to balance the deep desire with letting go? I like the mountain climbing analogy I read about in Robert Pirsig's *Zen and the Art of Motorcycle Maintenance*, in which he describes how a Zen master climbs a mountain. The master is determined to reach the summit, which, in our case, is a metaphor for awakening. He then lets go of the goal, puts it in the back of his mind, and focuses on enjoying the journey.

So it is with you. You remember that awakening is your ultimate goal, but that the ongoing work is to be truly aware and present each and every moment of the day. When you start getting caught up in your story, in your beliefs, concepts, justifications, excuses, judgments, and rationalizations, notice it. Notice it, then breathe and come back to the present, to the awareness of your true nature.

Come back to the awareness of yourself as the consciousness that gives birth to the entire universe, expressing itself through this body, mind, and heart called you. Come back to enjoying the journey.

Letting Go of the Story

Awakening is the result of releasing one's story, of releasing all beliefs, concepts, and images of self and opening up to the beauty and power of the present moment. It is letting go of the attachment to the forms of consciousness—thoughts, emotions, experiences—and finding your identity in the formless ground of being itself.

This release happens naturally when you see that the story—this internal drama you have so identified with all these years—is not even real. Then you are awakened into the timeless present.

In a workshop once, a woman said to me, "How can you say my story is not real? As a child, I was physically and emotionally abused by my stepfather, and my mother did nothing to stop it. Even now, at the age of forty, I still have strong memories of those years. Sometimes I have nightmares about them."

I responded that the experience of being abused as a child, in her case, was undoubtedly real when it happened, and repeated abuse over many years certainly reinforces a story of anxiety, victimhood, and suffering.

As long as you keep telling yourself the story—for example, "My horrible childhood scarred me for life"—then it will continue to generate feelings of pain and numbness, of grief and fear. You will indeed feel scarred to some degree, and this emotional scarring may affect your ability to function as a mature, responsible adult.

When people do have this kind of heavy emotional wounding from the past, it does seem very much as if the person is their story. Such people often need some intensive, long-term psychotherapy in order to begin to heal their past and free themselves from it. But no matter how psychologically or emotionally wounded you were back then, it was in the past, and this is now. There is no person abusing you now. If there is, the wise thing would be to immediately remove yourself from that person's company.

If you want to be free of suffering, then you must begin to look within. You must see that identification with your story—the attachment to your memories from the past—keeps retriggering pain and hurt in the present.

In other words, you believe the past matters, so you get lost in the forms of the past. But the memories, stories, and beliefs you hold on to, no matter how true you might insist they are ("I had a rotten childhood," "I'm not worthy," "My mind, with its haunting memories, won't shut up") only serve to prevent new creative and healing possibilities from revealing themselves to you.

The more you learn to be present, expand your awareness, and see the entire inner drama for what it is—a self-generated story, a mish-mash of thoughts, beliefs, and perceptions that cannot actually be found anywhere, other than in your mind—the more it all drops away. Without the psychological and emotional holding your body relaxes, your mind clears, and you start to awaken to the experience of your true nature as openness, spaciousness, and freedom.

However, even though freedom is realizing you are not your story, you still have a story. We all have a story. We all have many stories. One of the delights of being human is this ability we have to share our stories. We have stories of our history and culture; stories of the things we have built, dreamed, or imagined; stories of our successes, failures, mistakes, and lessons; and stories of our loves, losses, joys, sorrows, and despair.

The beauty of awakening is that, as you release attachment to and identification with the stories you have used to describe who you are, you are then able to live with them and talk about them without personally suffering over them. This makes them a lot more fun and enjoyable—and, yes, sometimes poignant and sad. At the same time, because you are no longer caught up in all the drama around them, you are able to learn whatever lessons you need to learn much more effectively and speedily.

The more quickly you let go the attachment to your own story, and just listen and pay attention to what *is*, the clearer you will get about any lesson you are supposed to learn, and the closer you'll be to the freedom you seek. Then you can begin to write a new story for your life, except now you will be doing it consciously, without the personal identification or attachment.

Drop All Philosophies

Until you actually awaken to deeper levels of freedom, it's inevitable that you will try to hold on to a story—some thought, belief, concept, or philosophy—which gives you the flavor and feeling of the freedom you seek. This is okay up to a point, but eventually it will become clear to you that even the words and philosophies, no matter how accurate or succinct they may be, have to be released.

One of the last public talks I attended with Jean Klein was in a church hall in Sausalito, California. There were fifty or sixty people in the room, waiting patiently for Jean to come in and take his seat at the front. When he arrived, he had to be helped to his chair. He seemed very old, thin, and frail, yet his gracious European bearing was still very much in evidence, and he was dressed as elegantly as ever.

He sat down with some difficulty and smiled at us. A beautiful, clear light emanated from his eyes. We sat in silence for a while, and then he began to speak. He talked of the need to see through the person so we could come to our real presence, our true being. There were some questions, and subsequent dialogue. About halfway through the evening, a serious-looking young woman in a business suit raised her hand. When Jean acknowledged her, she stood up. She looked like a banker, or a stockbroker.

"Dr. Klein, may I ask, what is your philosophy of life?"

There was a long silence. Then Jean beamed one of those disarming smiles of his. "Madame, I have no philosophy . . . That is why I am a happy man."

Laughter rippled throughout the room. The young woman smiled rather self-consciously, and then sat down.

For months after the exchange, I found myself thinking about Jean's words. It was so simple. Forget the philosophies, the stories, the beliefs, the theories and just abide in the openness and freedom of our true nature. Then we really will be happy. We'll live out of wholeness, with wisdom and compassion, and we'll do what needs to be done—without fuss, without bother.

But if we hold on to a philosophy, a belief system, or an agenda of any kind, we create a barrier to the unfolding of something deeper, something more authentic, fresh, and alive. When our beliefs reinforce the idea of being a separate self, a lonely wave on the ocean of life, it is that separation that breeds feelings of isolation, insecurity, and fear. But when we let go of all philosophies, all stories, and just be, happiness is ours . . .

See if you can touch that place right now . . . Be present with whatever you are experiencing . . . Notice any thoughts or stories passing through your mind, and any sensations or feelings in your body, and see them for what they are . . . Just passing phenomena, coming and going . . . Now visualize yourself as empty space on the inside of your body, an emptiness that is at the same time infinitely full . . . Notice how you, as the one who is aware of all this, are still very much here . . . In this moment, you need no story or philosophy to define you . . . Then open your eyes and just be present as the beautiful, conscious person you are . . .

Lose Your Head

One morning, a year or two before I finally awakened to the freedom that is our true nature, I was meditating on the deck outside the small country cottage where I used to live. My mind was a little bit noisy, my thinking cloudy. I wasn't feeling totally aligned in body, mind, and spirit. A certain ease was missing. As I sat on my meditation cushion and looked eastward, over the richly verdant hills and valleys to the mountains beyond, the words came to me:

Supremely present, mind still,
I breathe in the beauty of this moment.

This mantra worked for me many times over the years. For me it always held a special power, a reminder to be present. Anyway, I became very still, very alert, with all my senses engaged. Then, suddenly, my head pierced through the scattered gray clouds of thought still in my mind, and my awareness became like the morning sky itself—vast, pristine, and empty. Everything was stunningly, vibrantly clear.

I say it was as if my head pierced through the clouds, but when I noticed my body, it was as if I didn't have a head. Above my shoulders there was only awareness, openness, a boundless clarity and radiance . . . And it was streaming with the world around me . . . The sky itself, the trees and the valley nearby, the mountains in the distance, the occasional crow flying by, a turkey vulture circling lazily overhead, all became one.

It was the strangest experience, and wholly illuminating. It was the first time I saw that everything between my ears was unreal. The stories aren't real. Thought is unreal. The pictures and images passing through the mind are unreal. They are just phantoms, ephemeral flashes, momentary appearances, which may have a symbolic or creative value, but have no separate reality in and of themselves.

As I sat there, breathing into the extraordinary feeling and freedom of being headless, I remembered a book I'd read many years before, by the English mystic Douglas Harding. It was called *On Having No Head*. In it he describes an experience similar to mine, which resulted in him realizing his true nature.

One day he was hiking in the Himalayas, and everything in his mind suddenly stopped. He looked down at his legs, passed his gaze upward to his shirtfront, and found a hole where his head was supposed to be. But the hole wasn't empty; it was filled with the vastness of the Himalayan panorama all around him. In his words, "I had lost a head and gained a world."

Throughout the day, periodically contemplate the notion that the world you've created between your ears is unreal—including your sense of self, of being a somebody with a personal history. This practice alone will bring you, sooner or later, to the headless state. In seeing that thought has no substantial reality, your head will start to clear.

Instead of having this solid, round, bowling-ball-like thing that worries, frets, and obsesses sitting on your shoulders, you'll start to experience a lightness, a spaciousness, a wonderful sense of emptiness and freedom where your head used to be.

The experience of headlessness brings you into your body, into your heart. It dissolves the illusion of fear and opens the door to love. As you begin to live more fully in your body, in your natural state of awareness, sensation, and feeling, you won't need a conceptual identity. You won't need to cling to stories and beliefs, to a self-image of any kind.

You'll use thinking as the creative instrument it is, but you won't be controlled by it.

You'll awaken to who and what you really are. The current of energy or spirit behind all creation will become a tangible presence for you. This will be all the proof you need of your own existence.

This ability to actually feel the beauty and power of the energy you are made of will be all the evidence you need of your life being inherently meaningful and worthwhile.

Loneliness and the Void

A forty-year-old man once shared with me, "I am going through a very difficult time. Whenever I sit to meditate, I get to a point where I start to feel a sense of peace, of well-being. And then, from somewhere deep inside me, a thought or image floats up having to do with my family, my friends, or my work, and it produces a feeling of anxiety.

"It makes me feel as if I am on the wrong path, and instead of bringing me more into life, meditation is somehow cutting me off from it. I find myself suddenly feeling very alone in the universe—achingly alone. It feels like this terrible void, and panic sets in. I have to immediately think about something positive, or stop meditating altogether. What should I do about this?"

Many, many years ago I went through something very similar. Like this man, I would sit and meditate, get to a certain depth of relaxation, and then an awful sense of emptiness, of the void, would loom. In my case, this went on for well over a year. It got to where I was almost afraid to sit and meditate any more.

Then, in 1982, I attended a retreat led by Richard Moss in Southern California's high Mojave Desert. Richard was a former medical doctor who became a transformational teacher. His work had a major impact on me at the time. He taught me to get out of my head, out of the realm of thought, and awaken to energy, sensation, feeling, to the nonverbal elements of experience.

As the retreat began, I made a pact with myself: for the next ten days I wouldn't try to intellectually understand the experiences I went through. I'd been experimenting with a new kind of awareness in my life and discovered how powerful it was to just be in the *experience* of whatever was happening, without the interference of the conceptual, analytical, story-making mind.

It turned out to be an extraordinary ten days, with many peak experiences, insights, breakthroughs, emotional highs, and a few lows. Then, on the last evening, about an hour before we were to attend our final dinner, I decided to meditate for a bit. I bundled up, for the night was cold, went out into the darkness, and sat on the porch of my cabin. It was utterly quiet and still. Above me, the night sky was black and immense, carpeted with the brilliant light of myriad stars. In the valley stretching out before me were a few scattered lights from the ranches in the area. Beyond the valley were the rugged mountains, darkly silhouetted against the night sky.

As I sat I began to get very still. At first there was peace, a gentle letting go of the tension I'd been carrying in my body from a long hike I'd taken that afternoon. But as I became more still, it began to happen again: the haunting emptiness and loneliness plaguing my meditations started to descend like a dark cloud. I found myself thinking of my parents who lived far, far away, in New Zealand, and of a brother who lived in Australia. I wondered whether I would ever see them again. Being in the desert, in the dark, barren emptiness, just magnified what I was feeling.

Suddenly, I had had enough. I didn't want to meditate any more. I didn't want to be a solitary seeker of truth. I didn't want to be enlightened. It was too lonely. It brought up too much fear, the fear of the unknown. I told myself I would think about something else, something normal. I'd had enough of cutting myself off from life in this way.

But something within told me not to run off into my mind, to just stay with the emptiness, to be very present with it. I remembered some words Richard quoted from the Bible about exalting the valleys. The message was to embrace whatever was happening.

Several years later, I heard Jean Klein say the same thing, but in different words: "Welcome your experience." The idea was not to run from whatever was happening, but to face it. To be supremely present with it, and not get lost in any story—not get into your head—about it.

In facing it and trusting it, the feeling or sensation undergoes a transformation and becomes something else. This is the way to freedom. In my case, I realized it was fear I was running from, especially the fear of not-being, the fear of "Who am I without my story?"

So, it was an innate trust, something deeper within me, which now whispered, "It's all right, Jim, this emptiness is showing you where you're not yet free. Let it be your friend. Don't reject it. You've been running from it for a long time. Why don't you just be with it?"

So I breathed slowly and deeply into every part of my body. Then I looked up at the cold night sky again, the brilliant stars. They seemed to take on a friendly twinkle. When I turned my attention within again, I found the emptiness was still there, but somehow it didn't feel quite so empty. The edge had been taken off. It didn't make me anxious as it did before.

After a while, I got up and went down to join the others for dinner. It was a happy evening, a celebration of all we'd been through together, and there was much joy and laughter. During the evening, I occasionally checked inside to see what I was feeling. The emptiness was hardly there. It was more like a vaguely felt memory.

After that desert retreat, the emptiness never came back again, at least not with any force behind it, and I was able to go to new depths in my meditations. When it did surface, I'd just face it, accept it, and breathe into it. It would always diminish and eventually dissipate. You'll find the same freedom too, if you learn to exalt the valleys and to welcome even the so-called negative experiences. Don't run from fear and it will become your friend.

No matter what you are experiencing, no matter what the sensation, feeling, or emotion, be very present with it. Treat it as a residue of the past. There is nothing to get upset about, so breathe into it and let your awareness expand. Don't get into your head, into some story about what is happening. If it helps, tell yourself: "Ah, I welcome this feeling. It is showing me where I am not yet free." Or you can just say, "This too shall pass," as it will. Then open yourself to it.

Open yourself not just to the residue of anxiety or fear, but to all you are aware of in this moment. Breathe deeply and be very present. Remember what you are here for: to awaken, to be free.

Do this, and the energy will shift. It will come into harmony. Then you will know the peace of your true nature. You will have a direct experience of it, and it won't depend on anything, not on any story, belief, condition, or circumstance.

How Do I Hold On to This?

One of the most common questions I am asked by people who have tasted their true, timeless nature is: "How do I hold on to this peace, harmony, or bliss I am feeling?" Of course the answer is you can't hold on to it, because it is what you fundamentally are.

It is only when you, as pure awareness or consciousness, see through the illusion of the ego, the little, mind-made me who wants to try and maintain the peaceful or blissful state, that you relax into the ease and spaciousness of your natural state of being. In other words, see that the very question itself is another story in your mind blocking you from being free.

Earlier, I spoke of Suzuki Roshi, and how he said it was important to have a beginner's mind. Beginner's mind is not something you acquire. It is your natural state of being. To return to it, let go of all the knowledge and all the stories you have accumulated, even if only for a minute or two, and just be very present in this moment. Be aware of yourself *as* the awareness, the consciousness behind everything. Do this and you are in beginner's mind. Then there will be no question about holding onto anything. You will simply be in the flow, at peace, one with life.

Let me tell you another Zen story, which speaks exquisitely about this practice of beginner's mind. Two monks were strolling down a path toward a river. The older one was an enlightened master. The other monk was much younger, but still a sincere seeker. As they drew near the water, they came across a young woman who, by her manner, was evidently distressed.

"I must get over the river without getting my kimono wet, but the recent rains have made it too deep for me to cross," the woman said. She looked at the two monks.

"I have to visit the parents of my fiancé. Will you please carry me? I would be most grateful."

"By all means," said the master, beckoning the younger man to help with lifting her. The young monk hesitated, frowning, but then held out his hands. Together, they made a seat out of their four clasped hands, and carried the young woman safely across.

"Thank you," she said, as she stepped onto the dry ground, gave a gracious bow, and went on her way.

The two monks walked off. After they walked a few miles the younger man, who had been internally stewing since the moment they stopped to help the woman, turned to the older monk.

"I don't understand it, Master," he said. "According to the rules of our monastery, we are not supposed to even talk to young unmarried women, let alone touch them."

"Ah," said the master, turning to the younger man, "You're still carrying her . . . I put her down by the river."

This has always been one of my favorite Zen teachings. Zen is a philosophy or spiritual path with its own set of traditions, rules and regulations. Yet Zen masters throughout history have been notorious for breaking them. They understand rules are meant to serve as guidelines only. In this story, the master was being guided by his heart, not his head. The young woman needing help took precedence over the rules about touching unmarried women. So, for him, there was no hesitation in providing assistance.

The attachment to wanting something to believe in, some principle, rule, or understanding to hold on to in order to feel a sense of security, is always strong at the beginning of the spiritual journey. However, such attachment invariably gets in the way of our responding intelligently, creatively, and lovingly to the very real needs of the present moment. Opening up to a deeper level of freedom and happiness in the present begins with the deliberate release of whatever you are holding onto from the past.

As you learn to put your baggage down, to empty your mind in this way, a tremendous gathering of energy happens, because it is no longer being fragmented or dissipated by thought. You find yourself being very aware in the present.

In this state of awareness and openness, thinking is liberated from all the psychological and emotional overlays, and is available as a powerful creative tool—a tool for wise and compassionate action.

Let Go of Your Attachment to Bliss

Like the question about holding onto the awakened state, I hear variations of this quite often: "When I started my own spiritual journey many years ago, I was moved by a burning desire not just for my own freedom, but also I really wanted to make a difference in the world. As time went by, it became easier and easier to quiet my mind in meditation.

"Then, more recently, I began to discover, in stillness and silence, a great sense of peace and bliss. Now I feel like I have become attached—almost addicted—to the bliss. I am really present when I meditate—supremely present, to use your term—but I find myself wanting to turn my back on the world and its insanity. Sometimes I feel like Nero, fiddling away while Rome burns."

If you are serious about your spiritual quest, then having a world where everyone has the freedom to be themselves, and to express themselves creatively, has to be important to you. After all, spirituality is about awakening to wisdom and love, to the oneness we share in common with all humanity—indeed, with all life.

But as you go deeper on the path, as you learn to be more present, to relax and open up to the beauty and power of the now moment, you do feel that power in your body as bliss. With deep muscular relaxation, a flood of endorphins, the pain-dissolving hormones, are released. I call endorphins "the bliss chemicals." They make you feel as if every cell in your body is vibrating with bliss, with ecstasy. It is incredibly healing and transformative. At the same time, you're opening up to the deeper, spiritual energy that infuses all creation itself. This presence is itself the source of profound harmony.

So, when this is new to you, it is understandable that you might forget about your original intention to help contribute to a freer and more loving world. It is easy to get lost in the delight of meditation, seduced by the mystery and wonder of your own travels through inner space. You begin to build a story about yourself as a seeker, as a meditator, an inner journeyer.

It happened to me. There's nothing wrong with this, for awhile. Just as teenagers have to push their edges and explore their limits, we must do the same when we are exploring our spirituality for the first time. Eventually you'll come to see even bliss has its limits. It's like sex. An orgasm would cease being enjoyable if it went on too long. Any sensation, feeling, or emotion lasting too long inevitably turns to suffering.

Bliss is a state; it comes and goes. When you get attached to a state through creating some story around it, you sow the seeds of suffering. The suffering arises either when the bliss is not there, or, the bliss *is* there but life is calling you, and now you've got this distraction taking you away from the bliss you've grown so addicted to.

Let me tell you a story. When my son Adam was about a year old, around the time I met Jean Klein, I reached a point in my meditations where it was easy for me to be completely present and to release all the tension in my mind and body, and open up to bliss. Waves of bliss just rolled through me, and I felt like I was in heaven. I fabricated a story around my new experience, convinced I had found enlightenment—not 100 percent convinced, but maybe 80 or 90.

Then, one morning as I sat to meditate, I was just beginning to cruise on the feeling of bliss when Adam started crying from the bedroom next door. His mother Barbara called out to me, "Jim, please go change Adam's diapers. I'm busy!" I remember cringing inside. The feeling of bliss was getting really strong, and the last thing I wanted to do was get up from my meditation and change my son's soiled diapers.

Then I heard a voice inside me—the voice of my conscience, no doubt!—saying: "Jim, your son is uncomfortable, he needs his diapers changed, and you don't want to go do it because it will interrupt your blissful meditation. And you call this *enlightenment*?"

So I got up and changed his diapers, and received a great lesson as well, a lesson now reinforced by my experience with having met Jean. Awakening, or enlightenment, as he said, is not about being attached to states of bliss, nor to states of peace, joy, stillness, or anything else.

It is about seeing through the illusion of the me. It is about getting free of identification with thought, with the world between our ears. It is about living in awareness, being supremely present, welcoming whatever is arising, and doing what needs to be done, whether it is changing diapers or going to the office every day, whether it is looking at ways to clean up the environment or help the homeless, eliminate poverty or solve any of the other countless problems facing us as human beings.

Sooner or later, you come to realize you're not on this path of freedom or spiritual awakening just for your own benefit. You're not doing it just for your own peace of mind, or to free yourself from your own conflict and stress—although it's an important first step, and is where most of us begin. Ultimately, you're doing it so the world can be a better place.

More and more, the liberation from fear, the awakening of the heart, becomes your guiding vision, your *raison d'être*. Then, as your freedom, fearlessness, and compassion deepen, you'll touch people in ways you cannot even imagine.

You'll understand what Oliver Wendell Holmes meant when he said, "The place for a man who is complete in all his parts is in the fight."

You may not do great things, you may not work on a very big scale or play in a big arena—very few of us will—but even to help your neighbor, to do good work in your own family or community, will be plenty. If each of us picked up our own garbage, spoke with kindness, and acted out of a genuine sense of respect and regard for our fellow human beings, even though we may not agree with their beliefs or condone their behavior, the world would soon change.

In any case, the delightful discovery is that when you release the attachment to bliss, you realize that bliss is always here. You just have to stop, get still, breathe, relax your body, and—presto!—peace, stillness, the bliss and fullness of *being*, it's right here. It has always been right here. It really is your true nature. It is *our* true nature . . .

See if you can experience it right now . . . Pause, and be very still, very alert, supremely present . . . Let go of any thoughts and stories in your mind, and just be right here, now . . . Then tune in to the vastness within, the vastness which is at the same time full . . . See if you can feel that fullness as bliss bubbling throughout every dimension of your being . . . Breathe and relax into it . . . Then, let the idea, the story of bliss go, open your eyes, and just be here . . .

Seeing from the Reality behind Reality

The 8th century's Shankara, from India, was one of the original masters of nondual wisdom, the understanding of reality as fundamentally one, indivisible Whole. He said, "The realization of truth is brought about by discrimination, and not in the least by ten millions of acts."

What he meant by this is all the spiritual techniques and practices, and all the good works in the world, will not set you free. Working with the body or engaging in breathing techniques won't do it. Meditation won't do it. Compassionate service to mankind won't do it. These practices are beneficial—and compassion, certainly, is needed throughout the world—but only the shift in perception, the clear discrimination that Shankara speaks of, will set you free: the shift from the limited, ego-bound perspective of me, myself, and my story into the expanded vision of clear, thought-free, present-time awareness.

The more aware of this you become, the more you intuitively realize you are not your body, mind, or senses because these can be observed. Rather, you are what is observing. What you actually are is pristine awareness or consciousness expressing through this unique instrument, this individual body/mind/self called you. You are the timeless, unchanging awareness noticing and responding to the endlessly changing drama that is life. You are the consciousness giving birth to the entire world between your ears, the world that you have always thought of as you.

The deeper the realization of yourself as the consciousness behind everything—as the ocean, expressing itself as the wave called you—the closer you draw to the perceptual shift that is true inner freedom.

Eventually, if you keep seeking the core truth about who you are, the realization becomes complete and you no longer have to work at being aware. You will see that the world between your ears really is a kind of dreamworld, a self-generated fiction, a story of your own making, and just through seeing this, it begins to fall away. You don't even have to actively drop it. Once you see the story you have been so attached to is not real, you will lose interest in it, in the same way a child lets go of the Santa Claus myth (albeit with much reluctance!) upon being told Santa is not real.

Your mind no longer controls you. Instead, you as consciousness are now fully in control of it. You still have thoughts, but you now know you are not your thoughts. You still have a story, but you now know you are not your story. You still have an ego, but now you know you are not your ego. From this place of inner freedom, you can then begin to use thought in a conscious, highly intentional way. You can use the creative power of thoughts to manifest the results you seek in your life. This is what it means to see, and to live, from the Reality behind reality.

As the teaching and the practice start to become more and more your way of life, your physical, mental, and emotional energies find their natural balance and harmony. Healing can then take place, often at very deep levels. If an illness or physical condition persists, it is much easier to live with and manage. Once you have awakened to your true nature, these kinds of things no longer get you down in the way they did before.

Whether it is a health problem or some other challenging or difficult circumstance, you do everything you can to address it, to heal it, to fix it, to change it, but you don't suffer because of it. If nothing can be done for the present, then you relax and accept it. You flow with it. You pay attention to the lessons to be learned, if any. You apply the learning in whatever way is appropriate.

The Teaching and Practice in Real Life

A young woman asked me, "For a long time I have been interested in spiritual matters, especially in the freedom you are speaking about. My husband doesn't support my interest. He thinks meditation and the pursuit of the spiritual life is a waste of time, just an escape, having little to do with real life. What do you say to this?"

I told her I was reminded of a cartoon I saw once about a young seeker who has just climbed to a mountaintop refuge, where a wise-looking, gray-bearded man is sitting on a mat. The seeker says to him, "Master, tell me please, what is the meaning of life?" The guy looks at him with his eyebrows raised, and says, "Beats me. I'm just up here hiding from my creditors."

No doubt about it, meditation and spiritual practices can be an escape from everyday life and responsibility. But as long as spirituality is taken up with the right attitude, it always brings us more fully into life. It helps us become more present because it gradually frees us from the identification with our ego and from the kinds of personal motives and agendas getting in the way of real, heartfelt communication.

Look at the current state of real life. The world is still in upheaval, with terrorist acts and clashes between warring factions ever on the rise. All wars cause an enormous amount of suffering, most of it inflicted on innocents, what the American military likes to euphemistically call "collateral damage." Regardless of who initiates the war or who is at fault, most wars are fueled by issues of money, power, greed, and the stories people hold on to and identify with around those issues.

Some wars are the result of ethnic, tribal, and religious conflicts, but ultimately they too are symptomatic of a deeper drive, the lust for both economic and political power. In turn, this lust for power comes out of a deep insecurity, the ego's story of what it is convinced it needs for its own survival.

Sincere seekers, like the young woman above, sometimes say to me that when they look at the world situation, it always seems so hopeless. It makes them want to escape, to seek refuge in a monastery or an ashram somewhere.

I tell them that, while retreat time in monasteries or ashrams is always beneficial, any illumination we find there must be brought into the world. We must bring it from the mountaintop into the marketplace; otherwise, what good is it?

When you really look at what is going on in politics and business, it is not so hard to figure out. In all countries, in all cities and towns, you have groups of men— for it is mostly men—who scheme, manipulate, and use force or violence to further their own personal interests. Meanwhile, inside themselves, they live in darkness. They have become disconnected from the light of truth they once knew when they were very young. Now, they only know reflected light, the light of bright, shiny, expensive objects, or of religious artifacts, "holy" books, and creeds invested with arbitrary meaning.

They are convinced the truth lies in such objects, and they can only find happiness through them. Thus they live in illusion, in their stories. As a result of identifying with their own dark story, they suffer tremendous anxiety and fear deep in their psyches. Through their willful and malicious actions, they inflict extraordinary amounts of suffering on innocent men, women, and children.

Awakening to inner freedom is the only way out of illusion. Awakening frees you from the ego's grip and its endless fears and insecurities. It brings you to the joy of your true nature, the joy not dependent on objects or reflected light, but the light shining from within you, the light which you *are*. This is the light Jesus spoke of when he said, "I am the Light."

It is important to remember that awakening is not just about your own bliss and freedom. The deeper you move into the enlightened awareness of your real nature, the more you feel your connection with the rest of humanity.

Then your motive for awakening becomes less personal, and more about the larger picture. You realize the sooner a critical mass of us wakes up to our true, divine nature, the sooner we'll have a world working for everyone and everything. If you have children, people, pets, or things you love, then having a world which is a safe, nurturing, and harmonious environment for all of us becomes a real priority.

The teaching and practice are powerful tools to bring you into the place where wisdom and love meet, where mind and heart become one. As more of us find this union within ourselves, then regardless of whether we live in relative anonymity or hold positions of leadership and influence, there is a cumulative effect.

The social atmosphere starts to become saturated with consciousness, and others, still not quite awake, pick up on it. It's beautiful how it works.

Helping People Get Free of Their Stories

When I do a workshop or private session, I am simply present with people as I guide them into the experience of being present with themselves and their environments. Sometimes, this process involves uncovering and facing the demons they haven't been willing to look at. If that is the case, I journey with them through the dark depths, and sometimes the raging inferno, of their own inner turmoil.

I guide the person through the practice—which, as you may be beginning to realize, is exquisitely simple yet powerfully transforming. As the person enters ever more deeply into the *now*, they find themselves freer of attachment to any story and the suffering it causes. They are clearer, more relaxed, more rooted in their own authentic being. Meanwhile, if it is in a workshop, the rest of the group, facing the issue they want to explore, is following along, experiencing their own little—and sometimes big—"Ah-ha!" moment.

The traumatic incident from the past is typically something that happened when they were very young—being left alone by their mothers on the first day of school, perhaps, and not feeling safe. Or maybe it is a memory of abandonment, sadness, guilt, or betrayal. That long ago event has been running their lives from the shadows ever since. I accompany them from a place of being very present. I am alert, calm, and relaxed. This encourages them to be the same. They get to explore their own pasts from the clear perspective of the present.

At one workshop, I worked with a middle-aged woman named Jane. Her story was that she was grieving the death of her dad, who had died just two months previously. He was mostly very mean to her throughout her life, as were her two brothers, who of course had learned their behavior from their father. Nevertheless, she wanted to be with him while he was dying. She said she wanted to show him unconditional love.

She was sobbing as she was telling this story, and I just listened, was very present with her. Then she said his last act, as he was lying on his deathbed, was to touch her with surprising tenderness on the cheek, and tell her he loved her.

A few other people in the workshop were weeping, too. As she finished telling her story, I gently directed her back to being present in this moment now. I encouraged her to be aware of her breathing, to feel the aliveness in her body, to notice her environment, the presence of the other participants in the workshop, the sound of my voice . . . Soon, she was deeply relaxed, and much more present. She was quite radiant, in fact, and looked at least ten years younger.

Then, about five days later, I received this email from her: "I can't tell you how different I feel. I feel like my life is changing . . . I feel such an amazing shift that it's hard to explain, but then, I don't need to explain it to you."

She didn't need to explain it to me because that is I why I do the work I do. When people release their stories of the past and the pent-up emotions around them, they are liberated in the present. They feel relaxed, alive, and always look younger than they did before.

Sophia was another woman I worked with privately. She was thirty-five years old and had been on a spiritual journey all her adult life. She had lived in an ashram and studied with many different teachers, yet still had not found freedom from the emotional pain of her childhood.

Her story was a familiar one, a story of abandonment, which she had tried to heal, unsuccessfully, through her years of spiritual seeking. Hers was a classic case of "spiritual bypass," using spirituality to deny, avoid, or try to transcend difficult and painful emotions.

When she was a child, her mother had ignored her emotional needs, and her father was never around, always busy with his work. Now, she fluctuated between experiences of real peace and bliss born of her years of spiritual practice, and times of extreme pain, sadness, and emotional trauma, such that she found herself feeling so alone, so lost, that she didn't want to live anymore.

When I met her, she was caught in the pain of her abandonment. She was wracked with grief, sobbing like a child. I looked into her eyes and encouraged her to honor her feelings, but not go into her usual story about them, which basically was: *I feel so alone . . . life is not worth living . . . I just want to die . . .*

Then I said, gently but firmly, "You can handle this, Sophia. These feelings are from your childhood, but you are now thirty-five years old. You are a grown woman, wise and powerful, and you are bigger than anything you are experiencing, including these feelings and emotions. So, *be* the wise, powerful woman you are . . . "

Soon, she stopped crying and began to breathe more calmly and evenly. She looked back at me with a steady, open-eyed gaze. Her dark brown eyes sparkled. Slowly, she smiled, and said, "I *can* handle it . . . It's true; I am bigger than the emotional pain I experience. Wow . . . "

Then she gave me a warm embrace and thanked me. I said to her, "No, thank *you*. Thank you for being vulnerable enough to share your pain with me. Now you have a new *mantra* to say to yourself whenever those feelings of abandonment, and the stories around it, start to surface."

She smiled again, and said, "Yes . . . I can handle it."

Now, maybe the emotion being triggered is a fear of something in the future. Then I invite the person to really look at the worst-case scenario, to play it out, visualize it actually happening, but again, always from the perspective of the *present*.

When seen from the present, you realize you are always okay in this moment. The stories and worst-case scenarios appearing between your ears are just imagined, made-up, although the feelings and sensations they evoke are real. But the minute you get that you are okay *now*— which is the essence of awakening, or self-realization—the stories dissolve, and the fear and other disturbing reactions fall away.

You can do it yourself. Maybe it has to do with nervousness. Sit with the question, "What is the cause of my nervousness?" suspended in your mind. Look at it from different angles. Notice what images, memories, or thoughts surface. Perhaps you will remember a time when you first asked a question, and the teacher scolded you or humiliated you.

You may need to probe into your past to find the emotional trauma or event, the origin of the story. Seeing the truth behind your old reactive patterns is the beginning of freedom. It takes courage to face yourself in this way. It takes trust in the process, trusting that what you get is going to be better than what you are letting go of. You don't know that going in. In a way, you have to free fall.

When you face the trauma, there may be emotion there, the experiencing of an old wound. You may get angry, sad, depressed. You have to be present with it. You have to learn to welcome whatever is there.

Once, in a workshop, a man had a memory spontaneously surface. He told me, "I remember this very crabby teacher from second grade, jabbing her finger at me and telling me if I had been paying attention like all the other boys and girls, I wouldn't need to ask such a stupid question. So, what do I do with this memory?"

I answered him by saying that there are many ways of addressing this, or any other problem. The decision of how to approach it is always yours. I teach the direct way, the direct path. When the forgotten memory—and the story around it—surfaces, and you realize that this is indeed where the nervousness or fear originated, simply hold it in your consciousness. Hold the past scene in your awareness. Remember all the details you can. See it vividly. Keep breathing as you do this.

If it brings up emotion and starts to get too intense, you can always let it go and come back to it later, maybe when you meditate tomorrow morning. Just make sure you come back to it, and quickly. You want to deal with this and be done with it. Our goal is to let go and release whatever gets in the way of our being here, fully present and available to life in this moment.

Basically, you just face the old wound and the story around it from this very clear, centered, grounded awareness. Welcome it. After all, it is showing you where you are not yet free.

You may notice that, because you are able to dispassionately observe this scene in your mind, the memory of the scene is *not* who you are. Who you really are is what is looking or observing, pure unbounded awareness, or consciousness itself. This is the shift in perception I have spoken of. The more you stand firm in this place of present-time awareness, the less charge and emotional reactivity the memory will generate.

When you shine the light of intense, present-time awareness on a story, thought, sensation, or feeling, what you are observing undergoes a change. Stories, thoughts, and pictures in the mind dissolve, uncomfortable sensations and feelings in the body unwind, and a feeling of true clarity and harmony begins to unfold throughout your entire being.

The Practice of Being Present

Step 1: Whenever upset, anxiety, or suffering arises, be present with it, even welcome it. Ask yourself, "What am I experiencing right now?" Pay attention to the feelings and sensations of the contraction or disturbance.

Step 2: Notice the story you are telling yourself, whatever the story is. If you like, you can step back with your awareness, out of the story. This helps you see it more clearly. If necessary, play out the worst-case scenario.

Step 3: See the truth. See that you are the one who sees. Take a deep, slow breath, and relax. Be very alert with your whole being. Continue to notice the sensations in your body. Feel the energy, the aliveness in your cells. Listen to the sounds around you. Look at the things, natural and human-made, in your environment.

See the connection between the story and the upset emotion in your body. Allow the emotion, which is real in this moment, to be there, but don't go into your head; don't go into any new stories or thoughts about it. Just be the spacious, present-time awareness you are, looking out through your eyes at the whole of life. Be the unchanging awareness behind the ever-changing stories, behind the ever-changing emotions.

Do this practice, and I promise you, your energy will soon shift. So long as you continue to be very alert and aware and don't go into concepts, into denial or rejection of the emotion, into analyzing or trying to understand, or anything else, the contracted emotion will unwind, dissolve. You will feel more relaxed, more at ease, more present.

Then you will find that, while you still have thoughts and feelings, you, as the awareness or consciousness that watches and experiences everything, will be senior to them. Your thoughts will not be a problem. They will have no emotional charge. Then you can use thinking for the powerful, creative tool it is. You can use it to manifest whatever your heart desires. That's its job. You can think of it as the "right use of thought."

⤳ 4 ⤳

Questioning This Me

ONCE YOU BECOME ACCUSTOMED to being present with whatever is happening and looking for the story behind your times of conflict, upset, or suffering, you will inevitably begin—if you are at all curious—to question the very me you think you are. This is where you take the fourth step I spoke about at the end of the introduction.

With deep self-inquiry, you'll see the me is just a story, too—the root of all stories, the storyteller—and that your true nature is the lucid, unchanging consciousness behind everything.

It is about looking into the very heart of who and what you take yourself to be. You have to understand, not just at an intellectual level, but with every fiber of your being, who you really are and what your place in the cosmos is. Paradoxically, you arrive at this understanding by observing and discovering who and what you are *not*.

This means seeing and understanding you are not your body, mind, story, thoughts, or senses. You cannot be them, in the most essential sense, because you are observing them. What you are is the consciousness aware of them, *seeing* them. Your true nature, in other words, *is* consciousness itself.

The practice we have been cultivating prepares you for this understanding. The teaching *is* the understanding. It is the simple yet elegant explanation of the true nature of reality, the metaphysical framework that informs and brings light to your mind, and points it in the right direction, back within, where truth lies.

There are two aspects to the teaching: the primary aspect and the secondary aspect. The primary aspect explores the principal barrier to presence, which is thinking. This exploration leads you to the realization you are not your thoughts, not your story, but rather you are the awareness or consciousness behind the thoughts. This is the discovery that frees you from your mind and leads to liberation.

The secondary aspect has to do with conscious creation, with the conscious use of thought and intention to create the reality you desire. When we understand thoughts have power, we can then use thinking in a conscious way, from a very clearheaded space. This is where awakening to inner mastery leads naturally to outer mastery, to success in the world of the marketplace.

Once you understand the teaching, know it at the core of your being, deeply enough to produce the shift in perception that sets you free, you won't need to keep it at the forefront of your mind any more. You won't need to contemplate it. It will have done its job. Once in a while, if some residue of self-doubt appears, you have the teaching—"I am not this story; I am the awareness *behind* the story"—to remind you of what is real. And the teaching is there to share with others who are still seeking and want to know what must happen if they are to be free.

The practice, however, is what you *do*, and is available as long as you need it. It is a practice both for finding freedom and for living itself. Residues from old patterns, from your story, can still arise when you are tired or sick, and you may have to make an effort to be present. Occasionally, during the first few years after awakening, old tendencies to resist or refuse something in your inner experience may also occur, but you will have these tools to gently remind yourself to be vulnerable, to accept what is, and to embrace it all.

Through the practice of presence, you embody the teaching and the understanding that has been revealed to you. This practice enables you to translate what you learn from meditation into the reality of the marketplace of daily life; it brings you into your heart and opens you to unconditional love. Once you are fully awake, then you are always present.

To understand the teaching, it helps to look again at the nature of suffering and how it arises. Suffering, in the way I define it, is the mental and emotional distress resulting from feeling victimized by some situation or circumstance in life.

Something happens, whether real or imagined—pain, illness, unexpected change, loss, a setback, or a difficult situation—and it provokes a reaction. It pushes a button, and you don't like it. You don't like what is happening. You already have a story about the event, and you create an even bigger, more dramatic story, which, in turn, increases stress and upset. As a result, you are discontented, unhappy, even more miserable. This is what it means to suffer.

Someone once asked me, "In what way is suffering different than just feeling your emotions? Isn't grieving the death of a loved one a kind of suffering too?"

Suffering is different than feeling your emotions deeply. Grieving the loss of someone you love, or feeling angry at the injustice in the world, at seeing someone harm another, is natural and normal. It is not suffering. When your heart is open to life, when you live in a state of acceptance or welcoming, you feel these things very deeply, and the feelings last as long as they last.

Some people may feel deep, intense grief at the loss of a loved one for a week or a month, and then it is basically over, except for residual waves of emotion, which may continue to wash over them from time to time. Others, perhaps because the bond with the loved one was so strong, may be in mourning for much longer. They need to take their time letting go. It is their way of honoring the remarkable connection, the story they shared with the person they loved, who is now gone. Again, this is not necessarily suffering.

Suffering is when you don't *like* what you are feeling or what is happening, and that makes you unhappy. It is always due to some form of resistance, which causes us to close down in some fashion. It is the exact opposite of being open, welcoming, and vulnerable. Conflict, self-doubt, anxiety, guilt, resentment, fear, loneliness, depression, and all other forms of discontent and unhappiness are always the result of resisting what is.

Resistance, in turn, is caused by holding onto beliefs, judgments, expectations, and pictures about the way things are or should be. It comes from fabricating, in your mind, some kind of story about what is happening. For example, you feel a numbing, tired sensation in your body, and you say to yourself, "I don't like this; I must be depressed." Or you notice someone look at you in a strange way. You think you are being judged and start to feel guilty or angry.

You can let go of the thoughts that are the source of the resistance, the story, and simply be present with what is. When you breathe into and flow with the ever-changing moods, feelings, and circumstances, you will no longer experience conflict or suffering. However, letting go of resistance to what is—of your assumptions, expectations, judgments, and so on—is not always easy. It is relatively easy for most people to let go of their inner agenda in some circumstances, but they find it very difficult in highly personal situations with an intense emotional charge.

To let go of resistance at the deepest level, so you can be fully open to life and other people in each moment—which is one of the signs of awakening—you must explore the very source of resistance itself. You must examine the ego, the personal I, the one inside you who is suffering. From the perspective of consciousness, your wholeness, you must look at this me who attaches meaning and importance to the story.

Another way of viewing this is to contemplate the notion that we are not our thoughts or our story, but rather we are the consciousness giving birth to it all. I call this the global or holistic approach. In Sanskrit, it is the *jnana* path to truth. It may also be termed the wisdom or discernment path to enlightenment. You orient the mind toward clarity. Give it a perspective or belief which is relatively true. It is true, because experiencing it radically transforms how you see reality. With this comprehension, you eventually realize what was previously only a belief for you is actually the way it really is.

You have literally stepped or popped outside the self, which, a moment ago, you believed that you were, and now you are viewing life from the perspective of the Whole. You have awakened to full consciousness. You know yourself *as* consciousness, and what this feels like is unlimited spaciousness, boundlessness, openness. It is love. There is no separation, only total connection to everything that is, ever was, and ever will be.

Speaking personally, there is no real difference between in here, inside my head, and out there, in the world. There is no me feeling separate, no center, and no border. There is just the flow of the universe, of life, and I, as consciousness, am one with it.

Consequently, I find myself open to all people and to all experiences. This is the essence or ground of unconditional love. I may not like the behavior of certain people, and may speak out against it or even reject it, but I am at least open to it. I may not like certain experiences, but I have learned the wisdom of not arguing with reality, of not struggling with what *is*. Thus, I live in peace and serenity.

Once you have awakened, while things may go on outwardly pretty much as they did before, your inner life is never the same again. At the same time, there will undoubtedly be some outward changes. You will approach life much more consciously.

Find Out Who Wants to Be Free

Meditation, as you know by now, brings clarity to the mind. Watching the breath, feeling the sensations move through the body, and witnessing the flow of thoughts and pictures as they move through the mind trains your power of attention. Meditation brings you to a place of inner tranquility, enabling you to see reality more clearly.

I meditated a lot during my time as a seeker. When I sat, I would watch my own mind and emotional reactions constantly, and pursue my own line of self-inquiry as I struggled inwardly to free myself of everything binding me.

Along the way, I formed a friendship with two men who became my *dharma*-buddies, or allies on the spiritual path—Erich Schiffmann and Darrell Price. The unique aspect of our relationship was its focus: all three of us wanted enlightenment, inner freedom, more than anything else. We spent a lot of time hanging out together, doing yoga, meditating in silence, and going for long hikes in nature. Above all, we found ourselves engaging in an ongoing, spirited dialogue about such subjects as the teachings of Krishnamurti, Ramana Maharshi, Zen, *A Course in Miracles*, and our own driving quest for freedom.

As serious as we were about awakening, we were still able to laugh at ourselves. In fact, we called our one-track conversation "the endless yarn." We used to wonder which of us was going to, as we put it, "go over the top" first. Those were heady times as we contemplated the vast spiritual possibilities before us!

Like many seekers, I had a number of other illuminating experiences and other breakthroughs during my years on the path, beginning with my very first taste of oneness that summer's morning. I was definitely a lot freer inwardly, more relaxed, more present. I still mostly believed in the possibility of inner freedom, in the reality of awakening. But sometimes I wondered.

Sometimes I questioned whether there really was a top to go over, and if this life of continuing meditation and inquiry, with its times of great peace and beauty, punctuated by periods of conflict and self-doubt, was as good as it was going to get.

Of course, as I found out, meditation alone won't set you free. If you want true freedom, you have to sit with the question: "*Who* is meditating?"

Once you have learned to easily shift states of stress and tension by doing the practice, then you have to look within and find the meditator. Find out where the urge to meditate, to seek refuge or peace, truly springs from. Discover who and what you are, who this person meditating really is. There is a Zen story that speaks to this.

The old master noticed his most eager student sitting hours and hours in meditation, way longer than any of the other practitioners who came to the *zendo* to meditate. He went up to him late one morning, after all the others left to go and prepare for lunch.

"What are you doing?" the master asked.

Without breaking his concentration, without even opening his eyes, the student replied, "I am meditating to get enlightened."

"Ah, so," said the master. He picked up a stone and a brick tile, sat down near the student, and began rubbing away at the tile with the stone. He made quite a noise, even huffing and puffing a little as he worked.

An hour passed, and when the student couldn't stand it anymore, he turned, opened his eyes, and inquired, "Master, can you please tell me what *you* are doing?"

"I am polishing this brick tile to make a mirror," the master responded, without interrupting his work.

The student's eyes widened. "But it's not possible. Nobody could make a mirror out of a brick tile."

"Just so," said the master, as he put the rock and tile down. He looked intently at the student. "And nobody ever got enlightened just by sitting and meditating."

This story says to me that once we are able to access the relaxed, clear presence meditation brings, we then have to look within. We then have to start looking at this I who wants freedom, who seeks meaning, who yearns for the secret of life. This is the art and practice of self-inquiry: to look deep within yourself to the very source of reality, of the I or me itself.

When you are worrying, stop and ask yourself, "*Who* is worrying?" Then dive deep within and really look. Find out where the I who says it is worrying comes from. When you are feeling bored or restless, ask yourself, "*Who* is bored? *Who* is restless?" Go within, and look for the source, the location of this I who insists it is bored. When you are suffering, when you are feeling a little blue or lonely, breathe consciously and ask yourself, "So, *who* is feeling lonely?" Then look inside. Seek the origin of the I thought.

Really stop and probe within, beyond the thought forms "I feel this" or "I feel that." Look beyond the story you are telling yourself about your suffering. Listen to the silence behind the thoughts. Feel yourself at the most essential level of your being *as* awareness, pure consciousness, the source, expressing itself through this body/mind/self called you. Find out who you are.

As you discover who this I is and from whence it arises, a day will come when you'll see it is not real. It is only a concept, an idea, albeit an extremely deep-rooted one. Then fear will leave you and love will become the dominant reality in your heart. Find out who wants to be free, and you'll no longer feel bound . . .

Pause right now . . . Take a deep breath, relax, and be very still, supremely alert, fully present . . . Now go within and see if you, as the awareness present, the pure consciousness that is aware of being here, can find this I you have taken yourself to be all these years . . . Can you find it anywhere within, other than as a fleeting ghost? Can you find any concept or thought? If you probe to the very core of your being, you'll come up empty-handed . . . There is nothing there, no thing, except your awareness, the awareness looking at everything within and without . . . So, look at the beauty within and around you, and be the awareness you are . . .

Breaking through the Story of Me

In 1983, my seeking and restlessness grew to the point where I knew I had to sell my practice and go to India. Other Western seekers had gone there and, if they hadn't found complete enlightenment, had at least deepened their spiritual experience.

At this point, I was very successful materially—which was what allowed me to take nine months off to travel and pay all the expenses for my new girlfriend, Barbara, and me. I was making a lot of money seeing patients just three days a week, owned a four-bedroom house with an in-ground pool, drove a brand new BMW, and had no debt other than the house. Several of my friends thought I was crazy to give it all up, but you have to understand the mindset of the true spiritual seeker, which I was: nothing else matters, least of all material success, as long as the Holy Grail of enlightenment, of inner freedom, is still being sought.

We traveled to China, Bali, Nepal, India, Australia, and back to New Zealand. I can sum up my experience of the journey in a few words: heat, dust, a sea of people, noise, cheap hotels, the thrill of strange and exotic sights, a lot of disillusion, and the glimmerings of an awakening to something new.

When we arrived back in California in 1984, Barbara got pregnant, we married, I started a small practice again, and at the end of that year I met the man who was to be my teacher or guide on the path of enlightenment, Jean

Klein. At the time, he was in his seventies, and his influence on me turned out to be profound.

I remember I really wanted the inner freedom Jean spoke about. I wanted it with all my heart, but I was often hesitant to ask him questions. I felt a little intimidated by his rather detached, austere, somewhat forbidding old-world European demeanor. Nevertheless, I'd eventually take a deep breath, muster up my courage, and put forth the question that was on my mind. Sometimes though, the questions arose spontaneously.

Once, without any forethought, I found myself asking him: "Do you ever experience fear?"

He looked at me for what seemed to be minutes (Jean lived in inner silence, and always took a long time to respond to questions). Then he said, with a smile, "Who is there to be afraid?"

I sat contemplating his answer. It was the essence of the whole teaching: when you don't take yourself to be anybody, when you're not holding on to any image or concept of self, there is nothing in you to resist the flow of life, to be in conflict with whatever is happening. There is nothing in you worrying about the future, or what may happen in the next moment, and so there is no fear. This is what it means to be free.

In order to fully realize the freedom that is your true nature, you have to turn inward and find out who and what is doing the looking. You have to find the looker. You have to be a fearless warrior to advance on this, the final leg of the journey. You have to really look deep within, and face yourself with rigorous honesty. But the rewards are there, awaiting your discovery, because this is the stage when consciousness fully evolves, becomes completely awakened within us.

In Zen, it is said of this final stage, "Mountains are once again mountains, and rivers are once again rivers." Now, however, the mountains shine with a radiance that could not be perceived before, and the rivers seem to flow right through us, cleansing our very souls. Moreover, it is always thus, for when we awaken to our true natures, everything, every day, seems fresh and new. The mountains, we realize, are no different in their essence than we are. They, like us, are expressions of the one universal energy, or consciousness, that is the source of all creation.

As we have seen, the beginning stages of the spiritual journey are addressed by religion, mythic stories, and belief systems. The intermediate stages are about spirituality itself, the direct and personal experience of what religion is talking about. The final phase is characterized by realization, by awakening to inner freedom.

True inner freedom is the fulfillment of the religious promise held out to us as we first set out on our journey. Religion, through its many stories and beliefs about personal redemption and salvation, has given way to this new freedom: the jewel of deep spiritual wisdom, of clear insight into the true nature of reality.

With this ultimate freedom, concepts, beliefs, and questions fall away. We let go of the identification with the personal story, which had previously given—or seemed to have given—such meaning to our lives. We let go of it because we see it isn't even real; it is just a fiction of our own making.

Whatever our particular story was, the fact is we made it up. We based it on all our past experiences, whether actual or imagined, and then added a smorgasbord of beliefs, opinions, and value judgments about what we thought we needed to do to survive. Yet once we see it is just a story, why would we want to persist in believing it? Why would any intelligent person cling to what is unreal?

By the time we get to this point in our evolution, we are ready to understand and embody the teaching. With the teaching, it becomes clear that to hold on to any concept or story prevents us from a deeper experience of truth in the now. But to get free of the holding, we have to explore how it comes about in the first place.

Thus, the primary spiritual practice at this stage is self-inquiry, or asking, "Who am I?" "Who is it that wants to believe?" "Who is it that worries?" and "Who is it that suffers?"

This is the technique known as *vichara*, self-inquiry, given to us by the great nondual sage, Ramana Maharshi, from southern India. Through self-inquiry, and with the understanding that we are no longer going to settle for any conceptual answers, we dive directly into the source of the mind, the ego, and the me.

As self-inquiry deepens, what we have already perceived in glimpses starts to become stunningly clear: we have thoughts, even the thought I or me, but we cannot be our thoughts. We are, instead, whatever is observing them. And what is that? Consciousness or awareness itself. All thoughts, sensations, and forms arise within the context of the pure, formless consciousness we are.

No matter what we are thinking or experiencing, what we fundamentally are is the awareness behind the thought, sensation, or feeling. Our true nature is pure awareness, or consciousness, being expressed through our body, mind, and personality.

Breathing happens; sensations, feelings, and emotions come and go; thoughts pass through the mind; and stories about our experiences form, but the only continuous, unbroken, and always present thing is consciousness itself. Consciousness is that which, in us, is *aware* of all these changing phenomena. This is the non-dual truth of existence . . .

So, relax into your true nature . . . Be present as the beautiful, shining awareness you are . . . Notice the flow of your breath, the sensations in your body, any feelings and emotions arising, the thoughts and stories in your mind, including the I or me thought . . . Notice whatever happens to be in your physical surroundings . . . Notice how you are the awareness that is aware of all these arising phenomena . . . And it all comes and goes, appears and disappears, in you . . . But you, as the awareness noticing it all, are always here . . .

The more we see from our true nature, the more the identification with mind-based identities—ego and ideas and images of self—falls away. Then the emotional baggage in the psyche, which is expressed in the body, starts to dissolve naturally. Our heads clear, in other words, and the psychologically and emotionally generated tension and stress start to leave our bodies.

With the releasing of tension, we feel a tremendous sense of inner spaciousness and ease. This expansiveness allows the pure light of consciousness to enter. We come to an authentic openness, a true vulnerability, where we hold on to nothing and allow everything to flow through us.

Eventually, we even let go of attachment to knowing, to the "Now I am awake!" story. We are content just to be the beautiful expression of consciousness we are. We no longer need to hold on to blissful or sacred experiences because we realize, at last, that bliss and the sacred are our true nature. We simply have to breathe, relax, and be open to the present, welcoming it all.

Now there is a new feeling of lightness, an ease of being, and with it the realization of the truth of the Zen saying, "After enlightenment, nothing changes, but everything is somehow different."

Life still goes on as before. Work needs to be done and responsibilities must be met. The difference is in the awareness now shining through us. We are simply wide awake in the present. With our ego and our personal history no longer in the way, it is as if we perceive everything and every moment with new eyes.

Toss the Ego a Bone

Some spiritual teachings support the idea of getting rid of the ego, even annihilating it, to become enlightened or free. Yet, upon awakening, we find that the ego is still here. Indeed, in terms of conscious creation, your ego will become your ally. Conscious use of the ego enables you to will specific actions to take place or manifest certain things into being. Ken Wilber, in his book, *One Taste*, has this to say about the ego:

> The ego is not an obstruction to Spirit, but a radiant manifestation of Spirit . . . [I]t remains as the functional self in the gross realm, and it might even appropriately be intensified and made more powerful, simply because it is now plugged into the entire Kosmos. Many of the great enlightened teachers had a big ego . . . in the sense of strong, forceful, powerful personalities.[5]

---

5 *One Taste*, 276, 278–279,

Perhaps Freud's influence is why people in the West often have a confused or incorrect idea of what the ego is. Ego can be thought of as something negative, as in, "That guy has a lot of ego," saying he is full of self-importance. Ego can mean an individual is very unsure of him- or herself, as in, "That person has a very insecure ego." Undoubtedly, ego is equated with self-image and self-worth. Inflated self-worth can indicate arrogance, and a lack of self-worth can indicate low self-esteem.

My use of the term ego simply refers to the personal sense of I or me. Whenever you say, "I must go and call my mother," or "I have to get to work," or "I need to fix dinner," it is your ego, your I, speaking. In this sense, everyone has an ego. Even though you may have realized your true nature and no longer feel separate from the timeless flow of creation, you still have an ego. You still need to be able to define your personal wants, needs, and desires, even though they may be minimal, and even though you are now no longer attached to them.

Developing a healthy ego and a clear set of boundaries at the personal level is a vital part of the growth and maturation process happening early in our life's journey. But the proof of maturation is when we begin to see the limitations of the ego. The ego can serve us in terms of our physical survival and well-being through its ability to remember, to project and plan, to analyze and reason, to intuit and create, and to define personal boundaries, but it cannot give us all we need.

The separate, stand-alone nature of the ego cannot provide us with the deeper nourishment, the feeling of love so vital to our spiritual well-being. For this, the heart must speak. And for the heart to speak and be heard, the ego must surrender its control. It must, in effect, fade into the background.

This is beautifully expressed in the wisdom of J. Krishnamurti, who said that you must die every day in order to be free. This means letting go of all the mental and emotional attachments that make up the ego or personal self—the attachment to beliefs, expectations, and desires. And the more you see such stories are not real, the more they fall away. When the ego gets out of the way, something new and vital is born. This something is your real self, the true I, the *I am* in you, standing on its own—clear, strong, and vibrant.

The ego needs a story, needs to identify with or call itself something: a member of this organization or that political party, a follower of this belief or that cause. The true *I*, that which you really are in your essence, needs no such label or identification in order to know itself or to feel secure. The true, pure *I* knows itself as itself, and that is enough. It knows itself to be an expression of the divine fullness of life, a fullness lacking nothing, which is one with all humanity, with all creation.

As you open up to a more relaxed and alert way of living in the present, as you become comfortable with the silence of your true nature, you have less need for the beliefs, concepts, and stories with which the ego loves to embellish itself. Then your ego, your personal I, will assume its rightful place in the totality of your being. Like your mind, your ego is an instrument, a tool existing for a very definite purpose. It is your personal boundary-setter. It is how you, as the ocean of consciousness, define and differentiate your individual waveness, your own personal creative expression.

The difference is, with the awakening to freedom, your ego becomes much more functional. It becomes transparent, a clear window. It is no longer caught up in any story about who and what you are, or what is important in your life. You are able to say, "I must buy groceries," or "I am going to the park," and there is no fuss, no unnecessary drama.

However, when you have not yet awakened to your true nature, your ego, your I or me, always has some kind of story attached to it. Whether you say it out loud or not, you are always feeling the need to justify, defend, affirm, or get validation for your point of view, your position, and for your sense of who you are. As your inner freedom deepens, your ego—like your hand, voice, or any tool you might use—is there when you need it. And when you don't need it, it's out of the way. It's not a problem.

And if your ego rears its head once in a while, as it is bound to—perhaps getting caught up in a moment of pride or self-congratulation—don't worry about it too much. Sunyata, a Danish man who lived much of his life in India and who embodied an inner silence and presence that attracted many people to him, said it was okay to toss the ego a bone once in a while. After all, it is part of who we are.

Acknowledge your ego's existence, and let it go. Come back to simply being open and aware in this moment now. Then your ego need not be a problem.

Embrace Change

In a moment of vulnerability, a young woman said to me, "Sometimes, when I think about it, I have a great fear of change. I want the people I love to continue to be in my life. I love the house I live in. I want to stay there always.

Yet I realize at some level it is just the story about change, about having to let go of things, that bothers me. Nevertheless, the fear of change still comes up . . . "

The Buddha taught three fundamental laws, or tenets, of life. The first was the law of *anicca*, or impermanence, which says everything is always changing. The seasons come and go, day turns into night, the climate changes, our body grows and matures and then, like all living things, begins eventually to wither and die. We can't stop change, and to resist it causes dissatisfaction or suffering. This is *dukkha*, the Buddha's second law.

So, when you see the truth of this, you don't hold on to things. You don't cling to *nama* and *rupa*, which are the Sanskrit terms for the world of name and form. You don't keep insisting things be a certain way. You learn to flow with the ups and downs of life, to take action when you need to, and to wait patiently when patience is what is required.

The well-known serenity prayer evokes this way of being: "God grant me the serenity to accept the things I cannot change, the courage to change the things I can, and the wisdom to know the difference."

A story the Buddhist teacher, Jack Kornfield, tells about his teacher, Achaan Chah, illustrates the same point in a different way. It revolves around a beautiful glass goblet he was given as a gift. He held and admired the goblet, while telling the gathered students that the glass was already broken. When they asked what he meant, he said one day, a year from now, or ten years, or a hundred years, something would happen—an accident, a fire, or someone would just drop the goblet—and it would break.

Because of this understanding, he could fully appreciate the goblet and enjoy using it without any attachment.

He had already said goodbye to it, so every day it was in his possession was a blessing.

Another, more colorful way of saying this is, "Shit happens." Wisdom is seeing the big picture, seeing the inevitable unfolding of events. It's looking ahead, and—to use a very practical expression—visualizing the worst-case scenarios. Then you are prepared. If the worst-case scenario does happen, you can take action to deal with it. You don't obsess about what might happen in the future, but you remain aware of and open to the possibilities.

You honor the past without clinging to it, you keep an eye on the future without obsessing over it, but all the time your awareness is grounded right here in the present.

The Buddha's third law is the law of *anatta*, or no-self. He said the self we take ourselves to be doesn't exist, except as an idea or concept in the mind. This is what all the great enlightenment traditions speak about and what Jean Klein taught as well.

The attachment to notions of self, to the idea of "I am this" or "I am that," to the whole inside-our-head drama called "me, myself, and my story," creates the resistance to change. You know what I mean: the fixed positions people take and cling to for security, whether they are religious or political beliefs, national identities, or something else.

Buddha's first law, anicca or impermanence, accurately describes everything as constantly changing. Yet we desperately try to cling to some part of it and keep it from changing. It is this clinging, this resistance (or its opposite, aversion, a pushing away of one thing while holding on to something else), which in turn results in dukkha, suffering.

But the real cause of suffering is the primary clinging to any idea of self, to being somebody, or identifying with "my" personal history. Let go of that, see it isn't even real, and you are free. Then you live without needing to cling to any concept of self, because you have turned your attention back in on yourself and have discovered you don't exist, except as a concept inside your head.

Then there is no struggle with self-esteem. You're not holding onto any image of a self needing validation or approval, or feeling pleased with itself on some days and hating itself on others. Then there is no more suffering. You always feel good inside because you're in touch with the underlying goodness of life. You use the words "I," "me," and "mine" purely in a utilitarian way, just as you use thinking for the practical, creative tool it is, but you no longer identify with thoughts or the thinker.

Carlos Castaneda's teacher, Don Juan, put it this way: "I don't have any personal history . . . One day I found out that personal history was no longer necessary for me and, like drinking, I dropped it."[6]

With the direct path approach, you learn to drop your personal history by seeing that it isn't real. It's only a story about something that *was* true, but isn't so now. Then an enormous weight leaves you. You don't have to prove yourself to anyone. You don't have to defend yourself, because no matter what anyone says, you don't feel attacked. Every moment is fresh and new.

A man asked me once, "Is there anything which doesn't change?" I replied yes. Consciousness itself does not change. It just *is*. Consciousness, or awareness—what is sensing and perceiving in you right now—is timeless, spaceless, causeless. It is ever-present, the silent background to the ever-changing flux and flow of creation. To understand this is to walk through the door to inner freedom.

---

6   Castaneda, *Journey to Ixtlan*, 11.

The Buddha did not really speak about consciousness being our true nature. He simply said enlightenment was the end of suffering. However, the direct path taught by Jean Klein did emphasize this aspect. We come to freedom through awakening to the changeless, timeless awareness behind all phenomena, to the fact that consciousness itself is our true nature, who and what we are.

At this point, you might ask, "How can I know this for sure?" Let's take a little trip. Look back at your life, as far back as you can remember, and think about all the changes you have gone through. Think about the friends and relationships you've had and let go of, the places you once lived, the schools you attended, the jobs you've had, the beliefs you once held so dear but have long since modified or downright rejected.

Now, see if this rings true. Notice if there is one thing which hasn't changed. Notice how your *awareness* of all these changes you have gone through has had a kind of constancy to it. It's as if, since the very beginning, there is something in you which has been watching the whole drama of your life unfold, shift, and go through its changes.

Most people understand this, and they often ask if that which doesn't change is the Witness, or the Observing Self. However, I prefer to call it simply awareness or consciousness. It is too easy to make an object out of the idea of a "Witness" or an "Observing Self," and then you are attached to another concept, another thing. This gets you back into your head and mind—into duality, into a story. When you live in duality, the seeds of conflict and suffering are sown.

It is not really your awareness or my awareness I am referring to; it is universal awareness or divine consciousness expressed through us. Remember, there is just one ocean, one energy manifesting in all these wave forms we are. There is just one consciousness here. Realize this and it will change your life forever . . .

See if you can feel or sense the one consciousness right now. . . Be very still and present . . . Be the awareness looking out through your open eyes . . . Notice everything within and around you . . . Tune into the vastness within and without . . . Notice how there is just the flow of energy, of consciousness, and you are simply one with the flow . . . Thoughts can come and go in the awareness you are, but you are not identified by them . . . You are just being here, breathing with the moment . . .

Don't Take Yourself to Be Anybody

Once, at a public dialogue with Jean Klein, a man raised his hand to speak. When Jean acknowledged him, the man said, "Every time I come to hear you, I notice you seem so clear and relaxed. You radiate a peaceful, loving warmth. You seem happy. Yet I am always discontented and often stressed out. There are times when I feel quite miserable. What is the difference between us?"

Jean looked at the man for awhile, and then said, with a smile, "You still take yourself to be somebody. I don't take myself to be anybody."

Until we have done it enough times, letting go of the need to be somebody can cause anxiety. We get used to relying on our thoughts, beliefs, and story to give our life meaning. It becomes our sense of identity, our sense of knowing who and what we are. Yet this very limited way of knowing keeps us in conflict. It keeps us divided from other human beings whose identities are based on different psychological, philosophical, or religious beliefs.

Early in my journey, I did not like hearing the American spiritual teacher Ram Dass say in order to be enlightened you had to be nobody. Since childhood, I had wanted to *be* somebody, to make my mark in life. I was always ambitious, probably due to my need for recognition and attention.

Eventually, though, I discovered Ram Dass was correct. The freest people don't take themselves to be anybody. Their ambition is less personal and more focused on just doing something worthwhile, something serving the greater good. They are not attached to any concept or image of self, because they see all such concepts and images as unreal, figments of our own creation. Nonattachment is the result of clearly seeing the true nature of reality. It frees us from worry and suffering.

Jean's strength as a teacher was in not giving any credence to the personal. People came to him with their personal problems, but he would seldom give direct answers or advice. Instead, he guided them back to the clarity, freedom, and vastness that was their true impersonal nature. From his perspective, once we are established in the impersonal and awake, knowing we really are nobody, then there is room for the personal—our personality—to emerge in an authentic, spontaneous way. The beauty of this approach is it allows us to be somebody without being attached to the *idea* of being somebody. This is what it means to be free.

Yet many had difficulty with Jean's style. They didn't want to let go of their personal story, their "I," their "me." They wanted quick fixes and immediate solutions, and they didn't want to have to give up anything in return, least of all their attachment to their beliefs and ideas about who they thought they were. They came to hear Jean speak thinking they wanted freedom, when all they really wanted was a bigger prison inside which their ego could roam.

If you want real freedom, it is very important to understand this. If the sometimes impersonal nature of the direct-path teachings triggers anxiety in you, it is just an indication of the degree of identification with your ego and your personal history. Letting go of your ideas about who you are can be unsettling, even scary, yet only when you let go can true freedom—and joy—be found. The letting go is made easier when you see that what you are identifying with is not even real.

Meister Eckhart once said the less there is of I, the more there is of God. He was referring to getting our ego out of the way. The ego, the me, is what gets in the way of anything new happening. Still, we need an ego to survive in the world. It is part of who and what we are. It is an instrument of the body/mind/self.

Doing the practice of freedom will help you to embody the teaching: you are not your thoughts or story. Gradually, the attachment to notions of I, me, and mine will loosen. You will start losing interest in this self you once attached such great importance to. You will see that clinging creates resistance to what is. Clinging is holding onto or believing in judgments, expectations, and attachment to outcomes. This resistance results in conflict, self-doubt, worry, fear, and suffering.

Instead of needing to hold on to any idea or image of self, you will live in openness and awareness in the present. You will neither be attached to the past, nor obsessing about the future. The deeper energy of creation itself will feed you, unfolding as an incredible dynamism each time you get still and tune in to the energy of now.

You will be free. Other people's approval will not matter to you, and their disapproval will have little or no effect. You will still have an ego, but it will be transparent. It will be a clear window through which your true wisdom, beauty, and essence will shine.

When you start to awaken, the ego has a tendency to keep sneaking in through the back door. With a sense of accomplishment and pride, it can say things like, "Hey, I'm enlightened," "I have arrived," or "I'm special." This is referred to as spiritual arrogance. But as long as your awakening is genuine, you will quickly notice this and ease right back into presence. You have the skills to successfully get your ego to back off and mind its own business. You will be more interested in meeting people at a heart level, rather than from the head.

A Native American elder once said knowledge divides the world and wisdom makes it whole. Knowledge is mainly of the head, but wisdom is very much of the heart. Listen to and trust your heart, and every step of your journey will be guided by wisdom.

My Realization

The first awakening I experienced with Jean was at a retreat at Mount Madonna Center, in the Santa Cruz Mountains of California, a few years after meeting him. I was walking down to the afternoon dialogue, contemplating the notion of not being the person I'd taken myself to be, when my I, my ego—with its whole storyline—suddenly jumped out into my awareness.

In an instant, I saw the game I'd been playing. I saw my attachment to the identity of myself as a spiritual seeker, and how much juice and meaning the seeker identity gave me for so many years. However, the attachment to being a seeker is as much a barrier to freedom as is the attachment to any other identity.

When I saw this about myself, I felt a great sadness. I knew I needed to let it go, and I sensed at a very deep level I would never be able to quite buy into my own story again. I told Jean what happened.

He said, "You have, in a certain way, understood that the existence of the person is an illusion, a fabrication from memory . . . Live completely in the absence of yourself, and you'll become a happy man."

Gradually, I felt myself getting freer of the mind's chatter. I was more awake, more open and present, more *here*.

Two events that occurred a couple of years before my final awakening were significant in my story. The first was a broken heart I experienced when a love affair with a much younger woman ended soon after I turned forty-six. My enlightenment was pretty intellectual still, and this heartbreak brought me into my emotions, my feelings, with a vengeance. I tell this story in chapter 6, in the section on forgiveness.

The second event, which marked the last liberation I needed to pass through, was when I filed for bankruptcy. I had gone through a costly divorce, and had gotten way behind on my credit card bills and tax payments. The IRS was threatening to levy my bank account.

Both my accountant and attorney had been urging me to file for bankruptcy protection for two years, but I resisted. Why? I was afraid of what people would think of me. When I looked this fear squarely in the face, I saw it was keeping me from the one thing I wanted most: inner, spiritual freedom. I realized, in the end, that it was only my ego, my self-image, that cared how people might judge me.

Who I really was, my true nature, did not care. I needed to find a way out of my burdensome debt. So, I filed a plan which would allow me to pay what I owed the IRS over a period of years.

Then, in the spring of my forty-ninth year, I woke up one morning feeling mildly depressed. I didn't like what I was feeling. As I lay in bed, I noticed a frustration about still being subject to negative states like depression, even after all these years of spiritual practice. Normally, I would have gotten out of bed and meditated, for I knew how to clear negative energy that way.

But this morning was different. I became very present, looked within, and faced the depression. I was curious. How come such a negative state could still visit me? How come I wasn't completely free yet? Then I remembered Jean's teaching that we are not the psychological or emotional person. I went deeply into the interior of my being with the question, "Okay, Jim, you say you are depressed. So, *who* is depressed?"

This wasn't just a mental exercise. This wasn't just some spiritual technique I was toying with. There was a definite urgency to my question. I *really* wanted to know. It was as if my entire life was on the line.

Yet as hard as I looked, I couldn't find the "person" who claimed he was depressed. The more I shone the clear light of awareness inside myself, the more all thought forms, including the thought "I feel depressed," just dissolved. The energy of depression cleared, I felt fine, and went about my day.

But the same thing happened to me the next morning, and the following morning. I awoke and noticed a slightly depressed feeling. Each time I went deeply into myself with the same inquiry—"So, *who* is depressed?"—and after the third morning, something shifted, permanently. Whatever sense of self remained in my consciousness dissolved, and I now knew myself as the Whole, as the awareness or consciousness behind all thoughts, forms, experiences—indeed, behind all manifest reality.

In the succeeding months, whenever I looked inside myself, I couldn't find a solid sense of a me anymore. I no longer believed my own story, whether it dealt with self-doubt, suffering, and still not being free, or my accomplishments, successes, and things in which I took pride. Instead, there was just clarity, openness, and a feeling of emptiness, which was simultaneously vibrant, full, and alive.

As the months passed, it dawned on me that I had finally found what I had been seeking for twenty years. What Jean told me, was guiding me toward, was now a bright, integrated reality. I saw once and for all that the psychological or emotional entity called "I" does not exist. My true nature is pure consciousness, expressing itself through this body, mind, and personality known as Jim Dreaver.

The difference was, before I awakened to the truth of my being, I was still identifying with my ego and thoughts, with my story about who I thought I was, with being somebody. Now I lived inwardly in luminous clarity, in openness, essentially free of any self-image or self-concept of any kind. I realized that my true nature was, and is, consciousness itself, which never changes.

The Practice of Self-Inquiry

This practice will help you release identification with the thoughts I and me, and with the ego itself. It will help you make the shift into what some traditions call the observer or witness consciousness—the awareness you are behind your body, mind, personality, thoughts, stories, sensations, feelings, emotions, and so on.

This practice is definitely useful during a time of conflict and suffering, but you can also do it when nothing is going on and you have a quiet moment or two just to look within, and examine this I, this me you take yourself to be.

Step 1: When conflict, upset, or suffering arises, close your eyes, go within and ask yourself, "So, who is this me that says it is suffering right now?"

Step 2: Be very still. Allow whatever feelings or emotions are there to be there. Just be very present and alert as you search within your psyche, your consciousness, for this me who is suffering. Make sure you don't settle for any conceptual answers, which is just more story. You are seeking something tangible: the actual location of the I or me thought.

Step 3: After a few minutes of looking into yourself in this way, and as long as you don't get lost in your mind, a truth will dawn on you: you cannot find the I or me thought anywhere—yet you, as awareness or consciousness, are still very much here!

What you will discover is that you cannot actually find any thought. This sense of self you have been constructing, and perhaps struggling with your whole life, can't be found. It doesn't exist, other than as a figment, a fiction, in your mind. Yet consider how much power you have given it to create and control your emotional reality!

So, with this realization, it will become increasingly clear: while you have the thoughts I and me, you are not those thoughts. What you are is the lucid, ever-present awareness that gives birth to the whole thinking process, and to this body, mind, and personality. Seeing this may result in a genuine epiphany, an "Ah-ha!" moment.

For at least a few moments, you will find yourself in clear, thought-free, present-time awareness. You will no longer experience yourself as an individual person, but as the universe itself—pure, unbounded consciousness, looking through these eyes and expressing through this body/mind/personality that is "you."

The Practice of Freeing Yourself from the I Thought

Do this practice throughout the day, whenever you think of it. You can do it when you sit to meditate, when you're taking a walk, when you're with others—you can do it at any time. Do it for a few minutes, or do it for an hour. The idea is to eventually come to the realization: "Wow, I am not my 'I' or 'me' thoughts . . . I am always the awareness, the conscious being, behind my thoughts!"

This is the practice: When you're thinking to yourself or talking with others, simply refrain from using the thoughts "I," "me," "my," or "mine." That's it. You'll be surprised at how difficult it is to do this, however—at least initially.

When you feel an emotion, like sadness, anger, or a particular sense of joy, just note to yourself: "There is sadness, anger, or joy arising in this being, in this body, right now." Note it without any personal identification. Experience the pure feeling or sensation and the conceptual label of the feeling without taking it personally.

When you hear something in your environment—a birdsong, a car, a plane flying overhead—again just note the sound, the experience, the sensation ("Ah, a mock-ingbird . . ." "A truck . . ." "A jet . . ."), without using the concepts "I" or "me."

When you are mulling something over, maybe some-thing you are doing, or have to do, or should have done, express yourself in this way: "This food tastes good," (rather than, "I'm enjoying the taste of this food"), "There's a need to go to the bathroom," "This being must go grocery shop-ping later," or "There should have been more patience and kindness shown to that old lady this being met yesterday."

You can make an exercise out of sitting and dialoguing with another person. One person goes first, taking maybe five minutes to label thoughts, feelings, and sensations without using the words "I," "me," "my," or "mine."

You might, for example, say "Thinking about the pain in this being's back," or "Contemplating a stiffness in the right knee," or "Remembering what this being had for breakfast this morning," or "Noticing how radiant your eyes look," or "Being aware of how relaxed you are." (It is perfectly fine to use the pronouns "you" and "your"—it is good practice in thinking about others, and taking the attention away from yourself!)

Then it's the other person's turn.

When both of you have finished, silently eye-gaze with each other for a few minutes and see how that feels. As you'll see in the practice of eye-gazing at the end of chapter 6, when you can gaze into another's eyes without fear or judgment—in other words, without "self" consciousness—that means you are, at least in that moment, very free.

⇜ 5 ⇝

Awakening to Freedom

To know you are not your stories, not even this I or me you have always taken yourself to be, is true freedom. It's the final perceptual shift resulting in awakening, enlightenment, or self-realization. You no longer seek your identity in the contents of your mind, in the state of your health, or in events or circumstances of any kind, but find it in the moment-by-moment flow of being. No matter what you do, you are always at one with life; you are always in the flow.

The Zen master D. T. Suzuki was said to define enlightenment as: "The lightning-and-thunder discovery that the universe and oneself are not remote and apart but an intimate, palpitating Whole."

Once you know yourself as the Whole, as one with the dance of the universe, the normal psychological and emotional fears rarely arise. If they do, they occur as brief residues of old ego patterns, rippling on the surface but not disturbing the deep waters of your inner peace. You just flow with whatever is happening and deal with it as skillfully and gracefully as possible.

We have the wisdom in a statement attributed to Idries Shah, the Sufi teacher: "No matter what point of truth or understanding I arrive at, there is always one beyond it." This beautifully expresses the point that the truth—the ultimate answer—does not lie in concepts.

We want to *know* the truth for ourselves, and the practice will bring us to the experience of it. Whenever we feel contracted or stuck, we learn to welcome the story and the conflict it produces, because they show us where we are not yet free. We notice the story and realize its impact on our emotional state. Then we become present, and just through our watching or witnessing the story, it loses some of its energetic hold over us, and we are freer.

As we saw in the last chapter, through deep self-inquiry we confront this I at the root of all the stories making up our personal history. We are the witness, the consciousness, the observer looking within, only to discover the ultimate truth: the I we were attached to and identified with for so long is not real. It never was.

I like the way Kunihiro Yamate puts it: "In this human, dream-like play we know what the feeling of being awake is like: It is awareness, clarity, a sharp, clearheaded feeling that 'I am awake. This is reality.' That is the way we will feel when we awaken or snap back to our full consciousness."[7]

You know you have awakened to the truth when it becomes stunningly clear to you that not only are you no longer identifying with your thoughts, but the very person you took yourself to be—the me, with all its history—does not exist. In other words, you don't take anything personally because you don't hold on to any idea or image of yourself as a person.

---

7   *The Way of No Thinking,* Robert C. Engler and Yuriko Hayashi, 206.

When you look inside you see only spaciousness and emptiness, an openness you realize is filled with the entire universe. It feels like there's no separate sense of me anywhere; you cannot find it because it cannot be found. The entire notion of a me is and always was an illusion, a mere concept. You cannot be located anywhere, yet you are everywhere. You are this vast, all-encompassing ocean of consciousness.

This realization results in a sense of lightness, freedom, and joy. Your basic state is one of ease, flow, and being alive in the present. All psychological and emotional suffering disappears, never to return—other than those occasional residues, triggered by periods of stress and illness, which can flare up from time to time. Your true purpose for being here becomes clear to you, and living itself takes on a whole new meaning and significance. Truly, every moment is new.

No one else can tell you whether or not you are awake or self-realized. When you look inside, only you can know for sure whether you are inwardly free of conflict, self-doubt, and fear. Only you can know there are no dark, scary places in your psyche anymore, and that thought processes no longer have power over you. There is no longer any separate belief in I or me, but only the light of universal consciousness shining through this body/mind/self appearing as "you."

Ultimately, only you can know whether you are free or not. This is where you have to be very honest with yourself. Another person who is already free can and will recognize and acknowledge your freedom, but only after you yourself have awakened to it.

He or she is able to discern exactly where you are on your path with a few well-placed questions:

"Do you still experience self-doubt?"

"Do you still have any suffering?"

"Are you still identifying with an idea or image of self?"

"Does your well-being depend on anything outside yourself?"

The bottom line is, if you are looking to have someone confirm or validate your realization, then you probably are not there yet. However, someone already awake will be able to guide you toward the next step. They cannot take the step for you, but they can direct you toward home.

Along these lines, a woman once expressed her concern to me about awakening being this "carrot in front of a lost and hungry soul." In her view, it presented the illusion of some end where all is known and there is no more to be learned, and therefore, no more growing.

Her words reminded me of the guru myth—the idea that the self-realized teacher/master/guru knows everything. It is prevalent in India and common among illiterate villagers, the educated middle class, and idealistic seekers. Ask the guru a question about economics, computer science, calculus, biotechnology, astrophysics, a foreign language, or what is going to happen in the future, and he or she will know the answer. Moreover, many believe the guru has the power, should he or she choose to use it, to fly through the air, walk through walls, and manifest sacred objects out of thin air.

Obviously, this is just a myth. Awakening to freedom does not mean you know everything or gain magical powers. On the contrary, it means you just know one thing: you truly are nobody.

Being nobody allows you to live in a relaxed body with a clear, focused mind and a joyful, loving heart. It allows you to be naturally centered and present wherever you are, opening you to accepting all points of view and learning all manner of new information.

Not until awakening happens, not until you see through the illusion of "I am this" or "I am that," does the real learning begin. This begins the process of growing into the fullness of your being, the unfolding of your deepest creative potential.

In other words, all concepts and ideas about who you are and what life supposedly means are just barriers to deeper levels of learning and communication. We so often think we are growing, but we just go around in circles, getting ever more stuck in whatever story or drama is currently running our lives. Awakening makes you realize how little you actually know, and *this* realization brings you into harmony with the endless beauty, wonder, and mystery of life.

When you realize you are nobody and don't have to try to be anybody, your body relaxes and your heart opens, making you receptive to the deeper layers of reality unfolding in each moment. Everything you need to know is available to you instantly, even the realization that the timing might not be right for receiving some answers. Sometimes, "later" is the right answer.

When you live in the present, you trust the flow. You are open to the signs and whispers of real intuition and can hear what life and other people are actually communicating to you.

Total trust in the flow is part of your secret. Trust awakens the master within. And while you are unlikely to ever levitate, walk through walls, or manifest objects out of thin air, the small miracles and synchronistic events occurring daily once you come into harmony with existence will definitely bring a quality of magic into your life.

The Power of Silence

The power of presence is an alertness or heightened awareness which brings you naturally to an inner silence, where the mind is no longer a problem. Jean Klein said, "Be knowingly silent as often as you can." In silence and stillness you hear the hum of creation itself, the Reality behind reality. You sense and experience your true nature, who and what you really are. Listen right now. See if you can hear it. See if you can feel it . . .

Be very still, eyes open, and tune into the silence within and without . . . Just listen, and become one with the silence . . . Notice you are this silence . . . Your true nature is the silent background to everything . . . Pure, shimmering stillness, within which all the sounds of creation are heard . . . Allow yourself to simply enjoy, bask in, the delicious silence of being for a few minutes . . .

Once in a workshop, a man said, "As I sit here, I definitely do feel—even hear—a kind of vibration, a presence . . . But I notice there always comes a point when the silence starts to get uncomfortable for me . . . It's happening now. I start to get restless. My mind says, 'What is this silence?' It's like there's nothing going on and it kind of scares me. Then I want to grab hold of something—some thought, concept, or story."

I told the man this: observe the tendency of your mind to try and create a thought or story to explain the silence. In acknowledging the story "What is this silence?" you are brought back into the awareness of the present. This observing or acknowledging is what I have been talking about all along: if you can look at the story you are telling yourself in your mind, then you cannot be the story; you are what is looking at the story. So, just *be* it. This is how simple it is to be who and what you are: consciousness, presence, an energy field which is simultaneously aware of everything, which *is* everything.

Below the surface noise in your mind lies the silence of your true nature. The truest communications come from this place of silent emptiness, which is rich in energy and awareness. When you listen within first, and then speak from the silence, your communication with others goes deep. What emanates from silence ultimately leads back to silence.

The deeper your silence, the stronger your words. Words springing from silence lead to real understanding, and then bring us back to silence itself. They bring us back to the beauty and fullness of *now*, to pure, radiant aware-ness. Such words bring us to the place where all creation and all love are birthed.

In silence, you feel the vibration of creation itself. You hear the sound of the source, the whisper of eternity. Within the silence, you rediscover your true nature. You experience firsthand that what is manifesting itself in this individual body, mind, and heart is indeed an expression of the one divine power behind the universe. Silence allows you to tap into your deepest creative power, which is no less than the source of all creation, consciousness itself. Silence is healing, nourishing. It is who and what you fundamentally are. In silence you discover the truth of interconnectedness and the priceless jewel of unconditional love.

When you know yourself as consciousness, the source of everything, you carry that inner silence with you as you go out into the noisy marketplace and engage in this wonderful, crazy, ever-fascinating drama called *life*. All awakened individuals share this one quality or characteristic: deep inner silence. It confirms what all the great texts extol: the sage dwells in inner silence.

People who are awake naturally become teachers just by the way they live and interact with others. Regardless of what form their worldly activities take—talking, laughing, playing, telling stories, engaging in all possible activities—they remain consciously in the depths of the silence. Teaching by example, they walk both worlds simultaneously.

It is not a forced silence, either. Silence unfolds quite naturally when you see all the mental chatter comprising the noise in your mind is entirely self-generated. Seeing your own story, your own incessant thinking getting in the way of your deeper peace and well-being, helps bring everything to a stop. Then the exquisite fragrance of stillness reveals itself. You *are* the stillness.

Most people fill their lives and environment with noise, whether it's music, television, video games, the Internet, endless telephone conversations, or being surrounded by other people. For many people, silence can be scary and uncomfortable. Lao Tzu put it this way: "One must get rid of knowledge; nothing is more powerful and creative than emptiness—from which men shrink."

Spending time in meditation and contemplation will help you overcome any fear of silence. Instead of running away from your fear, learn to face it. Remember the practice of breathing into it and welcoming it as a teacher and friend.

Of course, the fascinating thing is true silence is not empty at all. The emptiness out of which all sounds emerge, and back into which they disappear, only appears to be empty. David Bohm, the theoretical physicist, protégé of Einstein, and friend of J. Krishnamurti, said that in one cubic centimeter of empty space, there is the energy equivalent of twenty kilotons of TNT.

So, the silence we start to notice when we get quiet and still is not empty. It is not a lonely and barren place after all. In true silence you discover the energy, the core vibration of creation itself—the hum, the pulse of the universe. The yogis call it the *Nada*, the breath of God. The quieter you get, the louder it gets. Buddhists refer to our true nature or emptiness of mind as the plenum-void or the full-nothingness. The silence from which creation is manifested has a density and physicality to it. It is teeming with possibility and potential.

To access the gift of awakening, it is vital to take frequent time for inner silence. Until you awaken to its presence within, one of the best places to find it is to go out into nature. Being in nature connects you with your inner, essential nature. The experience of being in nature is invariably transforming, healing, and renewing.

There are so many choices: hike up into the hills or mountains, walk in a forest, visit a public park, feel the spaciousness of an open field, or sink in the sand along the seashore. The seashore, of course, is not always so silent, with the waves crashing on the beach, but it is very cleansing. I have often described the experience of going to the wild Northern California coast, near where I used to live, as "getting the cobwebs blown out of my system." It is simply very healing to feel the wind blow through you and to smell the salt air.

Nature, as the Zen master Shunryu Suzuki said, is the true teacher of Zen. Out in nature, your consciousness expands beyond the borders of the ego and its story and you begin to merge with the universal consciousness, the larger sense of beingness, which is who and what we all really are. Here, you get a larger, truer perspective on things. I call it the mountaintop perspective, because it leads you toward detachment, so you can see more clearly, more widely.

This is essential for making the shift in perception you are seeking. Instead of being mired in your own story, your own drama, you want to be able to step outside it in order to see it is not who you really are. Your true nature is consciousness, pure, timeless awareness. Nature helps you discover and connect with it.

Even if you can't go out into nature, you can pause frequently throughout the day—before you open your car door, get up from a chair, make the next phone call, or go into a meeting—to stop, be very present, be very still, and remember. You can remember to breathe, feel yourself in your body, be aware of your immediate environment, and open yourself to the stillness, the silence behind all the noises you hear. You can take the time to remember you are not your ego, your story, or your circumstances, but you are the awareness recognizing all of these phenomena.

If you are in a meeting and the other people are open to it, you can invite everyone to share a minute or two of conscious silence. Communing in silence in this way will help everyone present to get on the same energetic wavelength. You will be amazed at the creativity unleashed in the whole group once you start to talk and get into the agenda which has brought you together.

Many years ago, I was inspired to write down a short mantra. It was my guide in meditation for some time. Listen to the spirit behind it, make it your own, and the secret of those who have found freedom will be yours:

The fewer words, the better.
Let silence be your teacher.
It is the true power.

Take a Stand for Truth

Regardless of the spiritual tradition or lineage, if you go deeply into what any true teaching is communicating, you will find it is some variation of this: We live in difficult and uncertain times. There is much unrest, fear, and suffering in our world. This fear exists because people feel separate from one another, divided by their social, political, and religious beliefs. More than ever, we need to see beyond separateness into the unity, the love which is our true spiritual nature.

To see beyond separation, or duality, into unity requires a perceptual shift. We realize while each of us has a personal history, our own self-defining story and beliefs, these are not who we really are. Who and what we really are is the consciousness, the clear, creative awareness, that gives birth to all the beliefs, concepts, and stories. The more we see this—see *from* the perspective of consciousness—the freer we become, and the closer we move to the place where wisdom and love meet.

This truth, the truth of love and unity, is the central message of this book. As you grow in presence, and come to know who you are behind all your beliefs, ideas, and stories about who you are, the truth of awakening will become more real for you. You will come to know yourself as much more than just an isolated person in a sea of relatively anonymous people.

You will come to understand you are universal consciousness itself—the Whole—being expressed through this unique part, this individual body/mind/self called "you." You will know yourself as the ocean, dancing over the course of your lifetime, in this particular wave form that is your current human incarnation.

With this knowing, you will no longer feel separate from creation or from the rest of humanity. You will feel the interconnectedness of all life, all phenomena, and you will be fearless. You will be free. Then you will live in the world in a way which is true for you. You will be an authentic human being, unafraid to speak the truth, unafraid to express your deepest creative urges. You will follow your bliss, your passion. You will do what you love.

Once I was having a private session with a woman, and she said, "Why is it so difficult to discover and live the truth? I mean, I feel deep down I know what is true for me, but I still have all these fears and considerations going through my mind about why, if I follow my bliss, I am going to fail, or things won't work out. And then, whenever I go to speak my truth, sometimes I can't even get the words out. My voice literally chokes up. I know you are saying these are all just stories, and they are not what I am. I do glimpse my true nature, pure consciousness, in moments. But still, the fears, the choking up, arise."

I responded by saying, "Let's explore it right now. Be present with the choking up. Pay attention to the feelings and sensations. Even welcome them. After all, they are showing you where you are not yet free."

I told her to notice the fears and considerations going through her mind, but not to give them any energy. "Just be present with the whole of your being," I said. "Have your eyes open and all your senses awake. Breathe, and just be with whatever feelings and emotions are there. Be as present and as relaxed as you can be."

"When I do as you say, I must admit I feel more present, more here," she said. "I feel more at ease . . . But still, the question comes to mind: what about the future?"

"What about the future?"

"Well, what if the fear, or the choking up, happens again?"

"I am sure they will. Even when you fully awaken, residues of the fears that were once so real for you will surface. This may include the tendency to choke up. When it happens, do exactly what you are doing now. Be present with your experience, and then notice the story, the fear triggering the nervousness, the choking up. You can tell yourself, 'I am *not* my story . . . I am the pure awareness present right now . . . ' Then be *it*. Be the clear, very present awareness you are. Let the choking up feelings be there, but don't go into your head, don't go into any story about them."

Choking up is a classic fifth chakra symptom. The fifth chakra, the throat chakra, is the center of self-expression. When people are blocked here, they can experience a cracking or catching of the voice in the throat and find it difficult to get their words out. They literally struggle to speak their truth. Other physical manifestations, such as a sore or raspy throat, swollen glands, thyroid problems, and chronic neck pain and stiffness can also occur with blockage in the fifth chakra.

When I was a chiropractor, I occasionally saw this occur with women who were married to controlling, dominating men. These women did not feel they could freely express their deepest creative truth. They could not be who they really were because their husbands insisted they conform to some idealized model of "wife," and they were too afraid or too programmed to think or be different. The repressed energy manifested itself psychosomatically in the kinds of problems I just mentioned.

Sometimes, just a woman's plucking up the courage to finally tell her husband to get lost or back off was enough to create a breakthrough and bring about a healing. When we start being honest with ourselves, ridding our lives of the lies and lack of authenticity, it is amazing how much healing happens. As soon as we realize that to *not* express ourselves truthfully, we are actually hurting and making ourselves sick, we are then on the path to freedom. All of a sudden, we discover we no longer care what the other person says or does.

I learned a long time ago, in relationships, it is best to tell the truth right at the beginning and risk the small pain of hurt or rejection. If you lie, there will come a point, perhaps weeks, months, or years later, when the deception will be revealed. Once the other person realizes he or she has been deceived all this time, the pain of betrayal goes much deeper, is longer-lasting, and can be devastating.

There is a cleanness, lightness, and openness to living with this depth of truth and honesty. You know what it is like to tell a lie and then have to keep telling it, hoping you remember the story correctly to avoid getting caught. You also know what it feels like to be lied to. Living this way creates suffering for yourself and the other person. It's not liberating at all.

But as you awaken to freedom, you will naturally tell the truth. You couldn't do otherwise. You wouldn't do anything to cause your own suffering, and you wouldn't do anything to cause another to suffer. Practicing being present and truthful frees you from the attachment to your story and brings you closer to genuine freedom.

The Truth Is What Is

Communication, as my friend Phil Salyer once said, is the wonder drug of relationships. And the key to communication is the truth—being willing to hear it and to speak it. It takes courage to speak the truth. The head wants to reason, to be right, and will play all sorts of games in order to be right, but the heart yearns for truth. Without rigorous self-honesty, there can be no awakening, no enlightenment. The truth shall indeed set you free.

There are many reasons why we close down and suppress our aliveness and authenticity. Invariably they have to do with a past history of invalidation, rejection, judgment, ridicule, humiliation, or shame from when we were young. Therapists' offices throughout the country are filled with clients who are struggling to work through these issues.

Psychotherapy is a useful tool for healing the mind and emotions, but without the transpersonal perspective, it doesn't bring about true freedom. You just rearrange the contents in your mind, so you feel a little more at ease, a little more comfortable inside yourself. But you are still a prisoner of your own story. You still believe in the dreamworld you've created inside your head. The difference is you just now have a bigger prison cell to roam around in.

To be true to yourself means going deeply into your own psyche to see if there is anything you haven't been looking at which needs examining, anything which is blocking your freedom of expression. Then you've got to look and see if there is something you haven't said that you need to say to somebody.

The more willing you are to face the truth within yourself, to hear the truth from others, and to speak your truth without fear of the consequences, the more you tap into your passion. You connect with the source of courage within you, the boldness needed to take the risks in life that enable us to achieve great things. Then your destiny, your unique purpose in being here, starts to be fulfilled.

Being willing to hear the truth from others and to speak it confidently is one of the most empowering forms of self-expression available to us. It is one of the most critical skills or practices on the path of awakening. However, the truth is not found by sorting through the beliefs, assumptions, and judgments in your mind. All your mental considerations are what get in the way of truth. They cloud your perception of truth. Knowledge, as Lao Tzu said, is a barrier to truth.

Truth can be defined simply as what is. This means if you are hungry, that's what is, and hunger is your current truth. If you are angry, that's what is, and anger, in this moment, is your truth. If you are feeling lonely or afraid, then loneliness and fear are your truth. If you are feeling light and carefree, then this is your truth. If you know, deep inside yourself, that you love to play music, and you must do it on a regular basis, then that is your truth. It is not the only thing that is true about you, but definitely something that is true for you.

The truth, in other words, is whatever is being directly sensed, felt, or experienced. Zen, which is all about living in a true way, speaks of the suchness of life.

By suchness, Zen masters mean what is, or what is so. The moon is rising. Breathing is happening. The crickets are chirping. Maybe there's a creak in one of your joints when you move. All of these phenomena are the suchness. They are simply what is. If it's late at night, maybe you yawn, and you realize you are tired. That's the truth. It's what is. You're tired.

There is a wonderful and uniquely Zen saying describing the way enlightenment shows up in the world: "Eat when hungry, sleep when tired." Simple! If you understood the deep implications of that saying, there would no longer be conflicts or worries in your life. You would live like a Zen master, fully awake in the present, responding to whatever the situation or the real need in any given moment demands.

And, if there is nothing pressing right now, then you just relax and enjoy the flow of life.

Recognizing Truth

Problems arise not with the situation, but with our interpretation of it. Maybe you get a strange sensation in your chest and you start to panic, thinking you are about to have a heart attack. Or the rent is due in five days and you do not have the money, and you start to do a number on yourself. You begin to create a whole story around what will happen if you can't pay the rent: what your landlord may do, what happens if you get evicted and end up homeless. Maybe you start to shame yourself.

This is an example of what the ego does with what is. It interprets the situation and builds a story around whatever *it* is. Whether it's a pain in the chest, not having the rent money, or uncertainty about a relationship, the ego will create an elaborate drama, which often has little basis in fact or reality.

But when you live with what is, when you are in harmony with the suchness of life, there is no need for conflict when a challenging situation presents itself. You just deal with it; you respond. You make whatever changes are needed if you can, or just accept things as they are, but all without building an internal drama around it. Live like this and you are on your way to true freedom.

If, for example, you *don't* have the rent money, tell the truth. No games, just the truth. I remember being late with the rent a few times. I would call the landlord and say, "Look, I'm sorry, but I am going to be late this month." When there is genuinely no fear or embarrassment in your voice, no guilt, no blame, then those you are dealing with will most often relax, too. They open up and are willing to negotiate with you.

Be levelheaded and responsible. Make payment arrangements or work it out somehow. If the landlord gets angry, that's his or her problem, not yours. You certainly care about meeting your obligations, but you don't worry or lose any sleep if you can't. After all, your financial condition is just that—a condition. On this path, you don't depend on conditions for your well-being. Your happiness comes from a much deeper place. It comes from within you.

If speaking the truth is going to bring actual harm to yourself or to another, if some person or institution would use the information to cause harm, if the truth was cruel or unkind, then you may have to conceal the truth, or some portion of it. Once in a while, you may have to downright lie. For instance, if you were a European citizen hiding a Jewish family from the Nazis during the last World War, you would obviously conceal that fact from the authorities.

In some cases, people may not be ready to face the truth within or about themselves. You may need to tell somebody something, but clearly the outright truth would be crushing to them. Maybe you have to drip-feed it to them. This is where mastery comes in, knowing exactly what to say at any given time, and how to say it. This takes wisdom, discernment, and love.

Now, I often hear this from people: "When I try to listen to what is true inside me, I often hear a number of voices—sometimes a barrage of voices—inside my head. How can I discern my true voice?"

If you take the time to listen carefully, you'll notice that in addition to the many voices that may be echoing around inside your head, there is a voice that resonates from deep down within your gut, your heart, your soul. This is the voice you want to listen to.

I discovered this deeper voice while traveling in Nepal in the early 1980s. I was staying in a cheap hotel in the tourist section of Kathmandu. I lay on my narrow cot in the hotel room to meditate, gradually becoming startlingly aware of two voices inside me.

There was the voice in my head, which was rather shrill, and very mental, and consisted mainly of tape-loops from the past, all my stories, beliefs, judgments, opinions, and so on. It was what Werner Erhard, the transformational guru who was big in the 1970s, called the "yammer-yammer" of the mind.

But there was another voice, one that came from deep inside me. When I got very quiet and still, I could hear this voice. It had a richer and more resonant sound. It felt very authentic, and was very present-time. It was not a voice I could second-guess, whereas the first voice, the ego's voice, was very predictable.

The insight into the two voices was an epiphany for me. From then on, I would notice which voice was speaking through me, and I would consciously practice shifting out of my head, down into my body, into a more present-time awareness, in which the deeper voice, the voice of truth, could reveal itself.

The more I lived with a heightened sense of awareness and inner silence, I discovered, the more clearly I could hear the voice of truth. Jean Klein always said that true communication comes out of silence and leads back to silence. If you don't know what to think or say, get very quiet on the inside, and just listen. Be totally present, and listen.

Your true voice will sooner or later reveal itself, in the form of an intuitive insight, a hunch, or maybe a profound thought or phrase that will rise forth into your awareness, seemingly out of nowhere . . .

See if you can hear the voice of truth now . . . Welcome whatever you are experiencing right now, and just be very still, present . . . Be the clear, lucid awareness you are . . . Then look deep within your body . . . As that awareness, listen for whatever voice arising from your heart or gut wants to be heard . . . It may say that nothing is needed right now, or it may voice a need, something wanting attention . . . Take note of it, and then simply be here . . .

Release Attachment to Outcomes

Some people fear that being awake and living in the now means letting go of goals and dreams, but that is an illusion, a story they have locked onto which keeps them from being present.

The attachment to outcomes, to getting a specific result, sets the stage for anxiety, the fear you won't achieve what you want. As you learn to release the attachment and become genuinely present, new creative energies—as well as feelings of courage and confidence—spring forth, and actually move you closer to your goal.

Worrying about the future is one of the main causes of stress in our lives. It is a habit that just perpetuates fear, the uncomfortable feeling of not being enough as we are. It keeps us stuck believing such and such *must* happen if we are going to be happy, and if it doesn't, our lives will be miserable.

A story about J. Krishnamurti speaks with crystal clarity about what it means to be free of this limiting, fear-based pattern of thinking. Every spring for over sixty years, he gave talks in a beautiful oak grove in the Southern California town of Ojai.

Hearing Krishnamurti speak in person was always an extraordinary experience. His friend Aldous Huxley described it thus: "Like listening to a discourse of the Buddha—such power, such intrinsic authority." It was no less moving when I went to hear him speak in the late 1970s, surrounded by nearly two thousand people, sitting on the grass or in folding chairs. Partway through this particular talk, Krishnamurti suddenly paused, leaned forward, and said, almost conspiratorially, "Do you want to know what my secret is?"

Almost as though we were one body, we sat up, even more alert than we had been, if possible. I could see people all around me lean forward, their ears straining and their mouths slowly opening in hushed anticipation. Krishnamurti rarely ever talked about himself or his own process, and now he was about to give us his *secret*. Why else did we come to Ojai every spring, but to see if we could find out just what his secret was? We wanted to know how he managed to be so aware and enlightened, while we struggled with conflict and our many problems.

There was a silence. Then he said in a soft, almost shy voice: "You see, I don't mind what happens."

We sat back as we contemplated his words, and considered the whole notion of what it would mean to not mind what happens.

A woman to whom I told this story said, "To me, not minding what happens sounds too passive. It's almost like you're allowing people and life to walk all over you. I mean, I have a five-year-old daughter. I would be devastated if something happened to her. I go out of my way to protect her, to take care of her."

I explained to her that, without a deeper understanding, it may seem so, yes. The deeper understanding we are talking about, of course, is inner freedom, total awakening. In the poem "Little Gidding," T. S. Eliot described the awakened state as "a condition of complete simplicity / (Costing not less than everything)."

Therefore, you have to let go of everything in your mind to be truly free. To use Krishnamurti's phrase, you have to not "mind" what happens, including your inner attachment to your daughter's well-being. But you are still human. You love your daughter and will naturally care for her and protect her. You just won't be obsessing about it or always thinking about it, which gives rise to the specter or paranoia about being devastated at the thought of possibly losing her.

Being awake does not mean you lose the normal human desires and preferences. You still feel and honor your creative urges. You still set out to do whatever you really want to do with your energy. If you don't like the circumstances you find yourself in, by all means take action to change them if they can be changed. The difference is they are now just circumstances, not problems.

Outwardly, for example, you might need to fiercely cling to a goal or objective in order to see it through to a successful conclusion. Yet inwardly, if you are truly free, there is no emotional attachment to what happens. You know yourself *as* the field of awareness, of presence. This knowledge, and the enduring peace it brings, is not dependent on whether you achieve your goals or not.

In other words, you are passionately committed to your goals and intentions, but you are ultimately unattached to the outcomes. This freedom from attachment liberates you from fear, from worrying about whether you are going to succeed or not. When you take the worry out of your work, you are actually more likely to succeed.

The process is exactly the same as the earlier example of how a Zen master climbs a mountain. Whether it's to make more money, learn a new skill, explore a new city, or attain enlightenment, first, set your goal, your intention, and then put it at the back of your mind and focus on the journey. Pay attention to the step you are taking right *now*. This is the best way to ensure your next step will be successful.

It is a timeless spiritual truth: release attachment to outcomes, and deep inside yourself, you will feel good no matter what. You feel good because you are connected to the energy of the universe, the beauty and power of creation itself. You will be one with the silence behind it all, and therein lies the true power . . .

Be one with the silence now . . . Be very alert and present, immersed in the flow of creation . . . Notice how you, as consciousness, are still very much here . . . Yet, right now, in this very moment, there is no need to think or to worry about the future . . . Soon, you can think about what you need or want to do, but right now, it is enough just to be the beautiful, present-time awareness you are . . .

The Proof Your True Nature Is Consciousness

In a workshop, a man said, "I understand that while I have a personal story, a psychological and emotional history, it is not who I really am. But what about cultural and ethnic identities? I am a Jew, and the whole of Jewish history makes me who I am. It is in my blood, my genes. I have a Muslim friend I've known since childhood who says the same thing about her background. Yet you say consciousness, and not my Jewishness, is my true nature. Can you prove this to me?"

I replied: "Without doubt your Jewishness is part of your personal story and your family history, your genetic lineage, so to speak. The body is what it is, the genes are what they are, and even the cultural conditioning is imprinted to a certain degree. But you don't have to be at the mercy of any of this. After all, you are *conscious* of being Jewish, right?"

"Yes."

"That proves my point," I said. "Consciousness, the awareness of body, mind, senses, and identity, comes *first*. Consciousness is the ground of being giving rise to all thoughts, sensations, beliefs, and experiences. No matter what is happening in your experience, no matter what you identify with, you are *aware* of it. Awareness, or consciousness, is primary. The practice we have been doing all along helps us come to this realization."

The difference between awakened and unawakened people is the former live from the ultimate Reality, the nondual reality. They dwell in awareness, in pure, silent consciousness itself, all the while acknowledging the relative reality of thoughts, beliefs, feelings, and experiences, including racial, ethnic, and religious differences, as well as genetic lineage.

Because they live from and embrace the ultimate perspective, the context of the whole, they are able to honor and work with the content, the day-to-day events and circumstances, without getting lost in it. By seeing the big picture, they see the intrinsic interrelationship of all the parts.

On the other hand, unawakened people are caught up in the relative reality, in the content, in one or more of the parts. Not having opened to and connected with the ultimate Reality, the consciousness that is the source of all thought, sensation, and feeling, they cling to what can be seen, felt, experienced.

This includes all the beliefs people hold on to regarding the value of a particular ethnic, national, religious, cultural, or social identity. When you factor in the personal history, all the subjective memories from the past, both painful and pleasant, you have this world between the ears I call "me, myself, and my story."

As long as people cling to their story or version of reality, be it Jewish, Muslim, Christian, Buddhist, Hindu, black, white, or gender-oriented, there is going to be conflict and suffering within and between individuals and groups. Conflict and suffering are then projected outwardly in various forms of religious, political, ethnic, and social strife. There is a resistance to the natural flow, the ups and downs of life. People are unable to see the truth: a *story* about something is not the truth of it.

It is happening right now all around the world in various hot spots of conflict and war. Human beings have been clashing and fighting with each other since they first learned how to wield a stick and throw a spear. Back then, they didn't even have religious stories to do battle over, but they had survival stories, they had stories of their clan or tribe.

A question I sometimes get asked when talking about the violence in the world is, "What's your solution, then? Surely you don't expect people to give up their Jewish, Muslim, Christian, or Hindu identities?"

I respond by saying it would be a huge step to at least give up the *attachment* to those identities. It would change the world if a large number of us began being more interested in what was actually, scientifically proven to be true—that is, the primacy and universality of consciousness—rather than the ethnic, cultural, nationalistic, or religious stories we've been programmed with down through the ages. Then we would experience a lot less war, and a lot more peace.

You can still honor any and all of your religious traditions, for tradition is a beautiful thing. However, it is important to see the inherent limitations in being attached to those traditions. If we try to overlay traditional values and ideals on whatever the current reality is, such an overlay prevents us from opening to something deeper, fresher, and newer in the present. We remain caught in duality and conflict.

The Role of Religion in a Conscious World

As people throughout the world awaken to the truth within them, religion itself, regardless of its form or expression, will undergo a transformation.

Because of the awakening or flowering of consciousness, religion will become a much more genuine expression for those who now pay homage to it. Instead of religion telling us how to live, we will shape it to serve us, to serve all of humanity, fully honoring the original beauty, truth, and goodness that initially gave birth to the religion.

After all, we created religion in the first place. Since we made up the story, we can revise it in any way we choose.

Religion, as I see it, has two vital functions. The first is the way in which it gets us started on the spiritual path, and offers us a helping hand, moral support, and guidance along the way. This is where our priests, pastors, rabbis, and mullahs can become important guides for us. The more awake they are, and the less caught up in the story, in dogma and rules, the more they can serve us by helping us see the light.

I am referring, of course, to the true light, the light of our innermost being, not just the reflected light glancing off the cross, sparkling on the chalice, or streaming through the stained glass window. These emanations of light off or through sacred objects are always beautiful to behold, but it is ever important to remember where the light comes from, otherwise we get seduced by objects and images outside ourselves. The light comes from the Source, of course. It comes from within us. We *are* the light.

The second great function of religion is community. Community brings people together, not just to worship the Source, the power behind creation, but to deal with conflict and crisis. When disaster, natural or man-made, strikes a community, the church, temple, or mosque becomes a rallying point, a center for collecting and focusing the energy, money, and talents of all those who have come to lend a hand. It becomes a resource for handling the logistics and supplies needed to address the particular crisis. It becomes a haven for sharing the burden of suffering, for giving and receiving physical, emotional, and spiritual sustenance and support.

During times of upheaval or disaster, or simply when there is a community need, governments are often ineffective or even powerless to help. It is ordinary people, concerned people, people of faith and compassion gathering at their local place of worship, who make the real difference.

So, awakening doesn't mean religion will go away. It just means religion will change, will undergo a transformation. Religion itself will become enlightened. Given the dark side of its history, all the death, terror, and suffering it has inflicted upon humanity in the name of "God"—and still does, in many parts of the world—such a change will be a good thing.

Many people wonder about prayer, and how that changes as we awaken more to our true nature. Instead of praying to some idea of God or a higher Power, you will be supremely alert in the present, fully attentive in this moment now, and you will *feel* as a palpable reality the immense silence behind creation. You will feel the power of it vibrating in every cell of your being, and you will know, beyond a shadow of a doubt, the Power you once prayed to actually exists. It is the very substratum of existence, the very energy and consciousness of which you are made.

Then your prayers will take on a different tone. Rather than beseeching or asking, you will be expressing the gratitude you feel for the grace continually being bestowed upon you, and upon all who have the eyes, the ears, and the sensitivity to notice it.

Instead of living in fear of not being "saved," not being good enough to make it to heaven when you die, or not belonging to the right religion, you will realize everything is perfectly okay. You will realize everything has *always* been perfectly okay. Heaven is here now, despite the seeming hell misguided human beings create.

It is just as Jesus said, that the kingdom is here. Or as the Sufi masters put it: "God and heaven live within your own heart." Or as the yogis and sages have always known, bliss, peace, and happiness are your true nature.

Grace Rains Down

With awakening there comes a profound sense of peace, trust, and happiness—a happiness not dependent on conditions or circumstances, but shining on its own, the very expression of the beautiful, conscious being you really are.

Personal conflict, fear, and discontent leave you, because you no longer take yourself to be a person. Rather, you have no concept or image of yourself making you need to proclaim, whether to yourself or others, "I am this," or "I am that."

You don't go through the day thinking about yourself in the old way anymore. You're just being what you are: pure, divine awareness, expressed through this body, these eyes, and this mind, which others perceive of as you. If you think about anything at all, it is just to remember to be present, should you get momentarily distracted, caught back up in a residue of your former self.

You still have your own unique personality and temperament, but now you are much more open, spontaneous, and authentic. Your personality is no longer rigid, reactive, and predictable, as it was when you were caught up in a story about who you thought you were.

With awakening, your work and unique destiny become clear. There are no rules, other than do no harm (you experience yourself as one with all of life, so to harm another would be to harm yourself). This leaves you with endless creative possibilities! You live each day, each hour, in gratitude for the gifts, big and small, which life continually showers upon you. Jean Klein always said as we get freer, gratitude becomes our predominant emotion. Without a doubt, this has been my experience.

The 19th century Bengali saint, Ramakrishna, said it slightly differently: "Grace rains down ceaselessly."

This grace is always available. Consciousness is who and what you are. Grace is your true nature. God is not out there in some place or state, as you were taught when you were young, but is the very substance of your being. God *is* consciousness. Consciousness is God.

Understanding this is what frees you from the fear of death. As you see the truth of everything more clearly and release the attachment to the rigid identification with I and me, you come to the realization that nobody is born and nobody dies. As a historical person, you exist only as an idea or concept inside your head. Your body is born, yes, but you are not your body. You are the consciousness giving birth to the body, the consciousness that brings it into being, into awareness.

When your body dies, it dissolves into dust, but the consciousness you *are* was not born and does not die. Consciousness has always been here, endlessly being incarnated, endlessly becoming aware of itself, endlessly manifesting itself in new forms, in new bodies. You are an individualized expression of divine consciousness, just as a wave is an expression of the ocean. But, like the wave, your true, timeless nature is the ocean, it *is* consciousness.

When you know yourself as consciousness, you realize you—as consciousness—have been here since the beginning of time. Your body, mind, and personality will die, but consciousness itself does not die. How can there be an extinction of consciousness? To know you are extinct, you would have to be aware of it—and if you are aware, you're not extinct! And if you're not aware of being extinct, or aware of anything else, then you're not aware of anything period, so clearly there is nothing to be afraid of or to worry about.

It is just like deep sleep. When you wake up from deep, dreamless sleep, you always feel wonderfully refreshed, so if death were a kind of deep sleep, and then you woke up somewhere else, why would it be any different? Whether you wake up back in this realm, in a new body, or in some other realm in an angelic form, you're always going to feel refreshed. And if you never do wake up, then you don't know anything about it, so again, what is there to fear?

This is the freedom, the liberation, the cosmic sigh of relief that awakening brings. Instead of fearing death, we look upon it as the last great adventure of this particular incarnation. We may even welcome it, when the time comes, with an attitude of, "Well, *this* is going to be interesting!"

This realization about consciousness not being separate from birth, life, or death brings with it an awesome responsibility. It means we can no longer look to a God out there for help or salvation, nor can we blame a God out there for what has gone wrong in our lives. God is us. Human beings created the whole concept of "God," and made Him in our image. It's just a word, a story we dreamed up to describe the indescribable power and intelligence of the consciousness behind everything.

Once we see and experience the truth of consciousness, our work here becomes clear: it is to guide others who are receptive on the journey of awakening. Maybe we do this directly, by sharing the practice and teaching with them. Maybe we do it indirectly by showing through example the way we embody consciousness and presence in our everyday lives.

Jean Klein put it this way: "In my teaching, one points directly to consciousness, the natural state; becomes established in it; and then moves down, so to speak, to the transforming of the relative nature."

This transformation of the relative nature, bringing the consciousness we are into every realm of daily life, is work that will go on till the day we die. After all, who can say they have mastered the art of living? I can't. In terms of living in the world, the marketplace, the learning goes on.

In many people who wake up, a fragment of the old self often reasserts itself and gets attached to the idea it is now enlightened—the ultimate ego trip, you might say. This happened to me, and it happened to other teachers I know.

In Zen, they call it "the stink of enlightenment." It's a phenomenon especially prevalent among men, who by nature are competitive and think they need to be one up on everyone else, even in the spiritual field.

But eventually you see through the "I am enlightened" story, too. You let go of the attachment to ideas of enlightenment, to yourself as the messenger, as the one who knows and who has arrived. Now you can just focus on the message. Not so much talking about it, but just *being* it. Being the knowing is what really matters.

The Practice of Being Awake

Take a minute or two right now to just be silent, alert, and aware of whatever is. Be present with whatever you are experiencing. Notice the stories, thoughts, and images passing through your mind, and realize you are not any of them. What you are is the consciousness, the awareness, that permeates your body, mind, and personality, and that sees everything.

If you like, you can affirm to yourself, "I am not my story. My true nature is pure consciousness, manifested in this body, mind, and personality that is me . . . " Then let the thought go, take a deep, conscious breath, and relax into being the pure, silent awareness you are.

When you are present like this, seeing without any story whatsoever, you are free. Everything in your universe, including all that you choose to create, flows out of this moment now . . .

~ 6 ~

The Power of Love

WITH THE AWAKENING TO our true natures as consciousness, each day becomes rich in love, meaning, and purpose. In this chapter, I want to speak about love.

Love, after all, is the most important and vital emotion we human beings can feel. The East Indian sage, Ramakrishna, said, "The mind will take you into the courtyard of the Beloved, but only the heart will get you into the bedroom."

Love is what humanity needs to show more of if there is ever to be any kind of global healing. Since long before the time of Jesus, whose teaching was all about love, prophets and sages have been telling us we needed to love each other more. Yet people everywhere seem to struggle with loving one another as much as they struggle internally with everything else.

Modern psychology is on the mark when it says we must learn to love ourselves first, and then we can love others. But so long as we remain in the realm of the psychological and emotional, it is not so easy. There are the selves we think we are, and the selves we are trying to improve, to love. It can be very confusing—as it usually is, when we are still identified with the personal, when we cannot see beyond our own ego concerns.

Through doing the practice of freedom I have presented here, through embodying the teaching that you are not your story, you are led to the understanding there is just one energy, one universal consciousness manifested in an endless diversity of forms. You are that energy, and its very nature, as it is expressed through the human heart, is love.

Reality is an indivisible Whole. Every living creature is a wave flowing out of and receding back into the one ocean of creation. Connecting with the oneness or wholeness of life paves the way for opening the heart. When you realize all fears are self-created, there is a deep relaxation or letting go at the somatic level. Then your heart will naturally feel the flowering of goodness, kindness, and love.

This is the very essence of love—to open our hearts and tap into our true compassion. It is to feel our energetic oneness, our interconnectedness, with every other human being and every living thing. However, in most of us, this flowering in the heart needs to be nurtured and brought forth.

The more we feel it, the more we extend our love outward, and the more our actions are governed by such heart qualities as empathy, kindness, affection, tenderness, compassion, forgiveness, generosity, gratitude, and courage.

This is where enlightenment comes down from the mountaintop and enters the marketplace. What I call the "mountaintop view" describes time spent in meditation, contemplation, self-inquiry to discover our true nature—the wisdom, love, and freedom inside us.

But this awakening to truth, to the divine love within you, is only the first step. Our ability to bring this love down from the mountaintop into the marketplace is the test of how deep and real our awakening is. It reveals our ability to be there with and for others; it shows the degree to which our hearts are truly open.

Inner freedom is absolutely attainable. Once you are free, you are always free. Other than those minor residues or echoes from the past occasionally cropping up, there is no getting stuck again. Residues are most likely to occur when the body is going through pain or illness of some kind, or survival is being threatened in some way.

But the mastery of love is something else altogether. In a way, we are all beginners at love. Mastery of your mind brings you to the experience of clarity and detachment, of freedom and openness, of spaciousness and presence. But opening and awakening the heart brings you into intimacy with life and with people.

As your heart opens and fear dissolves, your chest expands and is filled with warmth and love. This feeling of expansion is the sign that consciousness is entering your heart. When you trust and live from your heart, your true passion is liberated. The heart is the true healer.

Practical Love

Nisargadatta Maharaj said, "Wisdom is knowing I am nothing, love is knowing I am everything, and between the two my life moves." This is a beautiful expression of truth.

As you awaken, you will indeed discover you are nothing and everything. In that discovery, you will feel the power of the universe moving through you and realize you are connected to everyone and everything. True freedom arises in knowing, which is articulated in wisdom, and feeling, which is expressed as love.

Life then becomes very rich, because you are connected to the love within you, to the power of the universe itself. You still welcome love from other people—after all, you want to see the whole world awaken to this love within—but you no longer *need* it. The light and love shining in you are strong enough now. In fact, they overflow, so that you cannot help but share your radiant, loving presence with those who are open and receptive to it.

When I talk about love in this way, I often get this question: "What you are saying sounds true, but I still find it very hard to love certain people. I think many others would find it hard to love, too. I mean, what about terrorists, whose sole purpose is to kill and destroy? Are we supposed to love them? Or, closer to home, how can you expect a grieving mother to love her child's murderer?"

We have to look at love from a very practical perspective. Love is not necessarily about liking every human being on earth, or even your neighbor, especially if he or she is mean-spirited, malicious, or ill-willed. It is not about condoning harmful or destructive behavior. And even though people may be partially or almost totally disconnected from it, love is fundamentally about respecting the inherent humanity of all people and looking for the spark of truth, goodness, and light residing somewhere deep within everyone's heart and soul.

The ongoing work of awakening is to bring love from inside your heart out into the world, where it can make a difference. Learning to do this is a lifelong process. It requires you to be very conscious and aware throughout the day. When you notice you are not being aware, when you are caught up in distraction, in judgment, in

some story, take that as your cue to come back to awareness. Take it as your reminder to come back to being
here now.

You have to be vigilant. Sometimes you might have to
remind yourself to listen more carefully, to be more compassionate, to reach out and put your arm around someone. You may have seen through the illusion of the person,
of your own story, but opening your heart is an endless
process. It is a journey of growing *into* love, of learning to
express your true, compassionate nature ever more fully.
It's about being very aware, present, open, and grounded
in your body in each moment.

As freedom becomes more real for you, being centered
and grounded happens naturally and effortlessly. From this
place, you can reach out and share who you are with others. You can open your heart to them. If you are invited to
speak or someone asks you a question, you can introduce
the awakening conversation. Above all, you will be able to
share your silence, your stillness, and your peace.

As often as possible and as much as you can, let yourself be guided by awareness, presence, and love, and one
day true freedom will be yours. Then you will know how
to act and what to do—even in the face of a terrorist act,
even if, God forbid, your own child were murdered.

The Religion of the Heart

A man once said to me, "I want to open my heart more. I
often feel a kind of tightness in my chest, which I am sure
is fear. The doctors told me there is nothing wrong with
me physically, so I know it is not organic. You have given
us a good practice for facing fear, the story around it. I
have been doing that and the fear is definitely lessening.
Is there anything more you can tell me?"

Tightness in the chest is the somatic or physical manifestation of a heart that, at times, is still closed. It is a sign of an unresolved fear. The first step is learning to really welcome, or at least accept the fear from the perspective that it is showing you where you are still not free. It also helps to live inwardly with the question, "What am I afraid of?" and then notice what images, intuitions, and flashes of insight come into your awareness during the day.

Heart chakra issues become obvious in relationships, so pay particular attention to what happens whenever you are with people. Relationships test your ability to give or receive love.

You will probably find the fear has to do with rejection, issues of abandonment or entrapment, or being hurt or judged in some way. Like all such fears, it can be traced back to a pattern of emotional wounding in childhood. The more you learn to face the fear, to meet it head-on, the more insight you will get into how and why it has been running the story of your life all these years.

Then, as you realize you are not your story about fear, the freer you will become. No matter how true the story once was, you will know with increasing certainty that you are the awareness, the field of presence that watches or looks at the story *now*. You'll find yourself relaxing into your true nature. As you learn to be the beautiful, conscious person you are, the fear will drop away. While it definitely feels like a real emotion, it is based upon an illusory story and cannot exist in the light of truth, of your presence.

Take a few minutes to meditate on this right now . . . Look within . . . Notice that inside your head, you may have old memories surface, stories about childhood wounds and fears, and then corresponding emotions and feelings in your body . . . Let the story and the feeling or emotion be there, in the vastness of the awareness, the consciousness you are . . . These stories and feelings come and go, but who and what you really are—this spacious, luminous, and loving awareness—is timeless and ever-present . . . It is your true nature . . . So be that . . . Be who and what you really are . . .

Fear, the barrier to love, has its roots in beliefs and the stories about those beliefs. People believe in some things so fervently they are willing to die or kill for what they believe. In Jed McKenna's book, *Spiritual Enlightenment: The Damnedest Thing*, which is an excellent depiction of the nondual approach, he says:

> It's amazing how desperately we cling to our beliefs. As history shows, the fastest way to reduce otherwise decent, caring people to a state of savagery is by tampering with their belief system. The word for someone who does so is heretic, and the punishments reserved for him are more heinous than for any other type of criminal.

He describes people who identify with their stories and beliefs, people who are not at all open to anything new or different. Awakening, on the other hand, is all about getting beyond the stories and beliefs. It is about seeing that those stories and beliefs to which we cling are not even real. They are just concepts, assumptions about truth. Yet notice how, when it comes to religion, especially, people are willing to fight, kill, and die for their beliefs.

This was the Christianity of the Crusades and the Inquisition. Under the Inquisition, a hint of heresy meant you could be tortured in a horrible way. Just imagine Jesus' reaction had he seen what the church did with his teaching of love! However, Christianity had two thousand years in which to mature. Islam, by comparison, is a younger religion, and its fundamentalist elements display their own alarming degree of savagery when it comes to dealing with what the mullahs judge as heresy.

It is tragic and absurd when you think about it, stoning people to death because they don't agree with your story about God and creation, or because they have different sexual tendencies, or because they do something forbidden by some authority's interpretation of the rules of your religion or society.

Technologically, we live in an age of enlightenment, but there's still incredible darkness, prejudice, and bigotry in the world—all because people are caught up in believing some myth, some story about God and the meaning of life.

The most dangerous kind of religious fundamentalism thrives in places where there is extreme poverty, where there is both economic and social injustice. The fundamentalist religious cause becomes a rallying cry and brings meaning to otherwise hopeless, despairing lives. As the economic and social inequalities are righted, people become more interested in balance and moderation as a way of preserving and perpetuating the good they are beginning to enjoy.

But adjusting outer conditions and circumstances, while important, is just one level of freedom. At the deepest level, it comes down to making the adjustment individually—finding personal freedom.

Freedom starts right here, with each of us. Come back to your own situation, your own suffering, and inquire as to what is needed for *you* to free yourself. When you find freedom, you will no longer live in fear. The more of us who realize genuine inner freedom, the more this truth will spread outward in our world. Then, depending on your gifts and talents, you will make your contribution toward a more conscious world.

If you are a scientist, you will find a way through science. If you are a lawyer, you will find it through seeking justice for worthy causes. If you are a corporate CEO, you will build a corporation that values more than just the bottom line, that pays attention to the well-being of its employees, its customers, and the environment. If you are a politician, you will pursue policies that help transform our communities and our nation.

If you are a priest, a rabbi, a pastor, or a mullah, you will take what is genuinely good and true in your religion, and you will share it with your congregants. But you will not fill their heads with dogmas and threats of hell and damnation, which only make their hearts heavy and fearful.

When asked about his religion, an Indian teacher of mine named Dada said, "My religion is the religion of the heart." I have always remembered those words. When you practice presence and awareness and awaken to your true nature as consciousness, your heart opens. Then kindness, love, and generosity become the natural cornerstones of your behavior.

If everyone observed the religion of the heart, the world would be a beautiful and safe place for all of us. There would be room to express our competitive, striving natures in a healthy way, because they would be balanced by cooperation and sharing. If we lived like this, we wouldn't be in the fragmented place in which we find ourselves.

How, then, to practice the religion of the heart? Maghrabi Sahib, a spiritual master also from India, gave us this exquisite prescription:

> When I looked in, I found within me that which has been sought for ages by all mankind. We have been searching for it for many ages here and there, from one corner of the earth to the other, but we have found it only in our heart. Therefore do not search for your lost Beloved outside yourself. You will find Him [or Her] only in the recess of your heart.

Discover the Healing Power of Forgiveness

Forgiveness, simply defined, is the letting go of blame or resentment toward anybody who has hurt, offended, or slighted you in the past.

So long as you are still living from your ego, story, or image about who you are, you will always be subject to being hurt. Sooner or later, someone will do or say something to offend you. Then you will live with the feeling of being hurt, and of being angry because you were hurt, for some time. Some people nurse their hurt feelings and anger for weeks or months, while others do it for years or decades.

However, if you are on a path of personal or spiritual growth, you will, at some point, realize the hurt and anger you are holding onto are actually causing more harm to you than they are the other person. The other person is merrily going on with his or her life (which just pisses you off even further!), and here you are, suffering miserably because of what he or she said or did months or years ago.

But you can't deny it any longer. You've heard about forgiveness, you've read about it, and as much as you may hate doing it, you finally realize that for your own sanity and well-being you're going to have to get over it. You're going to have to let go. So, how do you do that? There are exercises, practices, and visualizations for learning to forgive. I share two such practices at the end of this chapter.

Let me tell you how I discovered these practices, and used them to let go of my own hurt feelings and anger. A few years before I awakened to my true nature, I met and fell in love with a much younger woman who fulfilled all my ideas about what a perfect mate would be like. That was undoubtedly my first mistake! I fabricated a whole story in my mind about who she was and what she represented to me—I projected my ideas onto her. To a large degree she became my identity. Thus I suffered terribly when I felt her disappearing from my life!

Also, the whole idea of "falling" in love suggests a kind of unconsciousness. Better, I think, to consciously *grow into* love with someone. Anyway, I had yet to learn those lessons.

After two years, my girlfriend fell in love with someone closer to her own age and this precipitated the end of our relationship. Since she failed to tell me about this other man, there were lies, deceptions, and betrayals. Heartbroken, I ended the relationship just to keep my sanity intact. I had fallen head-over-heels for this young woman. I had so completely identified with the story I'd fabricated around her that I experienced a tremendous emotional pain when it all fell apart.

Yet, as painful as the experience was, I knew it was necessary. My awakening, such as it was at the time, was pretty intellectual and quite detached. Going through the emotional pain brought me into my heart, into my feelings, into reality with a vengeance. Even during the worst of it, which lasted a couple of months, I knew it was for my highest good. The phrase going through my mind at the time was: "God is giving me a much-needed lesson in pain and feeling."

Surprising me the most was the feeling of anger that began to roil away inside me. While getting over the shock of her betrayal, I experienced an anger I never felt before, the kind which screamed inwardly, "How *dare* she do this to me!" I even found myself contemplating murderous thoughts. I am sure just about every spurned lover has felt something akin to this. It is the stuff of great drama.

In fact, it is the kind of drama that is best left to television, the stage, the pages of a novel, or the cinema screen. However, until we wake up to the beautiful, conscious people we really are, we seem destined to act out these dramas in real life.

I dealt with my anger and pain by going to the Sonoma Mountain Zen Center for a week. I rented a small cabin, I ate my meals with the others there and meditated a few times in the zendo, but mostly I just sat by myself in the cabin and took long, meditative walks around the beautiful property.

I sat with my feelings and welcomed everything that came up. Sitting on my *zafu*, my meditation cushion, in the tiny little cabin in the woods, I sometimes felt very vulnerable, sobbing over the loss of this woman I loved. At other times, I felt almost self-righteous. I'd view her with scorn and envision ways I could take out my anger on her. I gave myself free reign to do all this. It was what I needed to do for my healing.

Then there were times when the feelings of loss and anger would pass, leaving me sitting in clear, almost blissful freedom as I came home to myself. I was able to let go of all thoughts and images of her and simply rest in stillness, in the beauty and fullness of being. These clearer moments helped me to realize she had her own issues and was just following the call of her soul. She didn't hate me. She just needed to move on, and I needed to let her go. This brings me to the specific forgiveness process I wanted to share with you:

I visualized her standing before me as I surrounded her with light and wished her well. Inwardly, I thanked her for the gifts she brought into my life, and wished her all the best for her journey.

One of the keys to forgiveness is realizing the people who hurt you are only acting out of their own belief systems, their own stories of need and suffering. In the case of my former girlfriend, she was still exploring and trying to find herself. If I was the lover of inner truth and freedom I said I was, who was I to try and stop her? Heck, my whole life was about supporting people in waking up. This realization helped me get over my own pain fairly quickly.

Coming to the realization you are suffering and you want to be free from suffering more than anything else is the heart and soul of forgiveness. Your suffering is the result of the anger, hurt, and blame—the story—you are holding onto. You are smart enough to see that if you act out your anger, if you dump it on the person who hurt you, it is going to perpetuate the cycle of suffering—for yourself and the other person. You might feel a certain pleasure in acting out your anger, but so long as you remain attached to your self-righteous story, you will continue to attract people who offend or hurt you.

In the end, you come face-to-face with the cold, hard truth of the matter: you have to let your blame and self-righteousness go. You might practice kissing or waving goodbye to it, or visualize wrapping the anger and hurt in a silk cloth and tossing it into an imaginary fire. Do whatever works for you.

Ultimately though, it always comes back to the direct path. You breathe deeply, shrug your shoulders, and metaphorically shake off whatever you're holding onto, which is not you. You become supremely present, relaxed in your body, your heart open. You are right here in this moment—aware, alert, awake.

Through the power of clear, present-time awareness, you reconnect with the true beauty and vastness of life. You feel the energy of the universe moving through you again. You realize you are one with the universe. You *are* the universe.

In this oneness, all feelings of separation, hurt, and anger eventually dissolve and are replaced by clarity, light, presence, and a great feeling of peace . . .

Be the oneness right now . . . Go within and visualize your body as vast, empty space, space which is at the same time infinitely full . . . Connect with your heart, the love breathing within you, the love you are . . . Now think of someone who has hurt or betrayed you in the past . . . See them, the image of them, enveloped by the love you are . . . Whatever their intention was, they were clearly misguided . . . They were operating out of their own inner demons . . . Thus, it is easy for you to forgive them now. . . Send them love, radiate love, as you breathe out slowly, and then let the image of them go . . . Now just be here, as the awareness, the presence you are . . .

As you do this practice of being the loving awareness you are, a wonderful, relaxed feeling of ease, spaciousness, and well-being may unfold within you. Remember: you can't hold on to this feeling or keep it, because it is what you most essentially are. It is your natural state. So don't try.

If you feel yourself contracting—getting caught in conflict, stress, or upset—it is your cue to come back to presence. It is in presence, in the awareness of being here right now, that you rediscover your true universal nature. But to fully and completely awaken, you must inquire into who you are. You must investigate the I. You must look deep within to find its source or origin.

No matter how deeply you look, you'll discover you cannot find it. Your I, your ego, has no reality in and of itself. Only consciousness is ultimately real. This is the great liberation those who have awakened come to. This is the key to unlocking the secret of inner freedom.

Love Unconditionally

Toward the end of my time at the Zen Center, I felt much better, much clearer, more truly in a place of forgiveness. I processed all my feelings, and by and large, they fell away. The falling away or letting go is the essence of forgiveness. In the space that opened up, a whole new creative energy began to pour through me.

Somewhere around the same time, I read the book *The Chasm of Fire*, by Sufi teacher Irina Tweedie. The book is about her studies with a Sufi master in a small village in India—all her trials and difficulties, her amazing energy experiences, and her insights and breakthroughs.

On the first page of the book she says, "Only a heart which has burned itself empty is capable of love." This is a beautiful statement of truth. We have to empty ourselves of everything—our egos, personal histories, our stories of suffering and blame—and then we can, at last, open to the flowering of love. Then love can move through us.

In most traditional spiritual paths and in the psychological approach, this emptying happens progressively as you practice releasing the past and forgiving those who have hurt you. But in the direct path approach, the letting go happens naturally and effortlessly as you see what you were holding onto isn't even real.

Through doing the practice of freedom, and through contemplating the teaching, you realize if you can observe the stories, beliefs, and images causing you to suffer, you cannot *be* them. You are the vast, timeless awareness that observes and experiences.

Be who you are, then. Dwell in the freedom, clarity of mind, and openness of heart that are your true nature. Then the love flowing through you will always be unconditional for there is no you in it, no ego-self laying down rules, expectations, conditions, or agendas.

You just love because you love, plain and simple. What others do with your love is up to them. Those whose hearts are sufficiently open and whose levels of trust are deep enough will accept your love, appreciate it, and reciprocate. Those whose hearts are closed will not be able to receive the gift you have to give them. But it's okay. Remember, there are no conditions on your love. Maybe they will be ready next time.

The freer you are and the more your heart opens, the more naturally you feel compelled to reach out and connect with your fellow human beings. Because we are all part of an indivisible Whole, you feel their suffering, but you don't take it personally.

I remember British novelist and philosopher Aldous Huxley saying something beautiful about the interconnectedness of all people. He was comparing Christ's famous injunction to "Love your neighbor as yourself" with the great phrase from the Hindu Upanishads, "You are That."

Jesus was probably the greatest master of the way of the heart our world has ever seen. And his teaching was essentially nondual, as evidenced by his statement: "I and the Father are one,"[8] the word "Father" being a metaphor for consciousness. However, the Christian religion itself is based on duality. It was fashioned by men who were familiar with Christ's words, but for the most part did not share his experience of unity consciousness.

The governing powers of early Christendom decided man is separate from God and can find salvation only through accepting Christ as his savior—and only then through the agency of a priest and the church. I have no doubt they did this so the church could reign supreme and exert greater control over people's lives. So, in the dualistic interpretation of Christ's teaching, your neighbor is separate from you, but if you can love him as you love yourself, then there will be more peace on earth, and you will have fulfilled one of the requirements for salvation.

The Upanishad teaching, on the other hand, is a profoundly nondual statement. It is saying that you and God—That—are one. You and the divine energy, the consciousness behind creation, are one. It's the wave and the ocean again.

---

8   John 10:30

Huxley pointed to this intersection between Christ's *bhakti,* or heart injunction, and the *jnana,* or wisdom statement, from the Upanishads. He said to love your neighbor because he *is* yourself.

To see and understand this with the whole of your being, you have to see it from the perspective of consciousness, the vastness of your true nature. This is why I say there is something more important than love. That something is consciousness itself. After all, without consciousness, what is love? Without consciousness, love is always conditional. It is not pure. It is emotional. It has an agenda behind it. It can turn to coldness, dislike, even hate.

But with the light of consciousness and timeless awareness behind it, love is always unconditional. Look at everything in life, then, from the Whole, rather than from the parts. Get the big picture. Take the unconditional perspective, and your love will be unconditional.

Or, as Kunihiro Yamate put it: "The secret of this way is to look at everything from the perspective of self as pure Consciousness. It is the only real, true way to look at things."

Love Your Energies

A woman said to me once, "My husband complains I am too emotional because I feel things deeply, especially other people's suffering and the pain of the world. It is easy for me to be moved to tears by what I feel, and then I judge myself for being weepy, overly emotional. Sometimes I will get angry at the injustice of the world and then angry at my husband for judging me. How do I find the balance with my own emotional energy without becoming like my husband, who lives in his head and who seems so detached from his emotions?"

One of the main barriers to freedom is the conflict we often experience with our feeling, emotional selves. Like the woman's husband, whenever we live too much in our heads, whenever we repress any feeling, be it sadness, anger, fear, or even love, it eats away inside us. Over the long term, it can damage both our psyche and our health.

Many a case of high blood pressure, stomach ulcers, irritable bowel syndrome, or diabetes has its origins in the inability or reluctance to own our feelings and emotions. Men, who often tend to be more distant from their emotions than women, need to be aware of this. The fact is it is healthy to feel deeply and be emotionally vulnerable. Feelings, emotions, and even the energy of desire, are just part of what it means to be human. The more you awaken to freedom, the more these energies naturally come into balance and are therefore much less problematic.

In this regard, there is a story about a Zen master who was sitting on a rock, weeping profusely. His student came to him and said, "Master, you're crying! I don't understand. You're enlightened. I thought you were beyond tears."

"Nonsense," the master sniffled. "My oldest friend just died, and naturally I am sad."

A few years after my own spiritual journey begun, I went through my first divorce. One day my ex-wife, Briar, brought a friend with her when she came to visit. We were sitting having tea and talking, and as I looked at Briar, I started to think about what went wrong in our marriage. Before I knew it, I began to feel a great sadness inside me. Then tears started to well up. Not wanting to embarrass myself in front of my ex or her friend, I excused myself and went down the hall into the bathroom.

There I let the tears flow, all the pent-up emotion of my divorce, all the unresolved feelings I was still struggling with inside. Remember, I was fairly new to my spiritual journey and dealing with all kinds of inner demons. I didn't know myself very well at all.

Anyway, as I looked at myself in the bathroom mirror, tears streaming down my face, I noticed a small card pinned to the wall next to the mirror. It was a saying of Jesus' that I had put there, and I read the words, "Love your energies."

I remember blinking, unsure whether I read correctly or not. Surely Jesus hadn't said those words. I blinked again, wiped the tears from my eyes, and looked at the card more closely. Sure enough, it said, "Love your *enemies*."

But the real message was not lost on me. As far as I was concerned, it was a sign from the universe, and my first reading—Love your energies—was the real meaning behind Jesus' words.

After all, it is the enemy we perceive living within us, our own demons, conflicted feelings, and turbulent emotions—in short, our *energies*—that we must first love, else how can we begin to love those people whom we perceive as our enemies? How can we truly love another if we can't love ourselves first?

I remember smiling through my tears and saying to myself, "Hey, my sadness is one of my energies, and so is any embarrassment I might feel about being sad. It's time to start loving these energies, Jim." With that, I went back into the living room to join Briar and her friend and to share my feelings and my insight with them.

A friend once said to me he thought the spiritual journey was all about acceptance, and that it was the serene acceptance of whatever is happening that paved the way for unconditional love. This is an accurate insight. The more you learn to dwell in acceptance, the less you resist life and the less suffering you experience. Awakening, or inner freedom, is to live in total acceptance of life. To flow with it.

The more you are able to embrace, welcome, and accept as a gift each experience that happens in your life, the closer you move to true freedom. This does not mean you let the people in your life take advantage of you. Nor does it mean you don't act to bring about changes in unwanted experiences or you don't seek to improve your lot in life.

By learning this inward acceptance of what is, you no longer put up resistance. Without resistance there can be no conflict or suffering. Your heart opens more and you see everything more clearly, which means you take the most intelligent, creative, and loving action . . .

Practice inner acceptance now . . . Go within and connect with the spaciousness inside you . . . Breathe, and feel the energy and warmth of your heart . . . Notice if there is any story active in your mind causing stress or tension in you . . . See if you can just be with it, accept it, the way it is . . . You can quietly affirm to yourself, "I am not my story, I am the pure awareness present right now . . . " Then be the awareness looking through your eyes . . . You are just flowing with the moment, allowing the whole of life to wash through you . . . Everything you see, feel, hear, taste . . . You are open to all of it, resisting nothing, because you realize at an intuitive level, acceptance is the doorway to true inner freedom . . .

Don't Take Your Emotions Personally

People can feel overwhelmed by their emotions. Some-times being overwhelmed is what needs to happen. It is important to notice that the feelings and emotions come in waves.

If you are being overtaken by a wave of emotion, there is really nothing to do but let it happen. At the same time, be very aware of everything you are feeling. Whether you label it as fear, anger, sadness, or some other emotion, don't get lost in a story about it. Stay present with the feeling, and allow it to unfold, to have its expression.

In chapter 1, I spoke of the two contributions Jean Klein made to my spiritual understanding. One was the idea of welcoming whatever was happening. The other was stepping back with my awareness. This helped by giving me the capacity to be fully in an experience, and at the same time be detached from it, to be aware of the experience.

I did not include the stepping back process in the practice of freedom because many seekers could not successfully visualize it, or had difficulty doing it. Fortunately, it is not essential for awakening. What is essential is not resisting your suffering, noticing the story you are telling yourself, and being very present with your whole energy, and then seeing you are not the story, but rather what is looking at the story as well as everything else.

Nevertheless, I had my first taste of this stepping-back aspect of Jean's teaching when I was in a marriage counseling session concerning my impending divorce, my second, from my son's mother. I was feeling a lot of pain about the breakup of our little family, yet I knew it needed to happen because of the irreconcilable differences between us.

Sitting on the couch in the therapist's office, I started to weep. Then, suddenly, I remembered Jean's teaching. I sat up and positioned my awareness slightly behind and above myself. I was present as the witness of what I was experiencing. A remarkable thing happened. I was able to feel the sadness and watch the tears, and just let them flow without any judgment, without being caught up in them. I felt the grief, but wasn't lost in it.

It was an extraordinarily transforming moment. Thereafter, whenever I felt any emotion I was able to experience it fully and honestly, and yet some part of me was always free of it. Some part of me was always in pure awareness, the witness of what was happening.

It was then I discovered that no matter what was happening in this body/mind, I—as awareness, as consciousness—was bigger than it. I was bigger than whatever I was experiencing.

The key is allowing everything to arise, especially your emotions. Let the waves of feeling come when they come. Don't try to resist or get caught up in thinking, analyzing, judging, or trying to understand what is happening. Just stay present and be very aware. Notice if there are sensations in different parts of your body as the emotions ebb and flow. If it starts to get overwhelming, remind yourself, "This too shall pass."

The understanding always comes later, when the waves of intense feeling or emotion subside. The more you allow yourself to just experience whatever you're experiencing, staying completely present in the here and now with your awareness, the more the meaning of those experiences will be revealed. Perhaps you already know what I am talking about. Sometimes a situation is confusing, and not till much later does insight dawn.

What becomes clear on this path of awakening is the more you hold on to the need to have things be a certain way, the more you insist, "This isn't right," or "That should not be allowed," the more emotional charge you are storing up.

Then, when expectations are not met, there is pain and suffering. If your position is exposed as being hollow or false, you might experience sadness or embarrassment. If someone belittles you, puts you down in some way, or betrays you, it may be expressed as resentment or anger.

So the work is to welcome, or at least accept your suffering, and then look at what you are inwardly holding onto, the beliefs, expectations, pictures, and ideas. Look at the story you are telling yourself about who you are and what you need to be happy. Begin to see it is only a story, a story you are making up. It is a story entirely of your own creation.

Realize you are not the story, but the luminous everpresent consciousness that looks at the story, that creates the story, and you'll have a genuine experience, a taste, of freedom.

After all, the story you tell yourself keeps the emotions in a volatile state of readiness. As I said, when you cling to any point of view or psychological position, you are generating an emotional charge.

Freedom comes as you see the story for what it is: a figment of your own creation. When you're not holding onto any idea or image of yourself, there's no buildup of emotional energy. You are simply open to life in the present. The secret is in emphasizing awareness itself, having all your senses alert, and not getting lost in thinking. Then your head will be clear, and you will feel the deeper energy, the deeper beauty and power of creation itself, and it will nourish you. Then your emotions will come into balance. They will arise spontaneously and authentically.

You will feel sadness at the loss of a loved one, or perhaps in a moment of being confronted with the tremendous suffering of so many innocent people in our world.

Or you might feel anger whenever you are reminded of the terrible injustices still taking place, the brutality, the subjugation of one group of people by another.

But none of these feelings will be taken too personally. The I won't jump in and make some new kind of story out of them, such as a victim story, as in, "Woe is me, the world is too awful and I am too sensitive to live in it." People who really believe they are victims are always telling their tales of suffering to anyone who will listen, and this constant reinforcement of their stories just keeps them stuck.

As you grasp this teaching and let go of the attachment to and identification with your own story, you begin to know yourself as awareness, the pure consciousness behind everything. You start to free yourself. Emotions still arise and pass, but now they happen more spontaneously. The paradox of awakening or enlightenment is that while you feel very deeply, you don't take your feelings personally. Once you let go of the identification with your own story, you learn to let go of the attachment to other peoples' stories as well.

Then, in the clarity of your true nature, you see what action, if any, needs to be taken. If something needs to be done about the situation triggering the emotional response, you'll know what to do, and you'll do it. But you won't make a big drama out of it.

Now, if you choose to be involved in an intimate relationship, as most of us do, then, no matter how awake and free you are, your feelings are always going to be somewhat at risk. If you experience rejection, abandonment, or betrayal from a person you love, you will certainly feel some kind of a sting, and it may even last a while. Perhaps there is some lesson to be learned from the experience.

But know this: if your awakening is genuine, deep down you will still be at peace within. The peace never goes away.

In this regard, I am reminded of a Zen saying: "Now that my house has burned to the ground, I have an unobstructed view of the rising moon."

This is one of the most exquisite teachings on what it means to be inwardly free. You don't want your house to burn down (or your relationship to end), and if it's on fire, you do everything you can to save it. If your house does burn down, you will naturally grieve the loss. But then, at some point, you look up above the smoking ruins, and there—lo!—the huge, pale silver orb of the moon becomes visible, creeping slowly up into the night sky.

What a magnificent sight! Ah, such beauty, such beauty that is always here, even in the midst of sorrow.

The Relationship Mirror

A woman asked me this question about her relationship: "My boyfriend is often arrogant and controlling. It seems he always needs to be right. I have been with him for two years. The only reason I stay is he also has a sweet, tender side to him. How can I bring more of the sweetness out in him, and less of the arrogance?"

If you are a parent, and care about conscious parenting, you learn early on never to disapprove of your child, only of their behavior. It is the same with other people, including this woman's boyfriend. His behavior is the problem. True, someone may exhibit arrogant behavior so frequently it seems they are the very embodiment of arrogance. But on the journey of awakening, we are always looking for the deeper beauty in people, the interconnectedness that is our common thread.

Underneath the mask of arrogance you will find an insecure human being. And beneath the insecurity is the vastness, the beauty, the freedom of the person's true spiritual nature. Of course, he (for arrogance is usually a male problem) is disconnected from that truth. But the less you judge him for his arrogance, and the more able you are to relate to him in an open, friendly, nonthreatening way, the more likely he is to soften and see himself and his behavior more realistically.

However, here's something very useful to know: if another person's arrogance, resentment, anger, or confusion is a problem for you, it is a good time to ask yourself: "So, where does this emotion or state [whether it be arrogance, resentment, anger, confusion, or something else you dislike in the other person] exist in me?"

I call this the "relationship mirror." When we find something offensive or annoying in someone else, it is often because the same or similar trait exists within us. By focusing on judging the other person for it, we get to avoid looking at our own emotional patterns. We project out onto others what we don't wish to see in ourselves.

If you are experiencing conflict, anxiety, or suffering in a relationship, it's your clue that something is going on inside you that needs looking at. Again, simply say, "I welcome, or at least accept, this experience . . . It is showing me where I am not yet free."

The woman who asked about her boyfriend had, in fact, a subtle judgment toward him. I said to her, "The act of judging your boyfriend, which in itself is a kind of arrogance, creates suffering within you. You feel a certain tension when you are around him; you have this withheld energy toward him. You're holding up a barrier between you and him. You can't be open or authentic with him, perhaps because of your timidity.

"When you live like this, judging and distancing yourself from him, you may not feel like you are suffering, but by holding onto a fixed judgment, position, or point of view, it means there is resistance to the natural flow of communication. You can't be completely present and honest with him or yourself. Whenever there is a lack of authenticity in your life, the seeds of suffering are already germinating."

Then she responded by saying, "Couldn't the other person be at fault, though? If I am with someone—even someone other than my boyfriend—who is mean, who is unkind, even abusive, wouldn't it be natural to feel resentful?"

"Resentment is not natural," I replied. "It is a conditioned response. Conditioned, again, by the culturally and socially reinforced belief about happiness lying outside us, and in order for us to be happy—that is, not suffer internally in any way—the other person must exhibit at least a modicum of kindness and civility.

"Let's be clear here. This entire work we are exploring is about *your* freedom, *your* awakening. The freer you become, the less you will be affected by other people's stuck, reactive, unconscious patterns of behavior. Then you will be able to influence, guide, and lead others to freedom."

In other words, you could be having lunch with the angriest person in the world, and while the intensity of their energy may make you choose to not sit too close to them, you would not take any of their words or behaviors personally. Because you know yourself, and are genuinely relaxed and at peace within, you will not be providing any resistance to this other person's anger.

I was in a workshop once when the teacher gave us a wonderful phrase designed to immediately defuse relationship tension: "This doesn't mean anything about me." When someone starts attacking, accusing, or blaming you in some way, if you find yourself taking it personally, say to yourself, "This doesn't mean anything about me."

Even though other people may be convinced the problem is all because of you, they are just acting out their own inner suffering and projecting it all onto you. There may be an element of truth in what they are saying, so you can take the feedback and put it to good use. Apply it toward improving your communication skills or becoming a better human being.

When being given feedback about my own behavior, I did not always like what I was hearing, but I have grown a lot through my willingness to listen to it. Above all, don't start judging yourself just because others may be judging you. Listen carefully for the truth, but don't give undue meaning or weight to another's words or opinions. Don't believe their stories around you.

When you stop taking other people's criticism personally, when you no longer judge them or make them wrong, they will find being around you disarming. They are more likely to feel accepted and heard by you. Their anger will have nowhere to land. It will pass right by you. In that kind of nonthreatening openness, people are more likely to see themselves, their anger, or their arrogance more clearly. They may even experience healing or transformation.

But to come back to the point I was making a short while ago, here is the key to seeing what is true for you in terms of your inner emotional reality: any feelings or emotions you may be repressing or not acknowledging constitute suffering. If any situation or any person causes conflict or upset in you, ask yourself the kinds of questions that will lead you to the insight you seek, such as:

"So, what is going on with me?"
"Why am I am reacting this way?"
"What is it I need to look at it in myself?"

At the same time you ask yourself those questions, remember to say to yourself, "Ah, I welcome this situation, or this feeling, because it is showing me where I am not yet free."

Then be silent. Be quiet, be still. Listen inwardly for whatever comes up, whether new feelings, new insights, or something else. The secret of communication, both with yourself and with others, is silence. The deeper your silence, the clearer your thinking and the more potent your words. The willingness to be quietly, alertly present as you accept and embrace your own discomfort is the true doorway to freedom.

As I have said before, insight into your own emotional state may not come immediately. But just by living with the question, "What is causing this unhappiness within me?" sooner or later the answer will be revealed to you. It may appear in the form of some old story or some memory you still identify with. The moment you simultaneously realize you are *not* the story, not the memory, but you are the lucid ever-present awareness noticing the story, you will be free.

The proof that freedom is becoming more real for you will again show up in the relationship mirror. You will notice other people's insecurities, fears, and even the psychological and emotional games they play, but you will see past all that. You will see what they themselves do not see.

You will see into the truth of their beings, the beauty at their cores. You will see an expression of divine consciousness, the same consciousness manifesting itself through your body, mind, and self. Recognizing and honoring this is the essence of love.

In Zen, this is spoken of as the "empty mirror." It's one of the signs of enlightenment. You look into a mirror, and there's no one there. There's just the light and beauty of clear radiant consciousness shining back at you through two wide-open eyes.

Raising Children with Love

The more consciously and lovingly we raise our children, the less psychological and emotional baggage they grow up with, and the freer they are. However, our children still have their own karma, their own issues to work out. They need to find things out for themselves.

As the father of a son who is now a young man, one of the most important things I learned about raising children was also from Jean Klein. He said the people we love the most are those around whom we feel the freest to be ourselves. Meditate on this saying for a moment. Think of how it applies in your own life.

Isn't it true that the friends you value the most are the ones who give you the most space to be yourself, who truly accept you for who you are, and even when you act like a jerk, they still love you?

The main thing as a parent is to not become attached to the image of father or mother. For example, be a father when the father role is necessary. But don't get hung up on the "father knows best" dynamic in the way many fathers do, as if the father is somehow superior to the son or daughter.

Instead, just be there as a kind, loving, tremendously caring friend or ally. Give your children guidance when needed. Enter and learn about their worlds when invited. Provide a focus or direction for their energy until they are able to do it for themselves. Establish firm boundaries when they are needed.

I always gave my son a lot of freedom to explore and discover life for himself. Looking back from this perspective, I probably gave him too much freedom. If I were doing it again today, I would be more hands-on, more present as a guide for him. At the time, though, I was caught up in my own journey of self-discovery.

Nevertheless, I tried to make sure he understood that freedom and responsibility go hand-in-hand. I let him know that I would give him as much freedom as he was willing to be responsible for. It happened very rarely, but once in a while, when he was young, I had to discipline him. For example, I let him know that I had certain expectations about his level of performance at school.

When I once mentioned this to a friend, he said to me, "I thought awakening was about being free of expectations."

"Even with awakening, you can still have certain expectations, but you're just not *attached* to them," I replied. In other words, if my son doesn't fulfill the few but important expectations I have of him, it is not going to disturb my inner peace or well-being.

My expectations of him are really for him, not for me. As a parent, as someone who has been around the block many times, I know how the world works. It is demanding and competitive. Generally, the strong and educated flourish, while the weak and uneducated barely survive. As a parent, naturally I want my son to flourish, especially from within—to feel strong and confident, both in his inner being and in his ability to focus on and accomplish his goals in life. Most parents want this for their children.

So, when playing the role of father or mother, and when laying down certain rules, it may be necessary to be firm. But where the letting go comes in, where the consciousness becomes evident, is that it is all done without being emotionally attached to outcomes. You give your best to your children, but ultimately what happens is out of your hands.

A wise person once told me you are responsible for your efforts, not the results. You set your intention to ensure the best possible outcome, but you keep your attention right here, fully in the present.

One area where strong residues can arise from time to time (it was the only "real" residue I had) is around our kids. We are biologically, genetically, and emotionally connected to our children, so it is inevitable that we are going to be concerned about their well-being, and maybe even suffer a little because of that concern. Just to be aware of that, to notice when we are getting caught up in a story related to them, is liberating.

Do that in your parenting, and your kids will love being around you. You will have a special, unique, truly beautiful relationship, which will last a lifetime. Sounds good, doesn't it?

So, let's take a minute to breathe, relax, and simply accept, even welcome, whatever is. Feel into the silence, the love, the beauty that is here right now, all around us. The best and most creative actions always flow out of this clear sense of *being*. Whether it is parenting, exercising, making money, or indulging in the sheer joy of creating,

these activities flow effortlessly when we are fully established in the present moment.

Let's be here now.

Two Practices for Forgiveness

The Practice of Forgiving Your Parents

One of the main barriers to spiritual awakening, enlightenment, or self-realization is our unhealed relationships with
our parents, whether they are living or not. If you have an
issue with a parent, bring him or her into your daily meditations too, just like you learned to do with other upsetting
situations in the practice at the end of chapter 1.

If your parents evoke resentment, anger, guilt, abandonment, regret, blame, or fear, again, learn to welcome it
because it is showing you where you are not yet free. If the
relationship brings up a lot of intense feeling, you may have
to breathe deeply and slowly, very consciously, to stay present with it. If it gets to be too much for you, take a break and
come back the next day. Ultimately, though, you want to
be the spiritual warrior you are, and face this demon—the
unhealed relationship with your parent—within you.

Visualize yourself being with your mother or father (work
with one at a time) in past situations. Allow whatever wants
to come up to come up. Notice the stories you have and
the feelings they trigger, and see that you are not the story,
but rather the luminous, ever-present consciousness that is
always here, now. This is the essence of forgiveness: letting
go of your story of blame.

You will know the relationship with your parent is complete when you are at peace within yourself and you can
look into your mother's or father's eyes (face to face or in

your imagination) with affection, kindness, and love. This practice paves the way for others you may need to forgive. Bring them into your meditation, and follow the same process.

Or maybe there is someone you have wronged, done harm to, and you need to seek forgiveness from him or her. Bring that person into your meditation. Silently ask for forgiveness and, at the same time, visualize yourself beaming a wave of love and compassion in the person's direction. Surround him or her with love, light, and goodwill . . .

The Practice of Forgiving Yourself

Learning to forgive ourselves for the ways in which we have failed to perform, or have harmed someone, or haven't measured up to our own high expectations, is extremely important on this path of awakening. Forgiveness really does start within.

When you feel as if you have let someone down, or have failed to measure up to your own expectations, or are judging yourself for being a "bad" person in some other way, softening and opening your heart, and saying the following mantra can be powerful medicine: "I forgive myself for . . . "

Simply insert the appropriate words: "I forgive myself for [a particular harmful behavior, an action, a failure to act, being unkind, being a jerk, being an asshole, and so on]."

Say it as often as necessary, in a whole-hearted, self-embracing way, until you really have forgiven yourself for that particular failing or fault. You have let go the story of self-blame, and of course it lets go of you when you see that the story of why you've been so hard on yourself isn't even real. It's just a story, a memory about a long-ago past event you've been identifying with, clinging to, inside your head.

And you are not your story . . . You are always this beautiful, clear, conscious being who is reading these words right now!

Two Practices For Eye-Gazing

The most accurate gauge of how present and inwardly free we are is in our ability to connect with not just our parents, who may have hurt us, or people we may have harmed, but anybody, without fear or judgment, in a relaxed, non-threatening way. Our look is open and welcoming. We have nothing to hide or prove. We can apologize if necessary. The following two practices will help in the process of becoming free.

Eye-Gazing with Yourself

Most people spend time looking in the mirror, so this is the perfect practice for helping you awaken to the truth and beauty of who you really are—to the empty mirror experience I wrote about earlier.

Simply gaze at yourself in the mirror, paying attention to any self-judgments or self-criticisms or any other negative thoughts that arise. Then do the practice of freedom around these criticisms.

Step 1: Be present with the criticisms; learn to welcome them.

Step 2: Really notice your self-talk; you can tell yourself, Oh, I'm getting caught up in that judgment again . . .

Step 3: See the truth . . . and the truth is that judgments and self-criticisms come and go, just like the suffering they create comes and goes, but you, the beautiful, conscious being, are always here. So breathe, relax, and, as you look at yourself, be the beautiful person you are.

The ultimate goal of this practice is to be able to look at yourself with total acceptance and forgiveness, with genuine love and kindness. For that to happen, your ego, the little me, has to be out of the way. You have to have completed the fourth step of the practice of freedom.

As you gaze at yourself in the mirror, one positive saying, or mantra, that can help is this: I am pure, loving conscious-ness . . . or, My true nature is pure, loving awareness . . .

Eye-Gazing with Another

I use the following practice in my workshops. It can bring up our fears, anxieties, discomforts, judgments, and other negative feelings, particularly when we are meeting some-one for the first time. This allows us to see how much "stuff" gets in the way of our connecting genuinely with others. It can trigger the stories we are still internally identifying with.

However, the ultimate purpose of this practice is to give us the practical experience of being with others in a relaxed, open, nonjudgmental, and loving way—in a way that is entirely free of self-consciousness.

Step 1: Sit facing your partner (or a friend). You should be close enough that your knees are touching. Both of you close your eyes and establish a sense of calmness and spaciousness by simply welcoming everything— your body and the sensations, feelings, breath, arising thoughts, beliefs, stories . . .

When you feel sufficiently relaxed and clear, open your eyes and look at your partner. Let your eyes be soft, open, and receptive, as if you are inviting the whole world to come to you. Gently hold each other's gaze for a period of two to five minutes the first couple of times. As you get more used to it, hold your gaze for longer.

Step 2: Pay attention to any judgmental thoughts that may arise about yourself or your partner. Don't judge yourself for being judgmental; don't criticize yourself for being critical. If you notice this happening, just breathe and tell yourself, "Uh-oh, I'm doing it again—getting caught up in a story," and come back to being present with your partner.

Step 3: See the beauty and light in your partner's eyes. Recognize that what you see in them is a perfect mirror of your own beauty and light. After all, there is just one beautiful, radiant consciousness here, embodied in two separate people.

This can be an intense process, especially early on. If you need to periodically close your eyes and re-center, give yourself total permission to do so. Then, when you are ready, come back to gazing into your partner's eyes. When you and your partner feel like you've spent enough time connecting in this way, give each other a smile and a warm hug, and share your personal experience of the practice.

⁊ 7 ⟡

Creating a New
Story for Your Life

OTHERS BEFORE ME HAVE stated we are not our stories, so the teaching in this book is not new. Advaita itself, which dates back to Shankara in the 8th century, teaches us we are not the people we think we are.

However, this book combines the teaching and practice in a unique and new way, potent and relevant to our age. It blends the spiritual and material into one dynamic, unified or nondual whole. Its essential message is that life is happening right here, right now, and what has previously been considered spiritual is the material, and vice versa. It is all one reality, and we human beings are manifestations of this reality. It matters not what we may be or do in some as-yet-unknown future. It is how we are being and what we do right now that matters.

A different way of stating the teaching is this: Everything that can be seen changes, but you are the seeing, which never changes. Know yourself as the seeing, the changeless, and you'll always be fulfilled, at peace, and in the flow of life. You'll always be on purpose with your own unique mission or destiny here.

Let me explain in more depth. First, everything that can be seen changes. This becomes obvious the more closely you look at it. Our bodies change. They mature, age, and eventually die. Our thoughts, beliefs, sensations, and feelings change all the time. Our stories change. Even a devout religious story, whether about God or some other power, changes. It comes and goes, grows weaker or stronger over time, and is subject to vast numbers of interpretations. Then, of course, our friends and relationships change as they, too, come and go. And the world around us, both natural and man-made, is always changing.

The second key phrase of the teaching says you are the seeing, that which never changes. Think about it. Who or what in you is reading these words, words which themselves are changing, moving past your eyes as you read? You may say, "Well, I am." But then who is this I? Can you actually find the I anywhere in your mind, in your consciousness? Or is this I, too, just a concept, the storyteller, an object in consciousness just as elusive as any other object or concept?

You definitely have a sense of unique individuality. You know you exist. But when you look within and try to find this you that you take yourself to be, you won't be able to find it. Anything you say about yourself, no matter how true it may seem to be, will be just another concept—another story. And, as we have seen, all stories, no matter how true they seem to be, can be observed or seen—and, as a result, they change.

So again I ask: who or what in you sees the ever-changing stories you tell yourself?

This is the essential question, and many of you reading this have at least a taste of the answer, which of course is not found in words but only in being. One taste of the freedom, joy, and spaciousness of your true nature is all it really takes to orient you, to point you toward Home. And the practice of freedom we have been doing throughout this journey together helps you establish the sense of being Home.

What you are, then, is the seeing. You are pure, universal consciousness, the awareness looking out through your eyes. This seeing, in concert with all the other senses, perceives the unfolding reality of your life as it is happening right now.

For those of you who may still be struggling with this, just comprehending it intellectually is a good start. To understand you are not your story, that everything that can be seen changes, and you are the seeing, which never changes, is a big step. Living with this understanding and contemplating it daily helps bring it into the cells of your body, so that it gradually becomes your actual, felt experience.

The third key phrase of the message above is that once you know yourself as the seeing, you are free. This is the fourth step I have talked about: seeing through the illusion of the I, the me, the ego itself. Once you've made the shift from identifying yourself with your stories to recognizing your true identity as the unchanging consciousness looking through your eyes and giving rise to all the stories in your life, including the ego or storyteller itself, then you will be fulfilled and at peace with yourself.

When you know yourself as consciousness, you are in touch with the source of manifestation. Just being the consciousness you already are tends to bring forth whatever you focus on, whatever you truly need or want. And while thoughts themselves are unreal, in the sense you can't actually find them anywhere, they do serve a purpose. You use them for communication and creativity, for making good decisions, and for manifesting your goals or intentions in physical reality.

After all, everything man-made, from the biggest skyscrapers to the tiniest microchips, from forms of government to programs for feeding the poor, began with a thought, an idea, or a picture in someone's mind. So, be clear about your intentions. Be clear about what you want. Contemplate your purpose, goals, and objectives several times a day and then forget about them. Come back to the power of the present, and enjoy the flow of whatever you happen to be experiencing, whatever happens to be manifested in this moment.

Now, a question that arises from time to time is this: "Some people have told me that awakening or enlightenment is a process where we get freer and freer, but because we are human, there will always be some degree of suffering. However, you seem to be saying once we awaken, we are free, and there is no more suffering at the personal level. What is the truth here?"

My answer is this: once awakening happens, then it has happened. There is no going back. You don't get lost in separation again, although there will be times when those residues of past suffering may flare up and cause you to momentarily seem to forget your true nature.

However, the belief that it is a process is quite common. Perhaps this is because while we are still seeking, there is definitely a feeling of getting freer year by year. Some people assume the seeker just keeps going through different doors into greater levels of freedom, but there is still this you experiencing these different levels. This is where a guide, teacher, or someone who has actually gone through the last door can make a big difference. The guide holds up a mirror, metaphorically speaking, so the seeker can see him- or herself, and reality, more clearly. A Zen story illustrates how such a mirror can set someone free.

Keiji, a longtime student of Zen, came to his master and said, "I don't see how there can be any enlightenment setting you free once and for all. I think we just get ever greater glimpses of Buddha-nature, the vastness that is our true Being. It's an ever-expanding process."

"That may be what you think," the master replied, giving Keiji a fierce look. "But what is your experience? Your experience right now?"

Keiji looked momentarily confused. "My experience right now, Master?"

"Yes. Do you know yourself as Keiji, having ever-expanding experiences of Buddha-nature? Or do you know yourself as Buddha-nature, having the experience of Keiji?"

When the master said this, it was as if a switch tripped in Keiji's mind. Light suddenly flooded his consciousness. Gone were all his concepts and ideas. A huge smile lit up his face as he realized at last that he wasn't Keiji, but that he was Buddha-nature having the experience of Keiji— and that everyone and everything was, in their essence, Buddha-nature. In this way he finally discovered the enlightenment he was seeking.

Imagination and Positive Thinking

What are your goals and dreams, and what is the vision you have for your life? How do you want to serve?

Dr. Albert Schweitzer, the great humanitarian and Nobel Prize winner, made this statement when he addressed a group of young people after the Second World War: "I don't know what your destiny will be, but one thing I do know: the only ones among you who will be really happy are those who will have sought and found how to serve." These are true and powerful words, as inspiring today as when he first spoke them.

Once awakening happens, life becomes rich in love, meaning, and purpose. Awakening liberates you from self-concern, from self-obsession, from images and ideas of self, period. You don't take anything personally, because you no longer hold on to any idea or image of yourself as some kind of a person. Instead, you view everything from the perspective of pure consciousness. You see what needs to be done in any given moment, and you take action and do it. You see how you want to serve, how you are guided to serve from awareness, not from ego or personal agenda.

You feel moved to write a new, *conscious* story for your life. One of the joys of awakening is when you finally get clear about what you are here to do, what identity you now want to consciously assume in the marketplace of daily life. And it is different for every one of us. Some, like me, become teachers, guides, way-showers. Others volunteer, or make their contribution in the arts or business, a profession or trade, or in public or private life. The creative possibilities are endless. It doesn't matter what you do, just that you do it.

Now, imagination is a powerful function of the mind. It is the ability to form images and to visualize concepts and pictures of desired results. Imagination is the art of dreaming up new realities and consciously creating what you want.

Like intuition, reason, and logic, imagination is one of the mental tools we have available to help solve problems. With this mental paintbrush, you can do many things: visualize potential outcomes, picture whole scenarios, and play with possible solutions.

Perhaps you are feeling called to do something different, something more creative with your life. You can use your imagination to envision new possibilities. You can let your imagination run wild. It's fun to do this, to play around in your mind. Maybe you are making love with your partner, and want to explore new ways to please each other. Use your imagination. That's what it's there for.

The thing to remember, as Jean Klein said once, is that imagination is meant to enhance living, not be a substitute for it.

I was asked this question once: "What about fantasies, whether it's a sexual fantasy, a dream about the perfect relationship or job, or wishing to be rich and famous?"

A fantasy is really just an exaggerated feel-good story. The problem with fantasies is they don't go anywhere. They don't produce anything. But if you tend to fantasize a lot, there is a way you can honor your mind's tendency and still rein it in. I know this works because my mind frequently got caught in fantasies.

Here's the technique: allow yourself to indulge in a particular fantasy, any fantasy, for one minute, and then drop it. Come back to being very aware or conscious in the present. Come back to this moment now, to what you are sensing, feeling, perceiving now. Then, if you feel the need to revisit the fantasy, pick it up, but again only for one minute. Engage the fantasy as many times as you like during the day, but only for one minute at a time.

This technique starves the fantasy. You begin to lose interest in it. Soon, you are engaging with it for only thirty seconds, and then ten or fifteen seconds. Very quickly you start becoming more interested in the power and vitality of your actual living experience, what you are sensing and feeling right here, right now.

Don't forget, if you are using fantasy or imagination to reinforce your ego's insecurities, then your mind has you in its grip, in its story. Our goal here is to turn around and to become free of our minds, the nets of thought. Only then can we dwell effortlessly in clear present-time awareness, in what Zen refers to as empty mind or no-mind.

You'll experience an extraordinary feeling of openness and spaciousness inside you when you finally see you are not your thoughts, but rather that you are the consciousness giving rise to those thoughts. There will be no you in the way, no self-concept, no self-image obstructing the flow of life and creative energy. You'll know yourself as the universe, the ocean of universal consciousness, expressed through this body/mind, through this wave form you are.

Then thoughts will no longer be a problem. They will come and go as before, but you won't identify yourself using them. Your mind generates thoughts and stories, but when awakened, those thoughts emerge from awareness and you can take delight in freely using them to create all sorts of things. Since your mind is no longer a source of stress or anxiety, you can have a blast dancing around in it, playing with the images and ideas.

Once you are free of the addiction to fantasies, guess what? You can indulge them on occasion. A little fantasy once in a while is okay.

Take time to practice indulging a fantasy, then letting it go, right now . . . Go into your mind and consciously engage a favorite fantasy . . . Really dramatize it, picture it vividly in your mind. Feel the feelings it evokes in your body. Play with it . . . Then, just as consciously, let it go and simply be here . . . Know you have a mind that generates thoughts, stories, and fantasies . . . You have a body with feelings, emotions, and sensations . . . And you have a personality with qualities, quirks, and foibles . . . But who and what you really are is vastly bigger than anything you can see or experience . . . So relax, breathe, and be the awareness you are . . .

Another question I get is: "What about addictions? I mean to smoking, drinking, drugs, food, and so on? How best to deal with them?"

When facing addictions, you've got to really watch for the story you're telling yourself as you're about to reach for the object of your addiction, whether it's a cigarette, a drink, food, or whatever. Maybe you say, "I deserve this treat," or "A drink will help settle me down." Then see that it is just a story. It is not your true nature. It is not pure consciousness.

Telling yourself a new story about the negative consequences of your addictive behavior can be helpful and potentially healing, but it is only a stepping stone, because it is still a story. The main thing is, if you are going to indulge in the addiction, do it very *consciously*. Don't get lost in yet another story, such as, "I'll quit tomorrow." Be completely conscious and present even as you give in to the addiction.

A good practice to do as you are learning to be more conscious about your addictions is to pause for a moment before reaching for that cigarette, food, drink, or drug, and ask yourself a simple question: "Do I really want this right now?" Then listen carefully for the answer from deep within.

When you realize that the addiction is a way of numbing yourself out, of rendering yourself even *more* unconscious, then gradually you'll wean yourself from it. Or, rather, it will leave you. As Jean Klein said once, "Things leave us when they no longer fulfill their promises."

People sometimes ask me about the value of positive thinking. On another occasion, Jean said, "If you are going to think, it is better to think positively than negatively." The limitation of negative thinking is obvious: stressful, anxiety-producing thoughts like, "Oh, my God, everything seems so hopeless!" or "I just can't take this anymore!" result in feelings of unhappiness and depression.

The limitation of positive thinking is less obvious, because positive thoughts, such as "I *can* succeed at this," or "I feel wonderfully clear and relaxed inside," have a correspondingly positive effect on the psyche. They fill us with optimism. They can make us feel good. They give us a lift.

Yet what is the motive behind adopting positive thinking as a way of being? Invariably, it is to support and reinforce the ego's desire for meaning and security. This need is based on the belief that, if you just think positively, good things will happen to you, your life will improve, and you will be a happy human being.

It is coming from the old paradigm of *do, have, be,* where you are still looking outside yourself for fulfillment. *Do* this first—think and act positively—and you will *have* the circumstances allowing you to *be* happy. The problem is, your inner peace and happiness are then dependent upon what you have, and thus are always conditional.

The awakened paradigm for living is characterized by the rule of "*be* first, and then *do,* so you can *have.*" You learn to *be* at peace within yourself through the practice of freedom, and through learning you are not your thoughts or your story. The more you do the practice and remember the teaching, the more you are at peace, regardless of what is going on outside with other people or your life situation.

Lao Tzu said, in the *Tao Te Ching*, "The way to do is to be." Authentic action, doing, flows naturally out of being. Then, out of being content and at ease in the present, you not only do what you love to do, but what you feel called to do, or whatever needs to be done.

Awakened or not, what you do results in having certain outcomes manifested—the fruits of your actions, whether in relationships, work, health, recreation, or finances. The big difference with awakening is, since you are already at peace within and not dependent on these things for inner peace and well-being, you will be able to fully enjoy the results. The outer gifts are like a bonus, icing on the proverbial cake of life.

However, in answer to the question about positive thinking, affirming the statement, "To be awake and conscious is my natural state of being" is definitely more helpful than saying, "Life sucks," and then feeling hopeless.

But the awakening to inner freedom is our natural, felt state of being. We didn't create it. It already and always is. To truly discover it, the mind must be free of all thought, especially the I or me thought. Our true, awakened nature is discovered here, *now*.

Manifestation

A man opening up in a workshop said this:

> I was once very financially successful. I knew how to set goals and achieve them, to manifest things in material reality. Yet the truth was, I wasn't happy. Then, some years ago, a tragedy happened in my life, which caused

me to re-evaluate everything. It started me on the spiritual path.

I began meditating, reading spiritual books, going to workshops, and learning about living in the present, as you say. I am definitely more at peace now, but I seem to have lost the power—or maybe it is the interest—to make things happen in my life. Now I struggle financially in a way I never used to. What is going on?

Many people who embark upon the spiritual quest grapple with the issue of success. What happens to the worldly goals and desires they once had? What about their desire to accomplish something in life, or to leave a mark of some kind? Very often, when people turn their attention inward, it seems they lose their ability to manifest outer results, whether that be career goals or having the money needed to live comfortably, with income consistently exceeding expenses, instead of the other way around.

Soon after meeting Jean Klein, I met Ted, who was a student of Jean's. One day, Ted invited me back to the house in Marin County where his wife and daughter lived. Ted was in the process of getting a divorce, and while he was in the back talking to his daughter, I spoke to his wife. Picking up one of Jean's books, which happened to be lying on the table, I asked her, "So, what do you think of this stuff?"

She rolled her eyes. "Well, it's all very interesting, but it doesn't have much to do with real life, does it?"

Her answer didn't surprise me. Ted had already told me one of the reasons they were divorcing was that she didn't support his spiritual practice. For her, true happiness lay in the tangible reality of material objects, not in what she interpreted as ethereal notions of spiritual freedom. She wanted him to get a high-paying job and earn the kind of income that would allow them to enjoy the finer things in life. Living in Marin was expensive, after all.

As it happens, spiritual awakening is not incompatible with worldly success. Indeed, if it was, few would be interested in it! Fortunately, the same basic principles needed for material success are the same principles needed for awakening. One is focused outwardly, the other is directed inwardly. Once you realize this, then you can find a balance in your life.

If you really want freedom, you must make awakening to your inner being your primary goal. But you can also use the same energies to consciously create what you want in your outer, worldly life. The difference is now you are not attached to the outcome.

At first, mastering your mind leads to inner peace and freedom, but then you can harness the power of your mind for the purpose of shaping a better world. Ultimately, you come to realize there is no difference between the spiritual and the material. There is just one divine energy, consciousness, endlessly manifesting itself in different forms. That's the definition of nondual wisdom in a nutshell.

Manifestation is actually a very simple process. The more you know yourself as consciousness and live in the knowing, the more easily it happens. Sometimes all you have to do is just think of what you want, and before you know it, it shows up.

Just take a few minutes each day to sit down and visualize what you want to happen. Or go for a walk or a run and do it. But get clear about your intention. The more real you make it, the better. Involve as many senses as you can. You can even say a brief affirmation, as in, "I easily and effort-lessly manifest the perfect job [or relationship] right now."

Actually *see* and *feel* it happening, as if it were already so. This is an important key: to see the thing—what you have intended, what you want—as already having hap-pened. On the inside, in your mind and heart, it is already a vivid reality for you. Now, you are simply waiting to have it show up on the outside.

Then let go of the visualization or affirmation and any attachment to how it should be manifested. Completely let go, surrendering the goal or intention to universal will, as you come back to the experience of whatever is happen-ing right now. Then proceed with your day, making sure to focus your energies on any work needing to be done in order to manifest your goal, the thing you want, in reality.

Let's take a closer look at this. First, you must know what you want, whether it is building a successful busi-ness, getting in shape physically, finding the perfect mate, or completing some project like writing a book or master-ing creative skills in music or the arts.

You must set your goal or intention. After all, we generally get what we intend. When it comes to being successful in life, intention is everything. So, being very clear about what you want or intend to manifest is critical. Nothing productive can happen without such clarity and inner conviction. Then, as I said above, you must imagine it, see it, as already so. The goal or intention is already a living, breathing reality for you on the inside.

Management guru Peter Drucker put it like this: "The best way to predict the future is to create it." You create your future and the results you want through the clarity and power of your intention.

Second, you have to focus your attention and get passionately engaged in the process. You have to do the work. Sometimes it takes a lot of work to achieve a particular goal, and at other times not much at all. The clearer you get inside yourself, the more powerful your ability to manifest what you want.

The key here is focus. All successful people, no matter what their area of accomplishment, have sharpened their ability to focus on their goals and intentions. Those who do not succeed at their endeavors tend to be scattered with their energy. They generally lack focus.

Now, for creative, free-ranging thinking, it is necessary to be in an expanded state of awareness, which is the exact opposite of focus. There is definitely a time for this kind of inner exploration, for inwardly brainstorming new ideas and possibilities or just thinking contemplatively about things.

However, in order to actually *make* something happen in the world, you have to contract and focus your energy. You have to pull your energy in. This is how the law of attraction works. Like a magnet, when you pull your energy in, yet are supremely present, you tend to draw what you want to you.

If the process involves work, whether it is a little or a lot, you must totally commit yourself to it. You must throw your body, mind, and heart into it. In order to have anything worthwhile happen in your life, you have to have a passionate desire for it. You have to give energy and attention to it. To find your passion, look inside yourself. Ask yourself what matters to you.

Ask yourself, "If I knew I couldn't fail, what is it I would love to do, what is it I would love to accomplish?"

Many people read, see, or hear about someone else's success, and they set out trying to emulate it. They start chasing other people's goals, which never works. Everybody is passionate about something. If you don't already know, keep looking within. Keep trying different things until you discover what gets your creative juices flowing.

The third part of the process is sometimes the most difficult. It is a theme I have returned to again and again throughout this book. You must now let it go, releasing all attachment to the outcome. You must release it with an affirmation such as I suggest in the manifestation practice at the end of this chapter. You must surrender; get yourself, your ego, completely out of the way. You must realize that everything, ultimately, happens by grace, by a power beyond us, yet expressed through us.

In other words, you set your eyes on the mountaintop, you establish your intention to get there, and then you put it at the back of your mind and focus on the journey. If you don't release attachment, you just build a new story in your mind and worry, even obsess, about whether you are going to succeed or not. The energy of worry gets in the way of your chances of success.

It's important not to get in your own way and not to get ahead of yourself. What matters is *this* step, the one you are taking right now. Live this moment fully and completely, and the next moment will take care of itself. You will be guided every step of the way. You will intuitively know what to do.

Be Conscious about Money

I hear this question a lot: "I worry about money constantly—about not being able to pay my bills, about not having enough at the end of the month. How does someone who is awake relate to money?"

For the awakened person, the one who truly knows him- or herself, money is just another condition in life, albeit an important one. The awakened person manages his or her capital wisely, and usually will not spend more than he or she can afford.

Certainly, as your awakening deepens and matures, you worry less and less about money. However, money was one of my main residues. I was frequently worried about how I was going to pay my bills and meet my financial obligations. But over time, as I embodied my awakening ever more fully, even those worries dropped away. Now, I just make sure to live within my means.

However, money for the unawakened person is nearly always a major issue. Fears about survival, paying the bills, and making it financially cause at least as much stomach distress as, if not more than, relationship issues. Money is the number one issue people fight about in their relationships. In the face of the realities of the marketplace of daily life, it requires nothing less than awakening to be able to let go of worrying about money.

The struggle with money is often an issue for those who have consciously taken up a spiritual path in life. I've heard statements like this before, and have echoed similar sentiments myself at times in the past: "Sometimes I think my spirituality is a curse. I look at people I know who don't care about spiritual truths, who just focus on making money. They do well; they get to travel and live in nice homes, and seem pretty happy. Sometimes I think I made the wrong choice in life, and should have just gone for the money, the material prosperity, like most people."

It is true that people who look to money and material security for their happiness usually *are* quite happy—as long as things are going well for them. But it is an inescapable fact: if you are going to make your happiness dependent on outer circumstances, then, should those circumstances change or even threaten to change, it will trigger anxiety in you.

It is important to see the whole picture. Those who have no interest in inner freedom, who have put all their faith in the material, in controlling their outer circumstances, experience a very conditional happiness. In our culture, it is easy to be fooled by appearances. The sole mission of the advertising media is to lull us into believing if we have the purchasing power—that is, the cash or the credit—to buy lots of beautiful new objects, toys, or services, everything in our life will be rosy.

Obviously, money is a necessary ingredient in a whole and balanced life. You need to take care of your finances in the same way you care for your body, relationships, business, and all areas of your life. However, the more you are tapped into the real source of wealth—the wisdom, love, and creative energy inside you—the more clarity and passion you will bring to your work, and the greater the likelihood of financial success.

You need a vehicle to generate a flow of money, and this is where work comes in. If you do your work well, if you provide real value for those you serve, you will always find people willing to pay for what you have to offer. People will be drawn to your energy and enthusiasm for life, and that itself will bring more outer abundance to you.

Without inner clarity, you will likely be seduced by the promise of happiness coming from something outside of you, the glitz and the glitter. However, no matter how happy people seem, if their happiness is dependent on money, they will live with an undercurrent of anxiety.

A stockbroker friend told me once that she noticed that the more money her clients had, the more they lived in fear of losing it. This is not to say you can't be wealthy and be happy. I am sure there are people who are blessed with wealth but have also done a lot of inner work, have sought and maybe even found the source of peace within themselves.

Money has a vital place in our lives. We all need it to survive, to feed, clothe, house, and educate ourselves and our children. We might need it to care for our elderly parents. We can also enjoy everything else it does for us, like the things it buys us, and the freedom it gives us to spend time on purely creative, non-money-making pursuits. But when we are in the grip of addiction to it, believing it will save us or bring us the happiness we seek, we are making a mistake.

The more you face your fears and stories about money and your real or imagined needs, and realize you are *not* your stories, but rather you are the awareness *looking* at the stories, the freer you will become of anything binding you.

When I was in my thirties, my own particular fear was being out of work, out of money, and ending up homeless under a bridge. During my meditations, I faced this worst-case scenario over and over again in my mind, until eventually it no longer held any emotional charge.

I wasn't fully awake yet. I hadn't completely perceived my true nature as consciousness, as the ultimate perceiver, but I came to realize my connection to spirit, the energy behind creation, was strong. I knew how to be at peace in the present and this allowed me to be much freer of my fears around money.

Whether or not I lived under a bridge was certainly not going to take away my inner peace. Besides, there has been a whole tradition of Zen masters who lived under bridges, basking in freedom, enjoying the ever-present delights of nature, dharma-jousting with fellow travelers, writing haiku. I would have been in good company!

Once I knew this for sure, I had a clear choice. One option was to sit on my butt meditating in bliss all the time, but with the knowledge I might end up not being able to afford a decent roof over my head. The other was to get to work doing what I enjoyed doing—or at least tolerated doing—so I could generate the income needed to keep body and soul together in a comfortable way. Preferring middle-class comforts to the deprivation of poverty, I chose the work option.

Remember: the beliefs, images, and pictures in your mind drive the sensations and feelings of anxiety and fear and keep them alive. As you learn to live in the present, letting go of attachment to the story inside your head, you'll come to the realization that inner freedom is, and always has been, your true nature.

Someone once asked me this question: "As I feel myself drawing ever nearer to the freedom that is my true nature, I notice I want to teach this, to share it with others. Is it wrong to charge a fee for my services?"

I read an article by the Sufi teacher Kabir Helminski many years ago. In it he said that in Islam, knowledge isn't for sale. There can be no profit motive in sharing the knowledge of illumination; if there is, both sides are being poisoned. A professional class of spiritual advisers does not fit with the truth, and eventually corrupts it.

Unfortunately, this perspective, while honorable in its intent, is the reason why the spiritual and the material have never merged, and will always be at odds with each other. It maintains and perpetuates the division between the one and the other, and is an ongoing cause of conflict and suffering in people who are caught between their hunger for spiritual truth and their very real need for material survival.

The nondual or global viewpoint eliminates this division. It sees the spiritual and material as one unified reality. Thus, it is okay to charge money for the time you may spend delivering the teachings of freedom. After all, money is an essential part of life, and teachers of awakening need to earn a living, too. There needs to be an energy exchange. If the teacher is truly free, he or she will not be motivated by greed, and the fee will always be fair, one that the student can afford.

The good news for the student is that once he or she awakens to the truth within, no more money needs to be spent. It is an investment which, once made, truly pays dividends, and keeps on paying them, endlessly. The investment results in nothing less than your freedom . . .

See if you can taste the freedom of your true nature right now . . . Open up to the inner vastness, the spaciousness, expressing itself through your body, mind, and personality . . . Then notice how you have thoughts, beliefs, and stories in your mind, and feelings, emotions, and sensations in your body . . . Notice how you can observe all these phenomena, so you cannot be them . . . You are what is observing . . . You are the timeless, ever-present consciousness witnessing everything arising and falling away in the awareness you are . . . So, be the awareness . . . Dwell in the freedom of your true nature . . .

Lead the Way

A well-dressed man said to me, "I am a senior executive in a Fortune 500 company, and a serious student of the art of leadership. I am extremely busy, have an enormous amount of responsibility, work a minimum of twelve hours a day, and am generally under a lot of pressure. Yet I am interested in what you have to say. I am intrigued by the whole notion of awakening to inner freedom, and how it leads to serving people in a more authentic way. What do you have to say to me?"

Few people will argue against the need for more enlightened leaders in our world. This man was both a student and practitioner of the art of leadership, so it is good that he was thinking about how to apply these principles and lessons to his work and life.

I told him, "Doubtless you have been inspired by stories of great leadership. You have probably been moved by the example of individuals who embody such qualities as vision, courage, compassion, creative thinking, bold decision-making, and selfless service to humanity. Obviously you want to be the best leader and best person you can possibly be.

"I don't know what specifically motivates you, but I suspect it makes you feel good to be a positive force in helping influence, shape, and direct the creative energy of others. Evidently you like being of service. No doubt you like being part of a group, team, or organization with good chemistry, one where every member feels a sense of kinship, united around a common goal. Experience taught you how to create such unity, and you are clearly willing to take the responsibility for making it happen."

All true leaders understand the power of multiplication, and what can be accomplished when a group of conscious, focused people come together in pursuit of a shared vision. The best leaders use this power not only to produce great results, but to make their organization, their community—and ultimately, our world—a better place.

The greatest leaders in history, from Marcus Aurelius to Martin Luther King, Jr. to Nelson Mandela, have been the spiritually conscious ones. This has always been the case. The ancient Chinese philosopher Lao Tzu spoke about the secret of conscious leadership over two thousand years ago: "If you want to learn how to govern . . . Show people the way back to their own true nature."

If, as a leader, you want to be able to bring out the highest and best in others—show them the way back to themselves, as Lao Tzu said—you must achieve a certain level of mastery within yourself, a true meeting of wisdom and love. You don't have to be a saint or completely without ego, but your mind must be clear and your heart open, and you must know how to be present without any personal agenda.

Anyone can be present with an agenda—a self-centered motive—but it takes a very conscious and inwardly free person to be present without one. Only then can you be truly open and available to the untapped creative potential existing in each moment. Only from a place of clear, loving presence can you build, create, and nurture a conscious team or organization.

The philosopher-sage Nagarjuna, who lived in India about five hundred years after the Buddha, understood how critical enlightenment was in the art of leadership. He went so far as to say that if a ruler cannot implement a politics of enlightenment, then he or she must abandon the throne to pursue enlightenment first.

This does not need to be taken literally. It does not mean if you are trying to foster an enlightened and harmonious work environment, you need to resign your position or office and go off on a long spiritual retreat in a mountaintop monastery somewhere. But it does mean you must take time out from your busy schedule to do some inner work.

Make awakening, your own inner peace and clarity, *the* priority in your life. Draw upon the resources that will feed your soul, nourish your heart, and illuminate your mind. Read the books, take the trainings, and get the coaching or private work to support you in this process, allowing you to return to your leadership responsibilities with renewed clarity, vision, and passion.

Above all, spend time in meditation and contemplation. As you continue to work with the practice and study the teachings I have presented in this book, take your own inner counsel. Listen not to the voices in your head, the voices telling stories of fear and worry, but to the voice of truth resonating deep within your heart and soul. Heed that voice.

Realize you are not your ever-changing stories or your thoughts, but rather the luminous awareness, the boundless, ever-present consciousness that is the source of your moment-by-moment experience.

The more you embody this realization, the more you will naturally empower others to live it themselves. You will model conscious, awakened behavior for them. You will inspire them to dive more deeply within themselves. You will help them discover that for those who have eyes to see, every moment is new and rich in creative possibility.

This is how you become a great leader. This is how you become a great person—great in the sense of being a true master of your own mind and emotions, a genuinely self-realized human being.

This is how the world gets transformed: each of us discovering the greatness within us, the truth of consciousness and freedom, and then sharing that truth and light with others.

How You Know You Are Free

A woman came up to me after a lecture and asked me this: "How will I know when I am free?"

I said, "When you just don't take yourself to be anybody anymore. When you no longer hold on to any concept, story, or image of who you are. When you look inside yourself and there's no conflict, no darkness, no edges, no more tension, no fear. There's just this ever-fresh, ever-new clarity, spaciousness, ease—an inner stillness that is dynamic, vibrant, and alive. This is how you know you are free."

"And will that freedom be permanent?" she asked.

"Basically, yes. When realization happens, you know the truth of who and what you are, beyond all the beliefs and stories previously giving you your identity. And, once you know, you know. Like knowing your name, or where you live, you don't forget. Even when your body is tired, hurting, or sick, you always feel okay inside. Your fundamental peace and well-being remain untouched. And this is true whether you're waking, sleeping, or dreaming."

"You're always happy, then?"

"Not necessarily. If you just suffered a substantial loss—maybe someone you love died, or you just lost your life savings in a stock market crash or an investment gone bad—you are not going to be happy. But you will always be at peace. Nothing, not even a great loss, has the power to disturb your deep inner peace and equanimity anymore, other than momentarily."

Her eyes widened, and her face took on a dreamy, faraway look. "It sounds truly wonderful."

"It's just about being very present," I said, as I reached out and touched her hand, bringing her back to the now. "It's not about wonderful states in another dimension. It's not about being somewhere else. You know you're free when you realize there is only the present, this moment now, and you're always one with it. You're always at peace with this moment now. You, as an expression of consciousness, are juiced, turned on, by the unfolding of creation in this moment now."

She took a deep breath and started to relax, but then frowned. "What about ambition, hopes, dreams, the desire to do something with your life?" Suddenly, her voice rose again. "What happens to all of that?"

"Desire is still there, you're just no longer attached to it. You still have likes and dislikes, preferences, but they don't run you anymore. For example, if a desire arises to make love to your partner, and then it doesn't happen because he or she says no, there's no sense of frustration or disappointment. Or if there is, it is fleeting, and it falls away naturally. You're always in the moment, and there's always something new and interesting happening in every moment."

"What about ambition, having a sense of mission or purpose in life?"

"Ambition is there too, it's just no longer so personal; it no longer comes from the ego. As pure consciousness, you realize you are inhabiting this body, mind, and personality in order to do something. Once you find the freedom that is your true nature, what you are here to do—your personal mission, or destiny—becomes very clear. Startlingly so. Then you set about doing it. The beauty is you're no longer worried about success or failure. The joy truly is in the journey."

"And dreams at night? Do you still have them?"

"You'll still dream at night," I said, "because that's just what the brain does when the body is sleeping. Dreams are a way of discharging energy, of dealing with all the images and sensory input of the day. However, with awakening, just as during the day, you no longer identify with the dreams and stories inside your head, with thoughts of I and me, and there will be no identification with them at night when you are sleeping, either.

"Dreams will happen. You will enjoy the show. You may even get some useful or prophetic information, but you will not personally be caught up in the dream. Just as you are free of suffering during the day, so will you be free of bad dreams at night."

Our conversation took a different direction when she asked if a person who has realized his or her true nature ever has doubts. I explained that no matter how awake we are, since we're still human, there will be moments when we are dealing with stressful or challenging circumstances, where old ego patterns involving emotional reactivity may briefly flare up.

These are the residues Jean Klein spoke of. I mentioned earlier that Nisargadatta Maharaj occasionally had mental or emotional reactions, or residues. If such reactions happened to Nisargadatta, who embodied the truth of liberation as powerfully as anyone, then you can be sure they are going to happen to you and me.

Something definitely shifts once you have seen with total clarity that you are not your story. You no longer take yourself to be the person called Mary Smith or Bill Jones, but instead know yourself as the pure, shining consciousness *expressed* as Mary Smith or Bill Jones. The shift feels like passing through a final doorway, a point of no return, where you no longer identify with the personal.

As the years go by, whenever these residues or echoes from the past do appear, they are increasingly milder and less frequent. Consciousness is like the ocean. The echoes and residues are like waves or eddies, which cause a passing disturbance but don't affect the overall clarity and stillness of the ocean.

You notice the challenging problem or difficult circumstance and gently remind yourself, "This is not who I am." You become present and remember you are not your story, but rather you are the timeless, ever-present awareness looking at the story and experiencing the emotion surrounding the story.

Calmness and tranquility then soon return. This allows you to deal with whatever problem you are facing from a practical, creative, and focused place. Indeed, all you have to do is be fully present with the problem, attuned to what it is trying to tell you, and sooner or later it will reveal its own perfect solution.

As your awakening deepens and matures, you eventually come to the place where you don't even have to remind yourself. You live constantly in the knowledge of who you are. You will realize beyond a shadow of doubt that you are, in your essence, the same beautiful, conscious person that you took your teacher or guide to be. No longer will you place anyone on a pedestal, nor will you see them as lower or less than you.

In the meantime, the point to remember is that whenever there is conflict, it is because there is inside you this idea of being a person in conflict. After all, you say to yourself, "I am worried, I am upset, I am unhappy." Let go of the attachment to being somebody, to naming and labeling every experience, and you'll be free. You'll be free to share who and what you are with others as you take the action steps needed to fulfill your destiny here.

You will share the gift of freedom with others by just being who you are, whether or not you formally become a teacher of awakening. Your unconditional way of relating will give others permission to be free, whether they are consciously aware of it or not. Gone are the judgments, projections, agendas, and expectations that used to get in the way of your relating to others. They cannot help but feel this change in you, and will be changed because of it.

Awakening to freedom, as I have made clear, is a distinct event in time. It happens when you finally see that everything between your ears—the whole world of thought, belief, of me, myself, and my story—comes and goes, yet *you*, as awareness, the witnessing presence, are always here.

However, the embodiment of awakening, the deepening and maturing of it, is an ongoing, lifelong process. This is true of every one of us. Why do I say this? Because awakening or enlightenment is, above all, seeing the oneness of humanity, and the seeing and feeling give rise to our love of people.

It takes time to see and experience the one source, the pure consciousness, behind every pair of human eyes, particularly when people are motivated by fear, greed, and hate.

Facing Life's Challenges

During a period of several years after I awakened, occasionally, fear would come up, invariably related to money and material survival. When these residues from the past surfaced, I would get caught up in them for a while, thinking that maybe I was losing my awakening. But then I would remember my true nature, relax into knowing it, and soon be clear and present again.

Basically, my life since that spring of 1995 has been a smooth, harmonious flow. This is what happens when you wake up: you are mostly always in the flow, and it always feels good. There is little emotional reactivity, because you are not holding onto any personal story that could trigger a reaction. You truly identify with *being*, with the consciousness that is your true nature. You feel deeply humbled, and immensely grateful.

When the daily problems and challenges of life arise, as inevitably they do, you just face them from a clear, grounded, open, and present space. Consider, for example, what happened to me with the strokes I had, which I spoke of in the beginning of the introduction.

When I was in the emergency room at UCSF Hospital, just after the third stroke had occurred, a radiologist came by my gurney and said he wanted me to sign a waiver so he could do an angiogram. This was a procedure in which they place a catheter in the groin and go up through the carotid artery, and then inject a dye into the cerebral arteries. If he then found an area of constriction, he said, he would insert a stent to open the artery back up. However, there was a 25 percent risk of my having a major stroke or dying, which was why he wanted me to sign.

These didn't sound like very good odds to me at all! It was then that I experienced a brief but strong contraction of fear, an instinctual survival response, I later realized. But since my life was on the line anyway, I signed, and then I breathed and relaxed as much as I could. I came back to my normal way of being, of flowing with what was happening, one moment at a time. As it turned out, the radiologist made no intervention. I had several constricted areas in my arteries, but they were too deep to do anything about.

I remember lying in bed soon after coming home from the hospital, still in a state of extreme weakness and exhaustion, and thinking, "Thank God I'm free." If I was going to have another stroke, or even if I was going to die (and, at that point, both seemed in the realm of possibility), I was ready. Then, as the days passed and I regained a little strength, I realized I needed to make a decision: if I wanted to live, I needed to make a conscious choice to do so.

I was only fifty-seven. I had already spent four years working on a new book, an earlier version of this one. I wanted to finish it. I wanted to teach again, to share the good news, the benefits to ourselves individually and to humanity as a whole, of awakening to freedom.

So I formed a clear intention to get well. Daily, I used the power of visualization to create more blood flow in the corollary arteries beginning to develop in the left side of my brain after the strokes. Over the next six months, I had occupational and speech therapy to assist with my rehabilitation. The whole process took almost two years, but I have recovered to the point where everything except the function of my right hand and a slight, occasional limp in my right leg has pretty much returned to normal. My right hand was dominant, and it is still paralyzed to the degree where I can't use it very well, other than to shake hands, open doors, and pick up grocery bags.

The third stroke knocked me on my ass. My ego was still at times identifying with a story about being enlightened, and it was as if I were whacked on the side of my head with a cosmic two-by-four. As a result, I now have a much more relaxed way of being, and I am free of any story, even one about being free.

The strokes taught me several lessons and reinforced things I already knew. The lesson of gratitude was brought home to me. I was grateful for the friends who supported me with their love and energy, and with money when I really needed it.

I am also grateful that the strokes forced me to transition out of a career I wasn't passionate about (but was at peace with), into work that really is an authentic expression of me: writing about and teaching people how to be free, how to find the inner peace that does not depend upon outer circumstances.

Another lesson is the reaffirmation that life is always changing. One of the secrets of awakening is not to resist the changes, but to flow with them. In my case, I was relatively fit and healthy at the time of my first stroke. I jogged for exercise and worked out at the gym, and had practiced yoga for over thirty years. The strokes came with no warning signs, and the doctors are still not sure what caused them.

Anyway, I had to deal with the changes that took place in my life and learn to appreciate the gift in each new experience. This is the real meaning of the strokes and of my life now, I feel: supreme gratitude for still being here, for still being able to share my wisdom and love with others.

The Practice of Manifestation

This is a good practice to do first thing in the morning. You can even make it your meditation.

Close your eyes or keep them open. Become one with that expanded sense of pure consciousness, of radiant presence. Notice the thoughts that come and go. Do not identify with them, not even the I or me thought. Let your identity come from being itself. You are one with the beauty, harmony, and flow of this moment now.

Consciously use the power of your mind to think about something you really want to create or manifest. Pull your energy in like a magnet, and bring all the power of your presence to your manifestation. It could be anything: to create your ideal relationship, to make a certain amount of money, to find the perfect job, to build your business, to exercise or improve your health, to fulfill some creative urge, to plan something new, and so on. The more you are in integrity about your manifestation (that is, it serves the greater good by freeing you up in some way and allowing you to contribute more, rather than being completely self-serving), the more likely it is to be manifested.

Get very clear about your intention, and visualize it happening. Feel it as if it has already happened. Do an affirmation around it, if you wish, such as, "I now easily and effortlessly manifest more customers, or clients." See yourself conversing with the customers or clients, or the money coming in, or the plan taking effect. See it in your mind as already so.

When the visualization is very clear in your mind's eye, and you can feel it in your body as if it were already so, then let it go, using an affirmation like, "And so it is . . . " Such a statement, uttered with your whole being, helps take "you," your ego, out of the picture. It really is about surrender and allowing divine grace, or whatever you want to call the mysterious creative power of the universe, to have its way.

Then come back to simply being very aware and relaxed in the present. As you get up to go about your day, be aware of any action you need to take to manifest your intention into reality. Be proactive. Throughout the day, occasionally think of your intentions as a way of reminding yourself to stay focused. Otherwise, just be very present with whatever is happening and unfolding in this moment now.

Afterword

THERE IS A NATIVE American story I heard many years ago about a young brave who had bad dreams at night. In the dreams, he owned two dogs, a white dog named Love and a black dog named Fear. Every time he went out to feed them, the black dog snarled viciously and started attacking the white dog, such that the dreams turn into nightmares.

Desperate, the young brave went to the medicine man, the wisest man in the village. "The black dog in my dream keeps getting bigger and more ferocious. I'm afraid if he kills the white dog, it means love is going to die in my heart, and I will lose my courage as a warrior. What should I do?"

The medicine man thought for a moment. "It's simple," he said.

"What?" the brave pleaded.

"Just feed the white dog."

Feed the white dog. Focus on love, not on fear. Stop giving energy to the dark, fearful thoughts inside your head and feed only what is positive and true, what makes you feel inwardly confident and whole.

The lesson of this charming story is good to remember when you are struggling with issues of self-doubt, personal conflict, fear, or suffering. Just like the religious stories we were told when we were young, whether Christian, Jewish, Buddhist, Hindu, Islamic, or of some other tradition, this story has the power to shift our state of consciousness and give us a sense of peace and wholeness, if we let it.

But a story is still a story, no matter how charming, beautiful, or true it is. So long as our inner peace and well-being is dependent upon a story, it will always be conditional. When we no longer believe the story or the story just doesn't do it for us anymore, we are once again plunged into self-doubt and conflict.

In the book you have just read, I have presented a radically different approach to transformation, one promising to deliver you through the door to true freedom. I have described again and again the remarkably simple yet revolutionary practice, the essence of which is learning to face your inner conflicts, self-doubt, and fears without any story whatsoever. Here it is, one more time:

Step 1: Be Present with Your Experience

As you have learned by now, resistance to what is happening is the cause of personal suffering. When facing any inner conflict, struggle, or upset, be aware that that is your signal to become very present, very alert, and open to what is. Ask yourself, "What is my experience right now?" Better yet, you can even welcome the upset. After all, it is showing you where you are still not free.

Step 2: Notice the Story

Behind every reactive emotion, whether it is self-doubt, guilt, anger, envy, loneliness, anxiety, or depression, there is always a story, belief, or thought. Notice the story you are telling yourself. If it helps, you can affirm, "Uh-oh, I'm getting caught up in a story again . . . "

Step 3: See the Truth

Then see the truth. Observe how the thoughts, beliefs, and stories, just like the feelings and emotions they trigger, are ever-changing, appearing and disappearing, but you are the awareness that is always present, always here. So, breathe and be the clear, unchanging awareness you are . . .

When you do this practice enough, at some level you eventually realize that what you are is simply clear, radiant, present-time awareness itself. You are the luminous, unchanging consciousness manifesting itself in this body, mind, and personality called "you." As this realization deepens, it will impart a new sense of meaning, purpose, and power. When you are no longer identifying so much with the contents of your mind—with thoughts, beliefs, and stories—you are freer of emotional stress and reactivity, and you experience more ease and harmony.

However, in order to pass through the final door to awakening or inner freedom, you have to use this practice to face everything in yourself, including all your demons. You have to face fear itself. To use the metaphor in the story above, you have to confront the black dog. You have to look it in the eyes and discover for yourself just how real or unreal it is.

If you truly face it and stay with it long enough, you'll discover it isn't real. Nothing in your mind or in your dreams is real. Only consciousness or awareness is real. Only what is timeless, changeless, and always here is real.

Yes, you have thoughts, including the I and me thoughts. You have a personal history. You have concepts, beliefs, ideas about your life and what you want to do, what you want to achieve or accomplish. You have memories and stories about your life. You have sensations in your body. You have feelings and emotions. You have experiences. Events and circumstances come and go in your life.

But because they are always changing, none of these manifestations of consciousness can possibly be who and what you are. Who and what you are is the consciousness, the radiant presence that is aware of all these ever-changing phenomena. You are the entire ocean, the boundless awareness expressing in and through this unique mind/body/person appearing as you.

Realize the liberating truth of this notion, and you will be free; free of attachment to and identification with the personal pronouns I and me. Letting go of this identification, which is the fourth step of the practice, marks the final shift into freedom. You will be fully awake to your true nature. You will know yourself as consciousness, as an expression of the divine, the one Reality behind creation.

You will clearly see beyond all doubt the person you always considered yourself to be doesn't exist. It never did. It was only an idea or story in your mind that you had bought into, believed, for a lifetime. Then you will be truly present—naturally, easily, effortlessly.

After awakening, you will find your identity not in stories, not in thoughts or beliefs, not in emotions or feelings, and not in events and circumstances, but in being itself, in the beauty, harmony, and fullness of existence. You will still have an identity, a story in the world, as a business or professional person, as a laborer or mechanic, as an artist or musician, or as a mother or father. But now you will know, beyond a shadow of a doubt, that who and what you really are is much, much more than this.

The mind, with all of its thoughts, will no longer be a distraction. Instead, it will be a true ally, a magnificent tool for solving problems, communicating with others, and setting intentions about what you want to create. Your purpose will become clear. Love, gratitude, and affection will guide you in every aspect of your life.

This is the message in this book. This is the realization awaiting you.

Acknowledgments

HEARTFELT GRATITUDE TO Gaiakai Harris, Kari Taber, Christine Case, Cameron Pazirandeh, and Shari Faerman for their editorial feedback, and to Joe Kinnee for the great title. Special thanks to Shelley Warren, who graciously and painstakingly went through the manuscript twice, paragraph by paragraph, and suggested better ways of wording them.

I also want to thank my friends from Sonoma County, who helped me keep all this real: Karl and Satri Andersen, Eduardo Barr, Steve Brum, Larry Elsener, Frederic Ernst, Richard Koobatian, Richard Murphy, Sheldon Murphy, Phil Salyer and Julia Melody, and Glenn Siegel.

Much gratitude to Mary Criquet, who helped care for me when I was dealing with the most acute phase of stroke recovery. Thanks to Suzanne Taylor, who introduced me to her spiritual community in Los Angeles, and graciously hosted my gatherings in her home for more than ten years.

Many thanks, too, to my clients, students, and workshop participants. You are the reason why I am still here. Special thanks to Lee Chiacos, who assists me and leads the morning meditation and chi gong at my Esalen workshops, and to John Smith, who attended my 2008 Esalen workshop and gave me honest feedback on the practice, which helped refine it to what it is now.

Lastly, many thanks to Emile Trienekens of the Netherlands, who invested in the initial hardcover printing, and to Greg Brandenburgh of Hampton Roads, who read the hardcover, saw the value of the book's universal message, and is responsible for this edition.

Bibliography

Castaneda, Carlos. *Journey to Ixtlan: The Lessons of Don Juan*. New York: Washington Square Press, 1972.

Engler, Robert, and Yuriko Hayashi. *The Way of No Thinking: The Prophecies of Japan's Kunihiro Yamate*. Tulsa, OK: Council Oak Books, 1995.

Harding, Douglas E. *On Having No Head: Zen and the Rediscovery of the Obvious*. Carlsbad, CA: InnerTraditions Publishing, 2002.

Maharaj, Sri Nisargadatta. *I Am That: Dialogues of Sri Nisargadatta Maharaj*. Translated by Maurice Frydman. Durham, NC: Acorn Press, 1973.

McKenna, Jed. *Spiritual Enlightenment: The Damnedest Thing*. Wisefool Press, 2010.

Pirsig, Robert. *Zen and the Art of Motorcycle Maintenance: An Inquiry into Values*. New York: William Morrow, 1974.

Shakespeare, William. *As You Like It*. From the First Folio, 1623.

Tweedie, Irina. *The Chasm of Fire: A Woman's Experience of Liberation Through the Teaching of a Sufi Master*. Salisbury, England: Element Books, 1984.

Wilber, Ken. *One Taste: Daily Reflections on Integral Spirituality*. Boston, MA: Shambhala Publications, Inc., 2000.

About the Author

Cameron Pazirandeh

Jim, a native of New Zealand, is a writer and teacher in the nondual lineage, which says that the spiritual and material are one, and what is real is right here, now. His own inner journey took twenty years, and then he finally awoke to the freedom that is his true nature. His mission now is to guide others to the same realization but in a much shorter time. He currently teaches at Esalen Institute (*www.esalen.org*) near Big Sur, and in Los Angeles, New Zealand, and Australia.

Hampton Roads Publishing Company

. . . for the evolving human spirit

Hampton Roads Publishing Company publishes books on
a variety of subjects, including spirituality, health, and
other related topics.

For a copy of our latest trade catalog, call 978-465-0504
or visit our distributor's website at
www.redwheelweiser.com.

FLORIDAE AMERICAE Pr
Recens & exactiffima d
Auctore Iacobo le Moy
gnomen de Morgues, e
nierum, Altera Galloru
Prouinciam Nauigatio
eft,Atque adhibitis aliqu
Ob pericula,Regionis r
ora & Maritina dilig
Luftrauit,& Exactiffim
eft, Obferuata etiam fr
Fluminum inter fe difta
met redux Carolo.ix.
Regi, demonftra

SEPTENTRIO

OCCIDENS — ORIENS

MERIDIES

Pars Maris Antillarum.

Hicaranaoui

Caffi

Malica
Homoloathali
Caroli
Mora
Saguronib
Patica
Rabaldus fecunda
nauigatione hic appuli
rochoi

Cänaueral.

Yacaiouque fiue maior
Lucaya.

Bahata.

Zagareo.

F. Lygeri.
Leona. Inacana

Seguana

Serranahs
Timacani
Mari

Charenta
Guruana
Girolda
Belfini

Iris pars plena eft Infulis, fcopulis, breuibus et puluinis valde infidiofis.

Mons Chrifti

Iauana

S. deo Chrifti

Pocdus
Principis

Ifabella

Portus Patris

Cubandan

Alhaxhauui

THE ISLAND OF LOST MAPS

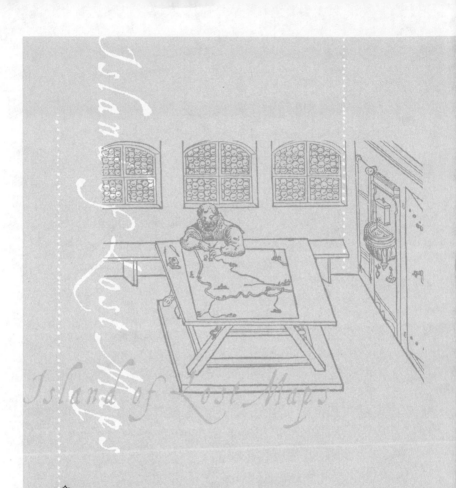

RANDOM HOUSE NEW YORK

MILES HARVEY

The Island of Lost Maps

A TRUE

STORY OF

CARTOGRAPHIC

CRIME

Library of Congress Cataloging-in-Publication Data
Harvey, Miles
　　The island of lost maps : a true story of cartographic crime / Miles Harvey.
　　　p.　　cm.
　　ISBN 0-375-50151-7
　　1. Libraries—United States—Special collections—Maps—History—20th century.　2. Map thefts—United States—History—20th Century.　I. Bland, Gilbert Joseph.　II. Title.

Z702.H37 2000
025.8'2—dc21　　　00-025604

Random House website address: www.atrandom.com
Printed in the United States of America on acid-free paper

9 8 7 6 5 4 3 2
First Edition

Book design by Barbara M. Bachman

Endpapers: map of Florida and Cuba, 1591, by Jacques Le Moyne, from the Geography and Map Division, Library of Congress.

IT IS NOT DOWN IN ANY MAP;

TRUE PLACES NEVER ARE.

HERMAN MELVILLE,

Moby-Dick

Contents

Island of Lost Maps

A PRINT FROM A 1537 EDITION OF A WORK
BY THE THIRTEENTH-CENTURY GEOGRAPHER
JOHANNES DE SACROBOSCO.

Strange Waters

EXPLORERS PIN MAPS TO THEIR WALLS; journalists tape stories to theirs. For both, doing so is a way of getting their bearings. As I sit down to write this book, the wall behind my computer is unadorned except for two photocopied articles, each of which helps me set the course for the journey ahead. The first one, which I ponder now while sipping coffee, is from a reference book called *Who Was Who in World Exploration:*

HOUTMAN, CORNELIUS (Cornelis de Houtman) (ca. 1540–1599). Dutch navigator and trader in the East Indies. Brother of Frederik Houtman. . . . In 1592, the Houtman brothers were commissioned by a group of nine Amsterdam merchants to journey to Portugal to learn what they could about newly developed sea routes to the East Indies. . . . In Lisbon that year, Houtman and his brother attempted to acquire classified Portuguese navigational charts detailing the sailing routes to the Indies. They were arrested and briefly held in a Portuguese jail when they were caught trying to smuggle the charts back to Holland.

The coffee I am drinking comes from a Chicago establishment called the Kopi café, a place where my life was transformed one day and this book was born. As it happens, the story of how the Houtman brothers wound up in jail is also the story of how the Kopi got its name. That, however, is not the primary reason this article hangs on my wall. I keep it there to serve as a constant reminder of the extraordinary power of maps—and the lengths to which human beings will go in obtaining them.

Shakespeare once used the term *mappery* to describe the passionate study of a map or chart. I am neither a map scholar nor a map collector, but if there's one thing I should make clear about myself from the start it's that I am an incorrigible *mapperist,* an ecstatic contemplator of things cartographic. On the desk in front of me now, in fact, is a reproduction of a very old and very famous map, one that, among other things, shows why the Houtman brothers felt compelled to spy on Portugal.

Published in 1569 by Gerard Mercator—the greatest cartographer of his era and a Dutch contemporary of the Houtmans—it was the first map to use a revolutionary system for projecting the three-dimensional world onto a flat plane. More than four hundred years later, this system is still in such common use that when most of us close our eyes and imagine a map of the world, we are seeing Mercator's rendition of the Earth. But for all the work's towering achievements, what I notice at first glance are its mistakes and misconceptions, its whimsies and wild stabs in the dark.

Gazing at Mercator's chart, I see a planet strikingly different from our own, a world full of blank spaces and never-never lands. North America turns into an amorphous blob that reaches so far west it is almost joined to Asia at the hip. South America has an unaccountable protrusion from its southwestern shores, a topographic tail feather that makes the continent look something like a giant waterfowl. This beast is, in turn, perched upon a very peculiar nest—a huge polar landmass, many times the size of present-day Antarctica. Known as the Great Southern Continent or the Unknown Southern Land (or, to more optimistic cartographers, the Country Not Yet Discovered), it was a place ancient geographers had dreamed up to complement their belief that the Earth was perfectly symmetrical. The Arctic region, meanwhile, is a massive donut of land, broken up by four rivers that lead into a polar ocean, through which water was thought to flow to the center of the Earth. From this strange sea rises a giant magnetic "black rock," which, according to ancient versions of the myth, destroyed ships by pulling out the nails that held them together.

It is easy, with centuries of hindsight, to chuckle at such notions. But for people like Mercator and the Houtmans the still-hazy outlines of the world were no laughing matter. Having refrained from widespread ocean exploration until the fifteenth century, Renaissance Europe was in a high-stakes rush to make up for lost time. Portugal had led the charge. Beginning in around 1420 under the direction of a prince who would be dubbed Henry the Navigator by later generations, the Portuguese launched a series of explorations down the west coast of Africa. Bartolomeu Dias arrived at what we now call the Cape of Good Hope in 1488, and ten years later Vasco da Gama became the first European to travel to India by sea. In so doing, he helped establish a Portuguese economic empire in the Far East, the realm of pepper, spices, drugs, pearls, and silk.

The Portuguese controlled the Indies because the Portuguese controlled the maps. Attempting to establish and preserve a trade monopoly, Henry the Navigator and his successors guarded their navigational secrets with an iron hand. "No foreign ship was allowed to sail to the Indies," wrote the historian George Masselman. "The penalty was confiscation of the ship and committal of the crew to a lifetime in the galleys." Nor were maps allowed to circulate. When Pedro Álvares Cabral returned from India in 1501—ending a trip in which he became, according to some scholars, the first European to sight Brazil—an Italian agent complained, "It is impossible to get a chart of the voyage, because the [Portuguese] King has decreed the death penalty for anyone sending one abroad."

On the browned surface of the Mercator chart, I can see signs of just how well Lisbon kept its secrets. Some scholars believe the Portuguese quietly discovered Australia in the early sixteenth century. If so, no word had leaked out to Mercator:

the entire continent is missing from his map. In its place, south
of Java, sit three entirely nonexistent kingdoms called Beach,
Lucach, and Maletur. Lacking firsthand accounts by contemporary explorers, Mercator based these lands on the fourteenth-
century descriptions of Marco Polo.

At first, the Dutch did not consider their ignorance about
the Indies to be a pressing issue, primarily because they were
close trading partners of the Portuguese. At the time Mercator
was making his map, however, that relationship was beginning
to change. In 1568 the Dutch, who were increasingly embrac-
ing Calvinism, started a long war of independence against
Catholic Spain, the great European power at the time. Yet just
as the Dutch were breaking from the Spanish empire, Portugal
was becoming part of it. In 1580 Spain invaded its neighbor,
routing Portuguese forces. Portugal and Holland had now become enemies. The Dutch, brilliant shipbuilders and sailors,
realized that they would need to go to the East Indies themselves—no easy task. "The route itself was almost completely
unknown," wrote Masselman. "Not a single Dutchman had yet
set foot in the Indies."

Their initial attempts to get to the East were by going north.
When Dutch merchants looked at world maps such as Mercator's, they saw a waterway passing over Europe and Asia to the
Pacific. When they ran their fingers along this route, as I am
doing now, they concluded that it was shorter than the passage
around Africa—and had the added advantage of being free
from heavily armed Portuguese ships. No one had actually
made the journey, of course; in fact, the whole concept of this

northern waterway—like the notion of the Unknown Southern Land—was based on the writings of ancient historians. It turned out that, for once, the ancient historians were right, but it also turned out that no ship would complete the northeast passage until 1879. The Dutch would make three unsuccessful attempts. In the meantime, they dispatched the Houtmans to Lisbon in search of sea charts. But for all their trouble, the brothers—who were eventually freed after their sponsors paid a considerable ransom—may not even have been particularly successful in their mission. Historians disagree about whether they succeeded in smuggling maps and charts out of the country and, if so, whether these maps provided any new information to Dutch cartographers, who had by this time begun to gain extensive knowledge about Portuguese sea routes from other sources.

What the experts do agree on is that the Houtmans and their associates were "the vanguard of the age of modern capitalism," as Masselman put it. The merchants they represented were in the process of pooling their resources in an innovative enterprise called the Company of the Far East, one of the earliest modern examples of the joint stock company, or corporation. This company was the predecessor of the famous Dutch East India Company, which in turn gave rise to the Amsterdam stock market, the first forum for what the historian Fernand Braudel called "speculation in a totally modern fashion." And as the Dutch East India Company thrived, this same class of merchants would figure out a way to use windmill technology for sawing lumber into the exact shapes and sizes needed in shipbuilding—one of the earliest examples of mass production. The Houtmans were helping to define both the geographic and the economic outlines of the modern world, but this probably never occurred to them. They were just a couple of businessmen trying to make a buck.

Today the brothers are mostly remembered as explorers. In 1595, a year after returning from Portugal, Cornelius Houtman served as "chief merchant" on the first Dutch expedition to the East Indies. In 1598 he and his brother led another journey, during which followers of a Sumatran sultan killed Cornelius and imprisoned Frederik. Over the course of his two-year confinement, Frederik Houtman wrote the first Dutch-Malay dictionary; later, in 1619, he made one of the earliest known sightings of the coast of western Australia. Thanks to efforts of adventurers like the Houtmans and a number of superb cartographers, the Dutch East India Company put together a collection of 180 navigational charts. It had the status of a state secret and was, in fact, called the Secret Atlas. With it the Dutch ousted the Portuguese and became the dominant colonial power in the southwestern Pacific.

They controlled the region for more than three hundred years—an entire empire built on getting one's hands on the right maps. By the end of the eighteenth century, that empire's most profitable export was a little bean, which the Dutch had begun to grow in Java in 1696. When brewed this bean produced an exhilarating beverage that the Dutch called *koffie*—a word passed on to the Malay and Indonesian languages as *kopi*.

HICH BRINGS ME TO THE SECOND STORY ON MY WALL, a December 21, 1995, *Chicago Tribune* report about another man who got into trouble for stealing maps:

TAMARAC, FLA.—The small, subdued man in khaki pants asked to visit the rare book room. Library curators checked his credentials, logging him as a visitor from Florida. He went inside.

Minutes later, pandemonium—the man fleeing, security guards chasing, police asking why anyone would steal a map from a 232-year-old library book and sprint through the streets of Baltimore.

Clues, it turns out, rest in Tamarac—home to Gilbert Bland, Jr., alias James Perry, a suspect in the theft . . . at Johns Hopkins University and perhaps scores more [burglaries of old maps] from libraries along the East Coast.

I had no idea, the first time I read those words, that they would soon be chiseled into my mind. Yet I do remember feeling an unusually intense jolt of curiosity, as fiery and bracing as the coffee I had raised to my lips. In those days I spent a great deal of time at the Kopi, a self-proclaimed "traveler's café" whose walls were adorned with masks from Bali and shelves were filled with Lonely Planet guides to far-flung destinations. I was then the literary critic for *Outside* magazine, a great job but one that was beginning to wear on my patience. The books I read were about people who climbed Himalayan peaks or rode bicycles through Africa or sailed wooden boats across the Atlantic or trekked into restricted areas of China. These tales of adventure filled my days and my imagination, yet my own life was anything but adventurous, the hours spent slogging through book after book in a dark corner of that coffeehouse or staring endlessly into a computer screen. The interior of the Kopi was ringed by clocks, each one showing the time in some distant locale, and as I watched the weeks tick away in Timbuktu and Juneau and Goa and Denpasar and Yogyakarta, I began to long for an adventure of my own. Or maybe adventure isn't quite the word. It was not that I had any particular desire to do something death-defying; what I wanted was a quest, a goal, a riddle to solve, a destination. My craving, I believe, was not unlike the one Joseph Conrad described in *Heart of Darkness:*

> Now when I was a little chap I had a passion for maps. I would look for hours at South America, or Africa, or Australia, and lose myself in all the glories of exploration. At that time there were many blank spaces on the earth, and when I saw one that looked particularly inviting on a map (but they all look that) I would put my finger on it and say, "When I grow up I will go there."

Looking back now, I think that what Conrad called "blank spaces" had much to do with why that article so completely commandeered my imagination from the start. In retrospect, I think I was intrigued not so much by what the story said but by what it left looming between the lines. What was it about these mysterious old maps that people found so alluring? And what kind of person would wander so far and put so much on the line for their acquisition? Who *was* this Gilbert Bland? I did not yet know how difficult these questions were. I did not yet know that trying to answer them would take up a huge portion of my life. I did not yet know that, even as I sat sipping coffee, my quest had begun.

All I knew was that I had to know more. I had heard about the bizarre case of Stephen Carrie Blumberg, who, during the 1970s and 1980s, removed as many as 23,600 books and manuscripts from 268 libraries in forty-five states, two Canadian provinces, and the District of Columbia. Consumed by what he called "the passion to collect," Blumberg employed an astonishing variety of tricks to build his illicit collection. He picked locks; he stole keys; he threw volumes out of library windows; he crawled through ductwork and hid in elevator shafts; he assumed the identity of a University of Minnesota professor; he even altered books, while still inside a library, so that they appeared to be his own. Then he would haul his takings to a house in rural Ottumwa, Iowa, where he filled nine thirteen-foot-high rooms with books shelved from floor to ceiling and meticulously arranged them according to a catalog system of his own making. He somehow convinced himself that he was not really stealing but "rescuing" the books from institutions that did not give them the attention and care they deserved. Although his collection was worth up to $20 million, Blumberg never sold a single book. I wondered if Gilbert Bland had a similar compulsion for hoarding hot maps.

But I was just as fascinated by the possibility that Bland was in it for the money. For centuries thieves have reaped big rewards by catering to the peculiar needs of collectors. In our own culture extensive black markets exist for everything from art to animals and sports memorabilia—but history offers some even more outlandish examples. In the twelfth and again in the sixteenth century, for instance, the popularity of a medicinal elixir made from, of all things, the flesh of Egyptian mummies led to a booming business in grave robbing. "Alas, poor Egypt!" wrote Louis Reutter de Rosement. "After having known civilization at its zenith, after having sacrificed its all to respect its dead, it was now forced to see the eternal dwellings of its venerated kings despoiled, profaned, and violated and the bodies of its sons turned into drugs for foreigners."

With our own tedious era sadly devoid of contraband pharaoh goo, Bland's alleged crime spree seemed about as interesting a subject as a writer—especially a writer with his own lifelong love of maps—could hope to find. I began to look into the caper and discovered that it was even more extensive than was originally reported. According to the FBI, Bland had stolen maps from at least seventeen libraries across the United States and two in Canada. He was, it turned out, the Al Capone of cartography, the greatest American map thief in history.

I took the story to my editors at *Outside,* who found the case deliciously offbeat and assigned a lengthy feature on Mr. Bland. I thought I would finish it in six weeks. But when it finally appeared in the June 1997 issue, I had worked on it for more than a year—and my labors had only just begun. By the time I completed research on this book, the investigation had consumed four years of my life.

Bland proved to be an extremely enigmatic and unwilling subject and, despite it all, a fascinating one. He was a chameleon. He changed careers and families without looking back; when a daughter from his first marriage asked him for help with buying a car, he refused, saying, "You're a stranger." He could seem to switch age before your eyes, appearing world-weary one minute and boyish the next. Medium height, medium weight, middle-aged, middle everything—he was a cipher, a blank slate; in cartographic terms, terra incognita. He was Bland: "1. Characterized by a moderate, undisturbing, or tranquil quality. 2. Lacking distinctive character."

Because he turned down all my requests to interview him—both for the article and, later, for this book—I was forced to build my profile the slow, hard way: visiting the places he worked and lived; walking through crime scenes; talking to family members, friends, business associates, and victims; methodically piecing together his past through criminal records, court documents, military files, computer databases, and other sources of public record. The more snooping I did, the more I began to see my quest for information as similar to that of the Houtman brothers, and my attempts to make sense of it like the task faced by Mercator. Filling in a life, it turned out, was like filling in a map, and my search for Gilbert Bland soon transformed from an investigation into an adventure. Along the way,

I happened upon a curious subculture made up of map historians, map librarians, map dealers, and map collectors—all gripped by an obsession both surreal and sublime. Like the explorers of old, I found myself heading farther and farther into strange waters, never quite sure if I had found what I was looking for, but endlessly filled with bemusement and wonder.

THE ISLAND OF LOST MAPS

A BIRD'S-EYE VIEW OF BALTIMORE'S
MT. VERNON NEIGHBORHOOD FROM 1850,
AROUND THE TIME GEORGE PEABODY BEGAN
MAKING PLANS FOR A LIBRARY THAT WOULD
ONE DAY STAND JUST LEFT (OR EAST) OF THE
WASHINGTON MONUMENT. ONE HUNDRED AND
FORTY-FIVE YEARS AFTER THIS ENGRAVING
APPEARED, GILBERT BLAND WAS APPRE-
HENDED ON THE FIRST PORCH TO THE RIGHT
OF THE MONUMENT.

CHAPTER 1

Mr. Peabody and
Mr. Nobody

*T*HE GEORGE PEABODY LIBRARY IN BALTI-more's historic Mount Vernon neighborhood is, by any measure, a remarkable place. "There is no other library like this in America, or anywhere else excepting the parallel universe of Jorge Luis Borges's fiction," the poet and essayist Daniel Mark Epstein wrote. From its lofty reading room, surrounded by gilt-framed portraits of long-dead librarians, to its Grand Stack Room—measuring sixty-one feet from the white marble floor to the latticed skylight, appointed in ornate cast iron and gold leaf, and containing 250,000 of the world's rarest and most important volumes—the Peabody has lived up to its original conception as "a cathedral of books."

The man who built the library was also remarkable. Born poor in South Danvers, Massachusetts, in 1795, and receiving no more than a fourth-grade education, George Peabody built a small fortune in the dry-goods business in Baltimore, then moved to London, where he made millions in the financial markets. But Peabody was equally adept at giving money away. In England he built more than forty thousand rent-free units of housing for poor people. In the United States he endowed seven cultural institutes and libraries, including the museum of archaeology and ethnology at Harvard and the natural history museum at Yale. At the end of the Civil War, he also established the Peabody Education Fund with $2 million (about $20 million in today's dollars) to provide schooling for the "destitute children of the Southern States." All told, his gifts totaled more than $7 million—something like $70 million in today's dollars.

In 1869, the year of the famous financier's death, the *American Annual Cyclopaedia* called Peabody "the most liberal philanthropist of ancient or modern time"—an overzealous description, maybe, but not by much. Mr. Peabody, as people around the library still respectfully refer to him, is widely acknowledged as the founder of modern philanthropy. He was extraordinary not only in the size of his gifts but in his philosophy of giving. Unlike most big-money benefactors of his day, Peabody did not promote religious beliefs. He had a different sort of evangelism in mind. In an 1831 letter to his nephew, he wrote:

Deprived as I was, of the opportunity of obtaining anything more than the most *common education* I am *well* qualified to estimate its value by the *disadvantages* I labour under in the society [in] which my business and

situation in life frequently throws me, and willingly
would I now give *twenty times* the expense of attending
a good education could I possess it, but it is now too late
for *me* to learn and I can only do to those that come
under my care, as I could have wished circumstances
had permitted others to have done by me.

Let others save souls; Peabody was interested in minds. And
so it happened that in 1857, during his first visit to the United
States in almost twenty years, he announced plans for a facility
which, he said, "I hope may become useful towards the im-
provement of the moral and intellectual culture of the inhabitants of Baltimore." The Peabody Institute was, wrote his
biographer Franklin Parker, "perhaps grander in its original design than any previous benefaction in America." Its audacious
goal was to jump-start the city's moribund cultural life on many
fronts at once. The institute would have an art gallery and a lecture series and an academy of music. Perhaps most important,
it would also have a library—but no ordinary one.

Peabody had two major stipulations for his library. First, he
insisted that it would be "for the free use of all persons who
may desire to consult it." But, although open to even the poorest and least educated Baltimorean, it would not be a lending library, cluttered with contemporary novels, how-to tracts, and
other popular forms of literature. The volumes, he declared,
would be only "the best works on every subject"—and they
would never leave the building. They would remain in the
stacks, always available "to satisfy the researches of Students

who may be engaged in the pursuit of knowledge not ordinarily attainable in the private libraries of the Country." What Peabody had in mind was a kind of modern-day athenaeum, a repository of wisdom and history that would survive the ages.

"Mr. Peabody's purpose," explained Epstein, "was to gather books that had made history and first recorded the thoughts and passions of humankind, in the belief that a book is something more than a locus of data, paper, glue, and ink; a book has supersensible power, and a great collection draws down a resonance endowing the reader of any book in it with special faculties of understanding."

Bringing such a library together was no small task. But library organizers had two huge advantages. The first was lots of money. Peabody eventually endowed the institute with $1.4 million, a huge sum for the time. The second was the Civil War. It delayed the library's official opening for nearly a decade—a vexation for just about everyone but John Morris, the first librarian. "Taking advantage of the delay, Morris and the Library Committee devised a long-range plan to systematically acquire the world's best books for the collection," wrote Elizabeth Schaaf, archivist and curator for the Peabody Institute. "Their model was no less than the combined catalogues of the finest libraries in Europe and America. The Peabody was a carefully planned collection, the scope of which was contingent neither on funds nor immediate availability in the book market."

Morris and his successor, Nathaniel Holmes Morison, carefully compiled massive desiderata—or wish lists—of books for the library. Publishing these lists in bound form, they sent them out to booksellers, bibliophiles, and librarians all over America and Europe in what surely must have been one of the greatest literary scavenger hunts in history. Ten years after the Peabody Institute opened its doors in 1866—an event attended by a crowd of twenty thousand and covered by newspapers on both sides of the Atlantic—there were more than sixty thousand volumes on the shelves, filling the library's original quarters to capacity and prompting the construction of the architect Edmund Lind's palatial Grand Stack Room.

The Peabody collection eventually totaled more than 250,000 volumes—including rare and vital works in U.S. and English history, Greek and Roman classical literature, romance languages, archaeology and art history, science, architecture, building and mechanical trades, genealogy, and, finally, geography and cartography. This amazing catalog has been well-used. H. L. Mencken sat in a reserved desk at the library when working on his monumental treatise, *The American Language*. The novelist John Dos Passos, whose books include *The 42d Parallel* and *1919*, spent countless hours there, along with thousands of less famous researchers and writers. Among them was Epstein, a poet, playwright, and biographer whose books include *The Boy in the Well, Sister Aimee: The Life of Aimee Semple McPherson, No Vacancies in Hell*, and *Nat King Cole*. In a 1993 essay, Epstein described the "magical library" as providing "the necessary environment for private education, the encounter between a person and a book." The Peabody is, he concluded, "a space where time stands still."

That is true in more ways than one. Because of shifting financial priorities at the Peabody Institute, few books have been added to the library's collection since the early part of this century. Today the library—now run by Johns Hopkins University—is something of a gilded warehouse of old books, a treasure-house of knowledge that goes largely unused. Only a few patrons visit the Peabody Library each day. Most of them are scholars, as has always been the case. Others are tourists, who come to gaze at the library's architecture, not its books. Many of the rest are eccentrics, following some odd fancy of intellect or simply killing time. But a few others, constituting a tiny but ominous minority, have darker reasons for being there.

On December 7, 1995, one such man entered the library. It is safe to say that George Peabody had just such a person in mind when he stipulated that the facility "should be guarded and preserved from abuse." It is also safe to say that the stranger was, in many ways, an opposite of the library's founder. Peabody's face—with its distinctive muttonchop whiskers, patrician nose, and wide-set eyes—is still familiar to many people more than a century after the philanthropist's death. The man who walked into the library that day, however, had built a career on anonymity. Few people who crossed paths with him could later recall the details of his appearance; many could not remember him at all. But Mr. Peabody and Mr. Nobody were opposites in even more fundamental ways. Peabody had spent millions preserving rare volumes for the betterment of all people; the man in the Grand Stack Room had come to gut those volumes for his own illicit financial gain.

The two of them, however, had one important thing in

common: a passion to collect. Like the men who assembled this library more than a century earlier, the stranger had come to the Peabody with a wish list. It was a red notebook, roughly the size of a steno pad, its cover bearing the initials U.S.C. and a picture of a gamecock, the mascot for the University of South Carolina, where the man had apparently paid a recent visit. Inside, in neat, well-spaced cursive, was a list of centuries-old books, most of them atlases. Next to many of the titles someone had scribbled the names of various libraries where the books could be found. Several of the entries were followed by "Peabody Inst." or simply "Peabody."

Now some of those same books were piled on a desk in the Grand Stack Room. Now the mystery man began to leaf through one of them. Now he stopped to examine a page. Now he took out a razor blade and carefully lowered his hand to the aged paper.

*O*N OCTOBER 11, 1492, CHRISTOPHER COLUMBUS, BE-lieving that he was nearing the shores of Japan, looked out across the ocean and saw a light "like a small candle that rose and lifted up." Ever since, historians have debated about what Columbus saw—or whether he saw anything at all. Was it a campfire on a distant shore? Was it the glow of native animals called Bermuda fireworms, which give off blinking green lights to attract mates? "Or was the mysterious light," wrote the Columbus biographer John Noble Wilford, "only an apparition in the eyes of the wishful mariner?" We will never know. What we do know is that four hours later, a lookout on the *Pinta* spotted white cliffs in the moonlight and shouted, *"Tierra! Tierra!"* Cartography would never be the same.

Like other discoveries, the discovery of a crime often depends on a combination of trained eyes, educated guesses, and good luck. Jennifer Bryan had all those things going for her as she sat in the Grand Stack Room that December day in 1995. But her visit to the Peabody would have been completely unremarkable—indeed, the whole saga documented in this book might never have been told—if not for another factor: "I was bored."

Bryan, who was then completing her Ph.D. in history at the University of Maryland, had come to the library to work on her dissertation. Her research that day involved scanning volume after volume of British legal documents from the fifteenth and sixteenth centuries. It was not a thrilling endeavor, even for a student with a sincere passion for her work, and Bryan soon found herself "just sort of staring into space."

From the skylight a gray winter glow washed down over the room. The air was cool and still and fragrant with the faint perfume of old volumes. The place was silent, save for the hush of the ventilation system, the occasional click of footsteps against the marble floor, and the squeal of the old-fashioned elevator. As Bryan sat absentmindedly, the elevator rose into the five upper floors of stacks, carrying a library staff member to collect books. When the elevator stopped, a light came on in one of the balconies, briefly illuminating shelves crammed with old volumes, then went off again. Then the elevator creaked back down to the main floor. This sound momentarily drew Bryan's attention, and when the elevator door opened she watched as a librarian took an armful of old volumes to a man sitting across the way. He was the only other patron in the room.

There was nothing unusual about his appearance—quite the contrary. A studious man in his mid-forties, wearing a blue blazer and khaki pants, he could have been mistaken for half the scholars who walk through the library's doors. He was unimposing and slight-framed, with a biggish nose and smallish chin, reddish hair and mustache—not the kind of person who normally draws stares. Yet Bryan found her eyes lingering on him as he flipped through the books.

"You know how it goes: this is distracting, so I'll watch it to break up the monotony," Bryan recalled about her fixation on the man. In truth, however, she was accustomed to observing other people at libraries. She had been trained to do so. In addition to her graduate work Bryan was employed as a manuscripts curator at the Maryland Historical Society, located just a few blocks from the Peabody. Her desk there faced a huge window that looked down over the James W. Foster Reading Room, and part of her job was to keep an eye on the patrons. She knew that there was good reason for such vigilance. Over the past few years rare books rooms all over the country had been plagued by thefts of increasingly valuable antiquities. The Library of Congress, for example, had announced in 1993 that thieves and "slashers" had stolen thousands of items from perhaps five hundred books in its collections. That august institution was less than fifty miles down Interstate 95 from the

Peabody: what happened there could happen here. Moreover, Bryan knew that the old saying about judging books by their covers also applied to crooks. Often those responsible for the thefts did not look like criminals; in a number of cases, in fact, they had been professors, even librarians. And although she had no obvious reason to distrust the man, she began to get an unsettling feeling about him. "Maybe I just have a suspicious nature," she said.

He quickly gave her good reason to worry. "I just happened to look up and over in that direction and thought I saw him tear a page out of a book," she remembered. But it happened so fast, and the man did it with such seeming nonchalance, that at first she did not completely trust her eyes. "I thought, well, *now* what do I do? Do I say something, or did I just imagine that?"

Bryan decided to wait—and watch. She did not like what she saw. "He was behaving very oddly," she said. "I mean, he wasn't behaving like a researcher. . . . He was just sitting there, riffling through the pages, so it was obvious that he was looking for illustrations."

By this time, the man had noticed her as well. He kept glancing over his shoulder, flashing her "surreptitious" looks. Bryan is an unassuming young woman whose face does not easily give away her thoughts. But behind a pair of glasses, her large blue eyes ache with intelligence and intensity. The man seemed to grow increasingly flustered under her steady stare. "It was weird," she said, "because he must have thought something was up, but he didn't think enough to run, to get out."

Instead, he stood up, pulled out a card catalog drawer, and

laid it alongside the books, purposely obstructing Bryan's view. This was a fatal mistake. She could doubt herself no longer. With that one false move, the man had given himself away.

WHEN MR. PEABODY AND MR. NOBODY CROSSED PATHS a few minutes later, there was no time for formal introductions. The encounter took place just outside the front door of the library, where George Peabody, or at least a bronze statue of him, sits leisurely in an armchair, permanently pondering the city he helped to create. At the time of their meeting, Mr. Peabody, wearing a vested business suit and a self-satisfied look, his legs comfortably crossed, had no special plans. Unfortunately, Mr. Nobody was in a rush. At that precise moment, in fact, he was fleeing security guards.

After Jennifer Bryan had told library officials of her concerns about the man, they quietly contacted security officials. Peabody librarian Carolyn Smith then asked the man to move from the Grand Stack Room to a front area, where she hoped to keep an eye on him without arousing his suspicions. The ploy was apparently successful. Even after being moved, the man requested a 1670 atlas of Africa by the cartographer John Ogilby, although perhaps this was simply an attempt to maintain an air of innocence. At any rate, he did not immediately flee—a bad decision. Within a few moments Donald Pfouts, director of security at the Peabody Institute, had entered the room, joined by two other officers. This time the mystery man decided not to stick around. He grabbed his notebook and

walked out the front door, followed by Pfouts and the other security officials.

On the library's steps Pfouts said, "Excuse me, sir . . ."

The man picked up his pace. The officers walked faster to
catch up—and the man hastened his gait to keep ahead of
them. In a scene that might have come from some odd amalga-
mation of *The Nutty Professor* and *The Fugitive,* the bookish des-
perado now led his pursuers on a slow-speed chase through
downtown Baltimore. Quickening his strides on Mount Vernon
Place, Mr. Nobody passed Mr. Peabody and headed toward another famous city landmark, the 178-foot-tall monument to
George Washington. "Great Washington . . . stands high aloft
on his towering main-mast in Baltimore," wrote Herman
Melville in *Moby-Dick,* "and like one of Hercules' pillars, his
column marks that point of human grandeur beyond which
few mortals will go."

The mortal now in question did venture beyond the column, but grandeur was far from his fate. With security officials
now closing in at a jog, an ignominious capture seemed more
likely with each moment. He pushed on, circling yet another
statue as he headed west across the broad boulevard of Washington Place. Above him a bronze marquis de Lafayette looked
down from his horse with a haughty stare. The general's steed,
a study in power and movement with muscles taut, mouth
chomping at the bit, neck twisting against the reins, tail flying,
seemed to be making mockery of the sluggish chase below.
Searching for an escape route on the far side of the boulevard,
the man spotted a nineteenth-century mansion that now serves

as a wing of the Walters Art Gallery. Approaching the building, he ditched his notebook into a row of shrubbery. Then he climbed a stairway onto the Ionic portico.

"That door doesn't go anywhere," Pfouts warned him. The man now realized he was trapped.

Pfouts spoke again: "I would really like to invite you back to the library, because I think there are some issues here that we have to deal with."

When the officers pulled the red spiral notebook from the bushes, they discovered that Jennifer Bryan's suspicions had been well-founded. Folded into its pages were four two-hundred-year-old maps.

SEA MONSTERS FROM A 1550 EDITION OF
SEBASTIAN MÜNSTER'S *COSMOGRAPHIA*.

CHAPTER 2

Imaginary Creatures

SOME OF THEM APPEAR TO HAVE THE TORSO of a unicorn, the paws of a weasel, the tail of an anchovy. Some look like Borneo-sized snapping turtles. Some resemble parrot-shark hybrids: the hellish spawn of Big Bird's one-night stand with Jaws. Some look like an amphibious Lucifer, an Evil One with webbed armpits. Some are huge and menacing aqua-dogs, ready to go fetch Madagascar. Some have fur, some have feathers, some have huge human-looking eyes scattered amid their scales. Some are snacking on entire ships. Some have naked ladies surfing on their backs. At least one is bridled like a horse and jockeyed by the king of Portugal. Another has a large sailing vessel beached on its tail, a group of sailors celebrating mass near its gills, and an altar, complete with candles and a crucifix, straddling its dorsal fin. My favorites come fully loaded: spouts, fangs, beaks, spikes, armor, opposable thumbs, the works.

Sea monsters are everywhere on old maps—loitering off Narragansett Bay and splashing around the Arctic Circle, slithering through the South Pacific and causing nothing but trouble near Tierra del Fuego. But they aren't the only unusual forms of life. Hartmann Schedel's 1493 world map, for example, is accompanied by prints depicting a variety of human monstrosities, from one man whose feet point backward to another with ears as big and floppy as Hefty trash bags. In the accompanying text, Schedel explained that in India some men have dog's heads, talk by barking, eat birds, and wear animal skins, while others have just one eye in the middle of their foreheads and eat only animals. Libya has a breed of people who are male on the right side of their bodies and female on the left. The western part of Ethiopia has people with just one mas-

HUMAN MONSTROSITIES ACCOMPANYING THE WORLD MAP IN HARTMANN SCHEDEL'S 1493 *NUREMBERG CHRONICLE.*

sive foot who can run as fast as wild animals. A land called
Eripia has beautiful people with the necks and bills of cranes.

Johannes Ruysch's 1507 map, one of the first to record the discoveries of the New World, shows a pair of islands off the coast
of Newfoundland said to be inhabited by evil spirits. In a legend
next to these isles, Ruysch—who is believed to have gone on one
of the early journeys to North America—offered what appears
to be an eyewitness account: "Demons assaulted ships near these
islands, which were avoided, but not without peril." He is not the
only explorer to have gone out into the great unknown and come
back telling great untruths. Christopher Columbus reported that
the New World contained "one-eyed men, and others, with the
snouts of dogs, who ate men," although he conceded he had not
seen them himself. He did, however, claim to have spotted three
mermaids on his historic 1492 journey but reported that they
"were not as pretty as they are depicted, for somehow in the face
they look like men." Likewise, Henry Hudson insisted that,
while exploring the Arctic in 1608, his crew saw a mermaid
whose "back and breasts were like a woman's, her body as big as
ours, her skin very white." Sir Walter Raleigh returned from
South America in 1596, repeating tales that the jungles were inhabited not only by the Ewaipanomas, a tribe of headless men
whose facial features were located in their chests, but by Amazons, a race of warrior women first described in Greek myth.
Antonio Pigafetta, a member of Ferdinand Magellan's historic
sixteenth-century journey around the world, later wrote that on
a beach in what is now Argentina, members of the mission saw a
half-naked giant so tall that human beings stood only to its waist.

The colossal beast, called a *patagón* (big-foot), is pictured on a number of seventeenth-century maps, including works made by the great Dutch cartographers Jodocus Hondius and Willem Janszoon Blaeu.

Of course, Patagonia never had Patagons and Amazonia never had Amazons. The explorers were liars. "It is easy enough to move from reporting [on a journey] to embellishing, adding details—perhaps to hold an audience's attention," wrote Steven Frimmer in *Neverland,* a book about nonexistent places and fictive creatures that have persisted as fact in the human imagination. "The next step must have been inventing. . . . The curious thing is that the stories had to be only moderately convincing, as long as they were fascinating. Distant places held a fascination all their own and human nature did the rest. It made the audiences want to believe in the unconvincing parts."

Maybe those early adventurers half-believed their own lies. As Bartolomé de Las Casas, the sixteenth-century missionary who documented the early period of Spanish New World discovery, once observed: "It is a wonder to see how, when a man greatly desires something and strongly attaches himself to it in his imagination, he has the impression at every moment that whatever he hears and sees argues in favor of that thing." Or maybe the explorers made up tales of sea serpents and demons and giants to scare off the competition. Or maybe they found that no one was interested in factual reports, that the public wanted monsters—just as today's public demands tabloid stories of UFO sightings and celebrity love affairs over hard news. Or maybe they created imaginary antagonists so that they could re-create themselves—and return as stronger, smarter, more heroic men. Or maybe they lied simply for the thrill of getting away with it.

Some of them might not even have bothered to leave home. Over the past few years, for example, some experts have begun to question whether Marco Polo ever actually traveled to the Far East. In her book *Did Marco Polo Go to China?* Frances Wood noted that no Chinese records of Polo can be found, despite his claims to have served as an official emissary for Kublai Khan. She also found it curious that, despite his travels, Polo didn't seem to learn much about Chinese geography and that he failed to mention even the most obvious aspects of Chinese culture, such as tea, bound feet, chopsticks, and the Great Wall. Wood, the head of the Chinese Department at the British Library, concluded that Polo probably based his book on the travel tales of other Italian merchants and on Persian accounts of China. It is "unlikely, even allowing for exaggeration," she wrote, that Polo himself ever made it much farther than Constantinople.

He would not have been alone in fabricating his adventures. One of the most important books of the late Middle Ages was *The Travels of Sir John Mandeville*, supposedly written by an English knight who journeyed to China and many other parts of the known world between 1322 and 1356. Like Polo's book, the *Travels* was hugely influential. Christopher Columbus read it in preparation for his 1492 journey. The English explorer Martin Frobisher took a copy of it with him on his 1576 attempt to find the Northwest Passage. The cartographer Abraham Cresques used it as a source for his monumental Catalan Atlas of 1375.

And Martin Behaim's globe of 1492, considered the oldest surviving European-made terrestrial sphere, includes text that quotes Mandeville extensively and respectfully. Details from the *Travels* were being incorporated into maps well into the sixteenth century.

But although the *Travels* was treated as fact for hundreds of years, many of the things John Mandeville reported seeing and doing now seem preposterous. He described walking through the Vale of Devils, for example, a place literally populated by Satan's minions, from which only "good Christian men . . . firm in faith" emerge alive. And he boasted not only of seeing the Well of Youth but of testing its miraculous waters: "I, John Mandeville, saw this well, and drank of it three times, and so did all my companions. Ever since that time I have felt the better and healthier."

Mandeville also claimed to have witnessed an amazing array of life-forms, including geese with two heads, thirty-foot-tall giants, people "who live just on the smell of a kind of apple; and if they lost that smell, they would die forthwith," ants "as big as dogs" that guard "great hills of gold" from human intruders, and "a kind of fruit as big as gourds," with a surprise inside: "an animal of flesh and blood and bone, like a little lamb without wool. And the people of that land eat the animal, and the fruit too. It is a great marvel."

But by far the most marvelous of Mandeville's inventions was his own life. On close analysis, his entire journey seems to have been fabricated, pasted together from other writers' travel narratives. "He was an unredeemable fraud: not only were his rare moments of accuracy stolen, but even his lies were plagiarized from others," wrote the literary scholar Stephen Greenblatt. Another critic conjectured that the longest journey Mandeville ever took was to the nearest library.

Even the name John Mandeville seems to have been a fabrication, leaving open—and probably unanswerable—the question of who wrote the *Travels,* and why. "The abundant identifying marks vanish on approach like mirages, and the extraordinarily ingenious efforts to name the author have failed," observed Greenblatt. "The actual identity, the training, the motives, even the nationality of the person who wrote *Mandeville's Travels* have become, under scholarly scrutiny, quite unclear. . . . Mandeville is radically empty."

ALTHOUGH THE STAFF AT THE PEABODY LIBRARY didn't know it at the time, the man they caught with the maps in his notebook also had a compulsion for creating imaginary creatures. The latest—the one whose face appeared on a fake University of Florida student ID card he had presented at the front desk—was named James Perry. But, according to police and court transcripts, there had been many others: James J. Edwards and James Morgan and Jason Pike and Jack Arnett and Richard M. Olinger and John David Rosche and Steven M. Spradling and James Bland.

He was no stranger to libraries. In the 1970s, when he was in his twenties, he had visited them often. But this, apparently, was long before he was interested in maps. According to one source who knew him at the time, he would use the libraries to track down the names of people who had died in childhood. Then he would create new identities, using the birth dates of the deceased.

He would invent these creatures, and then he would figure out ways to get people to send them free money. It worked for a while but then stopped working so well. In September 1973 the San Diego police arrested a man named Jason Michael Pike for grand theft. The charge, as the man would later admit in court, stemmed from the fact that "I applied for a credit card, and I used it to get money under false pretenses." At a bail hearing, however, the man conceded that Jason Michael Pike was just an alias. His true name, he told authorities, was Jack Arnett. But it later turned out that Jack Arnett was no more Jack Arnett than Jason Michael Pike was Jason Michael Pike. An alias on top of an alias—this led to an absurd moment in which the San Diego Municipal Court was transformed into a scene out of *Alice in Wonderland:*

The Clerk: Jack Arnett, aka Jason Pike. . . .
The Court: Is Gilbert Bland your true name?
The Defendant: Yes, sir.
The Court: You are also known as Jason Michael Pike?
The Defendant: Yes, sir.
The Court: Did Mr. Langford [the court-appointed de-
    fense lawyer] advise you of your constitutional
    rights, Mr. Arnett?
The Defendant: Yes, sir.

The Court: Mr. Bland, are you also known as Jack Arnett?

The Defendant: Yes, sir.

The Court: But your true name is Gilbert Bland?

The Defendant: Yes, sir.

The Court: What is your middle name?

The Defendant: Anthony.

The Court: Anthony?

The Defendant: Yes, sir.

But even Gilbert Anthony Bland was a persona of sorts. The
defendant was born Gilbert Lee Joseph Bland, Jr., a name he
had ditched many years before walking into that courtroom.
He pleaded guilty that day, receiving a sentence of five years'
probation, but his urge to create new selves did not stop.
Gilbert Anthony Bland soon transmogrified into John David
Rosche and Richard M. Olinger and Steven M. Spradling. And
like horror-movie monsters stitched together out of other people's corpses, these creatures got their inventor into trouble—
this time, serious legal trouble. On December 30, 1975, Bland
was arrested in Tampa, Florida, for using those identities to de-
fraud the U.S. government in a scheme to collect unemployment compensation for ex-servicemen. He pleaded guilty in
U.S. district court, where he was given a three-year sentence
and shipped off to the federal corrections institution in El Reno,
Oklahoma. He did not like it there, and when he got out he apparently vowed to begin anew.

He cut ties with his old family, started a new one, got a college degree, found work in the computer business, and began to lead a middle-class existence in suburban Maryland. With this new life came a new identity, and an old one at the same time. Gilbert Anthony Bland was now back to his birth name (minus the "Lee"): Gilbert Joseph Bland, Jr. I think he intended this to be his final creation. I think he wanted to leave the phantasms behind. But somewhere in his head they must have been calling to him, enticing him with easy money, adventure, escape.

Then one day in the early 1990s, they began to catch up with him. According to the FBI, it happened almost by accident. "His story is that he bought a bunch of items that someone had left unclaimed at one of these U-Store-It places," said Special Agent Gray Hill, the Bureau's point man on the case. "Included were a bunch of maps. And someone told him, 'Hey, there might be some value there.'"

ONG AFTER THE FBI AGENT TOLD ME THAT ANECDOTE about Gilbert Bland finding the maps, I was left with a vague feeling of déjà vu. Then one day I realized I had, in fact, heard the same story before—many times. On the desk in front of me, for example, is an open copy of *The Clue in the Embers,* the thirty-fifth installment of the Hardy Boys mystery series, a favorite of generation after generation of American children. In the chapter at hand, Joe and Frank Hardy, along with their "chubby pal" Chet Morton, have just discovered a missing medallion. The chums immediately realize that their new find, when matched with its companion, creates a map:

"It must show the area near the treasure that Luis Valez is looking for," Frank remarked.

"And the opal probably marks the place where the treasure is hidden," Joe added. "Boy, I'd like to find that spot myself!"

"But it's in Texichapi—the land of nowhere," Frank reminded him.

You don't have to read the rest of *The Clue in the Embers* to know what happens next. In about the time it takes chubby Chet to exclaim, "Wowee! What a treasure!" the brothers will locate the land of nowhere and uncover the long-buried Aztec palace there. This outcome is certain not only because the Hardy Boys are predestined to leave no mystery unsolved but also because the book is part of a larger literary tradition. So many adventure stories are set in motion by someone finding a map, in fact, that these narratives have assumed the status of myth, in which the buried treasure lies not only in the earth but deep in our collective unconscious. When I went back to read some of them, I was surprised to find how often these stories— like the real-life drama I was covering—were tales of temptation, exploring the perpetual contention between our good and evil selves, between our rational minds and the creatures that prowl the unexplored regions of our souls.

In the case of the Hardy Boys, of course, evil never stands a chance. Being the very embodiment of upstanding American youth, Joe and Frank refuse to exploit Texichapi's priceless antiquities for their own gain. (Frank: "These treasures are certainly government property! No one must be allowed to steal them. We must notify the Guatemalan government at once." Joe: "We don't expect a reward. We've had a grand time visiting your beautiful country.") In other such stories, however, the moral landscape becomes far more complex. At the heart of these narratives are two opposing icons, one symbolizing desire, the other knowledge. If the buried treasure is the forbidden fruit of these stories, the map is the serpent, prodding us to dream of a place beyond the borders of our innocence, pointing us to it, hissing, *X marks the spot*. Perhaps this explains why our culture uses cartographic and geographic language to express notions of sin and virtue. We speak of a moral compass. We describe good people as following the straight and narrow. We say sinners lost their way, lost their bearings. And in our fables of maps and money, characters are constantly torn between sticking to the path of righteousness and wandering into the wilderness of the soul, populated by all those wild animals.

The most celebrated of these stories, of course, is Robert Louis Stevenson's *Treasure Island*. This 1883 classic is often regarded as a harmless children's tale, but as the Stevenson biographer Frank McLynn pointed out, "There is a disturbing darkness about *Treasure Island* absurdly glossed over by those who continued to treat it as a mere 'boy's book.' . . . One of the most disturbing aspects of *Treasure Island* is its lack of a moral center."

The plot is well known. *Treasure Island* opens with the death of an old mariner, who leaves behind a sea chest. Jim Hawkins, a fatherless boy and the book's narrator, finds a mysterious packet of papers in the trunk and takes it to Squire Trelawney and Dr. Livesey for inspection:

> The doctor opened the seals with great care, and there fell out the map of an island, with latitude, longitude, soundings, names of hills, and bays and inlets, and every particular that would be needed to bring a ship to safe anchorage upon its shores. . . . There were several additions of a later date; but, above all, three crosses of red ink—two on the north part of the island, one in the southwest, and, beside this last, in the same red ink, and in a small, neat hand, very different from the captain's tottery characters, these words:—"Bulk of treasure here."

Jim and the men decide to hire a ship and search for the island. Before their vessel departs, however, the one-legged pirate Long John Silver and his associates secretly join the crew and plot to get the buried gold for themselves. This sets up a bloody battle when the ship arrives at Treasure Island. Jim and his friends are eventually able to overcome the buccaneers and find the treasure—but theirs is not a clear-cut triumph of good over evil.

Silver, for one, is a strangely paradoxical villain—especially given the simplistic moral framework of most children's literature. Both a "monstrous imposter" and a man of his word, a reckless killer and a careful compromiser (who, at one point, saves Jim from being murdered by the other mutineers), he is alternately a "prodigious villain" and a "bland, polite, obsequious seaman." The critic Ian Bell aptly described him as a "figure whose personality swings like a pendulum, whose character metamorphoses almost in an instant."

But *Treasure Island*'s hero is also oddly ambiguous. Despite the gee-whiz tone of his narrative, Jim is no Hardy Boy. In his worldview, love of money is not the root of all evil—far from it. Greed is good, and without consequences. Jim does not worry about where the buried treasure came from, who suffered by its accumulation, or whether he has the right to take possession of it. In fact, he revels in his avarice, providing a sensual description of the loot, one that might as easily have come from Long John Silver:

> It was a strange collection, like Billy Bones's hoard for the diversity of coinage, but so much larger and so much more varied that I think I never had more pleasure than in sorting them. English, French, Spanish, Portuguese, Georges, and Louises, doubloons and double guineas and moidores and sequins, the pictures of all the kings of Europe for the last hundred years, strange oriental pieces stamped with what looked like wisps of string or bits of spider's web, round pieces and square pieces, and pieces bored through the middle, as if to wear them around your neck—nearly every variety of money in the world must, I think, have found a place in that collection; and for number, I am sure they were like

autumn leaves, so that my back ached with stooping
and my fingers ached with sorting them out.

A villain capable of good, a hero who "never had more pleasure" than in fondling stolen money: in writing *Treasure Island,*
his first novel, Robert Louis Stevenson was already fascinated
by the notion of the divided self, a theme he would explore far
more thoroughly in *Dr. Jekyll and Mr. Hyde.* It's a subject that has
long captured the imagination of writers, not the least of them
being James Fenimore Cooper, creator of such masterpieces of
early American literature as *The Pioneers, The Last of the Mohi-
cans, The Pathfinder,* and *The Deerslayer.*

Cooper's 1849 novel, *The Sea Lions,* is an allegory about two
men on identical ships traveling the same route. If not quite
Jekyll and Hyde, these sailors are nonetheless doppelgängers—
alter egos embodying two very different kinds of human desire.
As in *Treasure Island,* this tale begins with the death of an old
sailor, who leaves behind a sea chest containing "two old, dirty,
and ragged charts." These are no ordinary maps, however. The
first shows the secret site of a seal-hunting paradise in the
Antarctic Circle; the other, the location of a West Indies island
where pirates have buried a "very considerable amount of treasure." Two schooners—both of them named *The Sea Lion*—set
sail in search of this double jackpot. The first ship is commanded by Roswell Gardiner, an honest, brave, and resourceful
Long Islander who, while diligent about making a profit, is primarily on a spiritual journey, having lost his belief in the divin-
ity of Christ. The second ship is led by Captain Jason Daggett, a

Martha's Vineyard sailor, also courageous and cunning—but whom "no dangers, no toil, no thoughts of future, could divert from a purpose that was colored by gold."

In the Antarctic Circle the ships harvest a fortune in sealskins, but because of misfortunes brought on mostly by Daggett's greed, both become trapped in icy waters. During a horrible winter Daggett perishes, confessing to his symbolic twin: "I'm afraid that I've loved money most too well." His alter ego done away with, Gardiner promptly learns humility, realizes that Christianity admits no "half-way belief," accepts Jesus as his savior—and survives. He recovers the buried treasure on his way home, but it proves to be worth only "a little more than two thousand dollars," much less than expected. And, unlike Jim Hawkins in *Treasure Island*, Gardiner understands that the money does not really belong to him. "Seeing the impossibility of restoring the gold to those from whom it had been forced in the first place," he decides on another course of action:

> The doubloons were distributed among the families of
> those who had lost their lives at Sealer's Land. The
> shares did not amount to much, it is true, but they did
> good, and cheered the hearts of two or three widows
> and dependent sisters.

A decidedly less happy, and less virtuous, fate befalls the split-personality protagonist of *The Treasure of the Sierra Madre,* a famous adventure tale by B. Traven—himself no stranger to imaginary creatures. The author's own life, in fact, was a study in the slippery nature of identity. B. Traven was a pseudonym—but for whom? That question, the travel writer Paul Theroux once observed, is "the greatest literary mystery of [the twentieth] century." Over the years, people have identified Traven as Jack London, a group of writers in Honduras, even the illegitimate son of Kaiser Wilhelm II. The most likely bet seems to be that he was the fugitive German anarchist Ret Marut (a name that itself was merely an alias for a man named Otto Feige, according to some researchers). Yet those obsessed with Traven's "real" identity overlook an important point—one that may offer insight into the life of Gilbert Bland. As the Traven biographer Karl S. Guthke observed: "Here was someone who had apparently realized the fantasy of millions. . . . He had enacted the adventure of vanishing into thin air and being reborn, phoenixlike, as someone else—literally a self-made man."

Not surprisingly, the idea of dual identity filters into *The Treasure of the Sierra Madre*, the 1927 novel that was later made into a film with Humphrey Bogart and Walter Huston. The treasure here is a lost gold mine, located somewhere in the Mexican state of Sonora and rumored to have been a primary source of the Aztec empire's wealth. All traces of the legendary mine disappear for hundreds of years, until the late nineteenth century, when college students on vacation in Arizona come across some old maps in the library of a priest:

One of the maps indicated a mine which was named La Mina Agua Verde. When [the students] asked the father about this, he told them the story of this mine. He ad-

mitted that the mine was one of the richest known, but
said that it was surely cursed, whether by the ancient
owners, the Indians, or by the Almighty he would not
venture to say. But cursed it was. Whoever went near
this mine was sure to be overtaken by misfortune.

The discovery of the map triggers a number of efforts to
find the mine—all of them ending in dissension and bloodshed.
Yet this fact only seems to strengthen the legend's allure and en-
tice more men to look for La Mina Agua Verde. One of them is
Dobbs, an American drifter in Mexico who is particularly fascinated by one part of the myth: a thing he describes as

that eternal curse on gold which changes the soul of a
man in a second. The moment he had said this he knew
he had said something that never had been in his mind
before. Never before had he had the idea that there was
a curse connected with gold. Now he had the feeling
that not he himself, but something inside him, the existence of which until now he had no knowledge of, had
spoken for him, using his voice. For a while he was
rather uneasy, feeling that inside his mind there was a
second person whom he had seen or heard for the first
time.

Dobbs and two other men head off in search of the mine.
They find it—but that "second person" takes stronger posses-

sion of Dobbs with each ounce of gold dust they pull from the hills. He becomes paranoid and unquenchably covetous, swindling one partner out of his share of the treasure and shooting the other, leaving him for dead. But before Dobbs can enjoy his wealth, he is attacked by bandits, who cut off his head with a machete. They steal his burros—and, thinking the sacks of gold dust are filled with mere sand, they empty the contents to scatter in the desert winds. The curse of La Mina Agua Verde lives on.

Curses are for legends. We rarely speak of them in nonfiction narratives. Still, I can't help feeling that there was a certain inevitability about Gilbert Bland's story from the very start, as if what would follow was both unavoidable and doomed. The superstitious might call this fate. Bland's lawyers described it as mental illness. Bland himself once hinted it had a lot to do with simple desperation. Whatever the case, it must have already been with him when he came upon those first old maps. As I try to picture that pivotal moment, I see him opening some long-sealed cardboard box to discover strange-looking manuscripts stacked inside. He takes them out into the light, blows the dust away, flattens them on a table, runs his fingers over the coarse paper, admires the craftsmanship of the printing and hand coloring. And, even at this early point, he is beginning to hear the voice inside his head, a whisper from the phantom who would become James Perry. Maybe these maps don't *lead* *to* treasure, this voice tells him, maybe they *are* treasure. And maybe you should find out where more of it is buried.

Then again, it may not have begun that way at all. It's quite possible that Gilbert Bland lied to the FBI about how he became interested in antique maps. The real story could be entirely different—and perhaps, as with the details of B. Traven's life, or John Mandeville's, the truth will never be known. That's the trouble with people who make up imaginary creatures.

I SUPPOSE ALL OF US HAVE STRANGE VOICES IN OUR heads, quirks of cognition that defy simple explanation. When I was a boy, my parents were convinced I had a sixth sense. My father was a schoolteacher with a lot of vacation time and a mean case of wanderlust, so our family would spend much of the summer exploring the U.S. interstate highway system, a great barn of a travel trailer in tow. It was during these long trips that my supposed gift was discovered. Soon, testing it became a kind of game.

I would be fast asleep in the backseat, drooling on my big brother's shoulder, when my father would turn to shake me awake. "Quick," he would say as I blinked my eyes open. "Which direction are we going?"

"Uh . . . north?"

He would look at my mother with a proud and conspiratorial smirk. "Amazing," he would say, shaking his head. "You're right once again."

It was true. As long as I can remember, I've had an excellent sense of direction. But, though I will never fully understand it,

I suspect my boyhood adventures as the Human Compass had a lot more to do with cartography than with clairvoyance. More than likely I simply made educated guesses about the direction we were headed, based on earlier perusals of the coffee-stained, mildew-fragranced highway maps that were as much a permanent fixture of our Chevy Bel Air station wagon as the steering wheel. I could read maps before I could read books—and that skill, combined with a knack for measuring the sun's angles, probably accounted for the better part of my so-called gift. If I was a prodigy at anything, it was cartographic comprehension.

I was good with maps, plain and simple. But what obsessed me about them was never their scientific utility. I did not look on them as mere tools but as mysterious and almost sentient beings. Maps spoke to me. They still do.

Having said that, I want to stress that I am not normally in the habit of listening to mute objects. Nor am I overlooking the obvious fact that a map is a visual medium. Nonetheless, when I need to think through some daunting problem, personal or professional, I often find myself flipping open an atlas and meditating on some random page. And after a few moments of blank contemplation, I no longer seem to be looking at the map so much as listening to it.

A map does not converse in sentences. Its language is a half-heard murmur, fractured, fitful, nondiscursive, nonlinear. "It is almost as if one had to read from a page where all the words had been assembled in random order: obviously there could be no fixed starting point or sequence of perception," wrote Arthur H. Robinson and Barbara Bartz Petchenik in *The Nature of Maps*. A map has no vocabulary, no lexicon of precise meanings. It communicates in lines, hues, tones, coded symbols, and empty spaces, much like music. Nor does a map have its own voice. It is many-tongued, a chorus reciting centuries of accumulated knowledge in echoed chants. A map provides no answers. It only suggests where to look: *discover this, reexamine that, put one thing in relation to another, orient yourself, begin here* . . . Sometimes a map speaks in terms of physical geography, but just as often it muses on the jagged terrain of the heart, the distant vistas of memory, or the fantastic landscapes of dreams.

I use a map to get from one place to another in my mind in the same way that someone else might use it to get from Omaha to Oskaloosa. It's a peculiar kind of travel, I admit, but I suspect many others embark on similar journeys. Robert Louis Stevenson, for one, believed maps had the power of "infinite, eloquent suggestion." Before he wrote *Treasure Island*, he sketched a map of its imaginary shorelines. Soon, he was practically taking dictation from the thing:

As I pored upon my map of *Treasure Island,* the future characters of the book began to appear there visibly among imaginary woods; and their brown faces and bright weapons peeped out upon me from unexpected quarters, as they passed to and fro, fighting and hunting treasure, on these few square inches of a flat projection. The next thing I knew, I had some paper before me and was writing out a list of chapters.

So important was this map in the genesis of *Treasure Island*, in fact, that Stevenson was reluctant to take too much credit for writing the book. "The map," he wrote, "was the chief part of my plot." He offered this advice to other writers:

> It is my contention—my superstition, if you like—that he who is faithful to his map, and consults it, and draws from it his inspiration, daily and hourly, gains positive support. . . . The tale has a root there: it grows in that soil; it has a spine of its own behind the words. . . . As he studies [the map], relations will appear that he had not thought upon.

Like Stevenson, I often find myself ruminating on maps before I sit down to write. Often, little more comes of this exercise than a sense of relaxation and focus, a general freeing up of the imagination. But once—just as I was beginning work on this book—a seven-hundred-year-old map suddenly seemed to be speaking about Gilbert Bland. *Mappa mundi:* that's the mellifluous expression for a medieval work of cartography—and, despite appearances, it does not mean "map of the world." It more accurately translates as "napkin of the world," a reference to the fact that *mappae mundi* were often painted on cloth.

During the Middle Ages, in fact, there was no word for "map," either in the everyday languages of Europe or in Latin— evidence of how different the medieval conception of geography was from our own. The *mappae mundi* were intended more to diagram history and anthropology, myth and scripture, dreams and nightmares, than to provide geometrically precise representations of the physical world. Not surprisingly, they can look bizarre to modern eyes.

The *mappa mundi* that spoke of Bland was a reproduction of a brightly colored illustration found in a thirteenth-century book of psalms. The original, housed in the British Library and widely known as the Psalter Map, is less than six inches high and four inches wide—just the right size for a napkin of the world—but a much larger version of it is thought to have hung in the residence of the English king Henry III. At the exact middle of the map, like a bull's-eye on a dart board, is Jerusalem, the "navel of the world" in Christian teaching: "Thus saith the Lord God; This is Jerusalem: I have set it in the midst of the nation and countries that are round about her" (Ezekiel 5:5). From Jerusalem extends the known world—Europe, Africa, and Asia (with the last on top because the map is oriented to the east). The unknown world begins at the margins.

In these borderlands lie the spots that medieval Europeans had never actually seen but wanted to exist, the landmarks of their fondest hopes and darkest fears. At the top edge of the Psalter Map, for example, is the Garden of Eden, complete with the images of Adam and Eve standing by the Tree of Knowledge. On the northeastern border are the nations of Gog and

Magog, from which the dreaded servants of the Antichrist were expected to overrun Christendom on the Judgment Day. (Gog and Magog are surrounded on the map by a huge wall, which, according to legend, was built by Alexander the Great to keep those nations' flesh-eating citizens at bay.) And on the map's southernmost margins, standing side by side like criminals in a police lineup, are representatives of the various monstrous races: the Artibatirae, who walk on all fours; the Cynocephali, who have the heads of dogs; the Epiphagi, whose eyes are on their shoulders; the Maritimi, who have four eyes; the Sciopods, who have one giant foot; the Troglodytes, who live in caves. In the coming centuries the borders of the world would expand, and such monsters would move steadily farther from the civilized center, becoming extinct only when their natural habitat, terra incognita, finally ceased to exist.

In some very real ways, however, they are with us still, those monsters. We've added four new continents to our maps since the Middle Ages, subtracted Gog, Magog, and the Earthly Paradise, firmed up our ideas about sphericality, gravity, and heliocentricity. Yet, as I stared at the Psalter Map that day, I was struck not by its geographical failings but by its psychological accuracy. "Like the earth of a hundred years ago, our mind still has its darkest Africas, its unmapped Borneos and Amazonian basins," wrote Aldous Huxley, author of *Brave New World,* in his 1956 book, *Heaven and Hell.* Huxley called these regions "the antipodes of the mind"—a reference to a mythical landmass found on the southern edges of many *mappae mundi* (though, technically, not on the Psalter Map). Just as the geographical antipodes were thought to be inhabited by physical mutants, Huxley's antipodes of the mind are home to "strange psychological creatures leading an autonomous existence according to the law of their own being." Huxley, who found his own way to these antipodes by ingesting mescaline, insisted that we all have "an Old World of personal consciousness and, beyond a dividing sea, a series of New Worlds." For some, he wrote, seeking out "the mind's far continents" leads to a heaven of visionary experience; for others, a private hell.

I was meditating on such notions when the Psalter Map suddenly seemed to be telling me about Gilbert Bland's life, describing in vivid shades of green and red and blue a series of journeys back and forth between the center and the margins, between a mainstream middle-class existence and a criminal life on the edge, between a core identity and a pack of imaginary beings. Then it occurred to me that the map was also saying something about the kind of person drawn to such desperate excursions: you don't go unless you're either extremely self-delusional or self-destructive, unless you think you can reach an Earthly Paradise or are searching for your own version of Gog and Magog. You have to believe in other things, too: that there are places in the world where you can get lost, places where you can leave your old life behind, places where normal rules don't apply. And although I had never been prone to such adventures myself, I now realized that, in following Bland, I would be somehow traveling on a parallel journey to the margins. It struck me that mine, too, should begin at the center.

I knew that, in the antique maps business, no one is more central than a charismatic figure named W. Graham Arader III—though perhaps calling him the navel of the map world would be taking the metaphor too far. Some of his more cynical contemporaries might pick a different body part.

DETAIL FROM A MAP OF THE
TURKISH EMPIRE IN JOAN BLAEU'S
FAMOUS *ATLAS MAJOR*.

CHAPTER 3

The Map Mogul

*I*S THIS *BORING* OR WHAT?" GRAHAM ARADER growled at me as he entered a sales gallery at the elegant New York offices of Sotheby's, the venerable auction house. "Didn't I warn you? Didn't I say that this thing would be a big bore?"

It was late in the afternoon of a summer day so maniacally hot that even Manhattan seemed to have succumbed to a mood of small-town languor. A sale of rare books and manuscripts had been going on since morning, and now the gallery was less than half full, its chairs in disarray. A few hours earlier the place had been crammed with TV crews and scurrying newspaper reporters, all there to witness the much-publicized sale of some recently discovered love letters between Albert Einstein and a reputed Russian spy. The journalists, however, had gone home disappointed: the top bid on the Einstein correspondence— $180,000—proved to be less than the preestablished minimum price, prompting Sotheby's to take a pass on the sale. Since then a steady stream of literary curiosities had gone on the auction block: Sigmund Freud's note to an associate, begging for book royalties; galley proofs for a snippet of Marcel Proust's *Remembrance of Things Past;* Elvis Presley's epistolary vow that his love for a Memphis TV personality could not "be equaled or surpassed by anyone"; and the final shooting script for the second half of *Gone with the Wind,* complete with a proposal to change "Frankly, my dear, I don't give a damn" to "Frankly, my dear, I just don't care." Either line would have suited my mood at that moment. Coming from the Midwest, where auctions usually involve farm implements, I had expected to find this event completely entertaining if not engrossing. But as the afternoon wore on, I had grown tired of the practiced nonchalance of the clientele, who bid thousands of dollars on rare first editions with all the enthusiasm of someone ordering scrambled eggs, and of the endlessly solicitous patter of the auctioneer, a man with the prim voice of a BBC newsreader and the unctuous charm of an American game show host. By now, the pretensions of the place had begun to feel as stifling as the heat outside.

Arader was right: this *was* boring. I knew, however, that it was unlikely to remain that way now that he was on the scene. W. Graham Arader III has been accused of a lot of things by a lot of people, but no one has ever charged him with being dull. Brash and bombastic, brilliant and bigger than life, he has been the subject of lengthy profiles in such prominent publications as *The New Yorker* and *Smithsonian* magazine. He has also served as the thinly veiled model for the central character of a recent novel and is without question the most recognizable figure in the world of antique maps. When I began my research on that world, I quickly learned two things: (1) almost everybody in the business seemed to cherish the chance to discuss Arader, often in reproachful terms (and usually off the record), and (2) Arader had an equal enthusiasm for talking about himself, almost always in the most laudatory manner. "I'm the biggest map dealer in the twentieth century," he said in one typical moment of bravado. "There's no question about it. I sell $10 million in maps every year. I can pick up the phone and make $10,000 in a single hour. Yes, collecting has made me a very rich man."

And yet, as even Arader's worst critics would probably concede, these were not empty boasts. At the time of the Sotheby's auction, June 1998, I had been keeping in touch with this complex and contradictory man for two years. I was drawn to Arader in part because listening to him talk was like consuming a gallon of espresso in one sitting—an overwhelming sensation, to be sure, and one that could leave a decidedly bitter aftertaste, but also an experience that left you wired and, once the buzz wore off, wanting another cup. And, although Arader and Gilbert Bland had apparently never met, I realized from early on that if I wanted to understand the antique maps business I would first need to know something about its biggest player. Over the past few decades the market for old maps had spread steadily from the esoteric fringes to the mainstream. By Arader's own estimation, "It's straight up since I started collecting in 1971, increasing 5 to 20 percent each year." And no one had played a bigger role in this rise than Arader himself.

I had already talked with Arader many times over the phone and had twice traveled to his main residence—an eighty-six-acre estate in the rolling horse country of Middleburg, Virginia, one of three homes that he and his wife own—to sit in his map-filled den and talk with him. By now I felt that we were pretty much talked out. I had come to Sotheby's to see him in action.

The final event of the day—a sale devoted to natural history books and atlases, Arader's two main sources of wealth—was soon to begin. At long tables on either side of the auctioneer, flawlessly dressed young Sotheby's employees sat ready to take phone bids from clients around the world. Those who would be bidding on the premises were finding their seats. As he strode into the gallery, Arader was accompanied by his teenage daughter, Lilli, and his cell phone. He would dote on both of them in the moments to come, turning from one to the other with terse but lively observations about ongoing events. He took a conspicuously inconspicuous chair at the very back of the room, next to a couple of clients or maybe prospective clients—a pleasant middle-aged man who told me he was a novice collector of botanical prints and his wife, who was passing the time by doing needlework. They were clearly not regular auction-goers, and when Arader discovered that they did not even have a catalog by which to follow the action, he obligingly scooted off to get them one. A few moments later, as he flipped through its pages, briefing the man on the upcoming items for sale, I saw him stop and jab his finger at one of the images. "It's fabulous!" he whispered. "*Fabulous!*"

It's hard not to use exclamation marks when quoting Graham Arader: they seem to reflect not just the way he speaks (you get the feeling he even snores in superlatives) but his whole presence. Although his college sport was squash—he was captain of the Yale team—the forty-nine-year-old Arader has the hard-eyed, hard-boned look of a boxer, and a combative spirit to go with it. When he is making a particularly strong point about something, he tips back his head and sticks out his square jaw, as if expecting a punch from some unseen enemy and relishing the chance to return it. Even his name carries a certain belligerence: it's pronounced not *air-uh-der* but *uh-raider*, as in someone who attacks his target by storm. And that was precisely what he planned to do here at Sotheby's. "I won't start kicking ass until Lot 553," he had told me a few days earlier. "That's when I'll really start getting nasty. I'll be buying some things—or else prices are going to go very, very high."

Lot 553—a 1748 book of maps and maritime adventure tales by George Anson—was the very first item up for sale in this final phase of the auction. Its number was now posted on a big electronic tote board, designed to convert any bid instantly into its equivalent in pounds, francs, deutsche marks, lire, yen, and zlotys. As the bidding began, Arader's competitors turned toward the auctioneer's podium. Many of them were dressed in upscale suits, a measure of their respect for the august surroundings. Arader himself, I could not help but notice, was heading into battle in a tennis shirt, slightly rumpled green khakis, and a pair of Nikes.

THE FIRST TIME I INTERVIEWED GRAHAM ARADER—I WAS working on the *Outside* magazine story at the time—he used some extremely offensive language to describe a group of people he didn't like. One of the things I greatly admire about Arader is his willingness to speak his mind on almost any subject at almost any time, but these particular words were so objectionable, not to mention bizarre and beside the point, that I probably would not have been able to work them into the article even if I had wanted to. That, however, was not what I told Arader when he called me some time later, asking me to pull the quote. I simply reminded him that our entire conversation had been on the record and that, like any journalist, I could not allow a source to dictate what I wrote or didn't write. At first he began to lose his temper—a legendary trait—but then he calmed down and made me a simple offer: What if he gave me an even more quotable quote on the same general subject? Let me hear it, I said. He did just that. It was indeed more quotable—irresistibly so—and I ended up using it in the article, feeling that I had been very clever in my dealings with him. But months later, when I repeated this anecdote to Hugh Kennedy, a longtime Arader observer, he began to laugh. "See?" Kennedy said. "He's even got *you* buying and selling."

Kennedy knows plenty about such matters, having studied the controversial businessman for years, from the perspective of both employee and author. He worked for Arader from 1987 to 1990, starting out as a gallery assistant and later becoming the director of the Philadelphia office. (Arader also has galleries in Houston, San Francisco, and New York, as well as a kind of up-scale annex, an ornate Beaux Arts town house on Madison Avenue, which he modestly describes as "the single most beautiful house in New York City, without question.") After leaving Arader's service, Kennedy began a career as a novelist. His second book, *Original Color*, published in 1996, tells the story of a high-powered map and print dealer who "pitched fine art with the dogged persistence of a used-car salesman." Kennedy's Arader-inspired character terrifies employees, bends laws, lies to customers, bounces checks, and farts in public—not an entirely complimentary characterization, in short. Nonetheless, it was Graham Arader himself who had insisted that I read the book.

I asked Kennedy why Arader would do that. "Because, in some ways, the book is about him," he replied. "And he is, to a certain extent, self-obsessed. On the other hand, I've met very few people with his charisma. He's completely driven, and can do business any time of the day or night. He also blurs the lines with his clients between vendor-buyer and friend. In any market where you're selling something of premium value, you often need to sell yourself as well as the product. And the entertainment value of Graham is huge. When he's on, he's an enormously fun person to be around, and I think a lot of his clients have stuck with him just for that. They're amused and occasionally delighted by him."

I shared those feelings. Arader could be a shameless flatterer and an equally shameless bully, but there was something very arresting about him nonetheless—not charm, exactly, but a kind of infectious exuberance for everything he said, did, thought, bought, or sold. And somehow, underneath all his seeming self-absorption, he had a skill for listening, for feeling out the needs of others and telling them exactly what they wanted to hear. Even a skeptic like Kennedy was not immune to his almost magical powers of persuasion. Once, on a book tour visit to Philadelphia, Kennedy stopped by to say hello to his former employer. "Within five minutes," Kennedy remembered, "he was offering me a hundred-thousand-dollar-a-year job in the New York gallery, doing sales. I just felt like, 'If I don't get out of this room in five minutes, I'm going to say yes, and I won't even be able to help myself.' There was something bizarre about it."

Arader has used his uncanny charisma to amass a fortune worth, by his own count, $100 million. In doing so, he has led a dramatic transformation in the market for antique maps over the past quarter century, turning a historical artifact into a hip commodity. Before he entered the business in the early 1970s, old maps were mostly the province of librarians, historians, and a few tweedy collectors. One of them was Arader's late father, Walter G. Arader, a successful banker and businessman who began collecting maps in the mid-1960s—a passion that stemmed from his days as a navigator in the Navy. Walter Arader typically paid one or two hundred dollars for individual maps from atlases by great Age of Discovery cartographers such as Willem Janszoon Blaeu, Gerard Mercator, and Abraham Ortelius. Today those same maps are listed in Graham Arader's catalogs for prices ranging from five thousand to fifteen thousand dollars.

The younger Arader got his feet wet in collecting as a teenager, during a year he spent in England before college. While studying at the Canford School in Dorset, he made frequent visits to map and book shops in London, where he carried out buying assignments for his father. It was during this time that he began to become enamored of maps himself. "The first map that I remember being wildly excited about was a map by Christopher Saxton of Dorset, which was printed in London in 1579," Arader remembered. "It had beautiful late Renaissance designs on it and wonderful color. And it also showed where I went to school. Like most people, my interest in maps was very provincial. It was just incredibly exciting for me to buy."

But if Walter Arader saw maps as a fun way to *spend* his riches, his son viewed them as a potential way to *make* his own. When he enrolled at Yale, Graham Arader started to turn his enthusiasm for maps into an enterprise. The school has two great cartographic collections, the Beinecke Rare Book and Manuscript Library and the map room at the Sterling Memorial Library. Together, they house literally hundreds of thousands of rare maps and atlases, including the controversial Vinland Map, reputed (by a dwindling number of experts) to be the only pre-Columbian map showing Norse discoveries in America; groundbreaking New World maps by Henricus Martellus and

Johannes Ruysch; and a one-of-a-kind atlas previously owned by George Washington. The young Arader immediately sought these libraries out, determined to give himself a crash course in cartographic history. The scholars who worked in those secluded haunts were stunned to find a college freshman in their midst, but, as Arader would later explain: "That was my advantage. There were thirty world-class rare book librarians, historians, curators of collections—and nobody had any interest in what they were doing. So here were these lonely men and women, without anyone exhibiting any interest in their work, and then here comes this bright, young, aggressive man deluging them with questions. I'm the only guy in history who used Yale as a trade school."

He was still living in a dormitory when he began his career as a dealer. His initial break came when he cajoled a New Haven bookseller into giving him the names of three members of the Yale medical faculty who had paid to have maps framed at the store: "That's how I got my first customers. I called them up and said, 'Are you interested in collecting maps?' They said they were—and they're still good customers to this day."

In 1973, using a $150,000 loan from his father, Arader set up shop in earnest, issuing his first catalog. Business boomed. "It was incredible," he said of those early days. "You could buy the things very cheaply. You'd buy something for a hundred bucks and sell it for two hundred. You know, you doubled your money pretty easily back then."

But why settle for only two hundred dollars, when you might get a whole lot more for a given map? Arader understood that antique maps prices were low because the market was tiny, and he was determined to expand the base of customers beyond the insular realm of aficionados. Some of his competitors probably had similar aspirations, but few of them had his capital, creativity, or connections—and none of them had his charisma. That was the important thing. Arader realized that through his own hustle, savvy, and force of personality, he could actually *create value.* An experienced collector might not be willing to pay three thousand dollars for a map that Arader had purchased for only a thousand. But a wealthy physician, looking for something interesting and fashionable to hang in his waiting room, might indeed be willing to spend that much—especially on a map that came with the imprimatur of W. Graham Arader III, a dealer known to carry only the finest merchandise and devote his considerable energy, talent, and knowledge to only the most exclusive clients. And eventually— after Arader was able to make a few more such sales, *and* after other dealers adjusted their prices accordingly—the map was no longer worth a thousand dollars in anyone's mind. It was now a three-thousand-dollar map—that is, until Arader decided to ask nine thousand for it.

By reaching out to nonexperts with cash to burn and corporations with offices to decorate, Arader has been able to steadily increase the demand for old maps. In so doing he has made many of his clients, not to mention some of his competitors, considerably more wealthy. He also has helped give antique maps unprecedented visibility, not only as investments ("These Old Maps Offer You a New Way to Double Your

Money," read one optimistic headline from the March 1997 issue of *Money* magazine) but as mass-media artifacts. You can now find images of historic maps on greeting cards and wrapping paper, T-shirts and photo albums, coffee mugs and clockfaces, popcorn canisters and computer mouse pads. You can see them in casinos and coffeehouses, children's books and *Playboy* magazine spreads. They have quietly become pop culture icons.

Arader has also helped transform other markets—most notably, the one for prints by John James Audubon and other natural history artists. These days, the biggest share of his business comes from such works. Antique maps total only about 20 percent of his trade. Nonetheless, he insists that "maps are my first love and always will be my first love."

Love, however, is a complicated thing. For all the time and passion Graham Arader has poured into the world of antique maps, the world of antique maps has shown him precious little gratitude. Respect, maybe, but not gratitude. And certainly not love.

ONE WAY OF MAKING A BID AT SOTHEBY'S IS TO TAKE THE little paddle provided by the auction house specifically for that purpose and raise it into the air. This is the method of the inexperienced and unhip. Those in the know rely on subtler techniques: the pointedly flicked wrist, for instance, or the pithily raised finger. Graham Arader doesn't use his hands at all. He bids with his head. A quick nod, accompanied by a fiery stare over his reading glasses, indicates that he is willing to top the previous bid; a side-to-side shake, so slight he seems to be experiencing nothing more than a sudden draft, means that he is bowing out. As the auction progressed that afternoon, Arader's skull was in a constant state of jiggle. He looked like a very tightly sprung version of one of those Bobbin' Heads dolls.

He did not purchase Lot 553, the first work up for bid, but he did buy the next two items—a nineteenth-century book of bird engravings by Jean Baptiste Audebert and Louis-Jean Pierre Vieillot for $7,500; and a first edition of John James Audubon and John Bachman's *The Viviparous Quadrupeds of North America* for $200,000. Arader was just getting started. In a flurry of spending over the next few minutes, he would snap up Mathew Carey's *Carey's American Atlas* for $2,000; Mark Catesby's *The Natural History of Carolina, Florida and the Bahama Islands* for $100,000; and John Gould's *A Monograph of the Trochilidae, or Family of Humming-Birds*, again for $100,000. On a number of other items—including natural history books by George Edwards and Gould; lithographs of Native Americans by George Catlin; and travelogues by Captain James Cook—he would help to drive the bidding up, often pulling out at the very last opportunity.

On Lot 585—the geologist and mapmaker Ferdinand V. Hayden's 1876 book on Yellowstone National Park—Arader won the bidding, then immediately reached for his cell phone. "You got it. One hundred and fifteen thousand," he barked to a client whom he was representing at the auction (and whom he later identified as Mark Rockefeller, Nelson's son). "Congratulations."

As he was finishing the call, another man strolled by him on his way out of the gallery. "Quiet, Graham," the man said, apparently in jest.

"You want me to be quiet? All right." I couldn't tell whether Arader had taken it as a friendly gibe or an insult. Whatever the case, his voice was noticeably louder when he added, ever so slowly, *"I'll be as quiet as you please."*

It was obvious that he did not consider the other bidders here his friends. He was not above slapping a few backs and shaking a few hands, but, in general, he kept his distance from them, and they kept their distance from him. (One of the other participants, who had noticed me taking notes on Arader, later pulled me aside. "That guy's crazy, you know," he said. "Did he use any foul language when you talked to him?") Taking all this in, I was reminded of a conversation I had had with Arader a few weeks earlier.

"What about the claim that you're abrasive?" I had asked.

"I *am* abrasive!" he replied. "I don't have time to be nice to my competitors. So I agree with that: I'm abrasive."

"Ruthless? Cutthroat?"

"I'm not ruthless. I'm a businessman. Tell the people who call me ruthless to get into the bond market or the stock market. You want to see ruthless? Tell them to try to compete against Bill Gates selling software. I'm a cupcake compared to real ruthlessness. I will buy whatever I can that's of high quality. So I guess they call it ruthless when I buy all the good things that come up at auction. They end up going home with nothing; I end up going home with everything. Is that ruthless? No. It's business."

I could not deny it: this pretty well described what was happening here at Sotheby's. But I also knew that while simple jealousy did explain some critics' resentment of Arader, others had real philosophical differences with him, not to mention longstanding concerns about his ethics. In 1983, for example, the Antiquarian Booksellers' Association of America drummed him from its ranks. The ouster stemmed from a feud between Arader and a Dutch bookseller who had sent him a five-volume set of John Gould hummingbirds (similar to the one he purchased today at Sotheby's for a cool hundred grand). Arader had decided that the books were in unsatisfactory condition—and, in a typical moment of pugnacity, returned them to Amsterdam third-class and uninsured. The genteel governors of the ABAA found this slight unpardonable. They booted Arader—after which he upped the stakes by filing suit against the group. He lost, and wound up having to pay the ABAA's legal fees as well as his own, to the tune of fifty thousand dollars.

If the incident cemented Arader's bad-boy reputation—an image he clearly relishes—it also added to concerns about his business practices. And of those practices few have been as controversial as a tactic he made famous early in his career. It is known by a number of euphemisms: book breaking, disbinding, discollating, and liberating from bound portfolio. Purists simply call it destroying books.

Graham Arader never claimed to be a purist, however, and when he was trying to make a name for himself in the 1970s, the sum value of the individual maps from an atlas was often greater than the value of the atlas itself. Predictably, Arader acted as businessman, not as bibliophile: he would buy up atlases and other art books, cut them apart, and sell off the plates one by one. He did not invent the concept—in fact, people have been breaking books for centuries—but he put it into practice so methodically and on such a large scale that, to this day, some lovers of literature still refuse to forgive him.

True, Arader's competitors might break an occasional atlas, especially if it already had missing plates or was otherwise damaged. But Arader systematically purchased pristine volumes with the express purpose of demolishing them. In one such instance, a fellow dealer named Bill Reese watched him break a first edition of John Smith's 1624 work, *Generall Historie of Virginia, New-England, and the Summer Isles.* Reese later told *The New Yorker* how Arader laid the book on a counter and began to massage its "gutter," or inner margins. "I said, 'Graham, what are you doing?' He said, 'What do you think I'm doing, Billy? I'm testing the strength of the binding.' Then—r-r-r-ip!—he razors the son of a bitch out."

It sounds ugly. Yet the more I looked into the matter, the more I wondered whether Arader really deserves to go down in infamy as the Bogeyman of Book Breaking. A great deal of hypocrisy surrounds this issue, as I once learned at a map fair where a California dealer named Robert Ross hosted a seminar on collecting. Someone asked Ross about the dreaded practice of cutting. He responded by telling a story about a time when he himself almost broke a low-quality atlas. "I had the knife out ready to go, but I couldn't do it," he said. "I put the knife back, because the atlas was complete."

But if Ross was hesitant to slice up atlases with his own hands, he seemed more than willing to let others do the dirty work. Most of the items hanging on the walls of his booth at the fair appeared to be from broken books, and the same was true for virtually every other dealer at the event. The reason was simple: precious few stand-alone antique maps are in circulation. Without broken books, the antique maps trade would virtually cease to exist.

So many atlases have been broken, in fact, the practice is becoming increasingly unprofitable—even for Graham Arader. "I don't break books anymore. I don't have to," he said. "Books are worth more than the sum of the parts at this point. Is it how I made my money in the first place? You bet your ass it is. Do I feel badly about it? Yes, I do feel badly about it. Looking back now from a very secure and lofty perch, I can say I wish I hadn't been able to do it. But I couldn't have made it without doing it. I mean, you could buy one of these atlases for ten thousand dollars and break it for a hundred thousand. It was wild. Now you buy one of these books for a hundred and fifty thousand and it breaks for ninety thousand. You just don't do it."

He insists he has not broken "a complete, perfect atlas" in more than ten years. And yet questions about his ethics linger— in part, because he keeps getting embroiled in new controversies. In 1996, for example, Arader reportedly sent a check for

$8,000 to a woman as payment for a 160-year-old map, believed to be the earliest plan of the city of Houston. He then had the piece restored and, in a quintessential application of Araderian economics, put it back on the market for $98,000. ("Yeah, I tried to buy it as cheaply as possible," he later told me. "Yeah, I low-balled it. . . . I paid as little as I could for it, to put it bluntly. Who am I going to take advantage of the most: the people I buy from or the people I sell to? . . . Because, boy, I'll sure as hell lose a client if I sell him something at more than it would go for at auction.") At that point the story took a strange turn. A Houston man named John Fox filed suit against Arader, claiming that the map rightfully belonged to him. Fox said that his sister-in-law had taken the map to Arader, and that she had done so to have it appraised, not to sell it. The suit was settled in Fox's favor: Arader agreed to ship it back and pay court costs. But then the story took a second curious twist. Employees of the Houston Title Company, who had read about the legal battle in a local newspaper, began to wonder whether the map was the same one that had disappeared some years earlier from their office, where Fox had once worked. It turned out that their suspicions were well-grounded. After confidential negotiations, Houston Title got back its map, and Fox (who claimed he had purchased the map from the company) never faced criminal charges.

For his part, Arader cooperated with police to ensure that the map was returned to its rightful owner—just as he had done in a number of similar cases. "To this day," he later said, "I am furious that they did not prosecute Fox. . . . The whole bad taste in my mouth from the thing is that the FBI and local police chose to let the case drop because the people at Houston Title wanted to sweep the thing under the rug, since they were embarrassed about it." Yet the incident also revived old questions about the dealer himself. Had he dealt honestly with the woman who brought him the map? Did he have clear ownership when he put it up for sale? Had he been aware that only one other copy of the map—a later version at the Houston Public Library—was known to exist? And, if so, had he done enough to check its provenance?

These are all, of course, important concerns. But what people will remember most about the incident, I suspect, is that whopping ninety-thousand-dollar markup on the map, that in-your-face 1,225 percent price hike. It may not be fair to hold Graham Arader entirely responsible for inflation in the antique maps trade. Yet as I watched him at Sotheby's that day, buying up many items and bidding up others, it occurred to me that nothing—not his egotism or abrasiveness, not his book breaking or business imbroglios—has earned him more enemies. Yes, the changing market has spawned some big winners, not the least of them being Arader himself. But it has also created a lot of losers, among them middle-class collectors who no longer have access to the kinds of maps they once could easily afford, and small-scale dealers who find themselves without the capital to maintain adequate inventory. These are the same people who used to form the backbone of the industry—scholars and aficionados who care about maps primarily for their historic and aesthetic, not economic, value. They may have helped kick

Arader out of the ABAA—but in a more profound way he not only forced his way into their refined little world but took it over. It's no wonder they regard him with contempt.

Arader seems well aware of this. I once asked him: "Has map collecting changed much since you began?"

"Yeah. You've got to be richer," he said. "Stuff has gone up faster than inflation. So a little librarian in Urbana, Illinois, who ten years ago was buying twenty maps with his twenty-thousand-dollar-per-year budget, is now buying one map."

True enough. But for librarians in particular that's not the worst thing about rising prices. The worst thing about rising prices is that they have transformed libraries into gold mines, books into illicit booty, and patrons into crooks. If the librarians hate Arader, it's not because he's made it harder for them to buy books but because they're having one hell of a time holding on to the ones already on their shelves.

A DRAMATIC EXAMPLE OF THE WAY IN WHICH OLD MAPS are becoming big business was about to play out at Sotheby's. Lot 599 was an edition of the ancient scholar Ptolemy's famous map book, *Geographia* (also known as *Cosmographia*), printed in Ulm in 1482. If you wanted to buy this volume in 1884, it would have set you back $85. It went for $350 in 1901, $3,000 in 1933, $5,000 in 1950, $28,000 in 1965, and $42,500 in 1984. Today, the catalog listed an estimated price range of between $200,000 and $300,000.

"On the other hand, it is an extraordinarily fine copy, it's in a contemporary binding, and it has already received a great deal of interest," Selby Kiffer, a Sotheby's official, had told me a few days earlier. "One never knows what will happen at an auction, but I do think that this is a case where competitive bidding could push price beyond estimate range."

From the start, it was clear that Kiffer's hunch was right. The bidding began at $100,000 but quickly moved past $150,000, then $200,000, then $250,000. A sense of urgency filled the gallery, as bids came in quick succession, from the floor and over the phone.

For once not even Graham Arader was willing to keep pace with the competition. He dropped out around $300,000.

The bidding continued to rise . . .

It was hardly the first time buyers had clamored to get their hands on a copy of *Geographia*. The work, in fact, holds a central place in the history of collecting, as well as the history of cartography. Its author, Claudius Ptolemy, was one of the ancient world's most intriguing and shadowy figures. Little is known about his life, other than that he lived in Alexandria during the second century A.D., was of Greek descent and was a Roman citizen. Nonetheless, he left behind a brilliant and wide-ranging body of work about astronomy, optics, mathematics, music, and geography. *Geographia*—a kind of empirical how-to guide for map drawing—is considered the high-water mark of ancient earth knowledge. Ptolemy systematized cartography by insisting that maps be drawn to scale and that they be oriented to the north. He was one of the first to offer a projection by which a spherical earth could be rendered on a flat surface.

Island of Lost Maps

WORLD MAP FROM
THE 1482 ULM
EDITION OF
PTOLEMY'S
GEOGRAPHIA.

He also abandoned the Homeric conception that the known world (Europe, Asia, and Africa) was surrounded by an uninhabitable ocean. This left open the theoretical possibility of further discoveries. "More than any one of the ancients," concluded the map historian Lloyd A. Brown, "Claudius Ptolemy succeeded in establishing the elements and form of scientific cartography."

But *Geographia* might not have been remembered that way if not for the efforts of some passionate collectors more than a thousand years later. It might not have been remembered at all. Like many great works of antiquity, *Geographia* simply disappeared from the European consciousness after the fall of Rome. Its concepts, meanwhile, were kept alive by Arab geographers, who translated Ptolemy's cartographic masterpiece around the ninth century and incorporated its concepts into their own maps. Then, in the thirteenth century, a Byzantine scholar and monk named Maximus Planudes found a long-forgotten copy of the work. According to Planudes' account of the discovery, the manuscript was not accompanied by maps. (Indeed, modern scholars doubt whether Ptolemy ever included maps with the work.) Nonetheless, Planudes set about drafting a series of maps designed to portray the world as Ptolemy would have drawn it himself. This was possible because Ptolemy had made the effort to include the geographical coordinates of eight thousand places throughout the world, so that someone in another place—even another century—could create maps on the basis of the text alone. I like to imagine Planudes in his little chamber, plotting coordinate after painstaking coordinate, then

at last stepping back from his work, the whole world suddenly
appearing before his eyes.

. . . $325,000.

$350,000.

$375,000.

$400,000 . . .

Planudes was an omnivorous collector of ancient manuscripts, who could often be found scouring the bazaars of Constantinople for the works of great classical writers. In addition
to translating many works from Latin into Greek, he put together a number of anthologies of lasting importance, including a compilation of Greek prose and poetry, a volume of
Aesop's fables, and the marvelously titled *Very Useful Collection
Gathered from Various Books.* In his determined pursuit of classical texts, Planudes was a spiritual and intellectual forerunner of
the great scholar-collectors of the fourteenth, fifteenth, and sixteenth centuries, who, through "grinding persistence . . . in the
recovery, collation, criticism, and publication of texts," transformed "the study of the ancient world into a cultural force,"
wrote the historian John Hale in *The Civilization of Europe in the
Renaissance.* Not the least of these men was the Italian poet Petrarch, famous for his collection of—and obsession with—ancient texts. "Please, if you love me," Petrarch wrote to a friend
sometime around the year 1346, "find people who are educated
and trustworthy and set them to scour Tuscany, to turn out the
book-cases of the monks and all the other scholars, and see if
anything comes to light which will serve to quench—or, shall I
say, increase—my thirst."

. . . $425,000.

$450,000.

$475,000.

$500,000 . . .

Petrarch confessed that his urge to obtain books was an "insatiable desire which I so far have been quite unable to control." Such compulsions would soon be the norm, as the Renaissance gave rise to an unprecedented culture of collecting. No longer did people seek out art and artifacts solely for their devotional purposes but for their intellectual, historical, scientific, aesthetic, nostalgic, or commercial significance. This collecting ethos—as exemplified by the "cabinets of curiosities" placed prominently in homes of the wealthy—began with an interest in ancient books, gems, coins, vases, and sculpture, then grew to encompass contemporary paintings, clocks, and scientific instruments, and, finally, expanded into what Hale described as "rare, valuable, or merely strange objects from the natural world," from shells and fossils to stuffed toucans and mummified Egyptian cats.

. . . $525,000.

$550,000.

$575,000.

$600,000 . . .

Geographia was at the center of this collecting craze. Around 1400 a copy of the text was brought from Constantinople to Florence, where, translated from Greek into Latin, it "caused an immediate and enormous stir," wrote Thomas Goldstein in *Dawn of Modern Science*. Hand-copied, hand-illustrated versions quickly began to circulate in Western Europe, usually with maps based on those of Planudes. As Lisa Jardine observed in *Worldly Goods: A New History of the Renaissance:*

> Apart from the extravagant Bibles, the ancient scientist and cartographer Ptolemy's *Geography,* complete with coloured and illuminated maps of the known world, took pride of place in a surprisingly large number of great men's libraries. The *Geography,* too, was an extremely expensive purchase, since some copies contained as many as sixty individual maps, each of which had to be accurately drawn and locations precisely marked before the delicate business of colouring and decorating could even be begun.

The first printed edition of *Geographia* appeared (without maps) in 1475, just two decades after the publication of Gutenberg's Bible, and the same year that presses were being set up for the first time in places like Holland and England. Numerous illustrated editions soon followed, making *Geographia* one of history's earliest bestsellers. The popular 1482 Ulm edition—the one on sale today at Sotheby's—was the first to be printed outside of Italy and helped spur the widespread dissemination of the book, with profound consequences. Wrote the historian Daniel J. Boorstin:

> The revival of Ptolemy . . . would mean the awakening, or the reawakening, of the empirical spirit. Now men

would use their experience to measure the whole earth, to mark off the known from the unknown, and to designate newfound places for return. The rediscovery of Ptolemy was a signal event in the revival of learning that marked the Renaissance, a prologue to the modern world.

Spain's King Ferdinand and Queen Isabella ordered their copy of *Geographia* from a Valencian bookseller. The monarchs' interest stemmed from their discussions with an ambitious Italian sailor who claimed he could reach the spice-rich Indies by heading west instead of east. Christopher Columbus had, in part, based these ideas on what would later prove to be two of Ptolemy's most famous mistakes: (1) a gross underestimate of the Earth's circumference, and (2) a gross overestimate of the eastward reach of Asia. In 1492, after much procrastination and debate, the Spanish sovereigns commissioned Columbus to sail with three caravels "toward the regions of India." He never reached his destination.

. . . $625,000.

$650,000.

$675,000.

$700,000 . . .

The Renaissance cult of acquisition had a dark side as well. Compulsive collecting could sometimes degenerate into theft—and some of the great writers and scholars of the age apparently succumbed to this urge. Giovanni Boccaccio, author of the *Decameron* and a friend of Petrarch, is thought to have pillaged a monastic library in his quest to obtain a previously undiscovered piece of classical literature. Poggio Bracciolini, one of the most famous bibliophiles of his time, justified his apparent theft from another monastic library by asserting that the books "were not housed according to their worth, but were lying in a most foul and obscure dungeon . . . a place into which condemned criminals would hardly have been thrust." Needless to say, those in charge of such collections had a different view—as expressed by an inscription at the library of the San Pedro monastery in Barcelona:

For him that steals, or borrows and returns not, a book from its owner, let it change into a serpent in his hand and rend him. Let him be struck with palsy, and all his members blasted. Let him languish in pain crying aloud for mercy, and let there be no surcease to his agony till he sing in dissolution. Let bookworms gnaw at his entrails in token of the Worm that dieth not. And when at last he goes to his final punishment, let the flames of Hell consume him for ever.

. . . $725,000.
$750,000.
$775,000.
$800,000 . . .

The month before the Sotheby's sale, another version of *Geographia* was to have gone on the auction block at Christie's in London. This was an even rarer edition, published in Bologna in 1477 and considered the first-ever printed atlas. Only a few copies survive, meaning the auction would have been an extraordinary event—if it had happened. But it did not happen. It was canceled at the last minute, when Christie's conceded the volume had been stolen nearly a year earlier from France's National Library. That disappearance itself had a bizarre twist: for about three months library officials had simply failed to notice that one of the most important volumes in history was gone. Yet after the theft was discovered in November 1997, it had been widely publicized. It is hard to imagine that Christie's officials did not know about it. Nonetheless, they had apparently accepted at face value the false ownership papers of a Frenchman who brought them the book. According to press reports, the sale had not been canceled until French authorities intervened.

Reading about this debacle a few weeks before the New York auction, I had naturally wondered about the provenance of the Sotheby's *Geographia*. I checked the auction catalog. The most recent owner it listed was a man named Georg Joachim Scherer. He had possessed the book in 1713.

I asked Selby Kiffer of Sotheby's whether his firm would provide me with information about the current owner. No luck. "The confidentiality of both our purchasers and our consignors is something we take seriously," he insisted.

Kiffer, however, was reassuring: "Knowing the consignor of this book as I do, and knowing the history of his family's collecting, there's certainly no doubt in my mind that it's a privately owned copy."

In other words, I would have to take his word for it. I had ab-

solutely no reason to doubt him. But I would have had no reason to doubt Christie's, either.

. . . $825,000

$850,000.

$875,000.

$900,000 . . .

The auctioneer was speaking slowly now, leaving dramatic
pauses to underscore the immensity of the bids. His voice was
calibrated and quiet; it was the only sound in the room. The
competition had come down to two phone bidders, and all eyes
were on their respective representatives, seated on each side of
the podium.

. . . $925,000.

$950,000.

$975,000.

$1,000,000.

$1,050,000.

$1,100,000.

$1,150,000.

The auctioneer waited, but no new offer came. At last he
slammed down his hammer. *Sold.* There was a pause, and then
those in the gallery began to applaud, slowly at first and then
with real enthusiasm. They had just witnessed history. Once
mandatory fees were added, the sale would come to
$1,267,500—a world record for an atlas printed on paper. (In
1990, a scarce copy of the 1482 Ptolemy—printed on an animal-
skin parchment known as vellum—was sold for $1,925,000.)

If Arader was impressed, he didn't show it. I asked him if he was surprised by the sale. "Not a bit," he shot back cheerily. "I *knew* it was going to go for a million. It was a once-in-a-lifetime opportunity for somebody."

Others, however, were clearly in a state of shock. One dealer was slouching out of the gallery when his eyes caught Arader's.

"Twilight Zone," he mumbled, in a dazed, singsongy voice. And then he left, shaking his head.

BY THE END OF THE AFTERNOON, THE BILL FOR Graham Arader's shopping spree at Sotheby's had come to nearly $800,000; roughly half of that was spent to increase his own inventory and half to purchase works on behalf of clients. One of his last purchases of the day was Christopher Saxton's 1579 book, *An Atlas of England and Wales*. It struck me as a perfect symbol of how far Arader had come. More than twenty-five years earlier a "wildly excited" teenager had got his start in collecting by purchasing a map of Dorset from the same edition of Saxton. He had paid $250 for it. Now that same map would sell for $5,500. Back then the entire atlas would have been worth $47,000. Today at Sotheby's, Arader paid $150,000 for it—and, in fairly short order, was asking $450,000.

Looking back on Arader's career, Hugh Kennedy once compared his former boss to Microsoft founder Bill Gates. Each man, he observed, had transformed his respective industry through his own vision and force of will. I thought the comparison was apt in another way, too. Like Arader, Gates had become a lightning rod for resentment. Some was well-justified and well-reasoned—but much was an unfocused rage, expressed in everything from the "Punch Bill Gates" Web page or "I Hate Bill Gates.com" to a real-life 1998 attack on the computer mogul by a group of cream-pie-wielding Belgian anarchists.

It occurred to me that beneath this anger was a lot of envy. We dislike successful entrepreneurs like Arader and Gates, in part, because somewhere in our dark hearts we want to be like them. We wish we had their foresight and confidence, maybe even their ruthlessness, their ability to spot an opportunity and grab it. It angers us that we came on the scene too late, that the doors are now closed, that the money has been made, the power taken, the fame handed out. In many ways these men are heirs to the explorers who first came to this country, brash mercenaries like de Soto and Coronado. We may revile them for their crassness, their avarice, their destructiveness, but who doesn't yearn to have been in their shoes as they strode deep into blank spots on the map?

Our resentment can take warped forms. According to the FBI, computer financial crimes and infrastructure attacks more than quadrupled between 1996 and 1998, as frustrated Bill Gates wanna-bes poured their energies into the electronic underworld of hacking. And Graham Arader wanna-bes? In the words of the map impresario himself: "Someone who comes along who's not well-educated, whose father beat them growing up, who's twisted, but has the same passion for maps I had without any of my advantages, is going to steal them."

DETAILS FROM A 1511
WORLD MAP BY
BERNARDO SYLVANUS.

Island of Lost Maps

CHAPTER 4

An Approaching Storm

ZEPHYRUS, FROM THE WEST; BOREAS, FROM the north; Notus, from the south; Eurus, from the east—in Greek mythology, these four deities shared the empire of the winds. Sons of Eos and Astraeus—the dawn and the starry sky—they provided the ancient world with a sense of order. True, Boreas could be nasty and vindictive, chilling the Earth with icy blasts from the north. But on the whole he and his brothers were a hugely positive force, helping to organize human labor, fertilize crops, and orient the routes of navigation. Such powerful icons were these wind gods, in fact, that they reappeared in the Middle Ages and Renaissance, this time on the edges of European maps.

On some maps they took the form of stern old fellows with shaggy beards; on others, flaxen-haired cherubs with playfully pursed lips; on still others, robust men with feathers blooming from their necks, symbolizing their role as God's "wings." Eventually, the original four wind blowers were joined by more of their kind, some shifting positions, others changing names, until there were as many as thirty-two faces surrounding some maps. They were not there merely for decoration, however. Their purpose was all-important: to serve as direction markers. "The Spanish sailors on Columbus' crew thought of direction not as degrees of compass bearings but as *los vientos,* the winds," wrote Daniel J. Boorstin in *The Discoverers.* "Portuguese sailors continued to call their compass card a *rosa dos ventos,* a wind rose. When the religious brotherhood of pilots commissioned the Madonna for their chapel in Cordova, it was no accident that she was *Nuestra Señora del Buen Aire,* 'Our Lady of the Fair Wind.' "

Not all winds were fair, however. Consider the Harpies. They, too, were classical wind deities, but you won't find them on old maps. That's because the sailors and adventurers wouldn't have wanted to think about these tempest-goddesses, much less look at them. The Harpies had the faces of old women, the ears of bears, and the bodies of birds, with long, hooked claws. Their stench was said to be so vile that it would sicken all living creatures. Even their names—Okypete (Rapid), Celaeno (Blackness), and Aello (Storm)—inspired fear. Combining the primitive concepts of wind spirits and predatory ghosts with the actual characteristics of carrion birds, the Harpies brought nothing but disaster and misfortune.

Fair winds or foul? The answer to this question has determined the fate of many a journey—even, perhaps, Gilbert

Bland's own odd version of an epic adventure. And up until that day in downtown Baltimore, we can only conclude that the gods had been extremely kind to our mysterious hero. Zephyrus and his brothers had ushered him safely to and fro across the continent, with stops in Seattle and Charlottesville and Chicago and Vancouver and several other apparent ports of plunder. He had been lucky. Any of a million little things could have failed him—a fumbled razor blade, an inopportune rustling of paper, an unseen security camera—but, miraculously, everything had gone off without a hitch. Or maybe he considered it a matter not of miracles but of his own skill. Maybe, as he emerged undetected from the tenth, eleventh, twelfth, thirteenth, fourteenth, or fifteenth library, he began to feel invincible—or, even more intoxicating to him, invisible. Yes, that seems right: he was suffering from hubris, that prideful arrogance which spelled doom for so many a hero of Greek tragedy, causing him to ignore warnings that might have averted disaster.

Now it was too late for warnings. The winds had changed, and three foreboding figures suddenly stood before Gilbert Bland on the steps of the Walters Art Gallery. To you and me those three would have looked like slightly exhausted security guards. But Bland could be excused if, in his panic and confusion, they suddenly seemed like creatures surreal and terrifying, with whetted talons ready to tear him asunder. When the Baltimore city police arrived at the Peabody Library a short while later, they found a suspect who was sheepish and scared and apparently ready to cooperate. He admitted his name was not

James Perry, as indicated on the University of Florida ID card he had presented to library officials earlier in the day. (Like the name, the card would prove to be a complete fake.) His real identity, he confessed, was Gilbert Joseph Bland, Jr., and he showed police and security officials a Florida driver's license bearing that name. According to library staff members, the man offered no other excuse for taking the maps than that he "just wanted them."

It must have seemed to him just then that there was no way out. He had been caught red-handed with stolen maps, sliced from one of the books he was known to have examined earlier in the day, a 1763 work entitled *The General History of the Late War.* A reliable witness had seen the crime take place, and fingerprint and handwriting evidence would almost certainly further tie him to the scene. The winds of doom now seemed to be blasting through that library, swirling and shrieking. And then, just as it seemed they would lift him off his feet and batter him away to some horrible fate, they suddenly ceased their rage. A calm returned to the room. The police were talking about letting him go.

In his desperation Bland had offered to pay the library—on the spot and in cash—to repair the damaged books, and the cops seemed to think it was a pretty good deal. They had more important things to worry about than Gilbert Bland. Murders had risen nearly 9 percent in the city and its surrounding counties in the first nine months of 1995, compared with the same period of the previous year. Robbery, aggravated assault, and other crime categories were also on the rise. Nor was the

Mount Vernon neighborhood, which had once been among the city's most exclusive enclaves, immune from the problem. Tourists, students, and suburbanites—drawn to the area by attractions such as the famous Peabody Conservatory of Music— were often targeted for robbery or worse.

No wonder the officers did not seem particularly concerned about the meek and skittish man they found at the library. Well-dressed, polite, and obviously humiliated, he looked about as much like a menace to society as the Peabody Library looked like a crack house. And after all, what had he allegedly done? Taken a few pages out of a book? Stolen *four sheets of paper*? There were dangerous people out there—crazy, desperate, dangerous people with guns. This poor guy hardly seemed worth the bother.

But if the police had their own reasons for letting the matter slide, they also had some very practical concerns about how the case would play out, especially given that the suspect lived out of state and might skip out on his bail, with little practical possibility of extradition. "We were advised by the city officers who came that, with this kind of crime, we were running the risk that, if we placed charges, he would make bail and never show up [for trial] and we would get no recompense of any kind," Dennis O'Shea, a Johns Hopkins spokesman, later explained.

Wouldn't accepting the money in lieu of Bland's immediate arrest be easier for everyone involved? The library would get its book repaired; the crook would learn a frightening and costly lesson; the police would have that much less paperwork, that much more time to focus on real criminals. For their part, library officials thought the idea was at least worth considering. They telephoned a lawyer and mulled over their options, Gilbert Bland's fate still blowing in the wind.

*W*HAT TO DO ABOUT BLAND WAS JUST THE LATEST IN A series of difficult decisions that those who ran the Peabody had been forced to make in recent years. For the better part of this century, things at the library had been headed pretty steadily downhill. By 1910 the Peabody Institute was devoting more and more funds to its famous music conservatory, fewer and fewer to the collection. By 1940 new book buying had petered out almost entirely. By 1960 the library—full of dusty old books that no one could check out—had fallen into an alarming state of neglect. "Basically, nobody was using it," explained Cynthia Requardt, curator of special collections at Johns Hopkins University's Milton S. Eisenhower Library. Worse yet, the Peabody Institute no longer had the funds to adequately maintain the beautiful old building.

Cutting its losses, the Institute's board of trustees voted in 1966 to hand the Peabody over to Baltimore's public library system. It turned out to be an ill-suited marriage, one that the library barely survived intact. Shortly after the merger city officials gave serious thought to auctioning off the library's most valuable books, shuffling the rest into the public system, and converting the building into a study hall for high school students. If this caused a furious commotion inside the late Mr. Peabody's grave, it also triggered an uproar in the local academic community, and the scheme was duly abandoned. In the 1970s a fund-raising effort enabled the library to patch the building up a bit, install air-conditioning, and rebind a few hundred books. But as the city's budget tightened bureaucrats decided they could no longer justify the expense of the facility. In 1982 they turned it over to the special collections division at Johns Hopkins University.

This proved to be a much better match in terms of overall philosophy—but the library's financial troubles remained. The university reported that it was pumping between three and four hundred thousand dollars into the facility each year—and even that was not enough. Among other problems, the roof, with its hard-to-repair skylight, was leaking. "The [Grand Stack Room] was opened in 1878 and I'm not sure if the roof had ever been replaced," said Requardt, the Hopkins official who now oversees the Peabody.

To librarians a leaky roof is no small problem. Moisture is the enemy; it causes dampstaining, foxing, and mildew, all of which can stain and destroy paper and some of which are contagious, infecting nearby books with their harmful spores. It takes a lot of effort to defend against these foes, and a lot of money. The temperature and humidity must be precisely controlled—not an easy thing to do in balmy Baltimore, not with a leaky roof, and especially not in a place like the Peabody Library. "It's just an incredibly expensive building to run," explained Requardt. "It's a nineteenth-century building that's on the National Register of Historic Places, so there are certain restraints on what you can and cannot do."

By 1989 the building and the books were at such risk that university officials decided something drastic had to be done. They opted for an approach so controversial it is known in some quarters simply as the "D-word." That stands for deaccessioning, and if you are baffled by the euphemism, think uncollecting or anti-obtaining or conserving in reverse. Put simply, Hopkins was planning to sell rare books in order to save rare books. University officials announced that Sotheby's in New York would be auctioning off ten of the Peabody's books, consisting of sixty-seven volumes, as part of an effort to raise at least $2 million toward a $4 million endowment fund for the library. Included in that group were two copies of Hartmann Schedel's 1493 *Nuremberg Chronicle,* which contains one of the most important early printed maps of the world, as well as works by the photographer Edward Curtis and the nature artists John James Audubon, Mark Catesby, and John Gould.

Hopkins officials insisted they had no choice: the very future of the Peabody Library was at stake. "Our goal is to try to find ways to preserve [the library]," the university provost, John Lombardi, told the Baltimore *Sun.* He claimed the sale would maintain the library "with a minimum amount of change and a maximum amount of preservation and access." Officials also were quick to point out that all the books to be sold were duplicated in other Hopkins collections. Nonetheless, the announcement touched off a firestorm of criticism, typified by the blunt words of John Burgan, chief librarian at the public library in Hartford, Connecticut: "It borders on the rape of a great library collection."

To Burgan and other foes of the move, deaccessioning in order to preserve the library was like burning clapboards in order to warm a house. "The Peabody Library is one of the great treasures of the United States, and once you sell off the rare books you might as well close the library, because that's the uniqueness of it," declared Regina Soria, professor emeritus of modern languages at the College of Notre Dame.

But deaccessioning accounted for only part of the furor. Other museums and libraries had sold off some of their collections to make ends meet; in many people's minds the practice was ugly and unfortunate, but perhaps not unforgivable. No, what critics really found offensive was that Hopkins planned not just to sell historic old volumes but to cut them up beforehand. That's right: book breaking—not by some profit-obsessed dealer but by one of the oldest and most respected libraries in the United States. One of the books scheduled to go under the knife was Audubon's *Birds of America*. The Peabody's copy was extremely rare—one of only two in the world that contained Audubon's signature on all four volumes. Nonetheless, Hopkins and Sotheby's planned to gut the four-volume set so that its 435 prints could be sold separately. "That's disgraceful," Arthur Gutman, a member of the Johns Hopkins University Library Advisory Council, told the *Sun*. "It ought to be sold, if it has to be sold, to a sister institution, and not broken up."

Despite all objections, the sale went forward, raising a total of $2.4 million and allowing Hopkins to keep the building and the collection open to the public. One print alone, "American Flamingo" from *Birds of America,* fetched $66,550—a record at the time for a single Audubon. The buyer was a fellow named Graham Arader.

But while such head-snapping sums were a godsend for the Peabody in the short run—enabling Hopkins to pay for everything from staff salaries to upkeep of the physical plant—they posed a serious long-term threat to libraries across the country, which faced increasingly tough security concerns as the value of their collections skyrocketed. The Peabody itself had been saved, but its once stellar reputation had been noticeably damaged.

Now, as they questioned Gilbert Bland, Peabody officials faced yet another tough choice. Had they been aware that their decision would touch off another controversy, they would undoubtedly have given it more thought. But they had no notion of what—and whom—they were dealing with. "Frankly, my sense of it was that we had caught a bumbling, stumbling amateur," said Frederick DeKuyper, associate general counsel for Johns Hopkins University, whom Peabody officials consulted in the immediate aftermath of Bland's detention. "None of us at the time knew of his past activities."

After conferring with security officials, DeKuyper signed off on a plan to forgo Bland's arrest in return for seven hundred dollars in damages. The suspect, who was reportedly carrying large amounts of cash, was more than happy with the deal. With the gods apparently smiling down upon him once again, he fled the library in a hurry—too much of a hurry, as it turned out.

ERE'S THE THING ABOUT THE HARPIES: THEY SCREW with your head. Known by ancients as the Snatchers because they loved to steal children, souls, and other precious things, they were brilliant at torturing their victims. When Zeus condemned the soothsayer Phineus to everlasting hunger, it was the Harpies who served as enforcers. Each time Phineus attempted to eat, the Harpies would swoop in, stealing his food or fouling it with excrement just as he was about to put it in his mouth.

And now—just as Gilbert Bland was so close to freedom that he, too, could practically taste it—a similar fate befell our hero. Was it the Harpies who placed that notebook out of his mind and out of his reach as he left the Peabody Library? If so, it would be perfectly in keeping with their traditional role as tormentors of those with wicked obsessions. No matter: whether by intervention of the gods or simple forgetfulness, the fateful fact remains that Bland left his notebook behind. Within minutes of the thief's departure, the Peabody's security chief, Donald Pfouts, noticed the book and decided to give it a closer examination. He quickly made a discovery that would send shock waves through libraries all over America.

*T*O ILLUSTRATE THE SECURITY CHALLENGES FACED BY IN-
stitutions such as the Peabody Library, let us briefly return to
Baltimore's Washington Monument, that "towering main-
mast," which Bland had passed under during his unsuccessful
escape attempt. Completed in 1829, the monument is the nation's oldest public memorial to George Washington, and it
holds a central place in the city's history. In the words of one
tourist brochure, "It put Baltimore on the world map." Experts
still consider the design by the architect Robert Mills to be one
of the nation's foremost examples of Romantic neoclassi-
cism—but average people are passionate about it, too. When it
needed repairs in the 1980s, and the cash-strapped city ran out
of money to do the job right, a group of business leaders
stepped in, declaring the monument a "national treasure."

Now let us consider a different national treasure, this one
also the work of Robert Mills. I am not referring to his *other*
Washington Monument, the famous one in the nation's capital,
or to his Treasury Building, the famous one on the back of a
ten-dollar bill. I am referring to his *Atlas of the State of South Carolina*. It turns out that, in addition to being a noted architect,
Mills was an important mapmaker. His 1825 masterpiece was
not only a beautiful piece of art in its own right but a work of
real historical importance—the first state atlas ever produced in
the United States. Yet all national treasures are not the same.
We can be sure that if the monument were defaced, there

would be a public outcry. But few people would complain if someone desecrated a copy of the *Atlas of the State of South Carolina*. It's a pretty fair bet, in fact, that no one would even notice the crime had taken place.

But if the public at large knows virtually nothing—and cares even less—about the *Atlas of the State of South Carolina*, a small number of map collectors and dealers value it a great deal. Today a copy of the atlas in excellent condition might sell for upwards of $30,000. A single map of Charleston County from the atlas might fetch $2,000 or more. And, unfortunately, what collectors and dealers are willing to pay for, thieves are willing to steal.

So it was that, as he flipped through Gilbert Bland's notebook, Donald Pfouts came across the following passage:

> *For MD Dealer*
> 1. *Currier & Ives (90%)*
> 2. *Kellogg*
> 3. *Haskell & Allen*
> 4. *Baillie*
> *Mills County Atlas of S.C.*

Pfouts could not help but recognize the disturbing implications of such words. Almost every page was filled with lists, most of which contained the names of cartographers and the titles of specific maps (and a few of which, such as the preceding example, also included the names of artists and their prints). Next to many of these entries were prices. Pfouts quickly came to a startling conclusion: the notebook was essentially a hit list. Worse yet, there was ample evidence that, far from being an isolated incident, as library officials had assumed, Bland's visit to the Peabody was part of something much bigger. The book contained the names—and, in some cases, addresses—of other libraries where specific maps could be found. Moreover, folded into its pages were informational materials from institutions such as the University of Virginia's Alderman Library, a disturbing clue that other thefts may have already taken place. Then there were those ominous words "For MD Dealer"—a possible implication that the manuscripts were stolen on commission. And, finally, there were a number of potentially incriminating notes, which Bland had apparently written to himself or perhaps passed to an unknown accomplice. They strongly hinted that the intruder was a man on a mission, operating in a highly organized and deliberate fashion. "Can't these people leave? I can't do it now. OK now," read one of the neatly written passages. "These 2 are done now. Thank God!" read another. "Yes she's really slowing me down! Fat Bitch," read a third. And a final one: "The Bowen Atlas—of all the bad luck—What is going on here. Am I not going to get these Bowens? What [will] become of me?"

It was a question that was beginning to interest Peabody librarians a great deal—especially after they went back through their own records and discovered that more maps were missing from other texts that Bland had allegedly handled, during both this visit and one the previous September. Did he get his

Bowens? Apparently so. Four plates were missing from the now decidedly incomplete *Complete Atlas or Distinct View of the Known World* by the eighteenth-century cartographer Emanuel Bowen, along with material from works by Mathew Carey, Jacques Nicolas Bellin, Entick, and Pierre-François-Xavier de Charlevoix. In all, twenty-seven plates were missing from the Peabody alone. Had other institutions suffered similar losses? It was now becoming frighteningly clear to Hopkins officials that they might be dealing with a crime spree. Cynthia Requardt—who had not been in on the decision to free Bland—quickly began calling the libraries that appeared to have been targeted in the notebook. Then she went to her computer and sent out a message over ExLibris, an electronic discussion group for those interested in rare books and special collections:

On December 7, Gilbert Joseph Bland, Jr., was apprehended removing maps from eighteenth century books at the George Peabody Library of The Johns Hopkins University in Baltimore.

Bland was using the alias James Perry. He is a white male, 46 years of age, 5′ 9 or 10″, with light brown hair (receding) and a light brown moustache. A photograph is available.

When apprehended, Bland presented a Florida driver's license. In lieu of pressing charges, the library accepted payment for damages, and Bland was released. Since his release, we have reason to believe that Bland has visited other research libraries in the mid-Atlantic region.

For Requardt, Pfouts, and other Hopkins officials, there was little to do but wait—and hope that their worst fears would not be realized.

CHAPTER 5

How to Make a Map,
How to Take a Map

PART ONE

*I*T TAKES THOUSANDS OF YEARS. A SINGLE map, observed Denis Wood in *The Power of Maps,* is not a self-contained document but a compilation of what *"others have seen or found out or discovered, others often living but more often dead, the things they learned piled up in layer on top of layer so that to study even the simplest-looking image is to peer back through ages of cultural acquisition."*

Geographic discoveries are part of it, of course, but before you can explore the land you have to explore the heavens. "Progress in the science of cartography has never moved ahead of developments in astronomy," wrote the map historian Lloyd A. Brown, "and our world map of today has been made possible largely because of the high degree of accuracy achieved by

AN EIGHTEENTH-CENTURY
PRINTING PRESS.

astronomical observers." Coming to grips with this notion takes millennia all by itself, and then you still need the right tools. The sundial in ancient Babylonia and Egypt, the magnetic needle in ancient China, the astrolabe in ancient Greece, the cross-staff in the fourteenth century, the backstaff, telescope, and theodolite in the sixteenth century, the quadrant in the seventeenth century, the octant, sextant, and chronometer in the eighteenth century—these instruments make measuring the size and shape of the world possible. Nonetheless, they can only provide bits and pieces of information at any one time. In drafting your map, you will also need to depend on eyewitness reports of sailors, soldiers, merchants, adventurers, braggarts, and scam artists. You will have to consult the work of other cartographers and, when all else fails, rely on educated guesses and the occasional time-honored assumption (read: myth).

It's an incredibly difficult job. Let's say you're working in the seventeenth or eighteenth century, an age in which mapmakers were sometimes referred to as "world describers." In geometry, *describe* means to draw or trace the outline of something; in poetry, it means to get at the essence of something, to bring it to life in a way that's both startling and beautiful. You've got to do both kinds of description—and do it in a medium that's partially visual, partially mathematical, partially textual, a complicated miscellany of scale, orientation, projection, grids, signs, symbols, lines, colors, words. It's often been said that mapmakers combine science and art, but there's far more to it than that. Joan Blaeu, a legendary Dutch cartographer of the seventeenth century, wrote that "maps enable us to contemplate at home and right before our eyes things that are far away." Making the distant immediate, the unseen visible—that's far beyond science or art. That's alchemy.

It may take you months, even years, to draft a single map. It's not just the continents, oceans, mountains, lakes, rivers, and political borders you have to worry about. There's also the cartouche (a decorative box containing printed information, such as the title and the cartographer's name) and an array of other adornments—distance scales, compass roses, wind-heads, ships, sea monsters, important personages, characters from the Scriptures, quaint natives, menacing cannibal natives, sexy topless natives, planets, wonders of the ancient world, flora, fauna, rainbows, whirlpools, sphinxes, sirens, cherubs, heraldic emblems, strapwork, rollwork, and/or clusters of fruit.

And once you're finally finished describing the world, you have to transfer it to a copper plate for printing. This, too, takes time. You select a piece of copper that's not too soft, not too hard, and you planish it with a hammer to smooth it out and to ensure that it is firm and free from holes or flaws. Then you have to polish the smoothest side to a mirror-smooth finish, first with a piece of grinding stone and water, next with a pumice stone, then with a hone and water, then with hardened charcoal, and finally with a steel burnisher. Perfection is a must: any minor scratch might show up as a line on your map, possibly causing the accidental subdivision of one small nation into two smaller nations.

Next, you transfer the design of your map to the plate. This is a difficult process that involves heating the plate, spreading a layer of wax over it with a feather, then laboriously tracing the map, in reverse, onto the wax coating. Once that's done, you're ready to cut the design into the plate. You might do this by etching—using a needle to scratch the outlines of the map through the wax coating, then pouring acid into the needle marks to burn your design into the plate. More likely, however, you would engrave the plate—cut the design into it by hand—using a variety of tools: the burin (also known as the graver), the tint tool, the scauper, the threading tool, and the roulette. This is precision work, and it usually requires a number of people and a great deal of time, not the least because at several intervals in the process it is proofed and then corrected, by meticulously smoothing over the mistakes with a burnisher and then reengraving.

Next comes the ink. You spread it over the plate, then carefully wipe off the excess until the only remaining ink sits in the engraved grooves. You heat the plate until it is warm, lay it out on the printing press, and place a sheet of thick dampened paper over it. When the press is tightened, the moist paper draws the ink from the incised lines of the plate—and, at last, you are looking at a printed map.

But you might not be done. You might also need to color your engraved map—and there is no machine to help you with this. You must do it by hand, brushing watercolors onto the freshly printed map—meticulous detail work that, if done wrong, ruins all the labor that came before it, and, if done right, gives birth to bright-hued oceans and vibrant nations. On a particularly sumptuous map, you might also need to add gold-leaf highlights.

All that, and you've made only one map. What if you're making a whole atlas? The scholar C. Koeman once tried to estimate how long it took for the great Dutch mapmaker Joan Blaeu to print his famous *Atlas Major* of 1663. Assuming a relatively small press run of three hundred copies for each of the first three editions of the atlas (Latin, French, and Dutch), Koeman concluded that the composition (or typesetting), with eight full-time employees, would take 1,000 working days; the letterpress printing (of the text parts of the book), involving nine printing presses, would take 330 working days; the copperplate printing (of maps and other graphic elements), involving six printing presses, would take 900 working days; and the binding, involving three employees, would take 300 working days. "The planning involved in printing the three editions . . . within a span of three or four years," Koeman concluded, "exceeds the range of our imagination."

Making a map, in short, is a painstaking process, requiring extraordinary skill on the part of everyone involved, but there is a huge demand for your work. Members of a later generation will smugly call their era the Information Age, but it will be nothing compared with this one. The printing press is changing many aspects of life, none more so than the way people envision the Earth. This breakthrough invention not only allows for maps to be produced in accurate and standardized ways but makes possible the widespread dissemination of geographic images. For the first time the whole world is able to see the world as a whole.

PART TWO

*J*T TAKES NO TIME AT ALL. AND YOU NEED only one tool. An out-of-the-way spot is preferable but not necessary: with enough skill and daring, you can do this right in the middle of a busy rare books room. If making maps requires real magic, taking them involves only sleight of hand. Just listen to how Gilbert Bland did it. "When no one was looking he would proceed to take out a single-edged razor blade, like you would use to scrape stuff off glass," explained Lieutenant Detective Clay Williams of the University of North Carolina Department of Public Safety, who talked to Bland about the heists. "He could put the razor under his fingers so that you never really saw it. You just saw him take his hand and go down from the top of the page to the bottom. It would appear to be nothing unusual—maybe like he was just scanning text. But he would actually be cutting out the page. The whole operation would take just a matter of seconds."

Slide the page into your coat and you're through the door, hundreds of years of history gone in less time than it took the ink on the map to dry.

THE HARD PART ISN'T THE ACTUAL STEALING, IT'S THE getting in and getting out. Even at the least secure of libraries, you must present your identification, sign a register, perhaps even pass by a security guard and answer a few questions about your reasons for being there. This is usually when you feel the most trepidation and anxiety, like a smuggler at a border crossing. In fact, you are crossing a kind of border. As a map aficionado, you know about borders. You understand that they are not just lines on a piece of paper but powerful psychological metaphors. "The crossing of the border symbolizes transgressing against moral commands or trespassing into forbidden territory," observed Avner Falk, a clinical psychologist interested in the relationship between maps and the mind.

And make no mistake: a rare books room *is* forbidden territory. Scholars believe that libraries evolved from ancient "temple collections" that housed a religion's most important texts. "The theological collection was kept in a sacred place, and presided over by a priest," wrote Michael H. Harris in *History of Libraries in the Western World*. "Only the most important of the temple officials might have access to this library." In Judeo-Christian tradition, the temple collection was exemplified by the Holy of Holies, the innermost sanctum of the Jewish tabernacle and home to the Ark of the Covenant, which contained the original stone tablets of the Ten Commandments. The Ark was considered so sacred that God would smite dead those who touched it.

You have come to desecrate the modern equivalent of this temple, a largely off-limits chamber where our culture stores its rarest and most valued documents. But while penetrating this forbidden place no doubt fills you with apprehension, it might also give you a huge thrill. "Some people seem to seek the exhilaration of border crossing, and when conventional borders no longer seem exciting, more imposing ones are sought. . . . To even possess the ability to cross a dangerous border may be a necessary potency for some individuals," wrote the psychiatrist G. Raymond Babineau.

From 1967 to 1970 Babineau was the chief of psychiatric services at the U.S. Army Hospital in Berlin. There he had the opportunity to observe many "compulsive border crossers"—restless souls who repeatedly made dangerous journeys over the Iron Curtain in order "to be rid of one psychological state and catapulted into a newer and better one." Maybe you're driven by similar impulses. Maybe, like those Babineau interviewed (and, as court records indicate, like Gilbert Bland), you suffer from depression. Perhaps strolling through the doors of the library allows you to leave your feelings of low self-esteem and ineffectuality behind for a few moments and enter a world in which you are skilled and powerful. You may also, like Babineau's border crossers (and like Bland), come from a broken home. If so, your visit to the library might be what Babineau called a "search for identity." History shows that people often take on new personae when they cross borders, from the Old Testament, in which Jacob became Israel after crossing the Jabbok River, to Ellis Island, where countless immigrants likewise were given new names. It may be that by entering the library you, too, are trying to be reborn, just as Gilbert Bland became James Perry when he walked through the door.

In addition to the border crossers that Babineau studied firsthand, he also examined the case of a young man named Lee Harvey Oswald. You may have more in common with him than you think. True, stealing a few maps is a long way from killing a president. But look at *The Warren Commission Report*. See if you don't recognize something of yourself in it:

> Perhaps the most outstanding conclusion of such a study is that Oswald was profoundly alienated from the world in which he lived. His life was characterized by isolation, frustration, and failure. He had very few, if any, close relationships with other people and he appeared to have great difficulty in finding a meaningful place in the world. . . . [His wife] Marina Oswald thought that he would not be happy anywhere, "Only on the moon, perhaps."

Maybe you steal maps because you're searching for a home. Or perhaps you simply crave the dark joy of appropriation. Because that's another thing about borders: they are mighty tools of theft. "Countless governments have used map boundaries to subdue, displace, or annihilate native peoples," noted the geographic scholar Mark Monmonier in *Drawing the Line:*

Tales of Maps and Cartocontroversy. Talk about magic: with one teetery line, what was *ours* suddenly becomes *yours.* You understand how easy this is. That's why you are adding a new border to a map at this very moment. But you are not holding a pen. Your border is limned with cold steel.

THE PEABODY LIBRARY'S GRAND STACK
ROOM, FROM AN 1879 ENGRAVING.

CHAPTER 6

The Invisible Crime Spree

*T*HE GHOST OF LLOYD A. BROWN WAS NOT pleased. He floated invisible amid the mote-speckled air of the Grand Stack Room, nervously chewing his pipe or rubbing his bald pate, his bushy eyebrows arched with tension. In life, Brown had been head librarian at the Peabody. While there he introduced the first modern ventilation system to the building, overhauled the outdated card catalog, launched a campaign to degrime hundreds of books, and, as part of that effort, took it upon himself to personally inspect the contents of every shelf on all six tiers. But his biggest accomplishment, during a tenure that ran from 1942 until 1956, was his efforts not as a librarian but as an author. His groundbreaking book, *The Story of Maps,* published in 1949, set the standard for all cartographic histories to come—and is still in print more than fifty years later. With no formal training in cartography, Brown had not been an obvious candidate to write such a volume, but he'd had a couple of advantages going for him. The first was an obsession with old maps. "If you get bitten by a flea, I guess you have to live with it," he once joked. The second was his own library's extraordinary collection. In researching *The Story of Maps,* Brown had needed to consult more than five hundred books. He delighted in recounting that all but ten of them were found on the shelves of the Peabody.

Since his death in 1966, Lloyd A. Brown had led a happy spectral existence amid his beloved books. Or at least that's the way I imagine him. What a wonderful thing reading must have been, when unencumbered by the earthly pressures of time! One could linger on every word. No volume was too long, no passage too dense, no subject too unfamiliar, no metaphor too obscure, no foreign script too unintelligible. One need not despair, as in life, about the books one would never have the opportunity to open or reopen. Lloyd Brown had gone to heaven, and it was called the Grand Stack Room.

And so things might have remained, if not for the intruder—the hated one who crept into the library one day, seated himself at one of Brown's favorite old tables, and, as the ghost hovered helplessly above, began to slice up books. Worse: map books—the ones Brown had cradled so often, so tenderly, for so many years, the ones that had succored his intellect and imagination, the ones that had given him a sense of purpose, the ones that had ensured his name would live on long after he passed into the realm of the spirits. It was as if that razor blade was not just cutting paper but severing Brown's ties to the realm of the living. He raved, howled, shook incorporeal fists, shed invisible tears. None of it helped. I imagine that even after the man was apprehended, Lloyd A. Brown's ghost continued to wander disconsolately, muttering curses heard by no one—a spirit no longer at rest. The intruder had caused him to understand that while he would haunt this piece of air forever, all he had worked so hard to create could disappear, page by page, book by book, shelf by shelf, wall by wall, until the Peabody was nothing but a landmark on some old city plan, the last faded trace of his life. Of what use is eternity without the past?

MONG THE LIVING AT THE PEABODY, THE MOOD WAS not much brighter. In the days after Cynthia Requardt's Internet posting about Gilbert Bland, all news was bad news. Requardt had sent the message as "an attempt to warn people to watch out for Bland in the future," she later recalled. In so doing, however, she had unintentionally opened Hopkins officials to criticism—a torrent, as it would turn out. One writer after another filed messages to the ExLibris news group, lambasting the university for allowing Bland to go free. Such criticism pained Requardt. She would later concede that she was simply "not prepared" for the "candid assessments" of her peers. Yet as much as the attacks stung, she was even more devastated by the reports arriving from other libraries. James Perry had been to the University of Virginia. James Perry had been to Duke University. James Perry had been to the University of North Carolina and to Brown. At all of those stops, books handled by the mystery man now appeared to be missing maps and prints.

Perry's visit to the Regenstein Library at the University of Chicago on October 31, 1995—Halloween—came five weeks before Bland was detained in Baltimore. Walking calmly into the library, he sat down in the special collections room and opened one of the Western world's most extraordinary texts: a 1584 edition of *Theatrum Orbis Terrarum,* "Theater of the World," compiled and edited by Abraham Ortelius, the father of modern geography. Ortelius, a Flemish cartographer, lived during an unprecedented period of discovery. Columbus had landed in the Americas, Magellan's expedition had circumnavigated the globe, Copernicus had made his case for a sun-centered universe. Yet cartography was behind the times. Maps came in a slapdash variety of sizes and styles, many of them based on the ideas of Ptolemy and other ancient geographers, who, of course, had known nothing about the existence of North or South America. Ortelius set out to change that, painstakingly collecting the finest maps of places throughout the known world, then bringing them together in a uniform size and format. Originally published in 1570, *Theatrum Orbis Terrarum* was the first modern atlas. Ortelius put the whole world at the fingertips of the traveler in a standardized fashion—a milestone in the history of human imagination.

Yet now the great master's text had wound up in the hands of a kind of Anti-Ortelius, a professional scatterer of maps and destroyer of books. Bland apparently paged through the volume until he came to a map labeled *La Florida,* the first widely available map of the broad region that is now the southeastern United States. Ortelius added it to *Theatrum Orbis Terrarum* for the first time in this 1584 edition. And there it remained for the next 411 years—until the intruder allegedly flashed out his razor blade.

Although the book measures seventeen inches by twelve inches and its pages are so thick that they literally rumble when turned, Bland is believed to have removed *La Florida* and two more plates from that same atlas, as well as ten maps from another book. The Regenstein's special collections room is a kind of fish tank built expressly for security: its walls are made of

"LA FLORIDA" MAP FROM THE LANDMARK ORTELIUS ATLAS, *THEATRUM ORBIS TERRARUM.*

glass, and no briefcases or pens are allowed inside. Yet Bland seems to have sneaked the thirteen plates into his clothes and walked out undetected. For good measure, he also altered a librarian's pencil-written inventory at the front of the Ortelius book, making it appear that the maps he took had been missing for years.

But that wasn't his only alleged theft during his brief Chicago stay. Only the day before he'd paid a visit to Northwestern University's Charles Deering McCormick Library of Special Collections, a churchlike chamber with arched windows and cluttered old bookshelves adorned with busts of Dante, Einstein, Dylan Thomas, Samuel Johnson, and Ezra Pound. The curator R. Russell Maylone remembers the visitor as "the proverbial man in the raincoat" with "a pile of books on the table spread out in a not very orderly fashion." That day Bland is believed to have removed six separate maps from the pages of several antique atlases, including a 1681 map of New York and three maps of the Caribbean. As Perry got up to leave, Maylone said, "I hope you found what you were looking for."

He had, thank you. He certainly had.

As the weeks rolled on, more and more institutions reported visits from the dreaded Perry. Ultimately the count would rise to nineteen libraries, most of them in the East and Midwest but one in Seattle and two in British Columbia. The list would include such institutions as the University of Delaware, the University of Florida, Washington University in St. Louis, and the University of Rochester.

No one had called the police. No one, apparently, had noticed that the maps were gone. It was an invisible crime spree, hidden amid the seldom-opened pages of centuries-old books. And its perpetrator was the invisible criminal. Beyond a general physical description, the people who met him would later describe him in only the vaguest of terms: "clean-cut," "quiet," "polite," "mild-mannered," "nondescript and noncommunicative." Many simply had no memory of him at all.

WHAT A VAPID JOB TITLE OUR CULTURE GIVES TO those honorable laborers the ancient Egyptians and Sumerians variously called Learned Men of the Magic Library, Scribes of the Double House of Life, Mistresses of the House of Books, or Ordainers of the Universe. *Librarian*—that mouth-contorting, graceless grind of a word, that dry gulch in the dictionary between *libido* and *licentious*—it practically begs you to envision a stoop-shouldered loser, socks mismatched, eyes locked in a permanent squint from reading too much microfiche. If it were up to me, I would abolish the word entirely and turn back to the lexicological wisdom of the ancients, who saw librarians not as feeble sorters and shelvers but as heroic guardians. In Assyrian, Babylonian, and Egyptian cultures alike, those who toiled at the shelves were often bestowed with a proud, even soldierly, title: Keeper of the Books.

I think most librarians, especially rare books librarians, still secretly view themselves in this way. I met dozens of them as I retraced Bland's footsteps, and in the end I came to the conclusion that most view their work as what the scholar and novelist

Umberto Eco, writing about librarians of an earlier age, called a "war with the forces of oblivion." I think they wage this war because, like the historian Barbara Tuchman, they believe that "books are humanity in print" and that, as the Keepers of the Books, they are safeguarding not just pieces of paper but mortal flesh. The stakes are high: if they fail, the past dies.

Not that the librarians themselves are likely to talk in such terms. I found them to be a guarded, self-effacing, and often sardonic lot, a group decidedly short on Graham Arader types. As a result, I had a tough time getting a handle on what made them tick. I confess that this did not bother me too much in the beginning. Of the many mysteries surrounding the Bland case, the Secret Life of Librarians was not exactly the first I yearned to ferret out. But as the months wore on, and my respect for librarians grew, so did my curiosity about their craft. Yet, try as I might, I was unable to gain a good feel for their esprit de corps until I got to know Gary L. Menges, one of the last librarians I interviewed.

When I first contacted Menges over the phone, he sounded just as you might expect a librarian to sound, from the nasally voice to the precise, even persnickety, way of putting words together. But when I traveled to Seattle for a meeting with him at the University of Washington campus, I was greeted by a man much different than the one I had imagined. Far from being a tepid biblio-bureaucrat, Menges seemed full of vitality and purpose. He later told me that he was sixty-one years old; I had assumed he was a good fifteen years younger. His most memorable attribute, other than a tastefully radiant red-and-orange necktie, was a plush, meticulously maintained white beard. He reminded me of a very trim, very tidy version of Santa Claus, complete with a twinkle in the eye and a disarmingly robust laugh.

Menges led me to his basement office at the Kenneth S. Allen Library, where he worked as the head of the Special Collections and Preservation Division. On one wall hung a series of New Year's cards, which the department sent to its donors and supporters every winter. Each contained the work of a local artist, accompanied by a quotation about books. One read: "The world exists in order to become a book."—Stéphane Mallarmé. Another: "I have always imagined that paradise will be a kind of library."—Jorge Luis Borges. A third: "Handle a book as a bee does a flower, extract its sweetness but do not damage it."—John Muir. Menges told me the idea for the cards had been his; it would soon be clear to me that the sentiments were as well.

I had not come to talk about greeting cards, however. In the middle of the room sat a cart, holding a large, leather-bound volume.

"Ah," I said. "This must be *the book*."

"Yes," he replied. "I thought you'd want to see it."

It was true. I had already heard much about this particular book, and I was anxious to examine it for myself. But I also wanted to observe Menges as *he* looked at it, touched it, talked about it. Menges, I knew, had gone to extraordinary lengths to obtain and preserve this volume. I had come here to get a first-hand feel for one librarian's intense devotion to a single text.

The saga began in 1990, when Menges was contacted by a

University of Washington alumnus from Spokane. The man owned a collection of old books that had once belonged to his grandfather, a history professor at Northwestern University. He hoped the library might have use for the volumes. Menges, of course, welcomed the offer, but he realized, too, that nothing might come of it. Special collections libraries are, by their very nature, highly selective—and often the books people want to donate are either of little historical interest or already on the library's shelves. But you never know when and where you're going to strike gold. Once, for instance, somebody had fished some old architectural drawings out of a dumpster and brought them to the library. They turned out to be the original plans for some important local buildings.

The Keeper of the Books must always keep his mind open. Menges hopped on a plane for Spokane, having concluded the man's collection was at least worth checking out in person. It was there that he first laid eyes on the book. Its ornately decorated leather spine was badly worn, but the gold-leaf title was still legible:

OGILBY'S
AMERICA

Menges did not need to be a rare books librarian to see that it was a beautiful work. That would have been obvious to anyone taking a cursory perusal of its 122 superb engravings, including many gorgeous maps. But Menges also recognized it as a historically important volume. Its author, the Scottish cartographer

John Ogilby, had served as royal cosmographer and geographic printer under England's King Charles II and had published *America* in 1671 as part of a series of works about other lands. It was not a particularly original work (most of the information was, in fact, lifted from other sources) nor a particularly accurate one (placing Montezuma's Aztec empire, for example, in Peru). Nonetheless, it had the distinction of being the first encyclopedia of the New World to be published in English. Moreover, Menges knew that Ogilby had authored several other map books, most notably *Britannia*, the first-ever national road atlas. Originally published in 1675, *Britannia* was later reprinted in a number of editions—including a 1762 version, revised by John Senex and retitled *The Roads Through England Delineated*, which now sat on his library's shelves. If nothing else, Menges relished the opportunity to bring two of Ogilby's most important works together under one roof. "This obviously was one of the nicest books—if not the nicest book—in the [Spokane] collection," he recalled. "I, of course, expressed a strong interest in it."

He understood, however, that in the thorny world of donor relations, interest does not always translate into acquisition. The Keeper of the Books must schmooze. Menges was not surprised that the man did not immediately relinquish the book, wanting some assurances before making the gift. "Because it had belonged to his grandfather, and there was this family tie to it," he explained, "he was concerned that it be in a good home."

Luckily, Menges was in an ideal position to talk about good homes just then. His Special Collections and Preservation Division was setting up shop in the brand-new Kenneth S. Allen

Library. The building had been named after a former university librarian, who (like most former university librarians) would not have had a large edifice built in his honor if not for one fact: he was the father of Microsoft cofounder Paul Allen. Thanks in large part to the computer magnate's $10 million gift (the largest in university history to that time), the architect Edward Larrabee Barnes had been able to fill the new facility with all sorts of state-of-the-art technology—from special filters on lights and windows, designed to guard books against damaging ultraviolet rays, to a computer-monitored, climate-controlled vault where rare works, such as the Ogilby, were to be stored.

"The book's going to be here forever," Menges could confidently promise the alumnus from Spokane. "It's going to be well cared for, and it's going to be used."

In making such assurances, Menges was putting not just the library's reputation but his own on the line. If anything happened to the book, he would be stuck with the unenviable task of explaining things to the donor—not to mention administrators, journalists, and, worst of all, other potential givers, who might consequently hesitate to put their own beloved volumes in his care. But his obligations did not end there. The Keeper of the Books must answer to the past and future, as well as to the present. In assuming responsibility for the book, Menges would be accountable to everyone who had ever read it, studied its maps, placed it lovingly on the shelf. They had kept the volume intact for more than three hundred years, and Gary Menges owed it to them to do no worse. Yet he had an even bigger responsibility—his most solemn duty of all, in fact: to keep the book in good condition for generations to come, readers not yet born.

This burden was one that Menges was only too happy to shoulder. I could see that right away as I sat in his office that morning—and it occurred to me that the donor from Spokane must have seen it, too. As I was, he had probably been reassured by the librarian's unpretentious enthusiasm for the book, all the more convincing for its lack of bluster, and by the careful but confident way Menges held it in his hands. And perhaps he was won over by the way Menges looked at it—not with the covetous stare of a lover, not even with the overly jealous eye of a parent, but with the proud and protective gaze of a good grandparent. The longer I talked to Menges, the more I suspected that the man's final decision to donate the book had less to do with the high-tech frills of the new library than with the quiet charisma of a certain old-fashioned librarian.

After the negotiations were completed, the legalities hashed out, and the paperwork signed, the book arrived in Seattle. But Menges's work was just beginning. His next job was to get the volume physically ready for the shelves—no small task. "This particular copy was not in the best condition," he explained. "The text block [the part made up of the actual pages] was intact, but the bindings had worn out. Most bindings do, if the book is heavily used for three hundred years."

As he told me this, Menges reached into a file and pulled out a couple of photographs, taken of the book when it first came to the library. It looked as if the volume had been chained to the back of a pickup and taken for an off-road adventure. The bind-ing—in layman's terms, the cover—was ripped, stained, and generally worn-out. The leather itself was cracked and brittle. The corners were frayed. The frontboard—the part of the cover you would open in order to read the book—was com-pletely detached. There were other problems as well, including some ripped maps. All told, Menges said, the estimated cost of repairing the damages had come to almost a thousand dollars—no small sum to plunk down on a single book, but manageable if you've got it in your budget. The trouble was, Gary Menges didn't have it in his budget. He would have to raise this money on his own.

One thing Menges did have, however, was a plan. He called it Save a Book. He had launched the program a year earlier, using a simple formula. First, select a beautiful old volume in a frightful state of disrepair. Then, put it in the display case that people nearly stumble over every time they walk into the read-ing room. Next, print up a bunch of flyers extolling the vol-ume's aesthetic and historical import. And finally, beg, cajole, and beg some more.

Menges has a subtle gift for this art—as I learned when, in the midst of our interview, I found myself reaching for my checkbook to help out poor old Sir Walter Raleigh, the Save a Book poster child du jour, whose *History of the World* had fallen on hard times. "All sorts of people donate," Menges cheerfully explained, moments before accepting my modest alms. "On our first Save a Book effort [for Hartmann Schedel's *Nuremberg Chronicle*], the donors ranged from the president of the university to a student who came in and gave me a dollar, saying that was all he could afford. I assured him that his dollar was most welcome."

The Keeper of the Books must enlist others to the cause. But the list of contributors for John Ogilby's *America* also included a Good Samaritan by the name of Gary Menges, who wrote a personal check for fifty dollars. When I asked him about this, he was dismissive. "I always contribute to the Save a Book," he simply explained. "I think it's an important program."

After the money had been raised, *America* was tenderly wrapped up and sent to the unlikely destination of Browns Summit, North Carolina, where it was unpacked with equal care. Gary Menges could not fight his war against oblivion alone; his efforts now hinged on the expertise of Don Etherington, a Book Keeper of a very high order. For the past fifty years the British-born Etherington has worked as a conservator, restoring countless old volumes with the steady hands of a surgeon and the mystic passion of a necromancer. This unlikely career began when, at age thirteen, Etherington enrolled in a special bookbinding curriculum at London's Central School of Arts and Crafts. What on earth would draw someone to such an arcane endeavor at so young an age? "I have no clue," Etherington told me with a laugh, during a phone interview. Perhaps it was simply in his blood. "My uncle was the head of the reading room at the British Library for many years," he said. "And in fact, as strange as it may seem, a few years ago I found out that my great-great-grandfather was the painting restorer for Queen Victoria."

Beginning with a seven-year apprenticeship at Harrison's & Sons, the printer for the royal family, Etherington worked his way to the top of his profession in England. In 1970 he came to the United States to help set up a conservation program at the Library of Congress, then took a similar position at the University of Texas in 1980. Since 1987 he has been president of the for-profit Etherington Conservation Center, a division of Information Conservation, Inc. During the course of his career, Etherington has worked on some of the Western world's most important documents. While at the Library of Congress, for example, he helped restore the Gettysburg Address. He has also done work on the Magna Carta of 1297 (owned by Ross Perot), the Carolina Charter of 1663, the Texas Declaration of Independence of 1836, and the State of Virginia's copy of the Bill of Rights. At the time I interviewed him—September 1998—Etherington was part of a team designing a new housing and display for the Declaration of Independence.

Working on such monumental—not to mention fragile—documents requires both a lot of talent and a lot of nerve. "You cannot allow emotion to get into it," Etherington explained. "You can't be overawed by the object. You have to be concerned about what you're doing and what's wrong with the object and what's needed to restore it. If you approached it as if you were scared of it, your hands wouldn't be so sure. And that's when all the accidents happen. You've got to have a certain surety of hand to deal with this type of material. And confidence—but not overconfidence."

You've also got to have decades of training. No university offers a specific major in book conservation, explained Etherington. Instead, it is largely "an artisan's job"—one of the last remaining professions in which skills are passed down from one generation to the next. He employs a wider variety of materials than his forebears did, but otherwise "the same procedures that they used in the fifth or sixth or seventh century we still use today."

With the book from Menges, Etherington's approach was the same as it has been on thousands of other old texts. The overall goal was to save as much of the old material as possible. In this case, however, some elements were beyond hope. "The binding had deteriorated and we couldn't restore it," said Etherington. "So that's the first decision: All right, we can't save this binding, so we're going to rebind it. And then, what you do is take off the old binding and clean the old spine. And then you go to the text block to see if it is sound—to see whether it needs restoring or whatever—because that's a major decision. If you get into taking the text block apart, it's what we call major intervention, because you are getting into the original structure and maybe changing it. Minimal intervention is when you don't do too much to change the original configuration of the book."

Only minimal intervention was needed on the Ogilby. Other than some torn maps, which had to be carefully patched with material known as Japanese paper, the text block did not need much work. Etherington and his staff could focus on the binding. "A new binding generally has new boards and new endpapers," he said. "Endpapers are the papers you put on either side of the text block. They're the connectors between the cover and the book. And then you decide what kind of cover you're going to put on the text block."

It was decided to use a leather binding that—while not as ornately decorated as the one that had preceded it—would be both faithful to the era in which the book was published and durable enough to be used widely by library patrons. But even such a no-frills cover required meticulous craftsmanship. "You have to pare the leather, which means you thin it down on the edges," he explained. "Then you paste the leather out, and then you form the leather around the boards of the book. You turn the leather in and then you let it dry, and once you've done that you put the endpapers down."

Once the binding was completed, the book was ready for shipment back to Seattle. Even though it had not been Etherington's most high-profile assignment, there was, as always, "that satisfaction of saving something from deterioration or the trash," he said. "And that's the difference between book conservators and other kinds of conservators. We're actually restoring objects to be reused, not just to be put in a museum . . . which I think is great. I don't think we should be restoring things to put in a glass case, never to be handled. Books were never designed to not be read."

And this one *would* be read, at long last. The cataloging process having been completed, *America* was made available to patrons of the Allen Library in June 1995. Gary Menges's effort to get it on the shelves had taken five years.

Perhaps you've already guessed what happened next. If so, it won't surprise you that on October 4, 1995, a stranger walked into the Special Collections and Preservation Division and approached the reference desk, where Menges was working. Nor will you be shocked that the man was wearing a blue blazer and, according to Menges, "looked very normal. He could have been a faculty member or a book collector. He wasn't anyone that you would be suspicious of from his appearance or the way he acted." Perhaps you've figured out by now that the man filled out a call slip for John Ogilby's *America* and that, as Menges recalled, "I told him that it was a wonderful book and went and got it for him." And if you've deduced all of this, then you need not be told that the stranger had identified himself as James Perry. There may be only one dark little detail you don't already know: he was the very first patron to handle the book.

On the day I interviewed Gary Menges at his office, he calmly recounted the story of the intruder's visit to the library, then stood and led me over to the book. Its thick new leather binding was magnificent, but beneath the cover much was amiss. One of the four maps the thief had sliced from the book was still missing, apparently gone forever. The three others had, in the intervening months, been returned by law enforcement officials and now lay next to the volume. They could be reattached—perhaps even well enough so that a casual observer might not notice any damage—but the book's integrity and monetary value had been irreparably harmed. That was especially true because a number of additional pages had been left half-mangled by deep slashes along the fold. "See how he cut the title page here?" Menges said, gesturing to one razor-scarred page. "He would cut very fast when somebody wasn't looking. And in doing so, he would cut through other pages like this one."

I had seen similarly mutilated books at other libraries but still found the sight chilling. And I wondered how it made someone like Menges feel. The conservator Don Etherington once confessed that it pains him to see even a cheap paperback ill-treated. "When you spend a whole life doing the work we do, you don't even like to see people turning the corners of books," he said. "You know how people turn in the corners to mark something when they're reading? Well, it gives you a little gut check. You feel like saying to the person, 'I wish you wouldn't do that.' That sounds a bit stupid, really—but that's the way you are. If you're in this business, you have that innate sense that you don't want these things to be mishandled."

And as for someone who would destroy a rare and beautiful book like the Ogilby? "You'd like to cut his balls off, basically," said Etherington.

As I watched Menges, however, I could see none of Etherington's ire. He looked concerned, to be sure, but calm. Nor had I perceived any great wrath during a phone interview a few days before my visit to Seattle, when I asked the librarian to describe his feelings about the theft. "Of course, one is angry," he said, choosing each word carefully. "You put personal effort into obtaining a book for the collection and getting it conserved and making it available to people. And then the first person who uses it comes in and cuts out maps. Obviously, one is not very happy about that."

By coming here, I had thought that I might get a more impassioned reaction. In the smarmy theatrics of my imagination, I had conjured up scenes in which Menges prostrated himself over the book, cursing the Library Gods and raining tears down upon the ruins of the text. Now, however, I realized just how silly such expectations had been. Gary Menges was not mourning the past. He was already looking to the future, telling me about his plans for repairing the book. He had saved it from oblivion once, and would do so again. The Keeper of the Books must never rest.

OW BIG IS THE WORLD? FOR ANYONE INTERESTED IN mapmaking, that question is about as fundamental as they come. The first person to make a scientific measurement of the Earth's circumference, however, was not a cartographer but a librarian.

His name was Eratosthenes, and, from about 235 B.C. until about 195 B.C., he was head of the library at Alexandria, one of the most legendary sites in all of antiquity. Alexandria was then the largest city in the world, a hub of Hellenistic trade and learning. The city had been founded around 332 B.C. by Alexander the Great; the library was established a few decades later—and quickly set about accumulating texts the way Alexander had acquired territory. Agents fanned out across the known world with orders to bring back the works of what one contemporary observer described as "poets and prose-writers, rhetoricians and sophists, doctors and soothsayers, historians and all the others too." Scholars were brought in to translate the texts of cultures from Europe to North Africa and India. Ships arriving in Alexandria's harbor were forced to lend the library any books they might have on board. Copies of the books—made on cheap papyrus—were eventually returned to the owners, but the originals remained in Alexandria. The library's goal was audacious: to gather, under one roof, every book ever written.

It never happened. Although, at its height, the great library built a collection of as many as seven hundred thousand rolls of papyrus, it was doomed to an inauspicious fate. No one can be precisely sure what became of it. Leading theories have the library being (a) burned by Julius Caesar in the first century B.C., (b) gutted by early Christian fanatics, (c) destroyed by Arab invaders in the seventh century A.D., (d) wasted slowly by the forces of time, or (e) all of the above. At any rate, the library vanished—but not before it helped the rest of the world to become visible. Claudius Ptolemy apparently studied there in preparation for his landmark *Geographia*. So did another prominent Greek geographer, Strabo, whose insistence that "it is possible to sail round the inhabited world on both sides, from the east as well as the west," inspired Columbus and other explorers to seek out new routes to the Indies. And then there was Eratosthenes. Thanks to a combination of brilliant abstract thinking and practical geometry (not to mention a bit of luck), he was able to deduce the Earth's circumference by measuring the shadow of a single obelisk. His estimate is hard to pin down because of our imprecise understanding of ancient Greek units of measurement. But modern scholars agree that his guess was astonishingly close to the mark. In fact, "Eratosthenes' measurement may have been within two hundred miles of the correct figure of the circumference of the earth," wrote the map historian Norman J. W. Thrower.

In those days, size mattered. Or, as the philosopher Hannah Arendt wrote in her 1958 work, *The Human Condition,* "distance ruled." It was perhaps the single most important issue for every cartographer and explorer until as late as the nineteenth century. Columbus, for example, believed that the distance between the Canary Islands, off the northwest coast of Africa, and Japan was only 2,760 miles. He might never have set sail—or been allowed to—had he known that his estimate was short by nearly 9,500 miles. And Magellan? He "had not the remotest idea of the width of the Pacific Ocean, uncrossed as yet by any European," wrote the historian Samuel Eliot Morison, who concluded that all authoritative estimates Magellan could have known about were at least 80 percent short of the actual distance. The captain and his crew were so ill-prepared for the vastness of the Pacific that during their one-hundred-day crossing they were forced to eat rats, leather, and sawdust.

In overcoming such hardships, those two journeys accomplished the miraculous: they made the world bigger. And for hundreds of years it continued to grow. But then—once the map was finally filled in—a curious thing happened: the world started getting smaller again. In *The Human Condition,* Arendt described "the shrinkage of space and the abolition of distance through railroads, steamships, and airplanes." And since her time the withering of the world has become even more profound. On the desk in front of me now is a book called *The Death of Distance*. Its bold thesis is summarized on the dust jacket: "Geography, borders, time zones—all are rapidly becoming irrelevant . . . courtesy of the communications revolution."

Geography *irrelevant*? Columbus and Magellan would have found such a concept both absurd and depressing. Yet I have to concede that Frances Cairncross, the author of *The Death of Distance*, makes a fairly convincing argument about how new telephone, television, and computer technologies "will help to shrink the world and to make people realize the extent to which, in John Donne's words, 'No man is an island, entire of itself; every man is a piece of the continent, a part of the main.'"

As I was reading *The Death of Distance*, it occurred to me that there are now two types of adventurers. The old breed—the kind who once slogged forth into the great unknown, back when there was enough unknown left to accurately describe it as "great"—is an endangered species, and not a happy one, either. The old breed does not want to be part of the main. It yearns for islands. It feels grounded in the global village. As the mountain climber Gaston Rébuffat once put it, "In this modern age, very little remains that is real: night has been banished, so have the cold, the wind, and the stars." And so the old breed finds itself jammed into the last fragments of true man versus nature wilderness, adventure ghettos like Mount Everest.

The new breed talks much the same game as the old, appropriating Age of Discovery language to describe Age of Information concepts (Netscape Navigator, Microsoft Explorer). But the similarities end there. The new breed has no need for physical wilderness. It celebrates the fact that, as Rébuffat put it, very little remains that is real. The new breed dances on the grave of poor old Distance, believing that in cyberspace all vistas are endless. At the beginning of the twentieth century, Theodore Roosevelt, one of the last great icons of the old breed, argued that the adventurer's heart "must thrill for the saddle and not the hearthstone." At the beginning of the twenty-first century, the new breed of adventurer must thrill only for the placid glow of a computer screen.

In his own curious quest, Gilbert Bland seems to have had in common with the old breed a certain compulsion toward risk. But for the most part he was solidly of the new breed. In the early 1990s, before turning his interest to maps, Bland ran a computer consulting firm, and he apparently put his technical knowledge to good use during his crime spree. He did not make his actual conquests on the Web, of course. But, according to law enforcement officials, he did do his exploration and discovery there—using the Internet, for example, to track down Ogilby's *America* at the University of Washington. Gary Menges found some bitter irony in that. "You tell the world you have something in order that people are aware of its existence and can come and use it," he said. "And then you have people who are not using this information for scholarly purposes. They're using it to put together their hit lists."

But if the death of distance helped Bland to stalk libraries, it also helped the libraries hunt down Bland. In the past, word of his apprehension in Baltimore would have traveled slowly, through gossip and other largely informal channels. But thanks to Cynthia Requardt's posting on ExLibris—a news group established in 1990 for discussion of rare books and manuscripts librarianship—institutions all over the country received notice of the crime only hours after it had taken place. "That made it a whole lot easier," Requardt later remembered. "If I didn't have ExLibris, I wouldn't have known how to contact people. I would have just stuck with the phone calls to people at the libraries I identified from the notebook. . . . The speed with which Bland's trail unfolded was amazing."

And as the librarians began to tally their losses, a collective rage spread through their ranks. "I felt like a real victim, like it was a personal assault," said Evelyn Walker of the University of Rochester. "I've been here about fifteen years, and quite a few of my colleagues have also been here for quite a while. We feel very responsible for our collections, and very connected to them. We work hard to develop them, and feel really happy when we find just the right item to fit into a little slot. It's more than a job. It's a calling, a passion, whatever you want to call it. The librarians here really are curators who treasure their materials and want to make them available. Anybody in the world would have been welcome to come here and look at those maps and use them. And now they're gone."

Added John E. Ingram of the University of Florida, "What I find to be the most difficult part is to realize that someone was coming in and destroying part of our heritage. We are a state institution, and the person who took the maps was robbing the entire state and the country, not just the library. For instance, for one of the titles—*Modern History, or, the Present State of All Nations* by Thomas Salmon—we have the only complete copy in the state of Florida. Well, we formerly had the only complete copy."

The librarians, a legendarily docile people, now wanted blood. "If Bland gets in front of my car," said Northwestern University's Russell Maylone, "I'll run over him—but in a nice way. . . . Oh, and then I'll back over him again."

But capturing Bland again did not prove to be a simple matter. After being detained in Baltimore, he apparently stayed on for a few days in his old hometown of Columbia, Maryland. While there, he called the Peabody Institute's security chief, Donald Pfouts, to request the return of his notebook. "He said he forgot his book and he really needed to get it," explained Pfouts. "Once he found out he wasn't getting his book back, I think that's when he really realized what the possibilities were. And that's when he fled."

It would take law enforcement officials nearly a month to capture him—a costly delay, as things turned out. The problem was not that the invisible man had disappeared once more. Police knew just where to find Gilbert Bland: at his home in Coral Springs, Florida. But getting there to arrest him proved to be a more arduous journey than anyone could have imagined. Bureaucracy, indifference, and disorganization can be more difficult to navigate than the widest ocean. And sometimes the world can still seem like a very big place indeed.

ex Deo, vincit mundum:
ue vicit mundum, nempe
t qui vincit mundum nisi
e filium Dei? 1 Ioan 5. 4

DIABOLUS

Sobrii estote, vigilate: nam
adversarius vester diabolus
tanquam leo rugiens, oham:
bulat: quærens quem devoret.
Cui resistite firmi per fidem.
1. Petr 5.

Subjicite igitur vos Deo,
resistite diabolo, et
fugiet a vobis. Iac. 4. 7

DETAIL FROM A WORLD MAP BY
JODOCUS HONDIUS, CIRCA 1597,
WARNING AGAINST THE TEMPTATIONS
OF SATAN. "BE SOBER, BE VIGI-
LANT," READS THE ACCOMPANYING
BIBLICAL TEXT, "BECAUSE YOUR
ADVERSARY THE DEVIL, AS A ROARING
LION, WALKETH ABOUT, SEEKING
WHOM HE MAY DEVOUR."

CHAPTER 7

A Brief History of
Cartographic Crime

S O THERE I WAS, STANDING IN AWE BEFORE the "monster camera," as one of its operators called it, a contraption of such massive proportions that it stretched across two large rooms, was able to snap a photo negative four feet wide and seven and a half feet long, could blow up an image to almost five hundred times its original size, and could reduce it by the same proportion. With one blink of its big reptilian eye, it could have transformed me from a six-foot-two-inch man into a half-mile-high colossus or a microorganism of about one eighth of an inch, just as it had once reduced all of Europe to the size of a postage stamp. It was a technological wonder, that camera. It was also, according to Vera Benson, a "white elephant," destined for the trash heap.

Benson is director of cartography for the American Map Corporation, part of the Langenscheidt Publishing Group, which competes with Rand McNally for retail primacy in the U.S. map market. A self-possessed woman with a wry sense of humor and a faint German accent, Benson was giving me a tour of the company's headquarters, a no-frills brick building in an industrial area of Queens, New York. If I had been following directly in the path of Gilbert Bland, this stop would not have been on my itinerary. To the best of my knowledge Bland neither came here nor had anything to do with American Map—unless, of course, he used one of the firm's popular road atlases to find his way from one library to the next. But in my journalistic travels, as in my personal wanderings, I'm a sucker for detours, back roads, tourist traps, scenic views, and historic landmarks. Invariably, these side trips enrich the journey, and every now and then they lead to an important discovery. I had come to Queens out of simple curiosity. Having spent so much time studying the profession's previous thousand years, I wanted to find out about the state of commercial mapmaking at the edge of the next millennium.

"We have traditional cartography and digital cartography going on down here," Benson explained, showing me into the mapmaking department, a long, open basement room with low ceilings. But even if she hadn't mentioned it, I could have seen that American Map was in a state of technological transition. One part of the room was filled with drafting tables, strewn with art supplies and staffed by slightly harried-looking designers. They were using a mapmaking process that was cutting edge not too long ago but that now struck even a casual observer like me as slow and inefficient—involving, among many other maddening details, the manual application of literally tens of thousands of street names to a page. American Map's colossal camera, that fading marvel of the mechanical age, was the central component in this kind of cartography, producing the negatives used to print everything from giant wall maps of the world to wallet-sized street maps of midtown Manhattan.

Another part of the room had a much more orderly appearance. Here, the tabletops were tidy and the faces serene. Instead of grappling with X-Acto knives, scribing tools, pens, paper, and unwieldy sheets of Mylar, the cartographers were drafting maps within the clean confines of their computer screens. "The advantage obviously is that digital maps are much easier to revise," Benson told me. "They're very time-consuming to create, unlike what people might expect. But then the benefits come in when you want to change the look of a map, eliminate features, alter it. Each feature is coded, so that, at will, you can just remove layers of information. You can take out a certain size of type, for instance, or you can change all the yellow roads to green. Previously, if you made a whole map and then decided the type you used was much too bold, there was nothing else to do but to scrap the whole thing and add on another fifteen thousand names by hand. Now, all you do is push a button."

It's not always quite that easy, of course. In another part of the room, Benson introduced me to a frustrated cartographer who was "looking at the fallout" from a computer-generated atlas that encompassed Bergen and Passaic Counties in New Jersey and Rockland County in New York. "We just got the index, and it has a lot of mistakes," Benson said. "There are twelve thousand street entries just for Bergen—and twenty-three hundred discrepancies. . . . Somehow the computer manages to create more problems on top of the ones we already have. We can't figure out why."

Because of such technical problems and other practical concerns, Benson predicted it would be years before the giant camera would snap its last shot. In the meantime, even workers who make maps the old-fashioned way were undergoing extensive computer training as the firm rushed to embrace the digital age.

Yet despite all the changes at American Map, what struck me most about the place was a sense not of disruption but of continuity. As Benson led me around the facility, I often felt like I was looking into the past, present, and future of mapmaking all at the same time. The decor, for example, mixed satellite photos of the Earth with reproductions of maps from the seventeenth and eighteenth centuries. And, glancing around the cartography department, I was amused to observe a state-of-the-art computer on one desk and a stack of books about the history of cartography on another. The texts were there, it turned out, because the firm was trying to cash in on the old maps craze. "We are turning one of our world maps into an antique-look map," Benson explained. "It's going to be an up-to-date world map, but it's going to look like an antique map, designed for those people who might not want some stark modern map in their office but may want something more traditional."

I wondered whether this computer-designed artifact would include sea monsters.

"Absolutely!"

Though she professed no expertise in the subject, Benson had an obvious appreciation for old maps. On the wall of her office hung a huge reproduction showing a bird's-eye view of Manhattan from the nineteenth century, and behind her desk stood a framed engraving of Johann Baptist Homann, a famous German mapmaker of the 1700s. "A friend of mine who is an antiques dealer thought I might like to have [Homann], because he was a German cartographer and I am a German cartographer," she explained with a shrug. "I had never heard of him."

The two mapmakers certainly *looked* nothing alike. The man on the engraving had a tight-lipped expression every bit as pompous as his lace cravat and cuffs, and wore a full-bottom wig so absurdly overblown that it looked like a sheep had crash-landed on his skull. Benson, by contrast, had short brown hair, sensible glasses, and simple elegance to go with her direct, low-key manner. Yet the more I listened to her talk, the more she seemed to have in common with Homann and other mapmakers from the past. Benson began her work life in Germany as an architectural draftsman and later studied to become a civil engineer. Those plans were cut short, however, when she married an American and moved to the United States. She then worked in the fine arts—"graphics, painting, lithography, photography, and the like"—before coming to American Map two decades ago. She freely conceded she was not a "classically trained cartographer" but made no apologies for it: "Map publishing, which is what we do here, is really an interdisciplinary field that combines cartography, printing, art, photography."

The man in the picture, it turned out, had not been classically trained, either. Although late in life Homann was given the title Geographer to the Holy Roman Emperor, he began his career as an ordinary engraver. Like Benson, he succeeded because he knew how to merge science and commerce and art, how to bring the physical world to the printed page in a way that was both useful and beautiful. The technology of publishing is now vastly different than it was in Homann's time, but the instincts and imagination required to make maps have not changed—nor, as Benson pointed out, has the fundamental objective: "information, how to get it right and get it in a timely way. . . . In cartography, that's the big word: new data."

New data was what had driven Ptolemy and Ortelius and Homann, just as it was what now drove Benson and her contemporaries. But if the quest to procure new data had remained constant, so had the need to protect it. Before I contacted American Map, Rand McNally had refused my request for a tour of its plant; a publicist hinted that the firm was worried about the loss of trade secrets. Benson was obviously less guarded, but she made it clear that security was also an issue for her company. American Map, she explained, uses a trick called trap streets to discourage competitors from infringing on its copyright. This practice, common to the industry, involves hiding a fictional roadway somewhere on each map. "We place the trap streets in areas that would be relatively harmless and would not mislead someone using the map—just a cul-de-sac at the end of some development," Benson said. "I let my researchers be creative in deciding on the names: they might name the street after their wife or dog or whatever. This allows us to do a quick spot check of our competitors' maps to see if they have stepped on our toes. It happens all the time. . . . Sometimes it's an innocent blunder, but more often, it's not so innocent."

And so, sitting in Benson's office and imagining maps with out-of-the-way streets such as Fido Lane or Fritzie the Good Puppy Boulevard, I realized that yet another big factor had remained constant throughout the history of cartography: larceny.

CALL ME OBSESSED, BUT THE MORE I LOOKED INTO MAP theft, the more I found it lurking behind the scenes during key moments of our collective past. And I'm not talking about *small* moments, either—unless you consider Columbus's voyage to America small or Magellan's circumnavigation of the globe small or the invasion of Normandy small. I started to think the historians had overlooked something important in their eternal search for those "hidden hands" that guide the course of human events. I kept coming upon hidden hands myself, all of them holding hot maps. It was not that I presumed to have hit on the answer to all life's mysteries, a Unified Theory of the Missing Map. It was just that I began to see Gilbert Bland as heir to an ancient though hardly noble tradition, one that has shaped our world more than we know.

Maps are big-time booty. Mapmaking has been going on since at least the Stone Age: a picture map painted on a wall of the famous Catal Huyuk settlement in south-central Turkey dates back to about 6200 B.C., nearly three thousand years before the first system of written language appeared. And recent studies have shown that even very young children have an uncanny ability to understand maps, fueling speculation that we are born with the skill. All cultures are thought to make maps in one form or another, and for good reason. Throughout history they have enabled their possessors to win military battles, gain access to precious economic resources, and claim new territories as their own.

As manna, maps predate even money. Cartographic crime also goes back thousands of years. "In the Roman Empire . . . maps of the world were exclusively for government use, and it was a crime for a private person to possess one," wrote the historian Daniel J. Boorstin. Augustus, emperor at the time of Jesus' birth, was so worried his maps of his empire might fall into the wrong hands that he had them locked in the innermost vaults of the palace. Rome's traditional rivals from Carthage were no less concerned about theft. According to legend, one Carthaginian sea captain sank his ship rather than let his sea charts fall into Roman hands. His crew drowned, but he was given a hero's welcome upon his return home.

In the Age of Discovery map theft literally changed the world. Sooner or later some European adventurer would have stumbled upon America, but it might not have been Christopher Columbus and it might not have happened in 1492 if not for some sticky fingers. Before beginning work for the Spanish crown, Columbus spent the better part of nine years in Portugal, where his brother Bartholomeo had established himself as a noted cartographer. In 1485, having failed to sell Portugal's King John II on his proposed Enterprise of the Indies, Columbus decided to solicit help for the plan in Spain. He left in secret, "fearing the king would send after him and hold him," according to the sixteenth-century chronicler Bartolomé de Las Casas. The reason for his furtive exit is unclear—but some historians have wondered whether Columbus absconded with a copy of the Florentine cosmographer Paolo del Pozzo Toscanelli's world map (no longer extant), which showed a possible westerly sea route to the Indies. If so, the mariner would have had good reason to worry about being stopped. Portugal was then the world's dominant seafaring nation, a status it guarded with an iron fist. Nautical writings and charts were considered state secrets, and to copy or divulge their contents was a capital crime. Yet despite these restrictions, an even bigger cartographic caper would soon follow. This time the perpetrator was Bartholomeo Columbus, who had remained behind in Lisbon to help compile a large world map that incorporated the latest top-secret information gleaned by Portuguese explorers. As Lisa Jardine explained in *Worldly Goods: A New History of the Renaissance:*

> Bartholomeo prepared to join [a cash-strapped Christopher Columbus] in Spain to help his project. Before he left Lisbon, however, he copied a number of Portuguese

maps from the secret archive, including the large world map (which he transferred on to eleven sheets of paper, because paper was lighter, and easier to conceal, than parchment). The Columbus brothers sold Bartholomeo's valuable stolen maps in Italy for substantial sums, thereby dispersing vital information hitherto held only by the Portuguese.

In Seville, their financial circumstances alleviated by their map sales, the two brothers reassembled the world map, and modified it to incorporate material not yet entered at the time of Bartholomeo's departure. Crucially, this additional information suggested that, once the Cape of Good Hope had been rounded, a significant mass of land remained still to be navigated around before ships could gain access to the Indian Ocean. Although factually incorrect, the Columbus brothers' map, thus modified, apparently offered strong concrete support for the argument that a westwards route to the Indies was a viable alternative option. On the strength of comparison of the Columbuses' map (with its exaggerated coastline of Africa) with their own Ptolemaic maps (on which calculation errors significantly reduced the Atlantic Ocean) the Spanish monarchs Ferdinand and Isabella finally agreed to finance the venture in 1492.

All this from a purloined map. No wonder Lisbon kept a tight lid on its secrets—so tight, in fact, that almost none of the empire's charts made before the sixteenth century have survived, meaning that much of what we know about Portuguese cartography comes from the relatively few maps that left the country illegally. The most famous of those is the so-called Cantino planisphere, a one-of-a-kind world map with a colorful and iniquitous history. Considered the earliest surviving map of Lisbon's discoveries east and west (and one of the first maps ever to show the Americas), the Cantino planisphere was named not after the unknown Portuguese cartographer who drafted it but after the Italian secret agent who smuggled it out in 1502. Alberto Cantino had gone to Lisbon masquerading as a dealer in purebred horses. His real mission, however, was to gather intelligence for the duke of Ferrara. Gather it he did, bribing a mapmaker for an up-to-the-moment copy of the *padrão real,* the standard cartographic prototype unto which new discoveries were constantly being added.

Prominent on this lavishly illustrated chart is a fragmentary outline of the Brazilian coast, marked by Portuguese flags and decorated with resplendent red macaws. Just two years earlier the adventurer Pedro Álvares Cabral had sighted this new land, which he "believed to be a continent," according to an inscription on the map. That was big news. Christopher Columbus went to his death in 1506 insisting that the land he had reached was Asia, but other European navigators were beginning to realize that the face of the Earth was drastically different from the three-continent version pictured on their Ptolemaic maps. This was one of the most sudden and dramatic jolts in the history of human thought, and it triggered a fierce competition for cutting-edge cartographic data, which, given the realities of the time, often meant contraband cartographic data.

Among those exploiting this emerging black market was Ferdinand Magellan, who departed his native Portugal for Spain in 1517, taking with him classified information that a navigable strait might exist at the extreme southern end of South America. At a meeting in Spain with Holy Roman Emperor Charles V, Magellan "brought with him a well-painted globe showing the entire world," wrote Las Casas, "and thereon traced the course he proposed to take, save that the Strait was purposely left blank so that nobody could anticipate him."

Scholars disagree about the origin of this globe. Some have argued that it was either a copy or an updated version of a famous 1492 work by Martin Behaim, today considered to be the oldest surviving European terrestrial sphere. Behaim was an enigmatic mathematician, merchant, and adventurer who had once been a government mapmaker in Portugal but had since sold his services to the city fathers of Nuremberg. "In making the globe for the Germans," explained Lisa Jardine, "Behaim had been involved in a substantial piece of commercial and industrial espionage. . . . Behaim incorporated the cartographical information he had access to in Lisbon—the most highly classified and inaccessible cartographical information currently available."

Other historians, however, have conjectured that what Las Casas loosely described as a "globe" was, in fact, a world map—most likely one made by the Portuguese cartographer Jorge Reinel, who had gotten into trouble in Lisbon and had since fled to Spain. This argument is bolstered by a report, made in 1519 by Lisbon's ambassador to Seville, which informed the Portuguese king that Reinel had made a map specifically to help Magellan prepare for his voyage. Reinel's father, the prominent mapmaker Pedro Reinel, had gone to Seville to bring his wayward son home. But according to the ambassador, the elder Reinel was also seen adding details to the Spanish map.

In any case, it is clear that Magellan benefited from carto-graphic secrets stolen from the Portuguese. A firsthand ac-count of his journey suggests that without access to such intelligence, he might never have located the famous strait that now bears his name. On October 21, 1520—more than a year after setting sail—he reached a cape where the South American coastline appeared to turn west. Was this, at last, the long-sought opening to the Pacific? Antonio Pigafetta, an Italian who sailed with the expedition and later wrote about it, was not con-vinced. Like others on the journey, he had expected the strait to be an open passageway that you could see through, like the Strait of Gibraltar. This cape, "closed on all sides," did not in-spire much hope. But Magellan was certain they were in the right place—apparently for good reason. As Pigafetta ex-plained, "He knew where to sail to find a well-hidden strait, which he saw on a map in the treasury of the king of Portugal."

Historians are still unsure which map Magellan had seen, or whether it actually could have provided him much useful infor-mation. And no map could have guided the ships through the unexplored strait that lay ahead, a maze of narrow passages and small islands, blasted by strange winds. Magellan's skills as a navigator should not be underestimated. Still, without the illicit information he procured from Lisbon, the first circumnavigation of the Earth might have been neither attempted nor completed.

But the Portuguese were not alone in their worries about map theft. Spain was quickly establishing a trade monopoly in the New World that rivaled the Portuguese hold on Africa and Asia. And as Daniel Boorstin noted in *The Discoverers,* the new empire had security problems of its own:

> The Spanish . . . kept their official charts in a lockbox secured with two locks and two keys, one held by the pilot-major (Amerigo Vespucci was the first), the other by the cosmographer-major. Fearing that their official maps would be deliberately corrupted or would not include the latest authentic information, in 1508 the government created a master chart, the *Padrón Real,* to be supervised by a commission of the ablest pilots. But all these precautions were not enough. The Venetian-born Sebastian Cabot . . . while serving as pilot-major to Emperor Charles V, tried to sell "The Secret of the Strait" both to Venice and to England.

Perhaps no one person was more hated by the Spanish than the man they called "master thief of the unknown world." In his fabled round-the-world voyage of 1577–1580, Francis Drake not only helped shatter Spain's hold on the Americas but came back to England with some forty tons of gold and silver bullion from Spanish ships and outposts. And yet those were not his only spoils. On March 20, 1579, while storming a small enemy vessel off Costa Rica, his men captured two large navigator's maps of the Pacific and a collection of charts detailing Spain's China route. Nuño da Silva, a Portuguese pilot Drake was then holding captive, later testified that the English buccaneer "prized these greatly and rejoiced over them." Drake had good reason to be pleased. Many historians believe that he had not left England with firm plans to circle the world. But now, with Spanish ships searching for him up and down the Pacific coast of South America, he was in no position to head back through the Strait of Magellan. The charts of the Pacific were "exactly what he required," wrote Alexander McKee in *The Queen's Corsair: Drake's Journey of Circumnavigation, 1577–1580*. Added the historian John Hampden, "Drake's smooth passage from the American coast to the East Indies was not due solely to his genius for navigation; he had [the] captured Spanish charts."

Other swashbucklers quested after similar booty, as Lloyd A. Brown observed in *The Story of Maps:*

> In the sixteenth century genuine Spanish charts of any part of the Americas were real maritime prizes, rated as highly by the French and English as the gold bullion which might be in the ships' strong rooms. One such priceless haul was made by the English adventurer and freebooter Woodes Rogers. While cruising on behalf of some merchants of Bristol along the coast of Peru and

Chile he captured some charts which were so "hot" that they were immediately engraved in London and published by John Senex.

In another celebrated case, a group of English pirates led by Bartholomew Sharp captured the Spanish ship *Rosario* off the Ecuadoran coast in 1681. On board they found what one buccaneer described as "a great Book full of Sea-Charts and Maps, containing a very accurate and exact description of all the Ports, Soundings, Creeks, Rivers, Capes, and Coasts belonging to the South Sea, and all the Navigations usually performed by the *Spaniards* in that Ocean." A Spanish mariner tried to cast this chart book—or *derrotero*—into the sea, but one of the pirates stopped him. "The Spaniards cried when I gott [*sic*] the book," Sharp later wrote.

Sharp did not know it at the time, but that *derrotero* may have saved him from the gallows upon his return home in 1682. Because England and Spain were then at peace, the buccaneer and two members of his crew were charged, at the behest of the Spanish ambassador, with piracy and murder. Before the trial, however, a copy of the stolen chart book was given to England's King Charles II, who took a personal interest in the case. Sharp and the others were soon acquitted—a verdict that may well have been due to "royal influence," according to Derek Howse and Norman J. W. Thrower, authors of *A Buccaneer's Atlas,* a book about the incident.

Charles II, by the way, seems to have had a real passion for the cloak-and-dagger side of cartography. In 1683 England's ambassador to France wrote the king to offer "the plans of some fortified places which I believe are very exact. If Your Majesty . . . approve of them, I do not question but to have draughts of all the other fortification of France in a little time." England and France were then allies. No matter: a reply soon came back informing the ambassador that Charles had received the plans and "carried them to his closet: where . . . he perused them . . . appeared extremely well pleased and . . . desire[d] you would goe on & procure as many as you could."

Another leader who appreciated a good secondhand map was George Washington. A former surveyor, the general was well aware of the military necessity of knowing one's terrain. In 1777 he lost more than twelve hundred men at the Battle of the Brandywine, partly because he had no accurate map of the area. "Spies directed by Washington were explicitly alerted to acquire maps whenever possible," wrote the map historian J. B. Harley, who added that "men were . . . prepared to risk their lives (and lost them) in acquiring suitable maps."

The crown had its own spies. Benedict Arnold's scheme to join the British was only discovered when his illicit maps—the plans for West Point—were found hidden in the boot of an accomplice. Other map-toting turncoats had better luck. In 1776 the British captured Fort Washington in New York City, thanks at least in part to the treachery of an American officer named William Demont, who later confessed that he had "brought in with me [to the British] the plans of Fort Washington, by which plans that fortress was taken by His Majesty's troops."

Stolen maps were again at a premium in the Civil War—

especially for the Confederacy, which generally lacked not only trained cartographers but mapmaking basics, such as surveying equipment, printing presses, paper, and ink. At times the situation was so bad that one Southern general declared his field officers "knew no more about the [local] topography of the country than they did about Central Africa." Southern spies coveted cartographic intelligence—and often had to look no further than Northern newspapers, whose accounts were regularly accompanied by battlefield maps. "I *know* that the principal northern papers reach the enemy regularly & promptly," fumed General William Tecumseh Sherman, who added that the problem had "brought our country to the brink of ruin."

Some Confederate operatives, however, had more prurient methods of obtaining maps. Rose O'Neal Greenhow was a beautiful and well-connected widow whose admirers included a number of powerful Northern politicians and military officers. From her richly appointed house in Washington, D.C., Greenhow ran a remarkably successful espionage operation—at one point charming a U.S. senator out of key military secrets that helped the South win the Battle of Bull Run. The person who finally exposed her as a spy was Allan Pinkerton, the famous private detective. On August 21, 1861, Pinkerton—perched on the shoulder of two assistants—watched through Greenhow's parlor window as the sultry secret agent entertained a young Union officer. As Pinkerton looked on, the soldier handed her a military map and described its contents in detail. Then, according to the detective's account of the event, Greenhow led the officer into another room—from which they returned "arm and arm" an hour later. "There was no doubt, if Pinkerton's report was to be believed, that the handsome widow had performed a sexual tryst with the officer in return for his delivery of the vital map," observed the writer Jay Robert Nash.

During World War I both sides were so concerned about secrecy that their maps of the front showed only the enemy's trenches, a practice that prompted troops to capture maps from the other side in order to get around their own fortifications. World War II military planners were also obsessed with safeguarding the maps of their defenses—sometimes in vain. In 1943 Nazi officials in the French town of Caen hired a man named René Duchez to redecorate their headquarters. While there Duchez noticed that, folded on the top of a desk, was a large map labeled "Special Blueprint—Top Secret." A normal housepainter would have minded his own business, but Duchez happened to have a sideline career with the French resistance. While the German commandant was distracted by other matters, Duchez hid the map within the office, retrieving it when he returned to work a few days later. The stolen map was a remarkable find, detailing the Germans' secret "Atlantic Wall" defense system, an elaborate network of underwater obstacles, tank traps, minefields, barbed wire, and gun installations—information that proved essential to the Allied invasion of Normandy. As General Omar Bradley later explained: "Securing the blueprint of the German Atlantic Wall was an incredible feat—so valuable that the landing operation succeeded with a minimum loss of men and material."

Not every map heist of World War II worked out so well, however. In 1944 twenty-five German POWs pulled off the largest and most spectacular escape from an American compound during the war, digging a 178-foot tunnel out of the Navy's Papago Park Prisoner of War Camp in Arizona. All of the men were eventually captured, but some remained at large for more than a month. Among the last to be brought in were three German soldiers who had based their own audacious but ill-fated escape plans on a stolen highway map of Arizona, which showed the Gila River leading to the Colorado River, which in turn led to Mexico. Devising a scheme to flee by water, they constructed a collapsible kayak under the noses of their captors, tested it in a makeshift pool within the prison compound, then snuck it out through the tunnel. Their plan was perfect—except for the map. The Gila, shown as a healthy blue waterway, turned out to be little more than a dry rut.

BECAUSE MAPS HAVE SO OFTEN PROVED INACCURATE, out-of-date, or just plain unavailable, military leaders have long searched for ways to get the lay of the land without them. Manned observation balloons were used for intelligence gathering as early as 1794 and played a vital role in both the Civil War and the Spanish-American War. In World War I, camera-equipped airplanes were providing information not available on old-fashioned maps, such as up-to-date images of troop movements and bomb damage. Aerial espionage continued to advance and flourish through World War II and the Cold War.

But by 1960, when Soviet forces shot down the U-2, an American ultrahigh-altitude aircraft specifically designed for spying, both superpowers were already hard at work on the next frontier of overhead observation. The space race was on, and soon the sky would be full of eyes.

Far from making maps obsolete, however, new satellite technologies have led to one of the most productive periods in the history of cartography, comparable only to the golden age of mapmaking in the sixteenth and seventeenth centuries. NASA's Landsat satellites—which, rather than taking photographs of the Earth, measure wavelengths of reflected energy—have "stood traditional cartography on its ear," according to Stephen S. Hall, author of *Mapping the Next Millennium.* "By seeing in electromagnetic increments beyond the normal range of human vision, Landsat revealed whole new worlds hidden within the folds of a familiar world we thought we knew so well." Among the many benefits of Landsat imagery has been the discovery of previously unknown lakes, a new isle (named Landsat Island) off Canada's Atlantic coast, and an uncharted reef in the Indian Ocean.

While such imagery greatly enhances maps, it won't replace them anytime soon—a point I grasped one day as I toured the Santa Barbara, California, headquarters of Map Link, Inc., the largest independent wholesale distributor of maps and atlases in North America. My host that day was the firm's publishing manager, Will Tefft, a man who regularly travels to distant corners of the Earth in search of cartographic treasure. As he led me around the facility, a cavernous former lemon-packing plant, Tefft explained that he and his associates chase a lofty goal: to stock every modern-day map by every map publisher on the planet. When a desired map cannot be obtained or does not exist, Map Link will often publish one itself. Among the firm's customers have been the Kuwaiti embassy in Washington, which purchased maps of its own country during the 1990 Iraqi invasion, and the U.S. military, which also placed large orders for maps of the region during the Gulf War.

Tefft, far more than most people, understands the importance of satellite photos in modern cartography—yet he insisted that no photograph alone can take the place of a map. "Perhaps people have been overwhelmed by movies, TV news, and all the other electronic media," he said. "There's a camera everywhere; it's just incredible. But a camera can't reveal the place names—anything that humans ascribe a word to, from Mount McKinley to the Los Angeles International Airport— and a camera can't help travelers, in terms of what they are looking at now and what they are aiming for over the horizon."

I remembered his words a short while later, when, during the height of the air war over Yugoslavia in 1999, NATO forces accidentally bombed the Chinese embassy in Belgrade, killing three people and touching off a messy diplomatic crisis. In preparing to deploy "smart bombs" for the attack, NATO commanders had made use of the most advanced satellite imagery available. What they did not have was something that could show them the correct locations of both the embassy and the intended target, the Yugoslav Federal Directorate of Supply and Procurement. The resulting tragedy was graphic proof that even in an age when satellites allow us to observe each other and our world in mind-boggling ways, there's sometimes still no substitute for a good map.

Not surprisingly, a black market for up-to-date maps still exists. In 1995, for example, a Michigan man named Bill Stewart was convicted of trying to sell classified U.S. government computer tapes containing three-dimensional maps of the Mideast. Nonetheless, in an era when you can switch on your laptop and find an adequate map of almost any place on Earth, and when, for a fee, you can buy satellite images of your own home or even spy from space on the backyard of a hated neighbor, contemporary maps have lost much of their contraband currency. These days a new kind of map thief has emerged—one who steals not to claim the future, like Columbus or Magellan, but to recapture a lost and longed-for past.

WHO COULD BE MORE TRUSTWORTHY AROUND OLD books than a couple of priests? When fathers Michael Huback and Stephen Chapo—members of the Eastern Rite of Greek Orthodox Catholicism, a Slavonic sect—began making frequent visits to Yale's Sterling Memorial Library in November 1970, they apparently received little scrutiny from staff members. The clergymen remained regulars in the stacks until March 1972, when a Chicago book dealer offered to sell Yale one of three extant copies of a 1670 atlas by the Dutch cartographer Hendrick Doncker. Library officials were shocked to discover that the sale item was, in fact, the copy they had thought to be sitting safely on their shelves. The stolen atlas was soon linked to Huback and Chapo, and when librarians did an inventory of their atlas collection they discovered that nearly two hundred other books were missing. But Yale, apparently, had not been the only victim. When FBI agents searched a New York City monastery where Huback and Chapo were living, they recovered books belonging to a number of other schools, including the University of Chicago, Dartmouth, Harvard, Notre Dame, Manhattan College, the University of Washington, and Indiana University. The motivation of the priestly pair, soon defrocked, seems to have been decidedly secular. As St. Jerome once quipped: "Avoid, as you would the plague, a clergyman who is also a man of business."

The recent annals of cartographic crime are full of such colorful tales. The offenders come from varied backgrounds and circumstances, but almost all of them have one thing in common. Like Gilbert Bland, they have all wrestled with bizarre alter egos, as if what those stolen maps showed them were secret routes to the furthest places in their hearts. Among the more notable figures in this unusual rogues' gallery are these:

- Andrew P. Antippas, a Tulane University English professor who "was regarded with that special undergraduate awe reserved for only a chosen few professors," according to a 1979 report in the New Orleans *States-Item*. A charismatic lecturer who sometimes fought back tears while reading the poetry of Keats aloud in class, Antippas was apparently held in such high esteem that the student board of the cam-

pus newspaper, *Hullabaloo*, voted not to report on his November 1978 guilty plea to charges resulting from the theft
of five antique maps—then valued at twenty thousand
dollars—from Yale University's Sterling Memorial Library.
He also admitted to stealing maps from the Newberry Library in Chicago. A map collector and part-time dealer, he
apparently succumbed to his demons. "I was there, I was
tempted. Who can explain something like this?" he said at
the time. In January 1979, upon being sentenced to a year in
prison, he declared that "I indeed ruined my life and career." But in retrospect he appears to have been overstating
the case. Today Antippas owns Barrister's Gallery, an up-
scale New Orleans establishment specializing in Southern
folk art.

• Charles Lynn Glaser, one of the most notorious Jekyll-and-
Hyde figures in cartographic crime. Glaser was a noted authority on antiquities whose 1970 book, *Engraved America*,
was once described by the trade publication *AB Bookman's
Weekly* as "the standard reference for early American
iconography." But he was also a compulsive map thief with
a criminal career that spanned three decades. Even before
his legal troubles began, Glaser exhibited a curious fascination with fraud. In his 1968 book, *Counterfeiting in America:
The History of an American Way to Wealth,* he took lengths to
praise the "few great counterfeiters . . . men of unusual
skill or cunning" who "ennobled the crime by demonstrating vision and industry." It's not clear why Glaser himself

turned to crime. He did sell the maps he stole—but when I tracked down his ex-wife, Nosta Boll Glaser, she said, "I don't think he did it for the money." Instead, she offered this theory: during the 1970s her former spouse, suffering from "delusions of grandeur," became deeply frustrated that his own map and print business floundered while a fellow Philadelphian, the loud and brash Graham Arader, thrived. "Arader was a younger guy who came on the scene like gangbusters. And I think my ex-husband couldn't quite deal with his success and his presence," she explained. "Lynn considered himself—and this is his expression and not mine—*morally superior* to Arader. And since he was morally superior he couldn't quite understand why Arader was having all this success. . . . I think he justified the thefts by telling himself he was morally superior but he wasn't being appreciated."

In July 1974 Glaser was arrested for stealing eight sixteenth-, seventeenth-, and eighteenth-century atlases—including Thomas Jefferys's famous *American Atlas* of 1776—from the map room at Dartmouth College. Sentenced to a three-to-seven-year prison term, he spent some seven months behind bars before being paroled. But that did not dissuade him from striking again. In 1978 Glaser stole two maps by the explorer Samuel de Champlain from the University of Minnesota's James Ford Bell Library. The maps—one published in 1613, the other in 1632—were each worth more than $10,000 at the time (and now might fetch upwards of $300,000 and $100,000, respectively).

Upon his guilty plea in 1982, Glaser, who also admitted stealing two maps from the Newberry Library in Chicago, was given six months in prison, ordered to pay $5,500 in restitution, and sentenced to four and a half years' probation. Yet he continued to pass himself off as a genteel bibliophile, publishing another book, *America on Paper,* in 1989. "For twenty-five years I have been handling browned bits of paper, usually bound in calf with ridged spines and gold stamping that somehow survived into the late 20th century," he wrote in that volume. "Sometimes, even if I could not read a work in the original, simply handling it made me imagine I was in touch with time."

Librarians must have fumed at the notion of a book destroyer lauding the survival of books, especially after he pleaded guilty in March 1992 to stealing a map from a 1628 edition of Sebastian Münster's famous *Cosmographia,* housed at the Free Library of Philadelphia. Less than one month later, while on probation, he was discovered again— reportedly wearing surgical gloves and carrying a hammer—in the stacks of Lehigh University. He might be out there in some rare books room today, still handling those beloved "browned bits of paper."

• Robert M. "Skeet" Willingham, Jr., librarian, author, Sunday school teacher, and city council member from Washington, Georgia, who was described by his friends and neighbors as "Mr. Straight," "a perfect gentleman," and "a very gentle fellow." Somewhere along the line, however, this exemplary citizen, the rare books curator for the University of Georgia, developed an alter ego. In the words of Katharine Leab, the editor of *American Book Prices Current* and an expert on library security: "He became his doppelgänger: the *bad* Willingham." In June 1986 a staffer at the university's Hargrett Rare Book and Manuscript Library noticed that a rare map of South Carolina was missing. Then a cursory inventory of the map collection indicated that others had been removed as well. Police—led to Willingham on a tip provided by the map mogul Graham Arader—soon searched the librarian's historic columned home and turned up seventeen framed maps, several of which were known to have been missing from the university. But that was just the tip of the iceberg. In September 1988, a jury convicted Willingham on thirteen of fourteen felony counts for the thefts of a huge cache of library property, including an eight-volume set of floral prints by Pierre-Joseph Redouté, valued at $500,000 (and now worth as much as $600,000).

• Fitzhugh Lee Opie, a descendant of the Confederate general Robert E. Lee and the legendary Virginia governor Henry "Light-Horse Harry" Lee, who liked to present himself as a guardian of history. When Virginia was considering adoption of the Martin Luther King holiday, Opie, an Alexandria bookstore owner, labeled the idea "a disgrace," arguing that the slain civil rights leader was "neither a Virginian nor a patriot." Opie's professed love of country, however, did not dissuade him from gutting the Library of

Congress over a period of ten years—visiting several times a week, according to prosecutors, to steal maps, books, and prints. The scam came to an end on March 7, 1992, when Opie was caught with two mid-nineteenth-century Pacific Railroad maps stuffed under his sweater.

- William Charles McCallum, a Yale University and Boston College Law School graduate, whom *The Boston Globe* described as "a rising star" at the New Hampshire attorney general's office. Thin, elegant, and sophisticated, with a taste for fine art and antiques, McCallum had such impressive legal credentials that the future U.S. Supreme Court justice David Souter—then on the state Supreme Court—once personally promoted him. But this outward success, his defense team would later argue, belied McCallum's bizarre private life, full of obsessive rituals such as eating his own hair, brushing his teeth up to fifty times a day . . . and stealing just about everything he could lay his hands on, including underwear and socks from laundromats. ("He only feels comfortable in stuff that's stolen," explained his attorney.) When police finally caught up with McCallum in 1996, they found his Colonial-style home in Londonderry packed with more than a hundred thousand dollars' worth of paintings, books, furniture, and prints, most of them stolen from local libraries and universities. Prominent in the ill-gotten collection were a number of cartographic curiosities, including Thomas Moule's 1845 map of Hampshire County, England, stolen from Saint Anselm College in Manchester, New

Hampshire; Jean-Baptiste Bourguignon d'Anville's 1755 map of North America, taken from the Thayer School of Engineering at Dartmouth; and two old editions of Strabo's *Geography* belonging to Dartmouth's Baker Library.

- Last but hardly least, the mysterious Daniel Spiegelman of Yonkers, New York. Among librarians Spiegelman is remembered as one of the biggest thieves in recent history, plundering the Rare Books and Manuscripts Library at New York's Columbia University for approximately $1.3 million in books, documents, and manuscripts, including more than 250 early maps. But among conspiracy theorists, especially those of the right-wing militia variety, he is even more legendary.

This much is known about the case for certain: in 1994 the staff at the rare books room at Columbia discovered that a large number of priceless documents—everything from one-of-a-kind medieval manuscripts to letters and documents signed by various American presidents—had been stolen. The perpetrator did not operate in public but broke into the secured stacks after hours, possibly via an abandoned conveyor belt, according to the library's director, Jean Ashton. When Ashton and other Columbia authorities discovered the thefts, they immediately started contacting book and print dealers worldwide—a strategy that soon paid off. In June 1995 authorities in the Netherlands arrested Spiegelman after he tried to sell a medieval manuscript to a Utrecht dealer, who recognized the item as stolen.

Then the story really got strange. Newspapers in the Netherlands, where the suspect was being held, began reporting that Spiegelman had possible links to Timothy McVeigh and Terry Nichols, suspects in the deadly 1995 bombing of the Alfred P. Murrah Federal Building in Oklahoma City. The reports quoted a Dutch Justice Ministry official as saying that Spiegelman was "suspected of delivering weaponry to the suspects of the Oklahoma bombings." The allegation—later retracted by the Dutch government—apparently stemmed from the fact that Spiegelman was wanted in the United States on charges of illegally purchasing several pistols from gun shops in Phoenix and Scottsdale, Arizona. Dutch newspapers also reported that a safe belonging to Spiegelman in New York contained a list of up to forty names of people allegedly linked to the blast.

The U.S. Justice Department, however, repeatedly denied a connection between the two cases. And Spiegelman himself disavowed any part in the Oklahoma City bombing, telling the Dutch media that "I was involved in it as much as I was involved in the assassination of John F. Kennedy." Nonetheless, the story soon took on a life of its own, encouraged by a member of McVeigh's defense team, who declared that Spiegelman bore a noteworthy resemblance to John Doe No. 2, the mystery man long sought in connection with the bombing. The Internet was soon abuzz with innuendo, as exemplified by one widely distributed posting, titled "Thirty Questions About Oklahoma City," which appeared on websites such as the Big Sky Patriot ("covering issues of government corruption . . . the militia movement, the Freemen"). According to the posting, whose writer was identified only as Monte, no "media blackout in the . . . case has been more complete than the blackout imposed over the name of Daniel Spiegelman; it is as if he has stepped off the face of the planet. Who is Daniel Spiegelman? What connection does he have with Oklahoma City? Is he John Doe Number Two?"

When I posed some of these questions to Jean Ashton during a phone interview in early 1999, she said she honestly didn't know—and what's more, she didn't particularly care. What mattered to her was, first, that Spiegelman had been extradited to the United States, where in April 1997 he pleaded guilty to a variety of charges at the U.S. District Court in Manhattan; second, that Judge Lewis A. Kaplan had set aside federal sentencing guidelines and handed out a harsher-than-normal prison sentence of five years, arguing that the crimes were more serious than "a simple theft of money"; and, third, that law enforcement agents had recovered much of the plunder.

All of that was good news, but when I asked her about the fate of the stolen maps, she turned glum. Of more than 250 maps Spiegelman was thought to have stolen, fewer than 50 had been recovered, she said. Worse still, many of those had come from an extremely rare copy of the Dutch cartographer Joan Blaeu's *Atlas Major* of 1667, valued, in its former state, at a minimum of three hundred thousand dollars. Only two intact German-language editions of the book had existed anywhere in the world, she explained, and Columbia's copy was all the more unique because it had once belonged to Alexander Anderson, a prominent early-nineteenth-century engraver who supplemented the original with his own maps. "In many ways," she said, "the Blaeu was the most serious part of the whole theft."

*T*HERE ONCE WAS A MAN WHO THOUGHT CLASSIFYING A criminal was as easy as assigning a Dewey decimal number to a book. His name was Johnny Jenkins, and he was famous in rare books circles, both as a flamboyant dealer from Texas and as president of the Antiquarian Booksellers Association of America. In 1982, when serving as head of security for that organization, Jenkins wrote an article claiming that all library thieves could be categorized into one of five "basic types." There was the Kleptomaniac, the Thief Who Steals for Himself, the Thief Who Steals in Anger, the Casual Thief, and the Thief Who Steals for Profit. It was simple to get inside the head of a crook, Johnny Jenkins declared, because criminals "tend to exhibit classifiable characteristics."

Six years after he wrote those words, this same Johnny Jenkins was found floating in the Colorado River, dead from an apparent suicide. Not long before that, news had broken that a number of the very rare and expensive documents Jenkins had been selling over the years were forgeries. Many mysteries surrounded the case—not the least of which were whether Jenkins was personally involved in creating the fakes, and, if so, why a man of his stature would have felt compelled to do such a thing. They remain mysteries still. In both his controversial career and his enigmatic demise, Johnny Jenkins would defy simple classification. "I suppose he was a man who lived two lives," one of his old friends told Calvin Trillin of *The New Yorker.* "Or maybe three."

I keep this tale in mind whenever I'm tempted to make generalizations about the motivations of modern-day map thieves. While at first glance a few of them do seem to fit nicely into those criminal categories Johnny Jenkins invented, on closer inspection most appear to have been driven by complex and contradictory impulses. (A New Hampshire jury, for instance, rejected William McCallum's insanity defense, determining that while he may have had a preference for stolen underwear and hot maps, he was not a kleptomaniac.) Still, if I had to pick out a single overriding motive for map theft, I would opt for the one that's been driving cartographic crime for centuries: simple greed. As a sixteenth-century Spanish diplomat wrote about Lopo Homem, official Portuguese Master of Sea Charts and unofficial smuggler: "[He and his assistant] have orders to make no chart for anybody but the King. But sometimes they venture at a price."

Yet there's another motivation, one that Johnny Jenkins failed to mention but that may have been a factor in his own fall from grace. Simply put: the chance of getting caught in a book-related crime is fairly small, and the chance of getting serious punishment is still smaller. This is especially true of map theft—in part because of the very structure of the trade. The

Columbia librarian Jean Ashton—who is not particularly hopeful that her missing maps will ever be returned—explained the situation like this: "The market for maps is—what shall I say?—much more *uncontrolled* than the market for medieval manuscripts, for example. These early printed maps are bought not just by scholars or the rarefied collector. They're sold as decorative objects, not as scholarly objects. And they may be sold in all kinds of ways that fall outside the system of security by the dealers and collectors of other kinds of rare materials—at flea markets, for example. So it's far less likely that people can track down an individual map."

Ashton stopped short of directly blaming dealers, aware that even the most scrupulous ones often find it impossible to recognize a stolen map once it has been cut out of a book. But when I discussed the issue with Graham Arader, the longtime alpha male of the map kingdom was not so diplomatic. He insisted that his competitors are often less than thorough about checking the provenance of their merchandise. "It's simple," he said. "All you say is, 'Where did you get this map?' Then you listen to the story and you say, 'Do you mind if I check your sources?' And then if he starts waffling, you say, 'Sir, get the hell out of my gallery!' And if you really think he stinks, then you turn him in."

On a number of occasions, Arader has practiced exactly what he preached. It was he, for example, who sparked the investigation into Skeet Willingham, notifying University of Georgia authorities in 1985 that someone had offered him a letter by the Revolutionary War hero Nathanael Greene—a manuscript ostensibly in the university's collection at the time. Still, Arader had to concede that even he has made mistakes, such as when he bought sixty-two maps from Andrew Antippas, unaware that more than forty of them had been stolen from his own alma mater. The fact that they were hot did not come to light until Arader offered some of them for sale to a Texas collector named Walter Reuben, who recognized the maps as belonging to Yale. "Antippas got me," Arader conceded. "He definitely tricked me."

But, in his usually pugnacious style, the map mogul laid much of the blame for the ongoing wave of thefts squarely on the shoulders of librarians, who he claimed are simply not vigilant enough. "Most librarians are incompetent, boring, and dull," he said. "And they have this easy life. Many of them view their collections as their personal fiefdoms. But really, they don't look after their material. You know, it's not hard to tell the difference between a thief and somebody who's legitimate. If you're not intelligent enough to see these guys coming, then you shouldn't be a curator."

It's easy to see why librarians don't care much for Arader. Even so, few of them would deny that rare books rooms face serious security problems. And while the curators—especially those who think they are somehow above the nuts-and-bolts work of preventing theft—certainly deserve a good part of the blame, so do the institutions themselves. Well into the 1990s, for example, many university libraries lacked surveillance cameras for even their most rare and valuable collections, a shortcoming school administrators largely chose to ignore. Protecting books is "simply not what we value as a society," observed the security expert Katharine Leab. "If there is a choice between providing funds to inventory the stacks or to get a new bus for the football team, what do we do? Well, we get a new bus for the football team."

But if the map industry and map libraries have not done enough to discourage theft, neither has the legal system. Willingham served only thirty months of a fifteen-year sentence before getting out on parole. Still, his punishment was comparatively harsh. McCallum, who could have served the rest of his life in prison for the nearly seventy counts against him, got a three-to-six-year term. Fathers Huback and Chapo each received only eighteen months. Antippas got one year, while Opie got just six months for his decade-long crime spree. Glaser, a habitual offender, received only three years of *probation* for his 1992 conviction. And even Spiegelman—whom the judge went out of his way to punish—got only five years in prison (of which he had already served more than half) plus a $314,150 fine (of which he may never get around to paying more than a small fraction).

"If you steal a Picasso or Rembrandt or any piece out of a museum," observed Carol Miller, the former head of security for the Free Library of Philadelphia, "there is going to be publicity and there is going to be serious time given. But if you steal things out of a book, the sentences are just ludicrously low. People say, 'Well, it's just a book.' What kind of message is this sending to people who are thinking about doing this? We're saying, 'Go ahead, because you're not going to get in too much trouble.' It's sort of a joke."

As the prices of rare maps soared in the mid-1990s, the security problems that had plagued libraries and the rare books trade for decades remained largely unsolved or unaddressed. Which meant that the stage was set for the most prolific cartographic criminal in American history to make his quiet entrance.

*G*ILBERT BLAND STOLE IT FROM THE UNIVERSITY OF Washington. John Ogilby stole it from Arnold Montanus, who stole it from somebody else. Ogilby's 1671 map of Virginia—one of those that Bland allegedly pilfered in Seattle—offers proof that the cartographers of yore were themselves shameless crooks. As the biographer Katherine S. Van Eerde so delicately put it, Ogilby "failed to mention" that he had borrowed the map from Montanus, who, in turn, forgot to announce that he had borrowed it from earlier cartographers. Save for a few decorative details, the Ogilby and Montanus maps of Virginia are dead ringers for a 1630 work by Willem Janszoon Blaeu, the leading Dutch cartographer of the seventeenth century (and father of the Joan Blaeu mentioned earlier in this chapter). For his part, Willem Blaeu tried to put a stop to such plagiarism. According to Lloyd A. Brown, Blaeu "made a special plea to . . . Holland and Friesland for protection against the vultures who were pirating his maps, asserting that he could support his family by honest means, with God's mercy, if certain persons would desist from copying all his newest maps before the ink on them was dry." But Blaeu himself was not above theft, as his own 1630 map of Virginia makes clear. He bought the plate for the map from the rival Hondius firm, replacing the Hondius name with his own (a change that left faint traces of the erased letters on his version). Yet the Hondius family had no rightful claim to the work either. Of all those who took credit for the map, the only legitimate one was the English adventurer John Smith, who drafted it in 1612.

Smith had a big advantage over his imitators: he had actually been to Virginia. But what differentiated the creators from the copiers often had nothing to do with firsthand familiarity with the terrain. Zebulon Montgomery Pike, for instance, made extensive explorations of the American West, whereas Alexander von Humboldt never set foot there. But Pike's 1810 work, *A Map of the Internal Provinces of New Spain,* presented as being based on "sketches of . . . Captain Zebulon M. Pike," was in fact plagiarized directly from a map that Humboldt had left at the State Department during a visit to Washington in 1804.

In an 1813 letter of apology to Humboldt, Thomas Jefferson regretted that Pike "made ungenerous use" of the map, insisting it had been done "on a principle of enlarging knolege [*sic*] and not for filthy shillings and pence." But in fact a hunger for "enlarging knowledge" was precisely what separated the two mapmakers. Pike, a career soldier in the U.S. Army, was good at following orders but lacked a necessary zeal for getting at the crux of things. During his 1806–7 expedition, he set out with much hoopla to climb a "Grand Peak" he had spotted in the distance. But after experiencing a bit of cold and hunger, he abandoned the project, miles short of the summit of what is now known as Pikes Peak. Humboldt, by contrast, was bent on penetrating the unknown. When faced with a daunting climb of his own—Ecuador's Mount Chimborazo—he braved rough weather to reach "the highest altitude ever attained by any human being in history until that time," according to his biographer Douglas Botting. He was not only a great explorer— covering more than six thousand miles of South America during one five-year period—but also a brilliant physiologist, zoologist, botanist, anthropologist, archaeologist, and meteorologist. Today he is perhaps best remembered as a founding figure in modern geography, a subject that fired his imagination even as a boy. "The study of maps and the perusal of travel books," he once wrote, "aroused a secret fascination that was at times almost irresistible, and seemed to bring me into close relationship with distant places and things."

It was this same inquisitiveness that enabled Humboldt to produce a map of the West that the expert Carl I. Wheat described as "a truly magnificent cartographic achievement." Humboldt could map a place he had never seen—using, in his own words, "a great variety of data" instead of "vague suppositions"—because he was blessed with the sort of intense curiosity that most of us experience so infrequently it often seems to come as a surprise. I'm not talking about the kind of curiosity that *invites* but about the kind that *demands,* not about the kind that says *I wonder* but the kind that says *I must know.* The kind that makes you immerse yourself in a subject, ponder it over and over until you are able to make sense of it for others and, in so doing, give your own life new meaning in some small way. Under such a spell, humans can accomplish the extraordinary. One need not be a genius like Alexander von Humboldt to make unseen worlds appear.

HE MAN WHO BROUGHT GILBERT BLAND TO JUSTICE was neither a high-profile FBI agent nor a flashy detective on a big-city police force. He was a campus cop, not too far up on the law enforcement food chain from the lowly private security guard. Nonetheless, Thomas W. Durrer had a keen mind and, more important, a roiling sense of curiosity. As an investigator for the University of Virginia Police Department, Durrer had little in common with the shoot-'em-up stars of tabloid TV cop shows; his work involved mostly mundane matters such as dormitory break-ins or stolen backpacks. But he took pleasure in the detail work that others might find boring, tracking down all the scattered little pieces of evidence, then putting seemingly unrelated facts together until they told a complete story. And, every now and then, something big would happen in Charlottesville and Durrer would luck into the kind of case where, as he put it, "you just have to kind of use your imagination and see how far you can go with it."

In early December 1995 he landed just such an assignment. Officials at the Alderman Library reported that at least seven rare maps were missing, including eighteenth-century works by the cartographers Herman Moll and Andrew Ellicott. Librarians had discovered the loss after hearing from Johns Hopkins officials, who had noticed references to the Alderman in the map thief's notebook. A check of the records confirmed that someone using the name James Perry had indeed paid visits to the Alderman on December 5 and 6, right before Gilbert Bland's ill-fated stop in Baltimore.

The case seemed tangled and slightly bizarre—everything Durrer could have wanted. "I knew this was probably going to be broader than some of the other cases I had worked," he said. "I knew it was going to be in-depth. And that type of investigation is, for me, fun to work. It's what I love to do."

Solid in stature, with a touch of both Southern gentleman formality and good-ol'-boy waggishness, the fifty-two-year-old Durrer has the air of a shrewd small-town sheriff. And in this investigation, at least, his hunches seem to have been dead-on from the start. Because the thief had apparently visited the library on two consecutive days, Durrer correctly concluded that he had spent the night in town. "I just started checking local motels and found out where Bland had stayed," he said. "It was a Howard Johnson's in Charlottesville, and he paid for his room by charge card. I tracked his address through his charge card and found out where he lived. I then confirmed his address and obtained a picture of him through the Florida Department of Motor Vehicles. People up here at the library made positive IDs on his picture."

Durrer quickly began to share his findings with other universities. "I don't think any of us knew how broad this would get before it was over," he said. "At the time, I thought maybe I had a collector who stole a few maps. Once I got into digging into him, I saw a pattern of him moving from one university to the next. It was obvious what he was doing."

Durrer said that some institutions, such as the University of Florida, were completely unaware that they had been robbed until he alerted them to the possibility. Such discoveries spurred him on. "As this case broadened out, it just made me go after it a little quicker, a little harder. As I found out one thing, two or three more things would show up."

His perseverance paid off. With the list of alleged victims growing nationwide, the FBI entered the investigation, armed with hard evidence linking Gilbert Bland to a crime scene. You could argue that collecting this evidence had been a matter of simple, solid police work, that any investigator from the dozens of places Bland had visited could have done the same thing. Yet the fact remains that only one man took the initiative. Thanks to Thomas Durrer's curiosity, the map thief would eventually wind up in jail.

FEW MONTHS AFTER MY VISIT WITH VERA BENSON AT the American Map Corporation, I called her with a tale to tell. I had just been looking at two early-eighteenth-century maps showing most of what is now the United States. The first one, by the cartographer Guillaume Delisle, was based on firsthand information gathered by French explorers. The second one was—with the exception of a priest, a pelican, a picture of Niagara Falls, a family of Indians, a couple of buffalo, and a pair of naked buttocks—a direct rip-off of the Delisle work. The man who made it was J. B. Homann, that foppish old cartographer whose portrait was perched behind Benson's desk.

When I informed her that she was harboring a known map thief, Benson began to chuckle. "Well, these things have happened throughout history"—she sighed—"but I'm terribly disappointed that my German countryman would have done such a thing."

As we both laughed, I remembered something Benson had told me during my trip to Queens. She had explained that these days a certain amount of cartographic appropriation is considered not only acceptable but necessary. Her company, like its competitors, copies maps all the time—the so-called base maps from the U.S. Geological Survey, which "everyone uses as sort of a framework or skeleton to build their own maps." With the basic shape of the world no longer a matter of debate, the challenge for cartographers now comes from accurately and stylishly modifying these base maps by eliminating "stuff we don't need, such as elevation lines or other features that are not appropriate for a street map," then adding the latest data from satellite photos and a variety of other sources.

"We are still refining the mapping that exists," Benson had concluded, "but nobody has to make a map by going out and surveying the land anymore."

Recalling those words, I laughed even harder—this time at the absurdity of my own situation. You see, the quest I had launched all those months ago at the coffeehouse—then a matter of simple curiosity—had become an increasingly complicated and frustrating endeavor. I now found myself in the midst of a peculiar cartographic project, one for which there were no base maps. My task was even more of a stretch than Alexander von Humboldt's attempt to chart a place he never saw. I was trying to map the life of a man—an anonymous and elusive man, a man I did not know, and a man who had demonstrated no desire to meet me. And even all that might not have been so bad if I had somehow been able to find a way inside his head, to put myself in his shoes. But Bland and I were very different people. Other than a few shared superficialities—both of us white males, both right-handers, both map lovers—our common frames of reference were few. We came from contrasting family backgrounds (Bland: broken home, me: two stable parents), were of different generations (Bland: turbulent 1960s, me: dull 1970s), had opposite dispositions (Bland: extreme introvert, me: strong extrovert), and battled dissimilar demons (Bland: risk taker, me: cautious to a fault). The more I knew of him, the more he seemed a stranger. *Stranger*—a word linked to notions of geography, its etymological root being "beyond the usual bounds or boundaries." That was Bland: beyond my boundaries. Searching for him had transformed me into a land surveyor of a land unknown and perhaps unknowable, never quite sure what I was doing or where I was going. In my most ludicrous moments I felt a creepy bond with another land surveyor—K., the protagonist of Franz Kafka's *The Castle*—a man *haunted by the feeling that he was losing himself or wandering into a strange country, farther than he had ever wandered before, a country so strange that not even the air had anything in common with his native air, where one might die of strangeness, and yet whose enchantment was such that one could only go on and lose oneself further . . .*

CHAPTER 8

Pathfinding

SILENCE IS A WILDERNESS. I TRUDGED THROUGH it many times as I tried to map Gilbert Bland's world. It was there after every letter I sent him, there when I wrote his lawyers and when I wrote his wife, there when I followed all those letters with phone calls. It loomed in front of me at every turn, vast and unyielding, making distances difficult to measure, directions hard to gauge, landscape tough to decipher. It was daunting, this wilderness, yet strangely seductive. The more I encountered it, the more I was determined to overcome it. Not that I particularly begrudged Gilbert Bland his silence. In an age when almost everyone is willing to go public about almost everything, I could not help but feel admiration for something so foreign as to seem exotic. Sometimes, as it spread out on every horizon like the sands of the Empty Quarter, obscuring all that lay below, I found it almost breathtaking. Eventually,

Horizon

de kimmen

A GRAPHIC FROM WILLEM JANSZOON
BLAEU'S *THE LIGHT OF NAVIGATION*
ILLUSTRATING HOW TO FIND YOUR
LATITUDE WITH A TOOL CALLED
A CROSS-STAFF.

though, I had to face the fact that it was not some sort of mirage, that it would not go away, and that if I did not conquer it, it would conquer me.

Curious to tell, it was the map thief himself who inadvertently showed me how I might do it. I had come to believe that when Gilbert Bland cut into all those books, he unloosed not just pieces of paper but stories, hundreds of stories centuries old, about the discoverers and scientists and surveyors and kings and queens and cartographers whose lives were pressed into those maps as firmly and indelibly as the ink, stories that were slowly intertwining in my imagination with the map thief's own tale. And so it was that I began to commune with the dead in search of a guide, someone whose past would light my journey through the shadowy wasteland of the present. Ultimately, I chose a man famous for navigating ground that was, as he once described it, "singularly unfavorable to travel." He was called the Pathfinder.

John Charles Frémont probably did more to popularize the American West than any other explorer of the nineteenth century. Friend and fellow adventurer of Kit Carson, son-in-law of the powerful Senator Thomas Hart Benton, and, later in life, first presidential candidate of the fledgling Republican Party, Frémont earned his legendary nickname by leading several Army Corps of Topographical Engineers expeditions to survey and map little-known parts of the West. He covered more ground than any other government explorer, including Meriwether Lewis and William Clark, and his published accounts of the journeys made him a national celebrity.

Historians love to point out that the Pathfinder did not, in fact, find many paths. The Pulitzer Prize winner Bernard DeVoto, for example, insisted that Frémont "did little of importance beyond determining the latitude and longitude of many sites which mountain men [already] knew." (Not to mention the Native Americans.) True enough—but this view ignores an important point. The Pathfinder understood that to truly conquer a wilderness you must not only survive in it yourself but make sense of it for others. His maps—usually drafted with or by the gifted cartographer Charles Preuss, who accompanied him on a number of missions—helped fuel one of the greatest migrations in American history. Most notable among them was the Preuss-Frémont map published with the 1845 *Report of the Exploring Expedition to the Rocky Mountains*. Presenting for the first time a coherent picture of the continent from Kansas City to the Pacific Coast, it took on vital importance for those who followed Frémont to the region—the builders of railroads, the settlers of land, the seekers of gold. "The map . . . radically and permanently altered western cartography," wrote Carl I. Wheat in his *Mapping the Transmississippi West*. "There would appear a few throwbacks, of course, but with thousands of copies of Frémont's authoritative report and map in print, no cartographer could find reasonable excuse for not fairly representing the main features of the West."

Frémont's philosophy of mapmaking was simple. He once offered the following instruction on "fixing on a small sheet the results of laborious travel over waste regions, and giving to them an enduring place on the world's surface:

First, the foundations must be laid in observations made
in the field; then the reduction of these observations to
latitude and longitude; afterward the projection of the
map, and the laying down upon it of positions fixed by
the observations; then the tracing from the sketch-
books of the lines of the rivers, the forms of the lakes,
the contours of the hills.

I wondered if this straightforward formula for charting unfamiliar land would also work for charting an unfamiliar life. By
this time I knew exactly what Frémont had meant by "laborious
travel over waste regions." I had accumulated stacks of newspaper and magazine articles about the case, interviewed scores
of people who had come in contact with Bland, retraced the
path of much of his crime spree, and brought together hundreds of pages of public documents relating to his personal, financial, and criminal history. At long last my fieldwork was
almost complete. It was time to begin "laying down . . . positions fixed by the observations."

Here, too, I took inspiration from the Pathfinder. Frémont
and Preuss were not afraid to leave huge white areas on their
maps. They understood that no single map can say everything
about a place, so they cautiously chose to incorporate only that
information which came from their own observations. Still,
they made some mistakes. On one map they combined the
Great Salt Lake and Utah Lake as a single body of water. On another they conveyed the false impression that the interior basin
of present-day Nevada was encircled by mountain ranges. They

knew that after all the measurements are complete, you still have to make some judgment calls. The Pathfinder inspired me to trust my own instincts in identifying the landmarks of Bland's life—and to let the blank spots stand.

So I set about the task of drafting my map, beginning with two coordinates close in time but half a world apart.

Latitude: 40.40 N. Longitude: 74.06 W. June 17, 1968

At 10:55 P.M., police in Bayonne, New Jersey, arrested a skinny, redheaded kid from nearby Ridgefield Park for possession of a stolen motor vehicle. He was eighteen years old but looked two or three years younger. In his now-faded mug shot, he sports a white T-shirt, a tight-lipped scowl, and a conservative mop top, half Beatles, half *My Three Sons*. His eyes are filled less with fear or anger than with numbness, as if he is looking through the camera instead of at it, as if he is trying to daydream himself right out of the police station.

He was in serious trouble. In 1968, conviction on the charge of possession of a stolen motor vehicle in New Jersey carried a maximum sentence of a five-thousand-dollar fine and ten years in prison—not a happy prospect for a kid who had just graduated from high school. Then again, the young Gilbert Bland was apparently no stranger to tough times. He had been born in 1949 in Indianapolis, where his father, Gilbert Lee Joseph Bland (listed on the boy's birth certificate as a baker), and his mother, a nineteen-year-old New Jersey native named Julia Patricia Bland, lived in a tiny, one-story house in the shadow of an

International Harvester foundry. Today that house sits in a bleak working-class neighborhood, around the corner from Ron & Deb's Tobacco Outlet and the Paradise Cove, a self-described "gentleman's club." Whatever happiness his parents found in that place did not last long. The couple separated when Bland was only three years old, according to Bland's lawyers in a later case. Some two years later, in 1954, Bland's father sued his mother for divorce. After Julia Bland failed to show up in court on three separate occasions, a Marion Superior Court judge ruled that "the allegations of the complaint alleging statutory grounds for a divorce are true." Surviving court records do not make the specific nature of those allegations clear. But whatever the case, Julia Bland, who was granted custody of the boy, took him back to her home state of New Jersey and at some point remarried.

By the time of his arrest, the teenager lived in a sturdy house in Ridgefield Park, a New York suburb on the banks of the Hackensack River. It was a pretty town with tree-lined streets, quaint slate sidewalks, and one of the longest-running continuous Fourth of July parades in the country. Bland's life there, however, appears to have been less than all-American. His mother's second husband "was both verbally and physically abusive to him," according to Bland's lawyers in a later case. No matter how bad his home life was, though, it could not have seemed worse to him than the prospect of prison. I don't imagine he slept well in the police lockup that night.

But in Bayonne Municipal Court the next day, Bland got a lucky break—the first of many he would receive in his dealings

with the law. Prosecutors amended the charge to the lesser offense of unlawful taking of a motor vehicle. He pleaded guilty
and was given a hundred-dollar fine. After reclaiming his personal effects—$1.25 in cash, keys, a wristwatch, and a comb—
Gilbert Bland emerged into the muggy Meadowlands air, a free
man.

How had he managed to get off with such a light sentence?
In plotting my map, this is one of those places where I have
trouble making sense of the terrain. Public records do not indicate why the charge was reduced, and when I tracked down retired judge Harvey L. Birne, who was on the bench that day, he
had no recollection of either the case or the defendant. "It's
more than thirty years ago," sighed Birne, who is now in private
legal practice.

He was, however, willing to venture a guess about what happened: "If there wasn't a good proof of intent to steal—if it was
just joyriding or taking of a friend's car—[prosecutors] would
downgrade it. If it's a downright theft, to my experience, they
wouldn't downgrade it. . . . The sentence seemed quite low. I
would imagine it was a minor case and first offense."

That makes sense. Yet I can't help but wonder whether a
much different scenario played out in court that day—one that
would have had a lasting impact on Bland's life. My suspicions
are based on a single tantalizing fact: just over a week after
Gilbert Bland walked out of jail in Bayonne, he walked into the
base at Fort Dix, New Jersey, for induction into the U.S. Army.
These two incidents may be unrelated—but then again they
may not. New Jersey law enforcement sources told me that,

during the Vietnam era, local prosecutors and judges were sometimes known to offer young defendants a deal. It went roughly like this: Son, you're going to serve time no matter what. You can serve it either in jail, wasting away your youth, or in the military, defending your country. It's your choice: join the U.S. Army or join the New Jersey penal system.

Was Bland offered such a deal? Apparently so, according to one source who knew him in the past. The source, who spoke on the condition of anonymity, said Bland himself had always insisted that the threat of jail was what drove him to the Army. Further—though hardly conclusive—support for this version of events comes from government documents. Although privacy laws prevent the military from disclosing whether a soldier signed up or was drafted, Bland's attorneys in a later case maintained their client had "enlisted in the United States Army." Bland's Army serial number, obtained from law enforcement records, also indicates that he was an enlistee. Yet the notion of a gung ho Gilbert Bland joining the military out of patriotism alone strikes me as out of character. He never seemed to be much of a joiner in anything, much less in the horror of Vietnam, and his political views were decidedly left-leaning, according to people who knew him later. It seems more likely that he was coerced to enlist, whether for economic, familial, or legal reasons.

For his part, Judge Birne claimed no memory of a deal with Bland (or anyone else) in which enlistment was offered as an alternative to prison—"not that I object to the proposition." If there was any special treatment, he said, it would have been because Bland was already Army-bound when he appeared in court. "If I knew he was going in [to the military] definitely," said Birne, "then perhaps we would have eased the pain and let him go."

But regardless of whether it led directly to his tour in the Army, the episode appears to have been a critical one for Bland. Arrested for the first time, he had learned an important lesson about how the judicial system could be manipulated to his advantage. He would not forget it. But there was another big lesson he had not learned. He had not been dissuaded from stealing things.

M Y FINGER IS RUNNING OVER ONE OF THOSE THINGS (or at least a reproduction of it) right now. It is titled *Map to illustrate an exploration of the country, lying between the Missouri River and the Rocky Mountains, on the line of the Nebraska or Platte River. By Lieut. J. C. Frémont, of the Corps of Topographical Engineers.* The Pathfinder drafted it, with the help of Preuss, to illustrate his report on the journey of 1842, his first great expedition of the West. My fingertip is lightly retracing the course of that trip, beginning at the point where the North Fork and South Fork of the Platte River break apart in what is now Nebraska, then gliding west to Fort Laramie in present-day Wyoming, and continuing on to the South Pass, the Oregon Trail's principal route through the Rockies. From there I run my finger north into the Wind River Range, drawn in dramatic hachure-style relief. This was where Frémont concluded the westward leg of his journey with typical bravura, scaling what he had determined to be the "loftiest peak of the Rocky Mountains" and planting a specially designed American flag on its summit. The mountain, it turned out, was not even close to being the tallest, but it was the symbolism that mattered. The climb became a rallying point for Manifest Destiny and helped make the Pathfinder's a household name.

Frémont's heroics, however, are not the reason I am now leaning over this map. Just the opposite, in fact. As I move my finger south, then east, following the expedition's return route, I am looking for a place where a dark and self-destructive side of the Pathfinder's personality emerged, a place that closely corresponds with the one I am trying to plot on my map of Gilbert Bland. Yes, here it is now—right where the Sweetwater River and North Fork of the Platte converge, a point southwest of present-day Casper, Wyoming. Don't bother looking for this spot on a modern map, because it's no longer there. In its place is something called the Pathfinder Reservoir—an odd double homage to John Charles Frémont, both memorializing his accomplishments and literally blotting out the site of one of his greatest blunders. This was where Frémont did something "stupid" and "foolhardy" (in the words of Preuss), something that risked not only the success of his expedition but his entire future.

You see, that was another reason I chose the Pathfinder as my guide: he reminded me a lot of Bland. Perhaps it was a matter not so much of common personality traits but of a shared emptiness—an emotional vacuum that both men seem to have spent their lives trying to fill. Like Bland, Frémont came from a broken home, in which his father was taken from him at a young age. The Pathfinder was the illegitimate child of a married Virginia society woman and her lover, the mysterious Charles Fremon, who, according to the varying accounts, taught French, gave lessons in swordsmanship, was a "dancing master," and/or did "occasional upholstering." Fremon ran off with the boy's mother—leaving her shamed and penniless— then died when John Charles was only five years old. Soon after, this young boy, like Bland, began dabbling in imaginary creatures. Early in life he re-created himself by adding a *t* to the end of his name, as well as an accent on the *e*. "No one ever knew why," wrote John Moring in *Men with Sand: Great Explorers of the North American West*.

But Andrew Rolle, author of *John Charles Frémont: Character as Destiny*, was willing to offer some clues. In his 1991 biography Rolle used "psychiatric techniques . . . to seek a better understanding of the man." He attributed much of the Pathfinder's adult behavior to a "fragmented sense of selfhood" stemming from the separation from his father. "Because Frémont's formative years of childhood were obscured by long shadows," concluded Rolle, "he fashioned an image of himself based in large measure upon fantasy."

That image, of course, was of a flamboyant adventurer. But in private the Pathfinder had a strikingly different demeanor. "In fact," wrote Rolle, "even while on his expeditions, some of Frémont's contemporaries used the terms *bland* and *gentlemanly* as well as *quiet* and *retiring* about him." The italics are Rolle's—

but the words sound like those used time and again to describe the map thief. And, like Bland, Frémont was a loner with a decidedly antiauthoritarian streak that often led him to break rules.

Frémont and Bland, however, were polar opposites in at least one important respect: the Pathfinder's life was as conspicuous as the map thief was silent and anonymous. But this, too, was to my advantage. It occurred to me that, like the best wilderness guides, Frémont might serve as my interpreter. I began studying his life, hoping that it would give me perspective on Bland's. This process, which took weeks, has led me to where I am now—at my desk, listening, once again, to the strange song of an old map, my finger tapping down on a spot that no longer exists.

It was there, on August 24, 1842, in what the biographer Allan Nevins called a moment of "reckless impetuosity," that Frémont decided to load the mission's precious records and scientific equipment into an experimental rubber boat and, without any advance scouting, run the swollen rapids of the Platte. There was only the flimsiest scientific justification for the effort; the Pathfinder seems to have been mostly interested in seeking thrills. He found them. Pushing off from shore with five other men—three of whom could not swim—he was soon battered out of control downstream. At one point Charles Preuss waded ashore with the expedition's chronometer and tried to walk with the precious longitude-measuring instrument to safety. Unable to traverse the rocks, the mapmaker had to climb back in the boat, which was now in a more perilous position than ever. "To go back," Frémont wrote in his report on the expedition, "was impossible; before us, the cataract was a sheet of foam; and shut up in the chasm by the rocks, which, in some places, seemed almost to meet overhead, the roar of the water was deafening. . . . We cleared rock after rock, and shot fall after fall, our little boat seeming to play with the cataract."

One more rock loomed ahead, hidden from view beneath the foam. This was the inevitable one, the one with the Pathfinder's name on it, the one that would flip the boat, nearly killing Frémont and his men and causing them to lose their sextant, their large telescope, two of their compasses, most of their food and clothing, and a journal containing important weather and cartographic data. But it could have done worse harm, that last rock. It spared not only his life but most of the scientific records. Had those observations disappeared beneath the rushing waters, Frémont's career might have sunk

DETAIL FROM THE TITLE PAGE OF A 1617 ATLAS BY PIETER VAN DEN KEERE.

with them. Yet as that underwater boulder drew near, the Pathfinder was not thinking about any possible disasters. When he recalled the event later, he remembered only the glorious feeling of being "flushed with success, and familiar with the danger."

I suspect some similar emotion was rushing through Gilbert Bland's mind when, according to the FBI, he crept out of the University of Rochester library, carrying a stolen copy of this same Frémont-Preuss map. The alleged incident took place on October 10, 1994—fairly early in his crime spree. But perhaps, like the Pathfinder on that river 152 years earlier, he already felt there was no going back. And maybe that was exactly what he craved: the rush of being pulled along by an overpowering current, of closing in on catastrophe at each turn, of defying the odds, of feeling intensely alive. *Flushed with success, and familiar with danger*—we've all known this particular joy at one time or another. Some people get it from rock climbing, skydiving, bungee jumping, or any of the other sports that allow us to flirt with our own funerals; others find it in more common pursuits, from speeding on highways or soaring on roller coasters to betting on horses or cheating on spouses. But while most of us require only the occasional taste of peril, others are addicted to it. The Pathfinder, for example, seemed to learn nothing from his near-disaster on the Platte. He sought out similar situations time and time again, both in his professional life (where, in 1848, his insistence on trying to cross the Rockies in midwinter left ten men dead and forced others to resort to cannibalism) and in his personal life (where his land speculation deals and other risky ventures left him penniless at his death in 1890). His biographer Andrew Rolle once again traced this behavior back to the loss of his father in boyhood:

> Bereft of two nurturing parents who could understand his needs, Frémont repeatedly, as we have seen, acted as though he wanted to validate his illegitimacy and lack of a complete family during childhood. . . . Child psychoanalysts, after studying hundreds of patients, have established the presence of unresolved bereavement stemming from loss of a parent in childhood. These modern clinicians have found that serious emotional impairment occurs throughout the lives of such patients.
>
> Recent findings regarding early separation and loss are thus crucial to understanding that later seemingly inexplicable conduct which often expresses a disguised repetition of early sadness. In such cases outbursts against authority are frequent. Also, persons who repeatedly place themselves in dangerous circumstances may be attempting to work their way back mentally to an unresolved conflict.

While I have no idea whether Rolle was right about the Pathfinder, I tend to be wary of writers who depend too heavily on pop psych generalizations about their subjects. And, since I have absolutely no professional expertise in matters of the mind, I am neither willing nor able to make any such sweeping statements about Bland. All I can safely conclude is that he, too, possessed a self-destructive attraction to danger, and that it had been with him for a long time. Perhaps it was already there on that summer night in Bayonne in 1968. If so, it would have been one more thing he had in common with John Charles Frémont—who also got in trouble at age eighteen, when he was dismissed from college for "habitual irregularity and incorrigible negligence." Both Frémont and Bland would then turn to the military—in which both would use their keen intelligence to earn technology-focused assignments, and which both would eventually leave under a dark cloud (in Frémont's case, resignation after a court-martial for "mutiny, disobedience, and conduct prejudicial to military discipline"). But, long before that happened, each man would head off to a place that would change his life—a place, as Frémont put it, "of strange scenes and occurrences." For the Pathfinder, of course, that place was the American West. For the map thief, it was a very different sort of wilderness.

Latitude: 13.46 N. Longitude: 109.14 E. May 4, 1969

This is the way Michael Herr began *Dispatches,* his landmark book on the Vietnam War:

> There was a map of Vietnam on the wall of my apart-
> ment in Saigon and some nights, coming back late to
> the city, I'd lie out on my bed and look at it, too tired to
> do anything more than just get my boots off. That map
> was a marvel, especially now that it wasn't real any-

more. For one thing, it was very old. It had been left
there years before by another tenant, probably a Frenchman, since the map had been made in Paris. The paper
had buckled in its frame after years in the wet Saigon
heat, laying a kind of veil over the countries it depicted.
Vietnam was divided into its older territories of Tonkin,
Annam and Cochin China, and to the west past Laos
and Cambodge sat Siam, a kingdom. That's old, I'd tell
visitors, that's a really old map.

If dead ground could come back and haunt you the
way dead people do, they'd have been able to mark my
map CURRENT and burn the ones they'd been using since
'64, but count on it, nothing like that was going to happen. It was late '67 now, even the most detailed maps
didn't reveal much anymore; reading them was like trying to read the faces of the Vietnamese, and that was
like trying to read the wind. We knew . . . that for years
now there had been no country here but the war.

I thought about those words often as I, too, lay in bed, trying to make sense of Vietnam, or at least the Vietnam experience of a certain Private First Class Bland. Like the regions
covered on Herr's map, the area I was trying to plot on mine no
longer really existed. It was a place where solid facts could not
be trusted and normal rules did not apply, where someone
might enter as one person and leave as another person entirely.
How could I hope to understand Bland's life in a country that
was no country but war? In Herr's words, it seemed like trying

to read the wind. Yet I had to try. The Vietnam conflict had a huge impact on all who took part in it—but in Bland's case it loomed especially large. At least that's what his lawyer would argue more than a quarter century later, when he stood up in a federal court and implied that the war had been at the root of Bland's string of map thefts. His attorney Paul R. Thomson, Jr., claimed that his client "has a pattern of problems . . . largely triggered by depression, a very common problem with post-traumatic stress syndrome." Not that Thomson was willing to supply me with any specifics. As usual, I would be navigating this strange landscape by dead reckoning.

HE MARINES WANT A FEW GOOD MEN. THE ARMY SIG-nal Corps wants a few smart ones. The Signal Corps is responsible for military communications, a demanding discipline as old as warfare itself. Ancient armies used drums, bells, banners, and flags to transmit intelligence, while later militaries employed lights, pistols, pyrotechnics, and homing pigeons, then the telegraph, teletype, radio, radar, and telephone. By Vietnam the Army Signal Corps was "actually ahead of the commercial phone companies at the time. They were the first to use communications satellites," John D. Bergen, an expert on the Signal Corps, told me.

To operate this state-of-the-art system, the Army needed to seek out exceptionally bright soldiers. It found them among incoming troops who were given tests to determine their intelligence and technical aptitude. "It was the equivalent of the college boards for the military. And the higher scores would get into this field," explained Bergen, who wrote *Military Communications: A Test for Technology,* a history of the corps in Vietnam.

Gilbert Bland apparently scored well enough on those tests to be offered the option of joining the Signal Corps and receiving advanced instruction after basic training. He accepted—perhaps because the offer was accompanied by an additional enticement. Joseph Zottarelli, Jr., who served in the same company as Bland, remembered getting "a lot of bullshit from the enrollment sergeants. You know, 'Hey, take these [tests] and you won't be going to Vietnam. You'll probably be going to Germany.'" But once Zottarelli arrived at Fort Monmouth, New Jersey—the same place Bland received his electronics training—he quickly discovered that "most of all the equipment they were teaching us how to use was in Vietnam. . . . I think about 90 percent of the guys that graduated from signal school went over there."

Bland was among them. His military records show that he arrived in Vietnam on May 4, 1969, for a one-year tour. He was a few months shy of his twentieth birthday. "They took guys over in commercial airlines," remembered Zottarelli, who arrived several months after Bland. "And when you got off the plane, they said, 'Hurry up and get off because the plane has to get off the ground.' They didn't want the plane to stay on the ground too long because it was taking mortar and rocket fire. So you got in country and you wondered, What the hell is going on?"

Bland could not have been happy to be there. But he must

have known that most soldiers in Vietnam had far worse jobs. Assigned to the 361st Signal Battalion, he had as his official mailing address Qui Nhon, a once-small fishing town that U.S. forces had transformed into a bustling port city, complete with a naval station and military base—a burg of such wartime decadence that the mayor reportedly turned his official residence into a massage parlor for American soldiers. It's unclear, however, whether Bland actually lived in Qui Nhon, or for how long. His records hint that he may have been reassigned to at least one other locale. This would not have been unusual for members of the 361st, who were spread out in small outposts, which provided communications links around the country. These "fixed station" sites usually consisted of two single-story prefabricated buildings filled with electronics equipment and surrounded by several large billboard or horn-shaped antennas. Some sites were located on the edges of huge military installations, others in more isolated areas. Either way it was not known as a particularly dangerous assignment.

"I really didn't come under fire that often," said Frank Dapuzzo, who served in the same company as Bland. "Occasionally, [the enemy] would lob in some rockets and some mortars—but believe me, there were a lot worse conditions than what I had to go through. Some of the people who really had to go through bad times there, they would look at us and say we were on the gravy train."

Dapuzzo, like several other former members of the company with whom I spoke, has no memory of Bland—which may have less to do with the map thief's inconspicuousness than with the unit being so spread out. Dapuzzo, for instance, was stationed at a Korean army base in Ninh Hoa and had little face-to-face contact with other members of the 361st. It's a safe bet, however, that Bland's day-in, day-out life in Vietnam did not differ much from that of the other members of the company. He worked as a fixed-station controller, a twelve-hour-on, twelve-hour-off assignment spent inside an air-conditioned building, in which the main enemy was likely to be boredom, not the Vietcong or North Vietnamese.

"The environment in the fixed stations in Vietnam by '68 or '69 was very civilized, at least on a base," Bergen told me. "The big fixed stations where these controllers worked were in most cases attached to bases that had sidewalks, PXs, and swimming pools. It would be just like being on a base in the United States. Some of the fixed stations—on places like Monkey Mountain outside of Da Nang—would be more isolated. But even those places, though they wouldn't have a PX or a swimming pool, would still have an environment with air-conditioned dormitories, safe water, generators, and all that kind of stuff. . . . The degree of danger in a job like that compared to an infantryman or a radio-telephone operator with an infantry unit was like night and day."

Gerald Streett, another former member of Bland's company, offered a similar perspective. "You got up; you ran your checks on your equipment; you did maintenance, things like cleaning up outside of the van; you did a daily calibration of your monitoring equipment. And that's about it. . . . If you had to go to a combat zone, this was kind of a nice job to have. I can't say they were fond memories, but there were one hell of a lot of worse places to be."

In fact, said Streett, the enemy actually went out of its way not to fire on his communications site on the edge of an air base, Nha Trang—and for good reason. "We had these sixty-foot billboard antennas. They had red anticollision lights on them, and [the enemy] used those lights as a reference for firing on anyone else in that geographic area. We were at one end of the airfield—and, of course, Charlie knew enough about that base to say, 'Okay, those lights are the 361st; if I go a quarter mile to the right I'm going to hit so-and-so; if I go an eighth of a mile to the left, I'm going to hit someone else.' It wasn't that they loved us, it was just that they thought, 'Hey, these antennas are great!' I mean, they were on twenty-four hours a day. So we were Charlie's best friend."

Nothing in Bland's military record indicates that he saw any direct combat. His medals, for example, were all perfunctory, most of them indicating only that he passed certain skill tests. It seems unlikely that his war experience was the sort that would traumatize a soldier for the rest of his life.

Unlikely, yes, but not impossible, according to Don R. Catherall, a psychologist who serves as executive director of the Phoenix Institute in Chicago, a clinic specializing in treating victims of post-traumatic stress disorder. "There have been cases in which it has been accepted that people in Vietnam suffered traumatic stress even though they were not exposed to a discrete trauma, such as being shot or being shot at, or being in a particular combat action," explained Catherall, himself a

Vietnam vet. "The state of the entire countryside was such that it would be possible for a person to go through a noncombat tour there and still never feel safe. There was a lot of guerrilla activity that couldn't be predicted, and of course there was terrorism going on. Even in the rear, where people didn't carry weapons, there was the possibility of rocket attacks. So it is possible that some individuals remained in a state of heightened arousal, similar to what happens when somebody is actually exposed to a trauma, but that their state of arousal was primarily geared toward anticipating a possible trauma happening. . . . The heart of trauma is often a feeling of helplessness."

And that feeling was not unfamiliar to other members of Bland's company. "You're not actively engaging the enemy, but yet you're not in any position to run, either," Gerald Streett said about working at the fixed-station sites.

In his book on the Signal Corps, John D. Bergen noted that life in the sites "held its own dangers and terrors," many of which stemmed from working day after day "in the windowless confines of a building . . . and being unaware of what was happening outside." Reading those words, it struck me how deathly claustrophobic it might have been for somebody trapped in one of those trailers, the war waiting somewhere in the unseen distance like a huge crimson-eyed beast. Fear of the unknown—is this not among the most ancient and awful of human horrors? Indeed, the scholar G. Malcolm Lewis has wondered whether it was the very thing that led to the invention of maps. For early humans, he wrote, mapping may have "served to achieve what in modern behavioral therapy is known as desensitization: lessening fear by the repeated representation of what is feared. Representing supposedly dangerous terrae incognitae in map form as an extension of familiar territory may well have served to lessen fear of the peripheral world."

It plagues us still, this dread of the dark beyond. "In some cases, the reaction is not to what's outside, it's to what you *perceive* to be outside," explained Catherall, author of *Back from the Brink: A Family Guide to Overcoming Traumatic Stress.* So it's at least possible that the war had a particularly strong impact on Bland. And, as his fellow soldier Joseph Zottarelli, Jr., observed, returning from Vietnam was tough on everyone, regardless of actual combat experience. "It kind of screws you up when you come back," he said. "All the time you were over there, you kind of missed out on everything over here. And there were a lot of changes going on in the States. It took a long time to get back into things."

One thing it did not take Gilbert Bland a long time to get back into, however, was trouble with the law. On October 20, 1970—less than six months after he had returned from Vietnam—he was arrested in Woodcliff Lake, New Jersey, for desertion from the Army. "We got a call of a suspicious vehicle in the orchards; in that era we had a lot of orchards," remembered Woodcliff Lake Police Chief Richard Poliey, a patrolman at the time. "I was given that call. I checked it out and observed a white male who was later identified as Gilbert A. Bland."

Poliey remembered Bland as being "kind of disheveled. He didn't fit the profile for the area. I thought he was a drunk driver." Upon discovering that the auto registration the suspect produced did not match his plates, Poliey ran Bland's name through the National Crime Information Center. "I got a hit that he was a deserter from the military. . . . The MPs came and got him, and that was the end of that."

Then as now, the maximum penalty for desertion was death. Such a punishment would have been extremely unlikely, given Bland's circumstances and the political realities of the time. Nonetheless, he was, by all indications, in serious trouble. Instead of being sent back to Fort Riley, Kansas, where he had previously been posted, he was assigned to nearby Fort Dix. There, according to military records, he was put in a special detachment that Daniel Zimmerman, curator of the Fort Dix Museum, described as "an organizational unit . . . where people would have been assigned who were awaiting a court-martial or awaiting discharge or awaiting transfer to some other custody, say the local police. He would not have been confined to prison, but he would have been confined to the barracks."

But that did not stop him from getting arrested again, on January 21, 1971, this time in his hometown of Ridgefield Park. According to police records, the charges—possession of burglary tools, failure to give good account, and trespassing on private property—stemmed from someone "trying all of the apartment doors" in a local building. He was found not guilty on those charges, but police records nonetheless indicate that he was AWOL at the time of his arrest. He was returned to Fort Dix, but some six months later, on July 6, 1971, the FBI arrested him for allegedly being AWOL once again. What happened next is something of a mystery. Bland's military records show that at least part of his final six months in the military was spent in a "pre-trial confinement facility"—but those same records show that no court-martial trial ever took place. Perhaps it was just too much trouble to court-martial a soldier whose military career was almost over (though privacy laws prevent the military from revealing such information). Whatever the case, Gilbert Bland left the armed services for good on August 31, 1971, at the age of twenty-two, apparently having dodged major legal problems for the second time in his short life.

*I*N THE PATHFINDER'S DAY, MANY MAPS OF THE AMERI-can West contained something called the Rio Buenaventura, a huge waterway flowing from the Rocky Mountains to the Pacific. It was the latest incarnation of a centuries-old myth known as the Great River of the West. Like any unexplored territory, the region had been home to many marvelous places never actually seen but nonetheless thought to be real. There was Cíbola, described by one purported visitor as "a land rich in gold, silver, and other wealth," with seven "great cities" whose residents were so prosperous that the women wore belts made of gold. There was Quivira, where, according to legend, common supper plates were made of gold and fish were as big as horses. And there was the land of the Madocians, a fair-skinned race thought to have descended from a Welsh prince whose reputed discovery of America in 1170 gave the British evidence that they had more claim to the continent than the Spanish. Like those places, the Great River of the West was the result more of desire than of reason. Ever since setting foot in North America, Europeans had fantasized about a waterway, or system of waterways, that would lead them neatly, safely, cheaply to the Pacific and the Orient beyond. "It must exist because it had to," wrote the historian Bernard DeVoto of this Great River. "The logic of deduction from known things required it to, and so did the syllogism of dream—both on no grounds whatever. So it did exist in personal narratives and speculative treatises, in treaties and on maps, under various names, flowing in various directions."

In 1776 a Franciscan friar named Silvestre Vélez de Escalante made a remarkable fifteen-hundred-mile trek through the Southwest, during which he crossed the site of the present-day Dinosaur National Monument between Colorado and Utah. There he came upon what is now known as the Green River. Escalante, however, gave it a different name: San Buenaventura. His cartographer, Bernardo de Miera, later placed this waterway on a map—but instead of making it head south, the direction in which the Green River actually flows, he sent it off southwesterly toward the sea. Miera never connected the Buenaventura to the Pacific, but the mapmakers who followed him were not so cautious. Before long, observed the author Carl I. Wheat, "it had become . . . a mighty stream, flowing, as befitted logic, into the San Francisco Bay or thereabout, and for many years even the most knowledgeable cartographers made this and other equally apocryphal streams flow westward from the central mountain range and from the Great Salt Lake to the Pacific."

By the spring of 1843, when John Charles Frémont launched his second big mapping expedition of the West, serious doubts had begun to emerge about whether there really was a Rio Buenaventura. The explorer Benjamin L. E. de Bonneville, for example, had returned from his extensive travels in the region claiming that no such body of water existed. Bonneville's map of 1837, as well as those of former Treasury Secretary Albert Gallatin in 1836 and Geographer to the House of Representatives David H. Burr in 1839, contained no Buenaventura, but the river remained intact on other popular maps of the period. In November 1843, having gone as far west as Fort Vancouver, near present-day Portland, the Pathfinder decided to put an end to the controversy once and for all. Instead of proceeding directly home along the Oregon Trail, he resolved to reroute his return trip to the south. He did this in large part, as he later explained, to make a final determination about "the existence of a great river flowing from the Rocky Mountains to the Bay of San Francisco." It was a typically rash and dangerous move. On no one's authority but his own, Frémont was leading his twenty-five men into a largely unknown wilderness just as winter set in. They wandered into the Sierra Nevada, expecting "with every stream . . . to see the great Buenaventura," Frémont later wrote. The higher they climbed, the more it snowed. As always with the Pathfinder, disaster awaited.

Critics often cite the journey as proof of Frémont's recklessness. His biographer Allan Nevins, for one, called it "appallingly foolhardy." Yet reading about the episode, I couldn't help but admire what the Pathfinder was trying to accomplish. At the time I was searching for my own waterway of sorts, a stream of events that coursed through more than twenty-five years of a man's life. If I were to believe Bland's lawyers, the Vietnam War had led to his crime spree just as surely as a great river flows to the sea. Bland's critics, by contrast, argued that his claim of post-traumatic stress disorder was nothing more than a convenient fiction, the courtroom equivalent of the Rio Buenaventura. Neither side, however, offered me much in the way of evidence. And so it was that I once again found myself following the Pathfinder's lead, on a mission to separate reality from myth.

I made a lot of discoveries on that journey. In the Bahamas I found a map dealer named Jonathan Ramsay, who had worked closely with Bland and seemed to know him as well as anyone in the industry. "One thing he did talk about was the war in Vietnam," Ramsay told me. "He had been over there and was quite affected by it. He didn't really like having been sent over there and he didn't really approve of the war and the way it was conducted. And he chatted a lot about his feelings about the Vietnam War and the people over there. . . . I can't remember the details exactly, but I thought that he was teaching at one of the local schools. He had the opportunity to teach the Vietnamese kids in this town, wherever it was that he was stationed, and he said that that was one of the most rewarding parts of being in Vietnam. I can't remember exactly what it was, a Catholic school or a government school for orphans or what.

But he was obviously very moved by that. He felt that he was contributing something very positive."

On the East Coast, I found one of Bland's daughters by his first wife, Carol Ann Talt Bland, whom he married in 1971 and divorced in 1978. Heather Bland told me she'd never had much contact with her father. Still, she was able to recall an old family tale about his days in Vietnam.

"I heard that the war did affect him," she said. "I heard a hearsay story about one of the things that happened to him. I don't know how true this is, but supposedly while in Vietnam he saw one of his higher-up officers doing something to some female, raping her or something like that. My father supposedly beat the hell out of him and was put in solitary confinement. Rumor has it that it really messed him up."

I found no confirmation of this story during the course of my expedition. But in Hackensack, New Jersey, I found a jail docket from Bland's July 6, 1971, arrest on charges of being AWOL. It indicated that he claimed to be suffering from a "nervous disorder," for which he was receiving medical care from the Army. The docket also listed him as a "drug addict." In those same files, however, I found another docket from an arrest some six months earlier, in which Bland "denie[d] illnesses" and "denie[d] drugs."

Whatever the case, I discovered plenty of evidence about the chaotic state of Bland's life after the war. In the New Jersey State Archives I found a letter he sent to then-Governor William T. Cahill on September 29, 1972, a few months before Heather Bland was born. Writing from the Sussex County Jail in Newton, New Jersey—where he had been booked the previous day for marijuana possession—Bland begged the governor to show mercy upon his pregnant, nineteen-year-old wife. Although she was with him at the Playboy Club during his arrest, he explained, she had nothing to do with the drugs that were found in his car. Nonetheless, she too had been tossed in jail, he claimed. Insisting that he was "going crazy" because of a situation that "I would expect to happen in Nazi Germany or Communist Russia," Bland implored the governor to halt the "persecut[ion]" of his wife.

It was hard not to feel sorry for the person who wrote this letter, hard not to see him as a deeply troubled and terribly naive young man—perhaps even as a victim. And it was equally difficult to imagine how such an unsophisticated individual would someday be able to talk his way into a blue-blood subculture dominated by Ivy League types. Or at least those were my first impressions. But, as I was quickly learning, first impressions—mine and other people's—about the map thief were often misleading. In police and court files in California and Florida, I found evidence of a Bland very different from the author of that forlorn missive. This was Gilbert Bland, inventor of imaginary creatures, exploiter of the system, professional con man—a persona that may have already been present in that jail cell in New Jersey. Files from the Sussex County case show that Bland, aka James J. Edwards, never showed up in court to face his drug charge, and that a warrant for his arrest (apparently still open to this day) was issued on June 22, 1973. (Those same court files, as well as local police records, indicate that, despite

Bland's implication to the contrary, no charges were ever filed against his wife.) The next time this alter ego surfaced was in California, where, in September 1973, Bland, aka Jason Michael Pike, aka Jack Arnett, was arrested on grand theft charges stemming from a credit card fraud scheme. And, unlike the Bland of a year earlier—a man so seemingly ignorant of the judicial process that Governor Cahill had to advise him to "give consideration to retaining legal counsel"—this one was a shrewd manipulator of the courts. Facing a maximum penalty of ten years in prison and a five-thousand-dollar fine, he agreed to a plea bargain and was given five years' probation. That, however, did not seem to slow his career as a scam artist. On December 30, 1975, federal agents nabbed him in Florida on charges stemming from his use of false identities to rip off unemployment benefits. This time, his long string of luck in the courtroom had finally run out. Even with another plea-bargain deal, he got a three-year sentence.

In files from that case, I found a letter he wrote shortly after arriving at the federal prison in El Reno, Oklahoma. In that note Bland begged the judge who had sentenced him for help, explaining that other prisoners had unjustly accused him of " 'snitching' as they call it, a crime in here punishable by death." He elaborated:

> *Everyone in here is associated in "clicks" or gangs. Since I am an outsider to these "clicks" I live a fearful existence. I pray before I go to sleep at night that I'll wake up the next morning. It's common knowledge among the inmates here that for [$]30*

worth of comissary [sic] items, a person could be arranged to
be killed. Weapons are not hard to come by in here. I know I am
obtaining a paranoia complex because I fear it's only a matter
of time before something happens to me. . . . I don't know how
long I can bear this pressure. I don't know who to talk to. My
counsellor said if I'm going to be in a fight to choose my own
place and time and make a lot of noise so the guards can come
and break it up before I'm hurt bad. I don't know if I can fight.
I'm not a violent person and I thought I was being sent to a
place with non-violent people, but that's not the case here. . . . I
don't think this pressure is the punishment you had in mind for
me. It's very hard to live in fear all the time . . .

Were these the words of a shell-shocked veteran who once
again found himself trapped in a windowless box, dreading
sounds in the darkness? Or were they simply the latest fictions
of a calculating flimflam man? I could never be sure. Nor could
I judge whether Gilbert Bland believed his own words when he
wrote that same judge eleven months later to vow, "I have no
intention of ever committing an illegal act again."

HE PATHFINDER SURVIVED THE SIERRAS, BUT JUST
barely. When he and his men became bogged down in snow as
deep as they were tall, their Indian guides deserted, and one
starving member of the expedition, suffering from hallucina-
tions, wandered off into the wilderness, never to be seen again.
The cartographer, Charles Preuss, lost from the main party for

three days, was forced to eat ants to survive. Yet when the dazed adventurers finally stumbled down into the Sacramento Valley, at least one thing was clear in their minds. As John Noble Wilford wrote in his book *The Mapmakers:* "Frémont's march south to California eliminated the Buenaventura from the map."

My own expedition was not so successful. I found a few promising streams and many dry riverbeds but discovered no unmistakable channel linking Bland's experience in Vietnam with his cartographic crime spree. Yet neither could I conclusively discount it as a myth. By now I had learned that sometimes you don't conquer the wilderness even when you have a guide. I would add many new coordinates to my map in the months to come, but this particular one would always resist my geography. In the end I was left to ponder one last story about the Rio Buenaventura. For centuries mapmakers theorized that the Great River of the West and all the other major rivers on the continent had their headwaters in the same place, a so-called height of land. At the beginning of the nineteenth century, this concept assumed a brief life as cartographic fact when Zebulon Montgomery Pike claimed "no hesitation in asserting" that, on a journey to present-day Colorado, he had come within a short distance of this "grand reservoir of snows and fountains." He should have known better. The true source of a thing is never so easy to find.

THIS MAP, WHICH ACCOMPANIED A
1614 EDITION OF WALTER RALEIGH'S
HISTORY OF THE WORLD, LOCATES
THE EARTHLY PARADISE IN
MESOPOTAMIA.

The Waters of Paradise

*F*LORIDA HAS ALWAYS BEEN A LAND OF new beginnings. Even the guy who put the place on the map came in search of metamorphosis. As a Spanish functionary in the West Indies, Juan Ponce de León had heard local legends about an island with "a spring of running water of such marvellous virtue, that the water therof being drunk, perhaps with some diet, makes old men young again," in the words of one sixteenth-century chronicler. Funny thing: European myths foretold a similar fountain, usually set in some far-off enchanted garden—sometimes Eden itself. You may remember, for example, that Sir John Mandeville, the enigmatic fourteenth-century figure we examined earlier, claimed to have visited a "noble and beautiful well, whose water has a sweet taste and smell, as if of different kinds of spices." Never one for understatement, Mandeville claimed that "he who drinks of it seems always young. They say this water comes from the Earthly Paradise, it is so full of goodness." Could it be mere coincidence that two legends half a world apart were so similar? Apparently Ponce de León didn't think so. Feeling past his prime at age fifty-three, he set sail from Puerto Rico in 1513, reportedly to search for gold and a cure for *el enflaquecimiento del sexo,* the debility of sex. He never located the Fountain of Youth, but he did stumble upon an even greater marvel: North America.

And, in a curious way, Ponce de León's quest has never ended. To this day Florida remains a mecca for those trying to make a new start. Possessing one of the country's lowest proportions of locally born citizens and highest rates of population growth, the state teems with wealthy Yankee retirees, ambitious Caribbean immigrants, and a hodgepodge of others who come in search of a new lease on life. The sense of rootlessness is as thick and ripe as the midsummer air.

Gilbert Bland, too, began his life all over again in Florida—not once but twice. The first time came upon his release from the federal penitentiary in late December 1977. After being discharged from a Florida halfway house in March 1978, Bland settled down in the Fort Lauderdale area, where, in May of that year, he went to court to divorce his first wife, Carol Ann Talt Bland. It would turn out that he was breaking not just with one person but with his whole past. According to Heather Bland, a daughter by that first marriage, her father rarely contacted her or her sister, Melissa, as they were growing up. "He's got two children that he totally abandoned and couldn't care less about," she told me.

Nonetheless, Bland appeared to turn his life around, at least for a few years. He married again, and he and his new wife, Karen Bland, had two more children. After receiving an associate's degree from Broward Community College in Fort Lauderdale and studying for three quarters at Florida Atlantic University, he moved to Maryland, where he worked for Allied Signal Corporation for five years during the 1980s. He may have also developed an interest in antiques during this period. Statements Bland later made to other dealers, as well as to police, indicate that his fascination with maps grew out of a more general interest in antiques, apparently including old stocks and bonds, as well as rare books. This notion was later confirmed by one of his attorneys, who wrote: "His interest in maps developed through his prior interest in and collection of older books, some of which contained maps in them."

In 1992 he and his wife opened their own computer training and leasing firm, Pacific Data Systems, in the town of Columbia. The firm, according to Maryland state records, was owned by Karen Bland—because, I would imagine, her husband's fraud convictions did not make for a particularly good credit rating. The couple apparently worked out of their home, since the company's mailing address was a postal box at Parcel Plus, a mail services outlet in Columbia. I could not find out much about the specific nature of Pacific Data's operations, but court documents from a later case offered a few fascinating details. One of Bland's "major customers," according to the documents, was an organization he would soon be dealing with in a vastly different capacity: the Federal Bureau of Investigation. The documents, drafted by Bland's attorneys, asserted that he "made a number of sales" to the FBI office in Maryland, where he "trained agents in the use of such equipment, and . . . assisted in a technical capacity with computers used during and for surveillance operations."

The FBI, prompted by a request I filed under the Freedom of Information Act, confirmed that a Pacific Data Systems of Columbia, Maryland, did indeed perform unspecified work for the Bureau in 1993. But even with a government contract, the firm was apparently far from a rousing success. Paul R. Thomson, Jr., one of the map thief's attorneys, would later assert in court that a changing market in the early 1990s made the concept of computer leasing "no longer . . . economically feasible." As Bland's business dried up, he and his wife decided to move to Florida to be with her mother, who "had been recently widowed," according to Thomson.

Bland departed from Maryland sometime in late 1993 or early 1994, leaving behind his usual share of unfinished business. At the Parcel Plus in Columbia, for example, an employee told me that Bland had pulled up stakes without paying his bill—and without leaving a forwarding address. It was yet another clean break from the past.

In February 1994, the Blands opened Antique Maps & Collectibles, Ltd., in the Gardens, a sleepy little office and retail complex located in the Fort Lauderdale exurb of Tamarac, whose open-air courtyard echoes not with the bustle of shoppers but with the listless gurgle of fountains that line the empty walkways. Perhaps, as he stared out at those fountains, Gilbert Bland thought that he had succeeded where Juan Ponce de León had failed, that he had discovered a way to wash away the past and reinvigorate a sense of potency. Perhaps, beginning a new career in a new town just months shy of his forty-fifth birthday, he felt almost young again.

Or perhaps he just wanted to be left alone. "Basically, the man stayed to himself," said Jan English, a bartender at the Beverly Hills Cafe, an eatery at the Gardens. Added one employee of a business that faced Bland's shop: "The place was basically always empty. We were sitting here one day thinking, I wonder how he makes money? And then we were wondering, Who would be interested in those old maps?"

The choice of location for the store must have seemed peculiar indeed to casual observers. Lost amid South Florida's vast formless expanse of strip malls and subdivisions—the kind of landscape where "everyplace looks like noplace in particular," in the words of James Howard Kunstler, author of the anti-sprawl tome *The Geography of Nowhere*—the Gardens was about the last spot you might expect to find an antique maps shop. Then again, this was one antique maps shop that had no desire to be found.

THE MAP DEALERS DID NOT TRUST ME; THAT MUCH WAS obvious from the start. When I called them they would often beg out of the conversation, some politely explaining that they were simply too busy to talk in the foreseeable future, others bluntly telling me to mind my own business. When I visited them at the 1998 Miami International Map Fair, once again following in Bland's footsteps, their eyes would sometimes dart to the floor as I approached, or their conversations would come to a sudden halt, rising again in whispers after I walked past. In some cases it took me years to gain their confidence, and even then they would usually speak to me only on the condition of anonymity.

At first I attributed their guardedness to simple embarrassment. Many of them had done a considerable amount of business with the now-notorious map thief, a fact that they hoped their colleagues would forget and their customers never learn. But as time wore on I began to see a more subtle factor at work. The world of antique maps is a very small and genteel one. Although their shops are located all over the globe, the dealers regularly attend the same gatherings (including the Miami map fair), read the same journals (such as the glossy *Mercator's World* or the scholarly *Imago mundi*), and keep in touch on the same Internet forums (most notably the Map History Discussion List), where they join librarians, scholars, and collectors in exchanging esoterica, debating map controversies, and trading cartographic jokes. *(What did the mapmaker send his sweetheart on Valentine's Day? A dozen compass roses.)* I was a complete stranger to this punctilious subculture. Even so, I had the feeling that in normal times I might have been made to feel welcome. These, however, were not normal times. Three years earlier, another outsider, someone the dealers had known no better than they knew me, had come into their midst asking for their trust. They had made the mistake of giving it to him. "It's a very close community," explained F. J. Manasek, a well-known Vermont dealer and industry observer who wrote *Collecting Old Maps*. "We're all friends, even though we compete in business. There's a lot of honor, which is probably why Bland could gain such easy entrée."

"The map trade is basically a handshake business," added George Ritzlin, another longtime dealer, based in Illinois. "People trust each other. Substantial amounts of valuable material travel thousands of miles based on a telephone call, without any other supporting documentation. And this is why Bland was able to be so successful. He was incredibly brazen by putting himself up to be a dealer. People just assumed that anyone acting as a dealer had obtained material honestly. Thieves don't normally work that way. Normally they are very surreptitious."

Having been burned once, the dealers now had little intention of exposing themselves to another outsider, especially one determined to open old wounds. I had not counted on them viewing me this way. Somehow I had convinced myself they would look upon me as an ally. It took a very long time to realize that when they glanced at me with those disdainful eyes, the man they saw looking back was Gilbert Bland.

ONE OF THE FEW DEALERS WHO WOULD DISCUSS THE matter openly was Barry Lawrence Ruderman, himself a relative newcomer to the trade. A bankruptcy lawyer by profession, the thirty-eight-year-old Ruderman discovered antique maps in his late twenties, when, during a ski trip to Taos, New Mexico, he "got bored" one day and wandered into a map shop. It was, said Ruderman, "love at first sight," and his passion soon developed into what he and other map junkies sometimes call cartomania.

"Cartomania is a sickness," he once told me. "It's obsessive. Once you're in up to your ankles, you want to be in up to your knees; once you're in up to your knees, you want to be in up to your waist. I like to think that it's sort of a beautiful sickness, because all human beings need things that stimulate them intellectually and drive them to passion. But the secondary aspect is that many of us spend insane amounts of time dedicating ourselves to map collecting. It's a twisted pursuit. But where's the problem in that?"

In 1992 Ruderman turned his "sickness" into a sideline vocation, opening Old Historic Maps & Prints, a La Jolla, California, venture that sold rare maps via mail and the Internet. Two years later he received a catalog from another fledgling map retailer, this one based in Tamarac, Florida. "It was semiprofessional looking, nothing real fancy," Ruderman remembered. Although the catalog contained "a bizarre mix" of materials, including a lot of worthless junk, Ruderman was intrigued by some of the offerings, especially maps of the American West. He would become one of Gilbert Bland's earliest clients.

But make no mistake: the fact that Ruderman was one of the only dealers candid enough to publicly discuss his dealings with Bland in no way means that he was the only one to have *had* such dealings. Indeed, the majority of Gilbert Bland's customers appear to have been dealers, including some of the most respected names in the trade. The map thief and his wife did little to encourage a walk-in business at their Florida store, which, like the brand-new home they bought for $151,400 in nearby Coral Springs, was owned by Karen Bland. Instead, they concentrated on developing a long-distance clientele, advertising in international trade publications and sending out catalogs. In retrospect, they seem to have penetrated the world of antique maps with startling speed and effectiveness.

Bland's inwardness worked to his advantage. Someone else in his position might have tried to ingratiate himself, make friends, become an indispensable member of the group—in short, to do what con men do: gain people's confidence. But whether by intent or natural inclination, Bland was less of a con man than an *un man,* inducing unmindfulness, lulling people into believing he was simply not worth much thought one way or another. As one dealer later put it: "Mr. Bland was bland. He looked bland, he sounded bland, he acted bland. There was no personality: nothing there."

Along the same lines, Ruderman remembered him as being "pleasant, not a fabulous conversationalist, but nice enough, friendly enough, a tad bit socially awkward, maybe. Just your average Joe. . . . There was nothing to raise an eyebrow about, other than the fact that here was a guy with a large cache of material whom nobody had dealt with before."

And, luckily for Bland, many in the industry were then in

need of a just such a "large cache." The map business was undergoing something of a sea change when Bland arrived on the scene. With big numbers of new collectors and traders entering the market, the demand for antique maps was higher than ever. For obvious reasons, however, the supply had remained pretty much stable. That meant not only higher prices but fewer maps in active circulation. This was no problem for major players like Graham Arader, who could afford a huge overhead. But for midsize and smaller dealers, the capital that had once bought five or ten maps now might purchase only one—*if* that item was even available. Hard-pressed to maintain an adequate inventory, these dealers found themselves scrambling for new sources of material. It was no wonder that word spread quickly about a Florida store with an incredible supply of low- to mid-priced maps.

For his own part, Ruderman "bought actively with Bland for probably six or eight months." On occasion he entertained doubts about his business associate, in part because he seemed to know so little about maps. One time Ruderman even "sort of cross-examined Bland" about the provenance of his materials. Bland replied that he and his wife had been involved in scripophily—the collecting of old stock certificates and bonds—and had incidentally been accumulating old maps. "That was an acceptable answer," said Ruderman, "because frankly there are two or three respected dealers who fit that general MO." In the end, Ruderman concluded, "Gil passed the smell test."

OR OTHERS, HOWEVER, THE ODOR EMANATING FROM South Florida had become increasingly foul. Among those who bought items from Bland were a pair of dealers who have operated a respected map store for several decades. The partners, who spoke on the condition of anonymity, became increasingly suspicious of Bland, eventually severing ties with him and privately informing other dealers of their concerns. We'll refer to them as Once Bitten and Twice Shy.

Their first contact with Gilbert and Karen Bland came in May 1994, just three months after Antique Maps & Collectibles had opened. "We heard about him from another dealer whom we're quite friendly with," recalled Once Bitten. "During a phone conversation, the fellow said, 'Well, this couple in Florida seems to have a lot of material. You probably want to get in touch with them.' So that's what we did. At first the Blands were very pleasant. . . . They didn't seem terribly knowledgeable, but they seemed to want to learn. So we tried to be helpful, just as people were helpful to us when we started."

Thus began a short-lived relationship in which the veteran dealers functioned both as customers and as mentors to the Blands, educating the newcomers on what they were doing wrong and how they might correct it. There was much to discuss. Among other problems, the Florida firm's early catalogs contained a number of descriptions that were "ignorantly inaccurate," according to Twice Shy. For example, the Blands misidentified the mapmaker of an eighteenth-century French map of China as Échelle. They had apparently found this word in the cartouche, the part of the map where the cartographer's name usually appears. Ah, but Monsieur Échelle, he was no mapmaker! Poor soul, he did not even exist! *Échelle*, the veteran partners dutifully informed the Blands, is the French word for "scale."

For their part, the newcomers always seemed grateful for such enlightenment, however humiliating. In one obsequious letter Gilbert Bland praised the partners' "eminence and experience in the field of cartography/map collecting," vowing to "accept and incorporate" their ideas "into my own limited knowledge of this business."

Karen Bland also had regular correspondence with the pair. It should be stressed that no criminal charges were ever filed against the map thief's wife; even so, observed Once Bitten and Twice Shy, she seemed to be intimately involved in the day-to-day operations of the store. "She knew as much as he did, that was my impression," said Once Bitten. "My feeling was that if we wanted to engage in any sort of business with them, we could talk to her as readily as him. I thought that she was an active part of the business."

Despite the cordial relationship, it did not take long for Once Bitten and Twice Shy to notice that some of their most important advice was being ignored. They became particularly frustrated with the Florida couple's continued failure to adequately describe the materials for sale in their catalogs. This was not a mere matter of snotty etiquette: the Blands were listing items in a way that implied that they were in top condition when in fact many of them were in "wretched shape," according to Twice Shy. "We'd send stuff back and say, 'Listen, we're not being picky. Here's what people want and here's how you should describe it.' Then the same items would appear on the next list with no correction at all. And Gil would always blame it on the computer—somehow it didn't catch in the computer when he made the correction."

Trying hard to give the newcomers the benefit of the doubt, Once Bitten and Twice Shy offered advice about which software might solve the problem—unaware that, in another, not-so-distant life, the Blands had been computer consultants. After a number of frustrating incidents, however, the veteran pair's patience finally wore out. "I remember one of the things they sent to us actually was missing a chunk," said Once Bitten. "We sent it back. And in the next catalog, there it was again without any description indicating it was incomplete. . . . At that point, it was pretty clear that they were being deceptive. When some-one is told in no uncertain terms that a map is incomplete, is missing a piece, and should not be described in the way they were describing it—and then chooses to do it again, it's hard to think of another excuse for their actions. They weren't stupid."

By the time they broke off ties with Antique Maps & Collectibles in late 1994, Once Bitten and Twice Shy had begun to have other suspicions about Gilbert Bland. They were troubled, for instance, by his "bizarre" style of negotiation. Bland's prices were fairly cheap to begin with, yet he always seemed willing to take a lower offer. "He never counteroffered," said Once Bitten.

"He'd just say, 'Well okay.' . . . In retrospect, we know that he didn't care so much about the price as long as he got *something*. It was all profit."

Worse, the partners had growing doubts about where Bland was getting his materials. At first, explained Once Bitten, they had assumed that he "lucked into something. Maybe he had bought an antique shop and there was a pile of stuff in the basement or something of that sort." But over time they began to suspect more ominous origins.

On the day I interviewed the partners at their store, they took out some of Bland's old catalogs, shaking their heads as they recalled the way his inventory mysteriously expanded to include multiple copies of fairly rare items. "It was frustrating to comprehend how this guy, whom I considered a classic jerk, was getting access to materials that we who had been in the trade for so long had to wait for years to pop up," said Twice Shy.

Because they had no hard evidence against Bland, the partners did not go to the police or denounce him in a public way. They did, however, begin to share their hunches with other dealers. "It was not like we called everybody up and said, 'Wow! We think this guy is rotten!' " explained Twice Shy. "People in this trade chat each other up all the time. We're as gossipy as a bunch of old ladies. And Bland's name would just come up in conversation."

They soon discovered that others had similar concerns. "As those of us old-timers in the trade started questioning how this guy was getting duplicates of some more interesting material, I was speaking with another dealer and I said, 'If I had money, I would hire a private detective to follow Bland,' " said Twice Shy. "I was *that* suspicious."

But if some dealers were beginning to steer clear of Gilbert Bland, others were becoming increasingly enamored of his growing stock of materials, which by now included a number of older, rarer, and more expensive items. His reputation on the rise, Bland and his wife made high-profile appearances at the two big industry conventions of 1995—the Miami International Map Fair in February and the International Map Collectors' Society fair, held in San Francisco during October. "Bland had a major presence at both fairs," recalled James Hess, who owns the Heritage Map Museum and Auction House in Lititz, Pennsylvania. "He was putting himself out there with the major dealers."

Barry Lawrence Ruderman, who had dinner with Bland at the San Francisco event, added: "Most of all, he was interested in being a wheeler-dealer. He was looking for big buys. He was definitely crunching numbers a lot more than he was learning maps."

"It got to the point," recalled one respected antiquarian, "that dealers would be saying, 'My goodness, maps of City X have been selling rather well. Do you have any maps of City X?' And Bland would say, 'Let me check and I'll get back to you.' And the very next week he'd call and say, 'Why yes, I just happen to have a map of City X.' "

Which, of course, is exactly why the dealers should have been wary. The fact that many continued to do business with him right up until his misadventure at the Peabody Library says less about the nature of the map trade than it does about that oldest of human afflictions, temptation. Almost no one I interviewed believed Bland's customers had firsthand knowledge of his crimes. More likely, the dealers were driven by what antiquarians sometimes describe as "a need not to know." In the words of Once Bitten: "I'm sure a number of people closed their eyes. It's very easy to do when there's a chance to make money."

OR GOD DOTH KNOW THAT IN THE DAY YE EAT THEREOF, *then your eyes shall be opened, and ye shall be as gods, knowing good and evil.* Such were the words laid down in ancient times about what transpired "eastward in Eden." Yes, wondered the people of later epochs, but where, exactly, was this Eden? Paradise was lost, quite literally—and for centuries theologians, scholars, pilgrims, and mapmakers were obsessed with finding it.

Earlier civilizations, from the Sumerians to the Greeks, had established a lush and fragrant garden as the basic setting of Paradise—a word that comes from the Old Persian *apiri-daeza,* an orchard surrounded by a wall. The Hebrew Scriptures fleshed out those myths, offering a seemingly solid clue as to this enchanted garden's whereabouts. According to the second chapter of Genesis, a stream flowed through the Earthly Paradise, then branched into four rivers—the Pishon, later thought to be the Indus, the Ganges, or the Danube; the Gihon, or Nile; the Hiddekel, or Tigris; and, finally, the Euphrates. This description, however, created more questions than answers—not the least of which being how four rivers whose headwaters were apparently so very far apart could possibly spring from the same source. Some early Christian scholars argued that such concerns were beside the point, since the Bible's description was merely figurative. But many medieval theologians insisted that the Garden was an actual place on Earth, one whose rivers flowed underground before reaching their apparent starting points. The learned St. Isidore of Seville, for instance, located Eden in the Far East, surrounded by a "wall of fire whose flames rise as high as heaven," making it "barred to humanity." Reflecting such ideas, the *mappae mundi* of the Middle Ages usually show the Garden at the easternmost edges (or top) of the world, sometimes as a walled-off region on the mainland, sometimes as an island above "farthest India." Such concepts remained pretty much standard until the Age of Exploration, when new possibilities arose, especially in the New World, where Christopher Columbus claimed to have seen "great evidence of the earthly Paradise" near the Orinoco River. The hunt would go on for centuries, although its focus would eventually shift from where Paradise *still was* to where it *had been.* Sir Walter Raleigh—who argued that the Garden itself could no longer be found, inasmuch as "the flood, and other accidents of time" had reduced Eden to the state of ordinary fields and pastures—placed its original location in Mesopotamia. Others put it in Armenia or Palestine or Africa or Ceylon. As late as the nineteenth century, a British general reported absolute proof of Eden's existence on Praslin Island in the Indian Ocean. Charles

Gordon, a war hero and religious zealot, was convinced that a species of palm on the island was none other than the Tree of Knowledge of Good and Evil. After all, he noted, the plant bore fruit of both sexes, the male resembling a phallus, the female "shaped . . . when opened like a [woman's] belly with thighs." How could such suggestive vegetation be anything but proof that Adam and Eve had lived on the island?

These days, of course, not even the truest of true believers would dare to put Paradise on a map. Yet despite the cynicism of our age, we humans have not lost our urge to quest after that place of perfect contentment, never quite finding it but never quite giving up hope, sometimes drawing so near that we can almost smell the faint sweet scent of its blossoms or spy the distant glimmer of its waters. I still don't know precisely what motivated Gilbert Bland to open that store in South Florida. His detractors argue that his intentions were evil from the start, pointing out that James Perry's visits to university libraries began just a few short months after the store opened. True enough, yet somehow I'd like to think Bland's motives were more complex. My hunch—or maybe it's just my hope—is that, in the beginning at least, his desire to start his life anew was sincere. But however the saga at the strip mall began, it ended as tragicomic trash-culture allegory: *And the sinner and his wife were driven forth from the Gardens retail center, and their sorrows were greatly multiplied, and they knew then that they were naked before the Almighty Media Juggernaut.*

The Fall of Bland came in mid-December 1995, a week after he was detained at Johns Hopkins. With the University of Virginia's Thomas Durrer and the FBI closing in on him, Bland had returned to Florida. At some point between the afternoon of December 14 and early morning of December 15, he cleaned out his store and left the Gardens forever, reportedly leaving a note for his landlord that said, "See you later."

"I came in and a lot of the maps were gone," said Laurie Bregman, a tenant at the Gardens whose business was just across from Antique Maps & Collectibles. "I thought that maybe he was just remodeling or that maybe he'd sold a lot of stuff. But it turned out that he had emptied the place in a middle-of-the-night kind of deal."

Although Bland had managed thus far to escape arrest, he had not escaped attention. A number of major media outlets, including the Baltimore *Sun* and Associated Press, had already run stories about the crime spree; many more, including *The Washington Post*, the *Chicago Tribune,* and National Public Radio, would soon follow.

The news spread quickly through the antique maps industry, prompting one of two sharply divergent reactions among dealers. For some, it was a fait accompli. "I was completely unsurprised when the story broke," remembered Twice Shy. For others, however, it was a complete shock. "My jaw dropped," said Jonathan Ramsay, the owner of a map and print business in the Bahamas. "I mean, the guy was straight as an arrow. When something like this happens, you say to yourself, 'Wow, I just don't understand human nature.' "

Ramsay, who had both a business and a social relationship with Bland, heard about the map thief's legal troubles when a friend from Florida faxed him a newspaper story. "I called my friend up and I said, 'You've got to be kidding me!' Just then I heard a noise in the shop and I turned around and there were these three guys standing there. And I said, 'Yes? Can I help you?' And one of them said, 'I'm an FBI agent.' He'd been standing right behind me as I talked on the phone. He said, 'Obviously I can hear from your phone conversation that you've heard the news.' "

Another dealer who bought maps from Bland and met him face-to-face shared Ramsay's surprise. "Bland was the most soft-spoken and considerate guy," he said. "It was like a contradiction. On the phone and in person, he was so quiet, and then on the other hand, the crimes he committed were incredibly nervy. I guess he was a hell of a con man."

Those who lived in the same upscale subdivision as the Bland family could be forgiven if they, too, were taken aback by the news. The four-bedroom, two-and-a-half-bath, Italian-style house, part of a development called the Classics at Kensington, projected an air of respectability and affluence. But Gilbert Bland's life had been full of misleading facades, and this one was no exception: The family's financial picture was nowhere near as rosy as it appeared from the outside. On November 3, 1995—a little more than a month before Bland's brief capture in Baltimore—Karen Bland, the owner of record for both the house and the store, had declared Chapter Seven bankruptcy. Court documents show that she owed more than forty thousand dollars in credit card debt alone.

Bland's lawyers would later argue that it was the failure of his computer leasing firm in Maryland that led to these financial troubles and eventually to his crime spree. But that might not have been the only factor. "I'll put another scenario in front of you," said Jonathan Ramsay. "He came over here [to the Bahamas] about four or five times—and he liked to gamble. He'd say to me, 'I'm over here on a gambling junket.' He would come in to see me and then he would go off to the casino."

Given Bland's apparent propensity for risk, an infatuation with gambling would hardly seem out of character. But whether to pay off casino debts or for some other reason entirely, he clearly found himself in desperate need of fast cash— and knew a way to get it. "He found an easy avenue to make some quick money, and he really overdid it," said Lieutenant Detective Clay Williams of the University of North Carolina Department of Public Safety, one of several law enforcement agencies that was by now getting involved in the case. "He got in way over his head. It became addictive. I don't think he had any conception of the federal charges that could come down on him."

Come down they did—but slowly, very slowly. While news of the crime was breaking all over the country, the FBI's attempts to get a search warrant for Bland's store had gotten bogged down in red tape. "A search warrant has to be originated in the same jurisdiction that it's going to be executed," explained Special Agent Henry F. Hanburger of the FBI office in Columbia, Maryland. "And timing was terrible with the

Christmas holidays and the absence of people at work both on the prosecutor's side and our side. . . . We just couldn't get the needed prosecutor to say, 'Damn right, let's get a search warrant.' That cost us a little bit."

In fact, the delay would end up costing investigators a great deal—and prosecutors even more. It was not until a day or two *after* Bland had cleaned out his store that FBI agents tracked him down in Florida. And it was not until two weeks later, January 2, 1996, that the map thief turned himself in to local police. At long last Bland was in custody. Now it was his maps that were nowhere to be found.

CHAPTER 10

The Joy of Discovery

*T*HE ADMIRAL SITS DOWN TO WRITE A LETTER. *From outside his cabin come sounds so familiar he does not even hear them: the creak of wood, the slap and flutter of sails, the hoarse lurch of the sea. He is on a ship called the Niña, heading east. As he leans over the page, his blue eyes narrow with excitement, and he indulges himself in a satisfied smile. The letter is dated "February 15 of the year 1493," and is addressed to a Spanish official. It contains thousands of words, only two of which really matter:*

I discovered . . .

The admiral does not know exactly what he discovered; he will go to his grave not knowing. (For now, he vaguely describes it as a great many islands inhabited by people without number.*) Nor does he understand how completely his discovery will change the world, or how fast. Within months copies of this same letter will be circulating*

Almirante de nauios para las Indias.

AN ALLEGORICAL COMMEMORATION OF
COLUMBUS'S DISCOVERIES IN THE
NEW WORLD, FROM A 1621 BOOK.

throughout Southern Europe, published in a dozen editions and in three languages. Within months the admiral will be a celebrity, cheered by throngs of well-wishers and feted by kings, queens, courtiers, and clergymen. Within months other explorers will be laying down plans to retrace the admiral's route. They, too, will make discoveries, but none of those will compare with his. The admiral has crossed an uncharted sea, visited an unmapped world: even though people may have spoken and written about these lands, all was conjecture, nobody actually having seen them. *To seek and to find—this has been his dream almost since childhood. ("He was charmed by the afterglow of legends that flashed from the unknown," the biographer Gianni Granzotto would later observe. "He began to fantasize about them, and they became the constant subject of his thoughts and dreams; he thus learned to travel the invisible roads that lay between wisdom and exaltation.") To seek and to find—and now, he writes, it has come to pass:* the conquest of what appears impossible. *The admiral has overcome all obstacles—the danger, the hardships, the terrifying uncertainty, the fact that learned and powerful men said it could not be done. To seek and to find—it is his triumph alone, he knows that, but he also knows that it means nothing unless it is shared, transformed from event to story and then to legend. That is why he is returning with specimens: gold, amber, cotton, herbs and chilies, caged parrots and other exotic birds, even human beings:* I bring Indians. *That is why he is writing this letter. That is why the still-wet ink glistens with these words:* The whole of Christendom should rejoice and make merry . . .

J TRY TO MAKE IT A RULE, DURING SOCIAL CALLS, TO RE-
frain from unsolicited comments about the attire of my hosts.
Then again, not every host comes to the door dressed in South
Seas islands.

"Your shirt," I blurted out, "is a map."

This unusual form of greeting did not seem to faze the
white-haired man who stood on the other side of the welcome
mat, studying me with a Cheshire-cat grin.

"Oh sure," he replied cheerily. "I've got map shirts, map ties,
map just about everything. Come on in."

And so began my visit to the extraordinary home of an even
more extraordinary person. For the next few hours my host
would lead me on a wide-ranging and high-spirited review of
the history of mapmaking, an astounding chunk of which happened to be hanging on the walls of his large house. Maps in
the bedrooms. Maps in the lounge. Maps in the dining room.
Maps in the living room. Maps in the hallways. ("There are a
few rooms that *don't* have maps," he observed, his boyish eyes
twinkling from behind a pair of big square glasses. "Fewer all
the time.") Maps on shelves and in cabinets and in cases. Maps
spread out on tables. But not just any maps—these were some
of the rarest and most significant maps ever printed, a collection of such scope and import that no less an expert than
Graham Arader had described it as "unbelievable." And Arader's
opinion of my host? "Oh, he's a giant! A giant collector!"

My visit here was yet another detour off Interstate Bland. Collectors in general had played only a small part in the map thief's saga; my host, to the best of my knowledge, had played none at all. Yet I had come to believe my research would be incomplete until I understood the nature of collecting. I knew, of course, that the collecting impulse was, in a general way, what created the market for Bland's stolen maps. I also thought this urge might help to explain why the map thief had built up his illicit hoard in the first place—and why he had then stashed it away from police. But I had a vague notion that it had an even deeper, if less immediate, significance to the story. I did not know then that my search for answers would turn into a journey of self-revelation. I simply had a hunch that an investigation was in order—and what better place to start than this bloated temple of cartographic wonders?

The house, I should note, was extremely well-secured—yet because its contents are literally irreplaceable I have decided to publish neither its location nor the name of its owner. Let's just call our "giant collector" Mr. Atlas, not only because he seemed to hold the whole universe aloft on his walls but because the house itself struck me as a kind of atlas—multiple views of the world making up a single worldview, an open book of one man's obsession.

And make no mistake: Mr. Atlas *is* obsessed. If you couldn't figure that out from his shirt (which, he complained, was not an accurate reproduction of any specific map but a "cobbled together" representation of "Cook's voyages of the South Pacific—though I've got lots of others"), you might have guessed it from the portraits hanging in the front hall. No, those bearded gents were not his ancestors. The pair in that double portrait, each of them holding a globe, were the legendary Dutch cartographer Gerard Mercator and Jodocus Hondius, the Amsterdam engraver and map seller whose atlases made Mercator's work famous. And hanging beside them, that fellow with the tiny little head perched atop the great big pleated ruff was none other than the great Abraham Ortelius, a name and face so familiar in the Atlas family that, recounted our giant collector, when "we visited a map dealer about a year ago, and my grandson saw a copy of the Ortelius portrait there, he just couldn't understand how it could be Ortelius because Grandpa already had Ortelius in his house."

In short, it was safe to conclude that Mr. Atlas suffered from a severe case of the malady described on a poster in his basement stairway:

WARNING
OLD MAP POX

Highly contagious!
There is no known cure!
Infection is characterized by dizziness and sweaty palms
when reading old map catalogues.
This is often accompanied by apnea and lust.
Additional pathognomonic signs are:
loss of free wall space and a self-induced poverty.

If infected, do not see your doctor, but
seek aid from an antiquarian map dealer who,
while unable to effect a cure,
can provide symptomatic relief.

But I would be loath to create the impression of Mr. Atlas as some sort of zoned-out eccentric. Articulate, dignified, and keenly intelligent, he was a man whose passion for maps was surpassed only by his knowledge of them. Retired from the business world, he now worked at an academic institution, where he researched and occasionally wrote about matters of cartographic history. He and his wife also helped to support various library acquisitions, as well as sponsoring a lecture series and occasional museum exhibitions. And, of course, his home was nothing less than a museum in its own right, painstakingly assembled over the course of some thirty-five years. As he led me on a tour of what he often referred to as "the treasures," I felt privileged not only to be in the presence of such marvelous artifacts—a few of which could literally be found only within those walls—but to get to know the man who had assembled them.

With a calm half smile fixed steadily on his full-lipped mouth, Mr. Atlas had the air of a slightly distracted sage—one happy to impart his wisdom upon a willing, if sometimes embarrassingly naive, pupil. "How many people can I share this with?" he said, gesturing to the walls. "Most people don't care." And so, in the slow cadence and indulging tones of a particularly patient grade school teacher, he began to speak about his maps and his life.

"Ever since I can remember I've collected something, whether it was seashells, minerals, postcards, stamps, coins—all at a child's level mostly," he explained. "I don't know whether you're just born with an interest in collecting or what. I guess either you're a person who accumulates things or one who gets rid of things. For example, if I have a file drawer, I'm not going to weed it out until it won't close anymore."

He discovered old maps while working as an investment counselor in the early 1960s. A business associate's office had recently been redone by an interior decorator who thought maps "created the right image." Two of the artifacts had thus appeared on the man's wall. "I think one was France and the other was Central Europe," Mr. Atlas said. "I don't even remember them exactly. But I said, 'Wow, those really are neat, Bob. Where'd you get those?' Well, he just mumbled something; he couldn't have cared less about maps. But for me, something clicked. I'd always been interested in art history and geography, and I thought, Gee, here's a product that brings both those interests together. And clearly it must be affordable also, or it wouldn't be on this guy's wall. So that got me started. I called the decorator and found out where the maps came from, and that led me to one of the most important dealers in the country. It was like a whole new thing opened up.

"When I started with maps," he added, "it was a miscellaneous assortment that had only a personal connection. I'd buy a map of a place because I'd taken a trip there or because I had relatives who lived there, something of that sort. And then after a few years I realized that really wasn't the right way to go about it. That's not a collection: it's an assembly of items. And the way I draw the distinction is that selecting a piece for a collection has nothing to do with the individual merits of the item. It's whether there's a potential of relating it to other items. That's what builds a collection: the sum is of greater interest than each of the individual pieces."

And then Mr. Atlas said something that has often occupied my thoughts since. His goal as a collector, he explained, was to tell a "comprehensive story." I confess that this idea escaped— and irritated—me at first. My general impression was that collectors were people with too much time on their hands and too much money in their checking accounts—passive consumers. Collecting had never struck me as a particularly creative act, much less a narrative form. And as a moderately hardworking writer, I was a tad miffed by my host's implication that owning a lot of cool stuff qualified him as some sort of auteur as well.

If Mr. Atlas sensed my skepticism, he did not say so. Nor did he waste time with arguments in support of his thesis. Instead, he set about proving it—with maps. One such demonstration began with a 1718 map of the Mississippi River by the French cartographer Nicolas de Fer. On the inset was a smaller map, showing the entire Gulf Coast region. This rendering of the coast, he explained, was far more accurate than those that had come before it, a big step forward in the cartography of the area. He then showed me other maps bearing that same general image of the coastline, including Guillaume Delisle's *Carte de la*

Louisiane of 1718, "which was widely copied by many other cartographers and was the mother map of that region for half a century."

Finally, with barely restrained excitement, Mr. Atlas led me to another part of the house. "Now, look at *this*," he said, carefully taking out one last document. "*This* is where *all of that* comes from."

On the table in front of me was a work produced not by a printing press but by hand—what historians call a manuscript map. Some of the edges had been slightly burned, but I could easily make out the outline of the Gulf Coast—the same outline I had seen on the other maps. Yes, said Mr. Atlas, I was indeed looking at a one-of-a-kind work, the original map drafted by the actual person who had surveyed the region nearly three hundred years ago.

There was something even more haunting about this document than the others I had looked at that day. Looking down at those uneven lines of ink, it was almost as if I could see the hand that drew them moving carefully across the page. Then I began to imagine all the other hands that might have held this fragile document during its long life: the hardened palms of sailors and explorers, the sinewy fingers of cartographers, the pampered mitts of royals, the loving clutches of collectors. Suddenly, I felt a powerful connection to the past—not so much that I was reliving history but that I was *part* of it, a continent taking shape right before my eyes.

"This map was done by Mr. Soupart, whom we know nothing about," Mr. Atlas said. Not even the first name of the cartographer has survived. Only his map—and only in this house. "It's so rare that you can know the exact source [of a cartographic tradition]. So this was really neat to come across. The other thing is, do you notice that it's burned? Well, we can't prove it but we do know that the ship which in all likelihood was involved in the surveying expedition burned in Pensacola Harbor in 1719. And it wouldn't surprise me a bit if this was one of the things that was rescued."

What a story, I thought. What an absolutely, undeniably marvelous yarn.

Not only did I feel a new admiration for my host but as the afternoon progressed I began to feel something else as well, something I would never have imagined when I walked in the door: I started to think that Mr. Atlas and I had a lot in common. It was not that I suddenly understood his obsession. But the more maps he showed me—relating each one's history, demonstrating its interconnectedness to others—the less his hobby seemed like some arcane and alien pursuit. Was not building a collection, I began to wonder, a little like writing a book? Did not his quest and mine have the same end, the acquisition of knowledge? Did not we each seek to organize this information—one of us on the page, the other on his walls—in such a way that we might, as he had put it, "know the exact source" of a thing? Wasn't a desire to know the source, in fact, precisely what had brought me here?

By the end of the day, I was ready to proclaim Mr. Atlas not only a storyteller but a chronicler of epic events, the Tolstoy of maps. He had devoted his efforts to documenting two sweeping historical narratives. The first one was the exploration of the American West. This period fascinated him in great part, he explained, because the people who did the exploring were often the same ones who made the maps. And since most of those maps were accompanied by diaries, "you can relive the entire trip."

To illustrate his point, he took out a work by Charles Preuss, cartographer for my old pal the Pathfinder. "Here you see all this commentary comes from the Frémont journal," he said, pointing to text within the map. "And some of it is very interesting—like here! 'First view of buffalo, June the thirtieth.' And the campsites are all marked, so you can see how much space they covered on any given day."

His other great passion was the Age of Discovery, a period from which his collection contained a mind-boggling blur of masterpieces. I saw a 1513 work by Martin Waldseemüller, one of the first atlas maps to depict the New World. (It was Waldseemüller who—under the mistaken impression that Amerigo Vespucci had discovered the New World—named the southern part of that landmass America in a 1507 map. He later discovered his error and deleted the name in further editions, but by then the name had stuck.) I saw a rare work from 1534, drafted by Diego Ribero and printed by Giovanni Battista Ramusio, containing the first clearly identified depiction of the Strait of Magellan. I saw the first printed map devoted to the Western Hemisphere, a work by the German humanist Sebastian Münster. I saw maps by Ortelius, Mercator, the French innovator Oronce Finé, the Dutchmen Gerard and Cornelius De Jode, the

Briton John Speed. The list went on and on. Pick a great map from the sixteenth, seventeenth, or eighteenth century, and it was probably in that house.

The one that really seized my imagination, however, was a smaller work by a lesser-known cartographer, Francesco Rosselli. Printed in Florence around 1508, this particular copy of the map had disappeared shortly thereafter. It remained hidden away for hundreds of years—and might never have surfaced, if not for a fortunate turn of fate. "Apparently this copy was discovered during the rebinding of an early book," Mr. Atlas said. "In past centuries, it was not uncommon for other prints, unrelated to the book at all, to be used as filler in the covers: the exterior of the cover would be an animal skin, and then to give it body there would often be paper inside that. And so when the book is being rebound, the conservators know enough to be careful because often there are prints and other things found that way. And that's how this one came to light."

Originally in the hands of a British dealer, the piece was purchased in the 1980s by a San Francisco map seller who, in turn, sold it to a collector in South America. Mr. Atlas became interested in the map when the South American, who "had to come up with lots of money due to a divorce settlement," decided to put it up for auction at Sotheby's.

He knew little about the piece at first. "I had to research it," he explained. "In fact, to me that's really the most interesting part: the work you do prior to making your decision whether to add a piece to the collection or not. And whichever way the decision goes, you've learned a lot. Really, that's what it's about, because it's only a piece of paper, after all. But the key thing is what that piece of paper *represents*. So if you don't know the historical and cultural elements that produced a map, I think you're missing most of the fun."

It turned out that those "historical and cultural elements" were plenty significant. Rosselli's map was the first one to use a projection system that incorporated 360 degrees of latitude and 180 degrees of longitude—making it, "in a very real sense, the first map of the whole world," according to the historian Peter Whitfield. (That "whole world," however, was a quirky one, containing a separate South American continent—labeled "Land of the Holy Cross or New World"—but no North America, only an elongated Asia.) It was also the first map to use the name Antarcticus (Latin for "opposite of the north") to describe what was then still a hypothetical southern continent. And it was the first map to incorporate discoveries made by Christopher Columbus during his fourth voyage of 1502–1504.

An important artifact, yes, but more: an extremely rare one. It turned out that only two other copies were known to exist— one at the British National Maritime Museum in Greenwich and the other at the Biblioteca Nazionale Centrale in Florence. Mr. Atlas determined that, if possible, the third one would be his: "It took a lot more digging than usual to find out what this one was. And I said, 'Well, yeah! That's definitely a great one to have. Absolutely!' "

Luck, as it turned out, was on his side. Instead of putting the work up for sale in an auction devoted solely to maps and prints—where it would likely have garnered a great deal of interest—Sotheby's offered it with an assortment of other antiques from the South American collector's holdings, including such unrelated items as furniture. "And it was not pictured in the Sotheby's catalog, either, so, again, attention was not drawn to it," explained Mr. Atlas.

How sweet it must have been to realize this gem was hidden from the view of other potential bidders! Yet how nerve-racking to think they might catch on! I knew enough about the lore of collecting to understand that the most coveted acquisitions are the "finds." There's the story of Henry Stevens, for instance, a prominent bookseller in the nineteenth century who, while visiting the home of an acquaintance, "chanced to notice a small copper globe, a child's plaything, rolling about the floor." Stevens, who later recounted that his host had "picked it up in some town in France for a song," realized that it was no mere knickknack but a world globe from the early 1500s—a priceless, one-of-a-kind artifact now housed at the New York Public Library. By comparison, of course, the reappearance of the Rosselli map was not quite so dramatic. Still, said Mr. Atlas: "I knew there would never be another chance to get it. And there, it's a question of how badly did you want it?"

Just badly enough. Though he refused to say how much he paid for the map, he did note—with discernible glee—that he "got it for a lot less" than the seller had shelled out in the first place. Still, it was clear that the map's monetary value was of relatively little importance to him. "The only time money matters," he insisted, "is at the decision point about whether you're going to buy something."

But if the commercial aspects of collecting weren't what kept him going, then why did he pursue a map like the Rosselli with such fervor? Its historical import? Sure. Its beauty? Of course. Its rarity? Doubtless. The stature it would bring him? Possibly. Yet something else seemed to matter more than all that—something that he never quite expressed but that I nonetheless began to recognize while I watched him pore over that map, his eyes dancing from one place to another as though in search of a previously unnoticed detail. Perhaps it was simple. Perhaps the impulse to collect maps and the impulse to make them arose from the same desire. Perhaps what drove aficionados like Mr. Atlas was precisely what had driven explorers like Columbus: the sheer joy of discovery.

The searching, the dreaming, the navigating of strange seas, the overcoming of obstacles—all leading up to that instant when the unknown is known, the unreachable reached, the unobtainable obtained. In an essay on collecting, the philosopher-critic Walter Benjamin—himself an incurable bibliophile—described that shining moment as "the final thrill, the thrill of acquisition." Columbus had put it another way: the conquest of what appears impossible.

An impossible conquest—I couldn't think of a better description of how Mr. Atlas had come to possess that long-lost document. But I also knew that not all journeys of discovery end so happily. If I needed proof, it was right there in front of me, on that map commemorating the last, lonely journey of history's most famous explorer.

HE ADMIRAL SITS DOWN TO WRITE ANOTHER LETTER. TEN years have passed and much has changed. He has fallen from favor with the crown, become an object of scorn among his peers. He has arthritis. He has malaria. His eyes bleed, leaving him blind for long periods. At the moment, he finds himself marooned in Jamaica, hundreds of miles from any hope of rescue, his men on the verge of revolt. He writes: I have not a hair upon me that is not grey, and my body is infirm. *He writes:* I am . . . ruined. *He could have avoided all this, if only he would have retired after his great discovery. ("Almost anyone, it might be thought, would rest content with so much fame, so much wealth, so many discoveries, so dramatic a social rise. But not Columbus," his biographer Felipe Fernández-Armesto would observe. "His sights were always fixed on unmade discoveries, unfinished initiatives, imperfect gains, and frustrated crusades.") The elation of that first triumph was so very sweet but so very short-lived, and he has tried to get it back ever since. Three times he has sailed across the sea, and three times his journeys have ended in frustration. (Once, he was taken back to Europe in chains, due to his misgovernance of the new colonies.) He has made many new discoveries, of course, but they do not satisfy him. He wants more: more land, more status, more fame, more wealth. He writes:* Gold is most excellent. *He writes:* Gold constitutes treasure, and he who possesses it may do what he will in the world. *To seek and to find and to keep on seeking—it's as if his dream has turned into an unquenchable obsession.*

ASING INTO THE SOFA OF WERNER MUENSTER-berger's midtown Manhattan apartment, I found myself surrounded by unsettlingly beautiful pieces of ancient African art: brooding figures that lurked in the corners like dim and disquieting memories, phallic totems, wild-eyed masks that stared at me so intently I almost blushed. They seemed to be carved out of solid id, those objects, which was only fitting because I had come here to discuss the shadowy nether regions of the human mind. Muensterberger, a charming, erudite, and meticulously attired octogenarian, was a leading expert on the psychology of collecting. With his bulky glasses, brushed-back white hair, and wiry eyebrows, he looked every bit like the psychoanalyst and retired professor of psychiatry that he was—and with his Teutonic accent, the result of a childhood spent in both Germany and the Netherlands, he somehow sounded the part as well. I had already become fairly familiar with Muensterberger's ideas on collecting through reading his work and interviewing him over the telephone. What I had not known was that his interest in the subject was obviously far more than clinical. Yet the fact that he was himself a confirmed aficionado only made me more anxious to talk to him. If Mr. Atlas had taught me about the beauty of collecting, I hoped that Dr. Muensterberger could give me some insight into the darker side of the obsession, a subject he had explored at length in his book *Collecting: An Unruly Passion.*

Fittingly, we began on the subject of African art. Muensterberger had just visited the home of a fellow collector of such objects—a man whose life story, he said, offered crucial insights into the mind of the collector. "It happened last night, so it's very fresh in my memory," he explained. "I walked into this house where he keeps his collection, a rather large suburban affair, and hanging on the walls were all these antlers. I said, 'Oh, you collect antlers, as well [as art]?' And he said, 'Well, I was a big hunter.' Then he took me to his basement, where he had an enormous collection of mounted and stuffed gazelles, antelopes, and lions, all of which he had shot himself in East Africa."

Muensterberger explained that the man had never been particularly interested in primitive art until one fateful visit to the western side of the African continent, when, "in a market, he suddenly saw pieces like these." Overcome by the strange beauty of the objects, the man eventually decided to put away his guns and abandon the bloody existence of the safari for the refined world of the auction house. His life had been turned upside down—or so it seemed. But on closer inspection, explained Muensterberger, it hadn't changed much at all: he had simply "switched from the collecting of animal skulls to collecting objects of African sculpture.

"I was sorry that I didn't know him when I was doing my book," he said, "because here is a very essential element of collecting—the hunting. When you talk to collectors, very often aggression, concealed as it may be, plays a role in the obtaining of the object."

Muensterberger believed that, like the hunt for big game, the hunt for rare objects involves what he described in his book as a "search—successful or not—that ever promises hope, suspense, excitement, and even danger." So it came as no surprise to him that his acquaintance demonstrated the same pattern of behavior in the art galleries as he had exhibited in the bush: having set off on an expedition, the man could not rest until he had bagged his prey.

"As a hunter, when he had two or three wonderful animals, he could take off and come back to America. The same is true now that he collects African objects," he said. "He told me he went to Europe to see some dealers in Paris and London and Brussels. Then he showed me an object he had bought. And, you see, when he had found that, he could take it under his arm and come back from the hunt."

Muensterberger felt that such behavior could be traced back to an ancient urge. In our past lives as hunters and gatherers, we humans practiced animism, the belief that when people or animals die, their remaining life force, or soul, is transferred onto ordinary objects. This philosophy, which eased the awful finality of death, has long since been replaced by those that purport to be more rational. Nonetheless, our animistic impulses remain—and, according to Muensterberger, are at the root of our compulsion to collect. As he put it in the book, "There is reason to believe that the true source of the habit is the emotional state leading to a more or less perpetual attempt to surround oneself with magically potent objects. . . . The compelling concern [is] to go in search, to discover, to add to one's store, or holding, or harem."

I asked him why the sense of discovery seemed to play such an important role for the collector. "Think of the word: *dis-*

cover—to take the cover off and see what's there," he told me. "It goes very deep for the collector: I want to find out. And what you really want to find is, Where do I come from? What is the source? That is discovery—finding something no one knew before, and you didn't know before."

That jibed with what I had learned from Mr. Atlas (whose pursuit of the long-hidden Rosselli map had begun—quite literally—with someone "taking off the cover"). But Muensterberger believed that such discoveries are not without a downside. While they can bring the collector much happiness, he noted, the elation is usually short-lived, giving way to renewed feelings of frustration. And so the hunt goes on. "The quest is never-ending," he wrote in his book. "It is, as one can see time and again, bound to repeat itself, while the ultimate pleasure always remains a mirage."

Most collectors seem to accept, even embrace, this contradiction—aware that for the aficionado, as for the adventurer, the journey is better than the destination. Mr. Atlas, for instance, seemed to have his habit well under control, buying only a few new maps each year at this point in his life. ("In fact," he had told me, "one of the reasons that I've gotten involved in exhibits and the lecture series and other aspects of maps is that . . . I didn't want my interest to be dependent on the next acquisition.")

But for a few aficionados what begins as harmless hobby can devolve into what Muensterberger described as "an all-consuming passion, not unlike the dedication of a compulsive gambler to the gaming table—to the point where it can affect a person's life and become *the* paramount concern . . . overshadowing all else: work, family, social obligations and responsibilities. We know of numerous cases in which moral standards, legal considerations, and societal taboos have been disregarded in the passion to collect."

History has seen more than a few out-of-control collectors, such as the notorious Don Vincente, a bookseller and former monk whose malignant bibliomania led him to commit no fewer than eight murders in nineteenth-century Barcelona. But while it is tempting to dismiss such zealots as a mentally disturbed minority, Muensterberger warned that even a generally well-adjusted and honest person can be tempted to transgress laws or moral codes—in part because overcoming the obstacles that lie between the collector and the desired object is exactly what makes the experience so rewarding. "Look, I spoke of the discovery," he said. "*Découvrir* in French, *entdecken* in German— I could use any number of languages, and it has more or less the same meaning: to take off the cover. So, as a collector, what you do is look for something that you're not supposed to see or possess. And so, intrinsically, whatever you discover or obtain by discovery is taboo in one way or another.

"There is always the chance of having trespassed," he added, glancing slowly around the room at his beloved possessions. "Even with these African objects it's true."

He had been collecting such pieces for no less than seven decades: "I discovered African art the first time consciously when I was eight years old in the house of a distant relative. I was so taken by it that, when I was thirteen, I went to the flea market in Amsterdam and saw a piece. The man said, 'It comes from the Dutch colonies—Indonesia.' I said, 'No, it comes from Africa.' He said, 'No, stupid boy.' But it clearly was a very nice African horse and rider. That was the first piece I ever bought."

In the years since then, he had tried to avoid buying items that are stolen from—or are sacred to—the people whose ancestors made them, instead purchasing only objects that either are meaningless to them or have been abandoned.

"But some of the objects have been discovered only recently, buried underground. Now, to whom do they belong? In Italy, anything in the ground belongs automatically to the state. In Africa, they have laws—but there are tribal laws and national laws and provincial laws," he said with a sigh.

"It's all very muddy," he added. And then, for a second, the old man's gaze seemed to lose itself on one of the sculptures. I have no idea where his thoughts had taken him at that moment. My own had drifted, as they did so often in those days, back to Gilbert Bland.

O F THE MANY WONDERFUL YARNS SURROUNDING THE LIFE of Christopher Columbus, my favorite is the story of the Unknown Pilot. The tale is said to have taken place around 1480, when Columbus lived on Porto Santo, one of the Madeira Islands off the North African coast. It begins when a crippled vessel, floating at the mercy of the waves, lands on the island. All of the ship's sailors have perished, except for the helmsman, who is on death's doorstep himself. Seeking to nurse the mariner back to health, Columbus takes him to his house. There, the ailing man reveals an astonishing secret: another world exists on the far side of the Ocean Sea (as the Atlantic was then known). The man has been to these distant shores himself, after his ship blew off course during a storm. With the pilot's help Columbus crafts a map showing the route to these new lands. Then the man dies, leaving our hero alone with the secret that will change the course of history.

The story of the Unknown Pilot is a myth. We can be fairly sure of this not only because it lacks supporting evidence but because it *sounds* so much like a myth. Substitute the Unknown Pilot for the Lady of the Lake and the secret map for Excalibur, and suddenly we're talking about not Christopher Columbus and the New World but King Arthur and the Holy Grail. In *The Hero with a Thousand Faces,* his classic study of legends, Joseph Campbell wrote that a key starting point for the hero's journey is "a protective figure (often a little old crone or old man) who provides the adventurer with amulets against the dragon forces he is about to pass. . . . What such a figure represents is the benign, protecting power of destiny. The fantasy is a reassurance—a promise that the peace of Paradise, which was known first within the mother womb, is not to be lost."

If, as has often been said, myths teach us fundamental truths about ourselves, then the Unknown Pilot legend demonstrates the powerful spell maps cast on the human imagination. Throughout the centuries people have viewed maps not just as useful navigational tools but as enchanted objects—what Campbell called "amulets" and Muensterberger described as "power-imbued fetish[es]." Columbus himself, for instance, seemed to think maps were endowed with a force that transcended mere matters of geography. They stoked his imagination, inspired the flights of fancy that made his great discovery possible. The sixteenth-century chronicler Bartolomé de Las Casas wrote that when Columbus gained access to a map from the Florentine scientist Paolo del Pozzo Toscanelli it "set [his] mind ablaze." Likewise, Ferdinand Columbus reported that after another acquisition of sea charts, his father's passion was "still more inflamed." A cartographer and dealer himself, Columbus drew maps, dreamed maps, meditated upon maps, listened to maps, acquired them at every opportunity (sometimes under very questionable circumstances). Even in 1492, after sailing into the unknown, far past the point where maps would be of any practical use to him, he continued to pore over them, fingering their edges the way a child might rub the satin lining of a blanket, as if their mere presence could ward off danger and make land appear on the horizon. I have no hesitation about labeling Christopher Columbus a cartomaniac.

In the centuries that followed his discovery, maps became ever more scientific and less whimsical. Even so, people continued to be drawn to them for reasons that had nothing to do with utility. In 1570, for example, John Dee, the Elizabethan mathematician and mystic, wrote this about why people collect maps:

> Some, to beautify their Halls, Parlors, Chambers, Galeries, Studies, or Libraries with, some other for their

own journeys directing into far lands, or to understand
other men's travels, liketh, loveth, getteth, and useth,
Maps, Charts and Geographical Globes . . .

But what is behind the liketh and the loveth, let alone the
getteth and the useth? What is the specific allure of maps, especially old maps? Why are some people drawn to maps instead
of, say, books, porcelain, beer cans, dolls, or any of a million
other objects they might collect?

When I put such questions to Muensterberger, he said the
map lovers he has met tend to come from broken homes or
families that have moved around a good deal. They throw
themselves into their hobby, at least in part, as a way to connect
with a parent or to ground themselves in a more permanent
sense of place. "Looking for maps, especially antique maps," he
told me, "is really looking for the past—Where do I come from?
Who were my ancestors?—and, symbolically, finding security."

Harriette Kaley, a Manhattan clinical psychologist and psychoanalyst who has also studied the phenomenon of collecting,
offered a similar view. "Analysts refer to a person's early childhood as his or her prehistory," said Kaley, herself a minor map
enthusiast. "And in fact, people remember that period of their
lives as a kind of fantasy, because an adult is unable to recapture
the way his or her thought process worked as a child. For each
of us, our early life seems like the distant past, and in that sense
it's like an ancient land—far-off, foreign, and unknown. It occurred to me that it's not unlike the way fairy tales begin: 'Once
upon a time in a faraway place.' And I think there must be

something in map collecting that taps into that. In some sense, old maps reach back into a part of life that you can't quite grasp, and give you a sense of where you've come from. They give you a feeling of being rooted."

Does any of this help explain the actions of our Antihero with a Thousand Faces, Gilbert Bland? His critics would probably say no. Most of those who came in contact with him told me that, in retrospect, they believed his interest in maps was never sincere; his only real passion was for a good scam. This view was somewhat bolstered by Bland himself, who reportedly told the FBI he had happened upon maps by accident. Nonetheless, I tend to agree with Joseph Campbell: "As Freud has shown, blunders are not the merest chance. They are the result of suppressed desires and conflicts. They are ripples on the surface of life, produced by unsuspected springs. And these may be very deep—as deep as the soul itself. The blunder may amount to the opening of a destiny."

Of all the criminal enterprises a would-be felon might select, I can't believe Bland chose map theft entirely on its merits as a racket. I won't presume to guess what "suppressed desires and conflicts" might have drawn Bland to maps, other than to note that his somewhat rootless childhood seems to fit a general pattern for cartographic connoisseurs as outlined by Muensterberger. And while he was not, strictly speaking, a collector, he did seem to exhibit the behavior of an obsessive aficionado. When I look through the entries of his notebook, for instance, I see someone who operates with the single-minded determination of a hunter. Each new map is like an elusive quarry, meticulously stalked down, first on the Internet and then in the library itself. The hunt is full of danger (*Can't these people leave? I can't do it now. OK now*), but it is this very risk, perhaps, that makes the eventual conquest so exhilarating (*These 2 are done now. Thank God!*). And by the end the thrill seems to have become addictive—so addictive that it's almost as if one's whole life hinges on the next conquest (*The Bowen Atlas—of all the bad luck—What is going on here. Am I not going to get these Bowens? What [will] become of me?*). Which brings us back to the tale of the Unknown Pilot. It turns out that there's a second version of the legend, one that offers a different lesson about the allure of maps. In this one the sailor does not die of natural causes. In this one Christopher Columbus bullies the man into supplying him with the map—then kills him to keep the secret all to himself. In this one the great discoverer becomes a common criminal.

ONCE DABBLED IN A SORT OF MAP COLLECTING MY-self. When I was twenty-five years old I covered the bedroom walls of my Chicago apartment with street maps of every place I had ever called home, a less than cosmopolitan list that, in addition to the Windy City, included the Illinois burgs of Downers Grove, Carbondale, Champaign-Urbana, and Springfield, as well as Washington, D.C., and Manchester, New Hampshire. I can't say for certain what prompted me to do this. Perhaps I was simply looking back at my childhood through those maps, aware that, with my father in failing health, the full weight of adult life's realities and responsibilities would soon be upon me. They were still on the walls when he died, but fate soon put an end to the collection. An arsonist set fire to the building, leaving the apartment in ruins. (I was lucky—in more ways than one— to be spending the night elsewhere.) I learned a lot from that blaze. It taught me that I could do without my possessions just fine, but I could not do without my friends and family. It also reminded me to look forward instead of dwelling on the past. I never retrieved those maps from the wreckage but left them hanging there, clouded with soot, like so many faded memories.

Nor was I seriously tempted, in all the time I spent working on this book, to purchase an antique map. Having reproductions of them in books was enough for me; unlike Mr. Atlas, I did not need direct contact. The truth is, I have never done much collecting at all. A few baseball cards as a kid, some 1950s-era slide projectors as an adult—but even these were half-hearted pursuits, inspired more by boredom than by any overriding passion. I always told myself that I was free from the compulsion.

I was wrong. That fact hit me like a bus during the afternoon I spent sitting on Werner Muensterberger's sofa in Manhattan. The elderly psychoanalyst was holding forth on the relationship between collecting and hunting when it suddenly occurred to me that, without really noticing it, I had devoted years of my life to building a collection, and a very extensive one at that. It was sitting on the shelves of my office back in Chicago, neatly displayed in a growing series of three-hole binders. Gilbert Bland's birth, marriage, and divorce records. Gilbert Bland's military documents. Gilbert Bland's criminal records. Transcripts from his trials. Gilbert Bland's prison correspondence. Documents related to his business and real estate dealings. Forms from his wife's bankruptcy case. A copy of the notebook Gilbert Bland left at the Peabody Library. Photographs of the maps he stole. Hundreds of pages of testimony from those who came in contact with him. I had never spent so much time, effort, or money acquiring any group of objects in my life.

All journalists keep records—but these scraps of paper had become much more than that. I realized that they were my amulets, my fetishes. Every time some new bit of Blandabilia arrived in the mail or turned up in an archive, I would rush to examine it with a feeling of giddy anticipation, sure that it would fill in some key corner of the map I was trying to create. Often it did just that—but invariably it would also raise new questions, so that as one blank space was filled another would open up, my map becoming simultaneously larger and smaller, Bland both more and less real. Excitement would then give way to disappointment—but just as quickly I would think of some new document or witness that, if tracked down, might provide just the right piece for the puzzle. And so the process would begin again, and I would set out in search of yet another discovery.

But in "taking off the cover," I sometimes saw more than I wanted to see. Prying into other people's lives is a necessary, if unpleasant, part of a reporter's job. In this case, however, it seemed even more disagreeable than usual. Not that I felt particularly sorry for Bland. His own actions had transformed him into a public figure, and, whether he liked it or not, public figures merit public scrutiny. Yet, because of a long-ago tragedy in my own family, I knew that the map thief would not be the only one to suffer. During the Great Depression my grandfather was sent to prison for bank embezzlement—a traumatizing event that left lasting scars on my mother's psyche and indirectly shaped my own personality. This incident, still a touchy subject in my family, assumed an increasingly central place in my thoughts as the investigation progressed.

Perhaps because of this, I felt particularly uncomfortable delving into matters that affected Bland's wife and children. When, for instance, one of Bland's daughters by his first marriage agreed to speak with me after much hesitation, the conversation turned out to be an awkward one for both of us. Heather Bland knew very little about her father, and the few memories she did recount were mostly unpleasant. I ended up learning more about her pain than I did about his life—and, though I was grateful to her, I was also relieved when our conversation concluded. I learned a similar lesson once in Florida. I was talking to people who lived on Bland's street, trying to add one more precious little piece to my collection, when a neighbor stopped me and pointed to a group of children playing with skateboards at the end of the block. "One of those kids is his," the man said sternly. "Is it really so important for you to be here right now?" I thought about it for a second, shook my head no, then got into my car and drove off.

Yet as unpleasant as such incidents could be, they were not the creepiest aspect of my pursuit. I simply cannot explain how surreal it was to spend years tracking down a man I'd never met, how disconcerting it felt to know someone so well and yet not know him at all. At first, Bland had seemed to me an exotic and intriguing figure—but, as is often the case with familiarity, the more I learned about him, the less interesting he became. He was, I ultimately determined, a fairly unexceptional person who had happened to commit a fascinating crime. At some point I realized he was not even someone I would normally want to know. But even that did not stop me from seeking him out. I had to face the fact that my search had become a compulsion—not so different from the one that lured Bland into those rare books rooms, perhaps, or the one that Rudyard Kipling described in his 1898 poem "The Explorer":

> "*Something hidden. Go and find it. Go and look*
>   *behind the Ranges—*
> "*Something lost behind the Ranges. Lost and waiting*
>   *for you. Go!*"

Then one day I came to an even more disturbing realization—that my identity and the map thief's were somehow starting to converge, that he had taken up permanent residence on the edges of my consciousness, a cipher on which I was projecting musings and misgivings and fears that had nothing to do with the case. And at that moment I understood that I was no longer searching only for the map thief. My quest had gone beyond Bland: I was now hunting down some enigmatic citizen of my own psyche, a persona I did not know and did not particularly look forward to meeting. There seemed to be no going back, however. Remembering what Aldous Huxley had written about what lurks in "the antipodes of the mind," I sensed that I was on a collision course with one of those "strange psychological creatures leading an autonomous existence according to the law of their own being." It was one discovery, I feared, that would bring no joy at all.

DETAIL FROM HERMAN MOLL'S 1719
MAP OF NORTH AMERICA, DEPICTING
CALIFORNIA AS AN ISLAND.

CHAPTER 11

The Island of Lost Maps

*T*HE HISTORY OF CARTOGRAPHY IS FULL OF PE-
culiar islands. One of the items Gilbert Bland stole from the
University of Virginia, for example, is the cartographer Herman Moll's eighteenth-century map of North America. It
shows a continent that looks a lot like the one we now inhabit,
except for one striking detail. Running parallel to the West
Coast all the way from what is now Canada to Mexico is a
sprawling independent landmass—a famous and widely repeated cartographic miscalculation known as the Island of
California. Other charts contain isles even more bizarre. A
twelfth-century map by the Arab geographer al-Idrīsī shows El
Wakwak, an island said to be filled with trees whose fruits,
shaped like the heads of women, continually cry out the meaningless chant "Wak-Wak." The famous Hereford *mappa mundi*,
drawn around 1300, has an isle on which "sirens abound," ac-

cording to the accompanying text, while another world map of the period contains an island inhabited by "men who murdered their fathers." The Catalan Atlas, made around 1375, shows one isle that "produces all crops and all fruits without any need to sow or plant" and a second where "there are trees that yield birds as other trees yield fruits." Martin Behaim's history-making globe of 1492 shows the Islands of the Satyrs, whose residents "have tails like animals," as well as a pair of Indian Ocean landmarks named Masculina and Feminea. "One of these islands [is] inhabited by men only, the other by women only, who [meet] once a year," reads the legend. Even the great Ortelius published a map in 1570 that depicts several completely mythical islands in the North Atlantic, including Drogeo, purported to be inhabited by cannibals; Icaria, whose king was said to be a direct descendant of Daedalus; and Saint Brendan, where the legendary Irishman is said to have brought a dead giant back to life.

From the earliest of times islands have had a special place in the human imagination. So close to our own world yet so out of reach, they have been the landscapes where no life-form was unimaginable, no occurrence impossible. Homer spattered *The Odyssey*'s oceans with isles such as Aeaea, where the sorceress Circe transformed men into pigs; Cyclopes Island, where one-eyed giants dined on human flesh; and Lotus-land, where visitors, having consumed the local flora, forgot their friends and lost all desire to return to their native lands. Other classical writers described islands on which those favored by the gods lived untouched by sorrow: Hesiod and Pindar called these the Isles of the Blessed, while Plato provided the first written account of Atlantis, the splendrous island that disappeared into the ocean. Celtic myth was full of enchanted outcroppings—islands of laughter, islands "full of men agrieving and lamenting," islands of women, islands shared by the living and the dead, islands where time stood still, and islands that could be seen only by the elect, rising out of the sea for one adventurer and vanishing back into the depths for another. Arthurian legend told of Avalon, a paradisal island inhabited by nine sorceresses, where the great king was taken after being mortally wounded. The *Arabian Nights* described one island that was home to "a bird of monstrous size called the roc, which fed its young on elephants," and another that was inhabited by the Old Man of the Sea, a huge beast that enslaved visitors. The Tantric books of medieval and modern India told of an Island of Jewels, where a goddess lived in a grove of wish-fulfilling trees. Thomas More put Utopia fifteen miles from the coast of the New World. Shakespeare set *The Tempest* on an island "full of noises, sounds and sweet airs," ruled by a noble magician. Native American island legends included the tale of Maushope, a giant on Martha's Vineyard, who pulled whales from the sea with his bare hands and ate them raw. J. M. Barrie set *Peter Pan* on the Never Land, an isle inhabited by lost children, "where all the four seasons may pass while you are filling a jug at the well." The film director Merian C. Cooper dreamed up an island "way west of Sumatra," then populated it with huge lizards and a petulant primate named King Kong. And while such enchanted islands no longer can be found on maps, they continue to dot the dark seas of our collective unconscious. It was no coincidence, for instance, that, when Michael Crichton needed a setting for his modern-day dinosaur epic *Jurassic Park,* he chose a volcanic seamount whose "forested slopes were wreathed in fog, giving the island a mysterious appearance."

Now let me tell you about another wondrous isle, one I saw with my own eyes. Like some evanescent island of legend, this one was elusive. Had you been with me when I first beheld it, you might not have noticed an island at all—just a mound of plastic bags, file folders, a zip-up art portfolio, and a U-Haul moving box, sitting in the middle of a vast conference table at the FBI office in Richmond, Virginia. In my eyes, however, it was a strange, sad world unto itself, full of marvels. All its inhabitants were exiles: Indians, Eskimos, cossacks, conquistadors, emperors, presidents, chieftains, queens, kings, soldiers, sailors, monsters, mermaids, serpents, seals, whales, lions, beavers, elephants, polar bears, fire-breathing horses, gods, and angels. As I approached its shores, they all seemed to be speaking to me at once, telling a million different stories in a thousand different tongues—tales of oceans crossed and shorelines glimpsed, of new worlds explored and old orthodoxies exploded, of empires gained and lost, of wars waged and genocides committed and peoples enslaved, of forests felled and cities built and borders drawn and railways laid and prairies cleared. They were chanting the whole history of the last five hundred years, the inhabitants of that tiny island, but they were also reciting another tale, one about how history can be untold with a few silent strokes of a razor blade. I had been seeking this place almost since my journey began. Now here it was, before me at last: the Island of Lost Maps.

The lord of this curious domain was seated across the way. Gray Hill was a lanky, middle-aged man who towered over his island the way Gulliver overshadowed Lilliput in Jonathan Swift's *Travels into Several Remote Nations of the World*. I knew that Hill had not come to these shores by choice. Like Gulliver and the heroes of a thousand other island tales, he was a castaway, brought here by the improbable tides of fate. Hill was an FBI agent, not a map collector—but, in the famous words of a shipwrecked traveler from *The Tempest*, "misery acquaints a man with strange bed-fellows." It was now July 1996, and he had already been stranded for some six months. He did not know it yet, but he was destined to remain for years, as if the Island of Lost Maps was enchanted and Hill was being held under the spell of a sorcerer. And, in a certain sense, that was exactly what was happening.

*I*N HIS BOOK ABOUT COLLECTING, WERNER MUENSTERberger wrote that the dealer of antiquities is sometimes endowed with almost magical powers. Many aficionados, he observed, view the materials they collect not as inanimate objects but as fetishes with "a soul or a life-force of their own." As a result, wrote Muensterberger, "the relationship between collector and dealer is different from any customary buyer-seller contact . . . largely due to the intrinsic power that accrues to the dispenser of magic provisions. This predicament is one of the most potent assets of the successful dealer, whose role is often closely akin to that of physician, priest, or shaman."

For those who had done business with Gilbert Bland, the mysterious dealer from South Florida must have indeed seemed like something of a shaman at times, able to conjure up maps as fast as he could snap his fingers. *Abracadabra, yield us an Ortelius! Open sesame, here comes a Jefferys!* One of those who got a firsthand demonstration of Bland's black art was a prominent Florida collector who visited the map thief's booth at the Miami International Map Fair in 1995. He came away—happy but perplexed—with two copies of a hard-to-find Florida map from 1845. "He had three of them," the collector said of Bland's inventory. "Those were the first three I'd seen [for sale] in six years."

To possess what others covet—what a heady feeling that must have been for the map thief, especially after his frustrations in the computer business. Systems integration, RAM upgrades, peripherals—people may need these things, but they do not hunger after them, do not stay awake at night aching for their feel, their look, their smell. Even before his computer firm went belly-up, Bland must have known that he was trafficking in mundane essentials—the same ones everybody else was trying to hawk during the 1990s. But to be the bearer of rare maps—well, that changed everything. Suddenly Bland was golden. Suddenly he was in demand. Suddenly he was a genie with the power to grant—or deny—people's fondest wishes.

I don't know how Bland felt about his newfound power, whether it thrilled him or scared him or gave him a good laugh.

What I'm quite sure about, however, is that he knew how to wield it. Even after he was arrested, his magic did not fail him. In a strange way, it became even more potent. Bland had been in legal trouble before, and he was skillful at working the courts. He knew that the judicial system was a lot like the antiques business: if you had something that the other side desperately wanted, you were likely to get a very favorable deal. And so, before surrendering to police, Voodoo-man Bland pulled off his most remarkable piece of prestidigitation: he made hundreds of old maps disappear, as if into thin air. Somewhere he was holding New Jersey, Virginia, and Maryland, as well as Italy, Sweden, and Norway. He had the fortifications of Montreal. He had the Missouri Territory. He had the Empire of China, the Empire of Japan, and India beyond the Ganges. He had the Eastern Hemisphere, the Western Hemisphere, and the North Pole. He even had the trade winds locked up somewhere.

I LIVE IN FEAR OF GETTING THESE THINGS WET."

As he carefully unfolded one fragile map after another, Special Agent Hill cast a suspicious glance at the can of soda in my hand. Spreading out on the table before us was a haphazard collection of cartographic gems. There were maps by Ortelius, Ogilby, and the Pathfinder. There were Hondius and Mercator. There were Jacques Le Moyne de Morgues, who visited Florida in 1564 and produced the first detailed map of the region; Guillaume Delisle and Jacques Nicolas Bellin, two leading French cartographers of the early eighteenth century; Thomas Jefferys, the official geographer of Britain's King George III and creator of one of the first important atlases of North America; and many others, including the great explorer James Cook. Glancing from one old map to another, I was once again struck by their strange beauty, a kinetic clash between austere grids and voluptuous contours, empirical reality and romantic fantasy, as if the cartographers could never decide whether to make rigorous scientific diagrams or erotic doodlings of Mother Earth. It was disconcerting to see them heaped up like that, centuries of mesmerizing and historically crucial documents scattered unceremoniously across the tabletop like a bunch of wallpaper samples. And, had the thief not been caught, that would have been their fate—decorating walls. Now it was Hill's job to undo Gilbert Bland's crime spree page by page, returning each of these orphaned masterworks to its proper home.

Hill pulled out a map from the 1607 edition of the famous Hondius-Mercator atlas. "This is another one that I don't have any idea where it came from," he said glumly. Then he turned to me, his frown slowly transforming into a conspiratorial grin.

"Hey," he said, holding out the map with a wink, "you got your checkbook with you?"

Hill kept surprising me. Prolonged childhood exposure to the TV series *The F.B.I.* had led me to sort of expect that all G-men would be like the stone-faced Efrem Zimbalist, Jr., who played his role as though possession of a personality could land you on the Ten Most Wanted List. But the amiable Hill, wearing a comfortable blue blazer as he reclined beneath a portrait of grim old J. Edgar Hoover (who looked like he had laced up his girdle a little too tight for the photo shoot), seemed to be a different sort of agent entirely. I had no doubt he could be a tough guy when the situation demanded, but at the moment Hill's most menacing quality was his booming tommy gun of a laugh.

Then again, everything seemed a little topsy-turvy on the Island of Lost Maps. Normally, Special Agent Hill's job was to track down lawbreakers, but now his role had been reversed: he hunted victims. This offbeat assignment had fallen into his lap shortly after Bland's arrest, when the map thief was extradited to Virginia. Federal prosecutors in Charlottesville—Hill's base of operations—indicted Bland on charges of stealing objects of significant cultural heritage and transporting stolen goods across state lines. If convicted on those charges, the map thief would have faced up to twenty years in prison without the possibility of parole and a fine of half a million dollars. Moreover, state courts in North Carolina and Delaware would soon file additional counts against Bland—and other states were threatening to follow. In short, the map thief was in what some old cartographer might have called an *orbis terrarum* of trouble. On the other hand, he had what one of Hill's associates later described as "a very effective bargaining chip."

Not only was Bland the only one who knew where the maps were hidden but he was also the only one who knew where they all came from. As a result, explained Hill, the feds faced a tough dilemma: "Do we take our pound of flesh, or do we say to the defendant, 'Okay, fine, we'll take eight ounces of flesh in return for information about what you had access to and what you have stolen'? We decided it was worth getting eight ounces of flesh, and maybe even a little bit less, if we could get all the maps returned."

Bland finally agreed to a plea bargain in which he would receive a reduced sentence and limited immunity from further prosecution. In return, he promised, among other things, to cooperate fully with FBI agents in their attempts to get the maps back to their rightful owners. So in February 1996, while jailed without bond, the map thief directed FBI agents to a storage locker in Palm Beach Gardens, Florida, that he had rented under an assumed name. When they looked behind its bright orange doors, they discovered an extraordinary booty: some 150 maps in all, a few of them more than four centuries old. Taken together with the 100 or so other maps that authorities would gather from Bland's clients across the country, the thief's total collection of some 250 maps had a market value estimated at as much as half a million dollars.

Federal authorities promptly held a self-congratulatory press conference to announce the maps had been "recovered, unharmed." But recovering them was one thing; returning them proved to be something else entirely. My visit came a full five months after the FBI had obtained the maps. Yet despite an exhaustive search, Hill had been able to positively identify the owners of only about seventy—less than one third of the total.

His efforts had been slowed by three big obstacles, the first having to do with the documents themselves. As a rule, maps are unmarked; many lack even a page number. Some institutions do, in fact, put stamps or other types of identification on their maps, but to many librarians this practice is repugnant, the equivalent of stenciling PROPERTY OF THE LOUVRE across the Mona Lisa. Nor do libraries always keep inventories of the maps that are bound in books—so even if they discover one missing, they can rarely be sure when it disappeared. As a result, FBI technicians were being forced to match each stolen map, jigsaw-puzzle style, with each damaged book, using ultraviolet-light technology to make sure the edges lined up precisely and the paper stock was exactly the same on both sides of the cut. It was a labor-intensive and time-consuming process—and, for all that, it did not always produce the desired results. "Just because someone is missing a map does not necessarily mean that the map I have matches that book," explained Hill. "I have duplicates—four or five of the same map. Some of the matches look good to the naked eye. But under the ultraviolet light, it's a different story."

A second problem was the attitude of certain librarians. Although the vast majority of institutions cooperated willingly with his investigation, Hill was surprised to find resistance from some quarters. A couple of libraries, for instance, had rebuffed his initial inquiries, asserting their records were private and Hill would need a subpoena to see them. "We explained to them, 'It's not *our* maps that are missing,' " Hill said, " 'And any information you have concerning the theft would be directly beneficial to you as well as to us.' "

Even so, at least one institution had chosen to remain in denial about the thefts, even when the evidence was incontrovertible. "I talked to one librarian who said, 'There's no way he could have stolen anything out of here.' Well, I said, 'I just know one thing. I know that Mr. Bland told me that he came to your library and stole maps.' But they won't accept it. They will not believe that they have had anything stolen."

Or maybe they believed it all too well. As Robert Karrow, curator of maps at the Newberry Library in Chicago, once told me: "A lot of library thefts have gone unreported in the past. You know—you're embarrassed, and maybe you say to yourself, 'What will the donors think?' And you're reluctant to talk about the whole issue because you don't want to give the crazies ideas."

Hill fretted that a similar rationale might now be keeping other victims from coming forward. But he knew that there was absolutely nothing he could do about it, except throw up his hands and say, "If you sit there and tell me that your security is so great that Bland can't possibly have stolen anything from you, well then, I have nothing to return to you."

The agent's other big frustration was Bland himself. Under the terms of his plea bargain, the map thief was required to provide full information about what libraries he had visited, what maps he had taken, and what had become of those items. To a great extent, he had done just that—but Hill knew that Bland was not being completely truthful. The thief was insisting, for example, that many items in the FBI's collection were rightfully his, having been legally obtained from other dealers. He could not provide documentation of the alleged purchases, however, and when Hill set a little trap for him—showing him a couple of items that FBI technicians already knew to be the property of a certain library—the map thief fell right into it. "Those are mine!" he reportedly declared.

"I have never seen anything proving that he had *any* legitimate purchases," sneered Hill. "Why buy something if you can steal it? It gives you a much higher margin of profit."

True, but if all those unaccounted-for maps weren't Bland's, whose were they? For now, Gray Hill had no answers. "Some universities," he said, glancing at the pile with a look of resignation, "may not even know they are missing these items."

ROBINSON CRUSOE ON THE ISLAND OF DESPAIR, Napoleon on Elba, Odysseus on Ogygia, Scarface Capone on Alcatraz, the souls of the dead on Dante's Purgatory—in literature, myth, and history alike, islands have frequently been places of waiting. And thus it was on the Island of Lost Maps. Time moved so slowly there that Special Agent Hill might have been forgiven if he, like Crusoe, sometimes felt that "all possibility of deliverance . . . seemed to be entirely taken from me."

It was not the maps that wore on his nerves. He found the history of cartography "an interesting field," about which he had become something of an accidental expert—able, for instance, to quickly spot the difference between almost identical maps. Nonetheless, Hill's job had become such a bureaucratic nightmare that it was starting to look like he would still be marooned on these shores long after Gilbert Bland got out of prison. "I'm getting to know my stock very well, going through it time and time again," he said with a sigh, placing another centuries-old piece of paper atop the heap.

In recent weeks the island had seen a number of visitors. Like adventurers in search of lost treasure, librarians from all over the country had come bearing slashed-up books. "Some people leave very happy," Hill reported, "and a few leave very upset."

At least one library got more maps from Hill than staff members had even known they were missing. But relatively few of the visitors were so lucky. Another institution was looking for "probably thirty or forty maps," all of which, in theory at least, corresponded with those in the FBI's collection. "Well, they came down and brought their books, and we started trying to match up maps," he said. "We matched up *nothing*. The books are missing these items—but they just didn't match up with the ones I have."

Despite such setbacks, Hill was not giving up. "It becomes an obsession," he told me, "to try to get rid of as many of these things as possible." His next step was to compile a volume containing photographs and precise descriptions of all the lost maps. Copies of this "big black book," as some librarians would later refer to it, were to be circulated all over the country. "Before, the way we were going about it was, 'You tell me what you're missing and we'll see if we can match it up,' " Hill explained. "Now we're going to go back out and say, 'Hey, we have these items; you look and tell us whether you're missing any of them.' "

Hill's persistence would eventually lead to a number of successes. Six months after my visit to Richmond, the British Columbia Archives in Victoria discovered that a certain James Perry had visited in October 1995, departing with twenty maps. Bland had not mentioned this episode to Hill. A similar stop at the University of British Columbia in Vancouver had also apparently slipped the thief's mind. With the help of Gray Hill's big black book, these two institutions would get back many of their maps. And, as the months wore on, Hill would find homes for dozens of other misbegotten documents. Even so, many mysteries would continue to hang over the Island of Lost Maps.

THERE'S A FAMOUS PASSAGE FROM *ROBINSON CRUSOE* in which the shipwrecked narrator discovers a single, inexplicable footprint in the sand. Having been alone for many years, he is instantly overcome by "wild ideas" and "strange unaccountable whimsies." At one point he concludes that cannibals have invaded his island, only to decide that, no, he himself left the print. Other times he "fancy'd it must be the devil . . . for how should any other thing in human shape come into this place?" Such "cogitations, apprehensions, and reflections" haunt him for "many hours, days, nay, I may say weeks and months."

It is no exaggeration to say that, like Crusoe, I had begun to experience "innumerable fluttering thoughts, like a man perfectly confused and out of my self." Increasingly, I felt as though I were chasing a ghost—traces of his presence all over, but he himself nowhere to be found. And in the months to come that ghost would begin to feel more and more like my own shadow, until it could sometimes seem as if Gilbert Bland was on my trail and not the other way around. But now, as I watched Gray Hill ponder one map after another, meditating on the mystery of each one's origin, I realized that at least I was not alone: the agent and I were following the same footprints. This was a strangely comforting thought, yet I knew that it was nothing he and I could discuss. Not only did the rules of our respective professions prevent us from comparing notes but Hill obviously had little time for small talk. He had more pressing cases to contend with, including the recent and widely publicized murders of two female hikers in Shenandoah National Park. And, to tell the truth, I was in a bit of a rush myself. At long last I hoped that those footprints might lead me face-to-face with the one who had left them.

CHAPTER 12

Eldorado

*T*HEN CAME THE HOUR WHEN I DISSOLVED INTO the map. Eighty miles an hour in a nice new rental car, and there I was, drinking my Dr Pepper and tapping my foot to something random on the radio, when all of a sudden— wooosh!—I'm hurtling backward through time and forward through space all at once. Part of me was still on Interstate 85, south of the Virginia–North Carolina state line, but part of me was on another road, a ghost road, the one that lay along this route before the concrete and cars, the horses, the white people. It was called the Great Indian Trading Path, one of the oldest travel routes in America, a byway that once snaked for more than five hundred miles from Virginia to Georgia. I had seen it on an old map of Carolina—engraved by James Moxon and published by John Ogilby in 1672—one of the same maps, in fact, that was in Special Agent Gray Hill's collection. The trad-

DETAIL FROM JOHN OGILBY-JAMES
MOXON'S CAROLINA MAP OF 1672.

ing path was only a thin gray line on that document, so sketchy that I had to squint to make it out, but now it seemed to be reaching out to me like a runway to an airplane, so real and so close that I could almost taste its hot dusty air. So this is what happens, I thought. This is what comes of so many hours spent peering over the edges of old maps. Sooner or later you fall in.

Or maybe it's just what comes of being tired and hungry and anxious about a meeting that may or may not take place an hour down the road. But whatever was causing this madness, I did not fight it. Give yourself over to the map, I told myself. March down that trading path. Scale those peaks—the ones labeled APALATHEAN MOUNTAINS. Frolic with those naked Indians pictured in that sparkling stream. What did I have to lose? This whole jaunt down I-85 was a giant crapshoot anyway. Might as well hitch a ride with the past, if only to see where it took me. And at that moment it was taking me to an Indian village illustrated on that map with thatched huts. These days, that same spot is known as Hillsborough, North Carolina, and if I could have stuck to the precise route of the trading path, it would have led me to within a block of Gilbert Bland's jail cell.

One of the first Europeans to visit the place Bland now calls home was John Lederer, a German-born adventurer whose geographical observations were later incorporated into the Ogilby-Moxon map. In June 1670, Lederer arrived at what was then a Native American settlement along the Eno River. He found the people of these parts to be "covetous and thievish, industrious to earn a peny [sic]"—which also struck me as a pretty fair description of the town's most recent resident. But the sad truth was, I didn't really understand the map thief a whole hell of a lot better than Lederer understood those Indians. Even after all these months, I still knew only the *what* of his story, not the *why*. So that's what I had come to find out. I had this idea that, away from the influence of his lawyers, Bland might be willing to talk with me, especially if I showed up unannounced at his appointed house of correction. Anyway, it was worth a try.

He was there to face state charges stemming from his heist at the University of North Carolina in nearby Chapel Hill. In addition, he still had to contend with state charges in Delaware, as well as the federal indictment in Virginia. At the time—July 1996—none of these cases had been resolved, so Bland, unable to make his $75,000 bond, was biding his time at the Orange County Jail in downtown Hillsborough. I went straight there, edgy to make contact with him, but was promptly told that there were no visiting hours on that day. To see the prisoner I would have to return the following morning. In the meantime, a couple of bored-looking jailers agreed to let him know that I was in town.

"Historic Hillsborough," as the travel brochures call this village of five thousand, is packed with late-eighteenth- and early-nineteenth-century buildings, making it something of a living museum, half Williamsburg, half Mayberry R.F.D. Wandering around town, the crape myrtle in full bloom, I had a renewed sense of being enveloped into the past. On one side street was a still-functioning inn, built in 1759 and rumored to have been frequented by such notables as the British general Charles

Cornwallis, who led his troops over the trading path during the waning months of the American Revolution. I drifted inside and a few moments later found myself settling into a room just a block down from Bland's jail cell.

That night it happened again. Lying there in the dark, the window air conditioner murmuring *aum* like some Hindu mystic, I stumbled into yet another locale from the Island of Lost Maps. This time I wasn't scampering down a footworn Piedmont trail but rushing headlong into the South American jungle, toward a place labeled "Manoa & el Dorado." Blame this weird waking dream on Sir Walter Raleigh, who had been at the back of my mind all day, his memory being nearly unavoidable in a state where even the capital city (to which I had driven for dinner a couple of hours back) bears his name. But if Carolinians remember Sir Walter for organizing the first English settlements in North America, the ill-fated Roanoke colonies of the 1580s, I was more interested in a different venture, his 1595 search for a legendary land of gold. He did not find it, of course—but that did not hinder him from writing a fanciful account of his trek, in which he claimed to have come within a short distance of "the great and Golden Citie of Manoa (which the Spanyards [*sic*] call El Dorado)." He was also the first explorer known to have put Manoa on a real map—and, thanks to Raleigh's fame and standing, his views commanded the respect of other cartographers. Jodocus Hondius, apparently using Raleigh's 1596 map as a model, included Manoa in his 1598 map of South America. In 1599 the Dutch publisher Theodore de Bry issued a Latin translation of Raleigh's book and included a map showing the city of gold with the caption "Manoa or Dorado, regarded as the greatest city in the entire world." The mythical metropolis continued to appear on many seventeenth-century maps—including Gerard a Schagen's *Totius Americae Descriptio,* into which I was at that moment fading—and would remain on some works until as late as 1808.

In addition to inventing imaginary places and people (including a tribe of headless men described in his El Dorado narrative), Raleigh had a habit of reinventing himself. He was, as the writer Robert Silverberg put it, "a man of many characters"—one of several traits he had in common with Bland. Each man was in his forties when he embarked on his quest for sudden riches. Each appeared to be on the verge of a financial collapse. ("There are many possible readings of his El Dorado quest," wrote Charles Nicholl in *The Creature in the Map: A Journey to El Dorado,* "but let us not forget the simple ones: for instance, that [Raleigh] was, or was going, broke.") Like Bland, Raleigh had a penchant for shady scams (having dabbled in both extortion and piracy). Like Bland, he had been to prison before and would go there again.

Yes, but I knew that I, too, shared something with old Sir Walter. For all his bluster, Raleigh seems to have sincerely believed his expedition ended just shy of a place where "the graves have not beene opened for gold, the mines not broken with sledges, nor [the] Images puld down out of [the] temples." The hope of reaching that promised land never left him. Haunted by an unfinished quest of my own, I could relate to that. I could put myself inside his head, dream his dreams, imagine how it feels to emerge from the dark jungle into a lush valley, "the deare crossing in every path, the birds towardes the evening singing on every tree with a thousand several tunes, cranes & herons of white, crimson, and carnation pearching on the rivers side, the ayre fresh with gentle easterlie wind, and every

THEODORE DE BRY'S SIXTEENTH-CENTURY MAP OF GUIANA SHOWS "MANOA OR DORADO . . . THE GREATEST CITY IN THE ENTIRE WORLD" (SEE INSET), TO SAY NOTHING OF A HEADLESS MAN AND AN AMAZON.

stone . . . eyther golde or silver by his complexion." And as that map rushed in at me, filled the corners of the room like darkness itself, I could almost see the glow of a "great and golden Citie" somewhere off in the misty hills. So there I was, chasing El Dorado all the way into the deepest part of sleep, and then it was morning, and there I was, off to visit Gilbert Bland.

The bored-looking jailers got straight to the point. He would not see me. This was not a surprise, and somehow not even much of a disappointment. If anything, my immediate reaction was a mild sense of liberation. I could finally relax: the quest was finished. Or so I now imagined. Later, I would begin to wonder if those bored-looking jailers had even bothered to pass along my message. Later, I would start to believe that, even if they did, only Bland's legal circumstances held him back. Later, I would begin to hope that he'd agree to speak with me once his court cases were resolved. But all that anxiety was for the future; for the moment, everything seemed simple. I had but one thing left to do in town. A tourist brochure reported that archaeologists digging along the Eno River near downtown Hillsborough had discovered Native American settlements going back to the Stone Age. This, I realized, was that village I had seen on the Ogilby-Moxon map—the original destination point of my pilgrimage into the past. If I accomplished nothing else on this sorry expedition, at least I would complete that journey. I would give myself over to the map one more time.

The dig site, it turned out, was only a few hundred yards from Bland's jail cell, sitting in a fallow field at a bend in the Eno

River, right down from a row of suburban-style homes. I walked out toward it, passing a rusty International Harvester tractor (itself so antique it could almost pass for the unearthed artifact of some forgotten culture), then pushing through a preternaturally large spiderweb, which hovered across my path like a phantom. The whole place, in fact, had a ghostly aura, an air of being more absent than present. The archaeologists had apparently gone home for the summer, covering their work with neat mounds of dirt that reminded me of fresh graves—the only outward signs of a Native American presence that dates back more than ten thousand years. So what happened to this place? Why its sudden demise in the early 1700s? The list of answers, I would later learn, included many of the usual suspects, such as warfare with other Indians and the devastating spread of European diseases (which, according to one early eighteenth-century chronicler, reduced some Piedmont-country populations by more than 80 percent in fifty years). But, standing there on that empty plain, I was already beginning to understand the role of another factor, less obvious but perhaps no less important: a clash of cartographies. When the adventurer John Lederer had rambled down the Great Indian Trading Path in 1670, for instance, he was not just sight-seeing. Working under the auspices of Virginia's governor, Lederer was at the vanguard of a systematic effort to appropriate land—an effort in which maps often played as big a role as guns. As the scholar Mark Monmonier wrote in *Drawing the Line: Tales of Maps and Cartocontroversy:*

Indigenous Americans communicated information about space and places through folktales, gestures, dances, and ephemeral drawings, but theirs was not the cartography of commerce, navigation, and warfare. Land ownership in the profane European sense of buying, selling, inheriting, recording, and taxing was an alien concept. American Indians, who considered land sacred and not "ownable," never developed a formal cartography focused on boundaries and surveys. This lack of maps—really a lack of what the European invaders recognized as maps—was one of many technological disadvantages that made the conquest of the New World not only quick and easy but also morally right in the minds of the colonists and their priests.

Even the map that had brought me here was made with pilferage in mind. Ogilby and Moxon's work was used as an advertisement to attract English settlers to the new province, whose colonization had begun only a few years earlier when King Charles II granted Carolina to eight wealthy lords proprietors. It was no accident that the new owners' names appeared all over the map (Ashley River, Cape Carteret, Clarendon County, Albemarle River, et cetera), obliterating the Native American identity of those places in the same way that Russian Communists would later try to purge the memory of their imperial predecessors by renaming perhaps half of the seven hundred thousand towns and cities in what became the Soviet Union. With the power to manipulate the land from afar—to hype it up, slice it up, divvy it up—the Ogilby-Moxon map gave colonizers a tool of theft every bit as sharp-edged and efficient as Gilbert Bland's razor blade. Indeed, it now occurred to me that not only did this one small document encapsulate the whole long saga of New World exploitation, but that when Bland laid his hands on it, he was reenacting that story in a very poignant way. His victims had almost the same relationship to their maps as the people of this site had to their land. For librarian and Indian alike, these were "sacred and not ownable" resources—a lovely ideal, which, like most lovely ideals, proved easy to exploit. I came here to find out why Bland did what he did. Well, maybe it was as simple as this: because he could. Until that moment I had viewed him as something of a cultural freak, a man whose actions were outside the normal course of human events. But now, as I stared across that haunted little patch of earth, he seemed very much a part of the landscape.

J HAD PACKED MY BAGS, DROPPED OFF MY KEYS. I HAD finished my breakfast, hopped into the car, and, just for the hell of it, cruised past the jail one last time. There was a plane to catch the next morning, hundreds of miles away. It was time to crank the AC and hit the road. But wait. Did I just see what I thought I saw? There, on Route 109 of my official North Carolina State Transportation Map, south of Healing Springs, north of Mount Gilead, east of Misenheimer, west of Spies, smack-dab in the middle of the Uwharrie National Forest, was a spot called Eldorado. Eldorado, the place that is always farther on. The land that exists only in a person's mind. The destination to which, as Charles Nicholl observed, "there is only the journey, the approach toward something that you cannot reach, something . . . that you dare not reach." Or . . . well, maybe I dared, after all. True, it was at least a hundred miles in the wrong direction. And true, I couldn't come up with one rational reason to undertake yet another wild-goose chase. But like some born-again who gets rich by heeding advice from random Bible passages, I was beginning to believe in the power of cartomancy. Maps had been talking to me even more than usual. Let this one be your Ouija board, I told myself. Close your eyes and ask whether to go or stay. Open them again. What do you see? A place not far from Eldorado: the town of Whynot.

And so I was off, like so many dreamers, desperadoes, and idiots before me: Raleigh, whose search for the golden city cost him his son and then his own head; Gonzalo Pizarro, whose men were reduced to eating horses, dogs, and saddle leather before abandoning their journey; Philipp von Hutten, whose expedition became what one chronicler called a "theater of miseries," the final act of which was the leader's decapitation with a blunt machete; Gonzalo Jiménez de Quesada, whose misadventure left 250 Spaniards and nearly 1,500 Indian porters dead and "achieved nothing," according to the survivors; and, finally, the infamous Lope de Aguirre, the crazed leader of a wilderness mutiny who declared himself "Wrath of God, Prince of Freedom, King of Tierra Firme," before his own followers killed and quartered him, then put his corpse on display in sections. "The reports are false," Aguirre wrote about El Dorado, not long before his death. "There is nothing . . . but despair." Not exactly a good omen for my little road trip—but if anything can be said for certain about the golden city, it's that the place brings out the optimist in a person. And so I turned up that country-and-western station and hit the pavement, just like Edgar Allan Poe's "gallant knight," who

> *. . . journeyed long,*
> *Singing a song,*
> *In search of Eldorado*

I followed the Great Indian Trading Path, aka I-85, west to Burlington, then cut down Route 62, past Julian and Climax, to Route 220 south. Everything was going just fine—but then a kamikaze rainstorm swooped out of the bright sky, making it difficult to keep track of the car in front of me and slowing my pace to a crawl. By the time I stopped for a dried-out chicken sandwich at the Hardee's in Randleman, I was beginning to lose steam.

> *But he grew old—*
> *This knight so bold—*
> *And o'er his heart a shadow*
> *Fell as he found*
> *No spot of ground*
> *That looked like Eldorado.*

I pushed on, past Asheboro, to Route 134 south, then followed that two-laner to Troy, a bleak town of textile and log mills. When I finally got on Route 109 and entered the Uwharrie National Forest, the afternoon and my patience were both seriously on the wane.

> *And, as his strength*
> *Failed him at length,*
> *He met a pilgrim shadow—*
> *"Shadow," said he,*
> *"Where can it be—*
> *This land of Eldorado?"*

> *"Over the Mountains*
> *Of the Moon,*
> *Down in the Valley of the Shadow,*
> *Ride, boldly ride,"*
> *The shade replied—*
> *"If you seek for Eldorado!"*

Oh, I was riding boldly, all right—thanks to another caffeine infusion from the kindly Dr Pepper. Somehow, though, I had managed to bypass the Mountains of the Moon and the Valley of the Shadow, winding up instead at a general store in the tiny burg of Uwharrie. Where can it be—this land of Eldorado? Well, shit, son. It's just up the road.

The first thing I learned about the place was this: even when you find it, it's not really there. The Macedonia Methodist

Church, the Adams Egg Farm, a few forlorn houses and ramshackle trailers—welcome to Eldorado (pronounced El-duh-RAY-doh by the locals), where the streets are not paved with gold and some are not paved at all. The most impressive edifice by far was the Eldorado Outpost, a new convenience store with deer and fish trophies on the walls, groceries and "Quality Gun Care Products" on the shelves, and Seen Better Days pizza under the heat lamps. I asked one of the girls at the cash register about the history of the town.

"Um, it's not really a *town*," she said with a giggle, before searching behind the counter for a photocopied "minihistory" by the county historical society. It informed me that Eldorado had been the site of a gold discovery in 1885. Whatever small riches were made here obviously did not last. Eldorado, I realized, was nothing but the last remnants of somebody's doomed schemes and blind greed. And, suddenly, I got a funny feeling that I'd been there before.

GILBERT BLAND OUTSIDE THE
COURTHOUSE IN HILLSBOROUGH,
NORTH CAROLINA, ON JULY 1, 1996.

CHAPTER 13

Mr. Bland, I Presume

*E*VEN AFTER ALL THE SETBACKS, I KNEW OF one last spot where I was sure to come across Bland. As his case shuffled toward completion in three jurisdictions, the map thief's calendar had begun to fill with events he could hardly refuse to attend. And so, on a bright, brisk day in December 1996, I found myself at a federal courtroom in Charlottesville, Virginia, where he was due to appear at a sentencing hearing. I would finally lay eyes on the man.

I had been awaiting this event with a kind of anticipation that bordered on frenzy. At times, I felt nearly as anxious as the explorer Henry Morton Stanley, who, on September 19, 1871, scribbled these words from somewhere deep in central Africa:

> I have taken a solemn, enduring oath, an oath to be kept while the least hope of life remains in me, not to be

tempted to break the resolution I have formed, never to give up the search, until I find Livingstone. . . . And something tells me, I do not know what it is—perhaps it is the ever-living hopefulness of my own nature, perhaps it is the natural presumption born out of an abundant and glowing vitality, or the outcome of an overweening confidence in one's self—anyhow and everyhow, something tells me . . . I shall find him, and— write it larger—FIND HIM! FIND HIM! Even the words are inspiring. I feel more happy. Have I uttered a prayer? I shall sleep calmly to-night.

Stanley's agitation was understandable. Having marched more than five hundred miles through vast swamps and dense jungles in search of the lost geographer-missionary David Livingstone, enduring 128-degree temperatures, torrential rains, unfriendly locals, mutinous underlings, bloodsucking tsetse flies, malaria-carrying mosquitoes, and beetles as large as mice, he was, at the time of his writing, half-loopy from "fevers without number." So what was my excuse? It was clear by now that my search had led me into dangerous emotional territory. And so, having invested many months in trying to figure out what made the map thief tick, I now began also to look at my *own* motivations. If I was going to keep pursuing this frustrating quest, I thought I owed it to myself—and perhaps to Bland as well—to figure out exactly what I was doing.

I realized that in spirit, at least, my search resembled a kind that popped up fairly often in the annals of discovery. As far back as Homer's time, when Telemachus set out after his long-lost father, Odysseus, much of our world has been mapped by explorers who were not actually seeking new lands but hunting for elusive human beings. In the Middle Ages, for instance, generations of European voyagers headed to Asia and later Africa in search of Prester John, an ever-elusive Christian king whose vast and wealthy dominions were said to have "no theft nor sycophancy nor greed nor divisions." We may now snicker at maps such as *The Kingdom of Prester John,* published by Ortelius in 1573, depicting a huge African empire. Nonetheless, the hunt for this mythical potentate unquestionably helped to end medieval Europe's isolation and spark the Age of Discovery.

Nor were other eras immune from what Eric Leed, author of *Shores of Discovery: How Expeditionaries Have Constructed the World,* described as "the Lost-Boy Complex." In 1805 the Scottish explorer Mungo Park vanished along the Niger River. He was never found, but those who attempted to track him down dispelled many geographical myths about the West African interior. Likewise, after British rear admiral Sir John Franklin disappeared during his 1845 attempt to find the elusive Northwest Passage, more than twenty expeditions were sent out in search of the mariner and his men (all of whom, it turned out, had perished). "The Franklin affair was the greatest disaster in the history of Polar exploration," wrote Peter Whitfield, "yet in drawing dozens of search-parties to the region in the 1850s, it was responsible for completing the map of the Arctic."

My own quest had many motivations, of course, not the least of them being money and professional pride. Like Stanley, who was sent to Africa as a reporter for the *New York Herald*, I was first and foremost a journalist on assignment. There was also an intellectual challenge. The more Bland had avoided me, the more I had learned to rely on my own resourcefulness and research skills to patch together the details of his life. But something else kept me going, an almost instinctual drive, seemingly linked to the allure of the unknown. It was beginning to remind me an awful lot of this Lost-Boy Complex. And as I read through the accounts of explorers, trying to make sense of the phenomenon, a curious pattern began to emerge. In a striking number of cases, the searcher—consciously or not—began to take on traits of the missing person, finishing his quest, meeting his same fate, or otherwise merging with his being. Stanley, for instance, had suffered a lifelong crisis of identity. An illegitimate child who was abandoned by his mother and never knew his father, he changed his name from John Rowlands to Henry Stanley, after a man whom he idolized as a father figure. His hunt for Livingstone was likewise a search for self, as if he were driven not only to *locate* the great adventurer but also to *become* him in some way. Stanley himself hinted at this very notion in his journal. In the older and more famous man's presence, he wrote, "I . . . begin to think myself somebody, though I never suspected it before."

Livingstone was, in many ways, worthy of emulation. As a physician he dedicated himself to using modern medicine to alleviate the suffering of the African people; as a Christian missionary he battled the slave trade; as an explorer he made sweeping contributions to geographical knowledge of the continent. I could see why Stanley would be drawn to him. But just what was I trying to find in a man like Gilbert Bland?

ACES HAVE OFTEN BEEN COMPARED TO MAPS. Ptolemy himself described mapmaking in terms of painting a portrait: in both disciplines, he wrote, one must be concerned not only with the whole head (the entire world) but with individual features (particular places). Likewise, the Dutch master Jan Vermeer—a contemporary of Golden Age cartographers such as Joan Blaeu, Jan Jansson, and Frederick de Wit—repeatedly counterposed the human face with the face of the Earth. In works like *The Art of Painting, The Soldier and a Laughing Girl, Young Woman in Blue, Young Woman with a Water Jug,* and *The Geographer,* Vermeer placed the face of his subject in front of a map—as if to show that the former charted the inner world just as the latter depicted the world at large. And this same metaphor was employed by any number of writers, including William Shakespeare in *Henry VI, Part II:*

> *In thy face I see*
> *The map of honor, truth, and loyalty*

So what sort of map, I wondered, as I sat anxiously in that courtroom, would I see on the face of the defendant? By now several photos of Bland were etched into my memory: the waif-like face from his first mug shot in 1968, cheeks angelic but eyes empty; the noticeably hardened face from a post-Vietnam mug shot in 1971; the dazed face from another arrest in 1972, hair shoulder-length and shaggy, mustache full and walrusy, à la David Crosby; and, finally, the face of a middle-aged criminal, mustache graying, hairline receding, eyes peering past the camera defiantly, one brow arched at a foreboding angle. But while those photos charted the changes that had taken place in Bland's outward appearance, they told me little about his soul: poker faces, every last one of them. If nothing else, I hoped that this long-awaited chance to observe him in person would allow me to decipher his features, as Stanley had done with Livingstone:

> I found myself gazing at him. . . . Every hair of his head and beard, every wrinkle of his face, the wanness of his features, and the slightly wearied look he wore, were all imparting intelligence to me—the knowledge I craved for so much ever since I heard the words [from my publisher], "Take what you want, but find Livingstone."

As the appointed hour approached, the courtroom filled with lawyers and clerks. There were no well-wishers or family members seated in the gallery—just a few reporters quietly readying their notebooks. And then, there he was, shuffling to his seat in blue prison scrubs. In a similar moment of encounter, H. M. Stanley had professed a desire to "vent [his] joy in some mad freak, such as . . . turning a somersault." But, despite months of anticipation, I now felt nothing but a vague sadness, whether at Bland's meager appearance or my own grandiose expectations, I could not be sure. Although I had hardly imagined a robust individual, I was taken aback by how sunken he looked. Five feet nine inches tall, with reddish brown hair that was beginning to go gray, he seemed hunched and frail, as if his body belonged to an old man. Yet he also had the look of someone far younger than his forty-seven years: without the mustache I had seen in so many of his photos, he seemed almost childlike. His skin was pulpy and lusterless, as though never exposed to sunlight. And his expression? Empty. Blank. Bland. It was simply not a face, I now realized, that gave itself away. The only thing vibrant about it was his piercing hazel eyes. A couple of times he leaned back and sneaked glances at me as I stared at him. I'm not sure he even knew who I was, but his look was not friendly. I could imagine how Jennifer Bryan must have felt when he darted his "surreptitious" eyes at her on that fateful day in the Peabody Library. It was the gaze of a man who intensely disliked to be observed.

Prison had not been good to the map thief. Earlier in his incarceration, while staying at the Albemarle-Charlottesville Regional Jail, he'd written the U.S. district judge to complain about having to live in crowded conditions with a number of violent criminals. He attempted to pass the days by reading, he said, but had trouble concentrating in a place where the television constantly blared, "with RAP music videos, cartoons, and wrestling. . . .

"I have tried, with the help of anti-depressant medication . . . to maintain and cope," he wrote, but "the stress is unbearable." Noting that two other inmates had hanged themselves since his arrival several months earlier, he said he was worried about "retain[ing] my sanity."

Knowing that Bland had written similar letters from prison in the past, I could not help but feel a certain skepticism about his claims of mental illness. But when the hearing got under way in court that morning, his attorney argued that the map thief's troubled emotions were indeed at the heart of this case. In urging a light sentence for his client, the Roanoke-based lawyer Paul R. Thomson, Jr., said Bland's "pattern of problems" was "largely triggered by depression, a very common problem with post traumatic stress syndrome and something that we saw a whole lot of during the Vietnam era." Thomson also cited Bland's financial troubles as motivation for the crimes. "He did it in large measure because his business that he owned in Maryland . . . was failing," he said, adding that Bland "could not feed his family." Thomson assured the court that his client would remain in an outpatient treatment program once he returned home to Florida. "He recognizes that this was a singularly poor judgment. . . . This has been an emotionally traumatic incident for him, for his family."

Any hopes I had entertained of Bland himself offering insight into the crimes proved sadly optimistic. Speaking in a meek voice that occasionally snagged with emotion, he gave what amounted to a stock repentant felon speech: "The first thing I'd like to say, Your Honor, is that I'm truly sorry for what

I've done. I'm ashamed of myself. I'd also like to say, Your Honor, that in the year just gone by, I've had a lot of time to think about why this has happened and also . . . about my responsibility to my family, to my wife and children when I get back home. I have a lot to make up to them. I'm forty-seven years old now and I realize that I can't make mistakes like this anymore. . . . It will never happen again."

Then he quietly slouched back to the defense table and seemed to melt into his chair, the soul of inconspicuousness.

UNITED STATES DISTRICT COURT JUDGE JAMES H. Michael, Jr., a tall, white-haired man with hawkish eyes, a resonant voice, and the stately air of an old-fashioned Southern gentleman, wanted Bland to know how much the thefts had offended him. "In the court's view, the loss is irreplaceable and unmeasurable," he told the map thief at that hearing. Nonetheless, a plea bargain had been signed, and the judge said he made it a rule to honor plea bargains. Accordingly, he sentenced the defendant to eight months in prison—time already served—and ordered him to pay seventy thousand dollars in restitution to the University of Virginia and Duke University. (Bland would later contest that amount, noting that the damages he had caused were easily remediable, since many of the maps could simply be glued back into their atlases—in response to which Judge Michael would accuse him of "a persistent misunderstanding of the gravity of the offense.")

Ten days after his sentencing in Virginia, Gilbert Bland was in court once again. Like their federal counterparts, North Carolina prosecutors had agreed to a plea bargain that would have let the map thief off with time served. This time, however, the judge had other ideas. Noting that Bland had stolen twenty-six maps and documents worth an estimated twenty thousand dollars from UNC–Chapel Hill, Superior Court Judge Robert Hobgood rejected the deal, insisting that "the penalty is not severe enough for what this man has done." It was a gutsy stand, so much appreciated by librarians that it earned Hobgood an award from the Smithsonian Institution's 1998 National Conference on Cultural Property Protection. But the practical impact of the decision proved minimal: even with the judge throwing the book at him, Bland would end up serving only five additional months in prison. After receiving a two-year suspended sentence in Delaware, where he was ordered to pay nine thousand dollars in restitution for the maps he took from the university, Bland was ready for release, having spent a total of less than seventeen months behind bars.

As the news of Bland's imminent freedom spread via the Internet, librarians from around the globe seethed at what they viewed as a laughably light sentence. "In my opinion, he should have got twenty years hard labor. . . . Those who talk their way into our confidence and then betray our trust are lower than the dirt," snarled P. D. Hingley, librarian for the Royal Astronomical Society in London.

"Since civility prevents us from chopping off his hand, any such thief should be stuck away for a year for each dollar's worth of stuff he stole and for each dollar it cost to apprehend, prosecute, and incarcerate him," added Sidney E. Berger, head of special collections at the University of California, Riverside.

Yet, despite such get-tough rhetoric, the librarians knew that their own peers were partly to blame for the situation. Of the nineteen institutions allegedly hit by Bland, only four had pressed charges. The others had simply let the matter drop. Why the unwillingness to act? "I've asked that same question many times, and I haven't gotten much of an answer," said Cynthia Requardt of Johns Hopkins, where Bland was apprehended but never charged. "I think it fell through the cracks. The legal counsel didn't think that there would be much gained by it, everyone else was waiting for the legal counsel to take the first step. . . . It dragged on so long, and then Virginia prosecuted, and then Delaware and North Carolina, and so the feeling became, Well, it's been taken care of."

True, Bland's federal plea bargain would have made additional state cases against him difficult to pursue—but by no means impossible. "Other libraries would have been able to prosecute if they had really pushed," insisted the FBI's Gray Hill.

Moreover, the U.S. plea bargain did not shield Bland in Canada, where he had allegedly walked off with a total of almost forty maps from the University of British Columbia in Vancouver and the British Columbia Archives in Victoria. Nonetheless, no charges from north of the border ever materialized. "I talked to the Royal Canadian Mounted Police about what our chances would be," said Brenda Peterson of the University of British Columbia. "And they said that in order to bring any sort of charges against him, we'd get into international law, and that would be very complicated. They didn't hold out much hope that the amount of effort and money that would be required to actually charge him in Canada would be worth it. Let's just put it this way: they did not urge me to pursue it."

And so, on May 23, 1997, less than a year and a half after entering jail, Bland strolled out into the spring air, a free man. In a curious twist of fate, his last days behind bars had been spent at Fort Dix, New Jersey—a federal prison established in 1993 on the site of a former military training facility that Bland knew all too well. It was into Fort Dix he had walked for induction into the Army in 1968, and it was out of Fort Dix he had come upon leaving the service in 1971, anxious to put the past behind him. Now he had reason to hope for another new start. The police and FBI were no longer after him. His victims had moved on to other concerns. And, as the weeks wore on, most of the media forgot about him, too. I was the last one on his trail.

*H*ELLO."

"Hi, Mr. Bland."

"Yes, who is speaking?"

"This is Miles Harvey calling."

I had waited more than eight months after his release to telephone him. His lawyers had told me he was not pleased with the publication of my magazine article and had given me no reason to believe he was any happier about the possibility of a book. Still, I hoped that, with the passage of time, I might find him in a reflective mood. I was mistaken.

"First of all," he said curtly, "do you mind if I record this conversation?"

"No. Do you mind if I go ahead and record it, too?"

"Be my guest."

"All right, thanks."

I was surprised at how shaky my voice sounded—and how calm his seemed. It was also deeper than I remembered it, and his slight New Jersey accent seemed to give it a toughness. There was a hint of menace in it, too. Even from the first few words I sensed that it was a voice that could persuade, a voice that could intimidate and injure—a voice, in short, entirely un-like the broken and barely audible one I had heard in court.

He demanded to know how I had found his phone number. I told him the source—a document on the public record—then fumbled for words. "I just wanted to introduce myself to you."

"Let me tell you something, first. I do not wish for you to communicate with me in any way and in any manner," he said flatly, as if reading from a prepared statement. "There are laws in the state of Florida that protect people. I do not wish for you to communicate with me any further. If you do, I will try to bring criminal charges against you, and I will certainly bring civil charges against you. Do you understand that? Is that clear?"

"I understand what you just said, yeah."

"Okay."

Although his legal threats were unfounded if not insincere, it was obvious the conversation was not going well. I knew this would be my last chance.

"Now, what I'd like to request is that we at least meet in person," I said. "I think you should meet me, even if you don't want to talk to me. I—I'm a good guy. I'm interested in getting to know whatever part of this story you want me to get to know. I just want to give you every opportunity; I just want to be fair here. It's part of my job. I have absolutely nothing against you. I have absolutely no interest in pestering you or invading your privacy. I'm just trying to do a good job as a reporter. Can you understand that?"

"Uh, you've been warned, and I suggest that you check Florida statutes regarding stalking before you try to communicate with me again. As I said before, I'm warning you and I have a tape recording of this conversation. If you continue to harass me or attempt to communicate with me in any way, I will file charges with the police and I will charge you in a civil action. Do you understand that?"

"Yep, I understand what you said."

"Is that clear to you?"

"It's absolutely clear. I'm still hoping to talk you out of it . . ."

"I have nothing more to say to you."

Then came a silence. A familiar silence. A final silence.

SEVENTY YEARS AGO, WHEN HER HUSBAND WAS CON-victed of embezzlement and shipped off to federal prison in Leavenworth, Kansas, my grandmother faced an agonizing decision: how to break the news to her young daughter. Family lore has it that my grandfather was guiltless, save for refusing to snitch on a friend who worked above him at the bank (and who later shot himself to death at a church in our hometown of Downers Grove, Illinois). But my grandmother knew that, even if her husband was innocent, his departure would devastate their youngest child, then about six years old. A levelheaded and resourceful woman who taught many generations of elementary school students, my grandmother was usually the type of person who knew precisely what to do in a crisis. This time, however, she felt overwhelmed, paralyzed by a combination of grief, loss, and the prospect of sudden poverty at the height of the Great Depression. For her teenage stepson, from whom news of the trial could not be kept, the situation was bad enough: he would have to abandon his college plans and look for work in the government-run Civilian Conservation Corps. But how could she possibly hope to explain the tragedy to her daughter, a sensitive little girl who idolized her father?

Desperate for help, my grandmother turned to an associate at her school and another friend with some supposed expertise in child psychology. Their advice was simple, rational, and, it turned out, tragically wrongheaded. Don't tell the girl anything, they said. There is no need to mention the word *prison;* a young child could not cope with the shame. Let her believe that her father has just gone away on a trip. Tell her he'll be home any day.

And so for years my mother went to sleep every night wondering whether the next morning would bring her father back from his journey into the shadows. She does not remember how long he was gone. She does not remember asking anyone where he went. She does not remember trying to picture him in a faraway place. He had simply disappeared, faded into some misty terra incognita, a place all the more terrifying because it was entirely undefined and undiscussed, as distant and incomprehensible as death itself.

He finally did return one day—but, in many ways, she waits for him still. I grew up with a mother who lived in constant fear that her loved ones would simply vanish. If her husband tarried too long on a trout stream, as he was prone to do, or if her teenage sons remained too long at a party, as was their wont, this normally vibrant and easygoing woman would dissolve into a panic. On nights when I came home far past my promised hour of return—there were too many of these, I regret to say—I would often find her sitting by the phone, sobbing, her terror so manifest it seemed to shrivel her six-foot frame. Yet if my grandfather's disappearance left her with a crippling fear of the unknown, it also left her with a very different, very healthy kind of dread: a fear of *not knowing.* My mother's fierce curiosity—a lifelong quest for answers, to both the world's problems and her own—has been, I think, her salvation, a sweet revenge on the forces of uncertainty that haunted her childhood.

I inherited, in equal and all-too-generous portions, her inquisitiveness and her skittishness. And, in retrospect, I realize how much these two contradictory traits colored my investigation of the map thief—one of them driving my search, the other filling me with trepidation about what I might find. Earlier in this book I wrote that Bland seemed such a stranger as to be "beyond my boundaries." I now understand that his remoteness, both psychological and physical, was the main part of my interest in him. I cannot say whether in seeking him out I was somehow looking for the grandfather I never met, a man who, like the map thief, had fallen from social grace in middle life. All I know is that, with each passing month, it seemed that I was searching less for an actual person named Gilbert Bland than for some dark and unexplored part of my own existence. And then one day, to my fascination and horror, I caught a glimpse of it. Him. Me. The thief. My years of attempting to get inside Bland's head had been a failure, I realized. I had not penetrated his thoughts, only imitated his actions—sneaking around the edges of his life just as he had crept around libraries, slicing away little pages of his past, then secreting them home. Although Bland's threat to sue me for stalking was all bluster, I could not really blame him for feeling misused. His sense of violation, in fact, must have been very much like that of his own victims.

And while I agreed with those victims that the judicial system had let Bland off easy, I also understood that punishment is not always measured in jail time alone. From my own family's experience, I was tempted to believe Bland's lawyer when he stood in federal court and told Judge Michael: "I think the biggest punishment that he will face is having to go back and face his teenaged son and explain to him how he made this decision."

Moreover, I knew there was yet another punishment awaiting Bland—one that I myself would be bound to administer.

I had hoped my search for the map thief would end with a discovery, some thunderbolt of truth that threw light upon all his actions. That never happened. Yet I came to understand that, at its most fundamental level, a discovery has less to do with revelation than with declaration. Just as the word *explore* comes from the Latin for "to cry out," discovery is the act of *making known*. Christopher Columbus was not the first to arrive in America: his genius was in introducing the New World to the old one. "To discover is to draw the veil," observed the Columbus scholar Mauricio Obregón. "It is not to run into something and keep it to oneself. It is to push back the frontier of infinity and to pass the news on to posterity."

But every discovery is also an act of appropriation. After all my years of research, the only thing I could say about Gilbert Bland with absolute certainty was that he cherished his anonymity. I had seen him nourish it through a succession of aliases, deploy it ingeniously in one rare books room after another, guard it like a pit bull against all outside forces. Even the courts had not taken it away from him. But I would. This book would. It was not that I meant him any harm: if anything, my feelings of compassion toward him had only grown over the years. But I had come to realize that, no matter what my intentions, the telling of his story would doom Bland to what was, for him, a most terrible fate: to be known.

I was confident that the penalty fit the crime. If nothing else, calling attention to Bland seemed likely to deter him (and other would-be library crooks, I hoped) from future pilferage. Nonetheless, over time I grew increasingly ambivalent about my pursuit of the map thief. I never considered abandoning the project entirely, but I did feel a growing moral fatigue, a creeping doubt about why I continued to rifle through Bland's life for ever more obscure details—especially after it was clear that, without his cooperation, those details would never add up to a complete picture of the man.

One last truth about the act of discovery: it's easy to get lost in the wilderness. Henry Morton Stanley went into the African jungle driven by curiosity, a reporter in search of a scoop. He came out years later, a cynical adventurer for hire, who, as a mercenary of Belgium's brutal King Leopold II, established the Congo Free State, a vast colony of forced labor, torture, and terror where literally millions of people perished. Perhaps it was also curiosity—"a genuine interest in and affinity for" old maps, in the words of one defense attorney—that first lured Gilbert Bland into the peculiar terrain of the rare books room. But curiosity, the desire to experience and understand a thing, has an unfortunate way of devolving into a need to possess it, to conquer it, to make it submit to one's will. And when that happens the explorer becomes the exploiter. I had tried to prevent that particular tragedy from befalling my own adventure. But one day, while transcribing the tape of the phone conversation with the map thief, I heard my voice strain at the words "I'm a good guy." It struck me that I had been trying not to convince Bland but to reassure myself. And I knew that I, too, was beginning to lose my way.

We rarely reach our destinations, at least not the ones we set out to find. More often, we arrive one day at a place unfamiliar and unexpected, where all roads suddenly seem to converge and something—the ineffable smell of fate or the stench of defeat or (likeliest of all) sheer exhaustion—tells us the journey is over. In my case it was the knowledge that I had wandered too far. We do not take trips so much as they take us, and this one had started to transform me into someone I did not want to become. It was time to head home.

OR WRITERS A PLOT IS A SERIES OF EVENTS; FOR cartographers a plot is a map. By either definition, this plot is now at an end. That does not mean it is complete: no plot ever really is. But there comes a point at which you must let the ink dry and step away from the drafting table, hang your work on the wall and see what's there.

Any attempt, whether in writing or mapping, to fit our three-dimensional world onto the flat page leads to distortions. Some elements receive too much space, others too little; still others become warped almost beyond recognition. As I examine my plot I see not only that it suffers from problems of projection but that much of its geography is speculative. Mountains undoubtedly have been sketched where molehills exist, and vice versa. Such guesswork is inescapable when one must depend almost entirely on other people's observations, often nothing more than a shoreward gaze from the crow's nest of a ship. And then, of course, there is the subjectivity of the plot maker himself. Although I have tried to be exacting, all cartographers occasionally succumb to myth and prejudice, thereby transforming entire landforms into Rorschach inkblots that reveal more about the draftsman than the terrain.

"Nature conceives of innumerable things, of which those known to us are fewer than those not known," wrote the fifteenth-century mapmaker Fra Mauro, "and this is so because nature exceeds understanding." To which I would add: especially human nature. As I study my plot, I see a land whose coastline is rendered with some degree of accuracy but whose interior, despite my best efforts, is still stamped *Lands Unknown*. I had hoped to do so much more. I had hoped to put things in exact relation and scale, to get at a single reality. Instead, I see only rumination and whimsy, arabesques of uncertainty. There have been times when, as I leaned over my work, I could make almost no sense of it. But as I step away now, the scattered details begin to merge into strangely familiar forms. And suddenly it no longer seems random at all, this ending. My plot, I realize, looks just like one of those wayward pages from the Island of Lost Maps.

DETAIL FROM A CELESTIAL CHART
PUBLISHED IN 1515 BY THE ARTIST
ALBRECHT DÜRER.

Island of Lost Maps

Lifting Off

THE WORLD WAS BEHIND ME, AND BEFORE ME was nothing but emptiness. What a fine spot it was, this rise overlooking the Pacific, to celebrate the end of my adventure. A crisp spring wind rustled through the low scrub on the hillside; it smelled, as sea air always does, of old tales and new dreams. On the horizon the dull ocean faded haltingly into a leaden sky. For a moment, peering past the outermost limit of the continent, unburdened of all those years of research and obsession at last, I felt almost weightless. Then a voice brought me back. Solemn and scratchy, it crackled from a pair of loudspeakers set up to my rear:

T-MINUS TWO MINUTES . . .

Mapmaking is an endless quest for perspective. From the earliest times human beings have gazed up with awe and envy as the birds spired overhead. What did those soaring creatures see? Where were they going, so far over the horizon? What could be found there, and what lay beyond? How big was the world? Who else lived in it? How was it shaped? Wings not being our evolutionary good fortune, the human mind evolved an ability to dream its way into the skies and peer down, then created a language of symbols to describe what it saw. The first maps came no later than the Stone Age, and the earliest extant map of the world was made about 600 B.C. The Babylonians who crafted that little clay tablet figured the Earth to be flat, but the Greeks realized it was a sphere and came up with a way to project it onto a two-dimensional plane. The Chinese, too, learned how to reduce space to a systematic grid, and threw in another innovation: the magnetic needle. Other cultures, meanwhile, came up with more navigational tools, using the sun and stars to define the Earth. The tools got better. So did the maps. Better maps begat bigger dreams. New continents came into view. Sailing vessels circled the globe. Balloons levitated above it, then airplanes, then rocket ships. Orbiting on one of those ships in 1962, the astronaut John Glenn observed: "I can see the whole state of Florida just laid out like a map." For the first time our perspective had outstripped that of the birds. Even so, we kept yearning for a better view.

I was about to witness the latest chapter in that quest. Gathered around me, hugging themselves against the ocean breeze, were a handful of reporters, space industry executives, and officials from Vandenberg Air Force Base. It was April 1999, and we all had come to this isolated edge of the base, some 170 miles north of Los Angeles, for a pivotal moment in the history of "remote sensing"—the geeky buzzword for examining the Earth from on high. To the south of us, past the Santa Ynez River, loomed a row of hills, behind which, just out of view, stood a ninety-three-foot-tall Athena II rocket, ready to roar into space. Its payload was the most sophisticated Earth-observation satellite ever built for the commercial market. Operated by Space Imaging, a cutting-edge Colorado firm, the *Ikonos I* would be able to produce photographs of objects as small as one meter—images equivalent in detail to maps drawn by the U.S. Geological Survey. From an orbit some 420 miles above the Earth, its camera could distinguish cars, homes, roads, bridges, individual trees, and even hot tubs. Previously the domain of only government spy satellites, these high-resolution images could then be merged with those of another onboard sensor, whose multispectral scans would reveal information not seen with the naked eye, such as the health of crops and the spread of plankton at sea, as well as earthquake fault lines and potential mineral deposits. Transmitted to Earth in digital form—meaning they could be easily stored in computers, then processed and converted into maps—these images would be available almost immediately to anyone willing to pay thirty to three hundred dollars per square mile photographed. Among the early customers was the National Imagery and Mapping Agency, the federal organization responsible for military maps and surveillance photos. But cartographers and spies were far from the only people interested in the *Ikonos I*. At the edge of the millennium, everyone from farmer to miner, urban planner to relief worker, was demanding a bird's-eye view of the world.

Personally, I had a different sort of perspective in mind. In this place where the land and sea and sky converged, where the past and present of cartography met its future, I wanted to take one last look back at a story that had consumed me for four years. Although the case had largely disappeared from public view, it remained very much alive for the people affected by it, many of whom had continued to pursue it behind the scenes. Of course, Bland had never been far from my thoughts, either. I had even had something of a last run-in with him. And so, as one countdown crackled in my ears, another one ticked off in my head, as I thought back on a parade of events that had transpired since the map thief's release from prison.

T-MINUS ONE MINUTE . . .

In February 1998 I had found myself in Florida, where organizers of the Miami International Map Fair were holding a panel discussion on security issues, focusing on the Bland case. Just three years earlier the map thief had passed himself off as a legitimate dealer at the event, trafficking his illicit stock to a number of unknowing map sellers and collectors. This fact was deeply embarrassing for all involved—but, to his credit, Joseph H. Fitzgerald, the fair's affable founder and chairman, chose not to hide from it. Unfortunately, although most of the dealers I met at the fair seemed well-meaning, little was said or done that day to convince me that the same thing could not happen at an event like this again.

Meeting in a basement lecture hall at the Historical Museum of Southern Florida, the panel included two rare books librarians, an art curator, a map seller, and a prominent collector. They covered a broad range of topics, from ways to keep thieves out of libraries to methods for getting maps back once the thieves got in. Noticeably absent from the discussion, however, was an honest examination of how Bland had so easily managed to gain the trust of dealers at this same fair. Such a discussion, however, would have fallen on deaf ears, since almost none of those dealers had bothered to attend the forum. They had better things to do just then. The workshop coincided with the opening of the fair—and in the lobby upstairs, where the dealers had set up their booths, there were customers to meet, deals to cut, maps to move.

"There's a feeding frenzy up there," I heard Fitzgerald tell an associate as he stood near the rostrum, "which is good, but . . ."

He finished his thought by casting a nervous glance at the rows of empty seats.

After the forum was over, I went upstairs and wandered from booth to booth. Dozens of dealers—from such far-flung spots as Argentina, Australia, Canada, England, Germany, and the Netherlands—busily hawked their goods, while hundreds of connoisseurs and other interested people shuffled about, gazing at maps on walls, flipping through maps in bins, holding maps at odd angles to get them in the best light, gathering in groups to discourse about a certain unusual specimen. Most of the fairgoers were middle-aged and older, but there were also twenty- and thirty-somethings, some of whom wore looks of delight and wonder, having just been initiated into the passion's quirky marvels. It was an unlikely event, half subdued art opening, half frenzied swap-o-rama. Maps were changing hands at a brisk pace: one dealer told me he moved $38,000 in product that day. No one seemed outwardly to be concerned about provenance.

Later that morning, away from the hubbub, a veteran dealer approached me in the museum's library. He had a story to tell—one that not even the FBI had heard. I'm not sure why he decided to let me in on it: perhaps he wanted to ease his conscience or perhaps he just figured I'd be interested. Three years earlier he had purchased an item from Gilbert Bland at a fair in San Francisco. He had not tried to get it back to the rightful owner. "The authorities never contacted me," he said with a shrug, "and, well, I'd already sold the map. I got lucky on that one, I guess."

T-MINUS FIFTY SECONDS . . .

"Librarians," said the woman with short red hair, "have an ostrich mentality when it comes to security: they have their heads in the sand and their tails in the air, and they're ripe to be screwed."

Four months had passed since the map fair in Miami, and I was at another workshop devoted to the bad deeds of Gil Bland. This time, the attendees were rare books librarians from around the country, who had gathered in Washington, D.C., for an annual meeting. In a conference room at the Library of Congress, some forty workshop participants had just heard from security experts and law enforcement personnel—including the FBI's Gray Hill—as well as officials from Johns Hopkins, who described Bland's capture and explained their controversial decision not to have him arrested.

Citing the confidential nature of the discussions about security, organizers had asked me not to attend the main body of the workshop. They did, however, invite me to speak at the end of the session, so that I could brief the librarians on my coverage of the case and ask for their input. Not long after stepping off the podium, I was confronted by the woman with the red hair and the vivid ostrich analogy.

Her name was Eileen E. Brady, and it turned out that she was not just blowing off steam. In addition to her work as a librarian at Washington State University, Brady was editor of *Focus on Security: The Magazine of Library, Archive, and Museum Security,* a position that had given her a "healthy paranoia" about the dangers that lurk in the stacks. Theft, she said, was not the only security problem; librarians have been raped and even murdered on the job in recent years. Nonetheless, she reported, many of them would still prefer to ignore the problem. "The attitude that the library is a safe haven, a quiet place, that nothing bad will happen there, that we must not do anything to offend our so-called 'user' or patron—whether or not that patron is legitimate—is very common. And it's difficult to overcome this mind-set.

"My position is militant; there are no two ways about it," she added. But, unlike most militants, Brady was not being shunned by her peers. She had, in fact, been one of the featured speakers at the day's workshop—which struck me as a very healthy sign. Yes, the librarians had a long way to go in defending themselves against the Gilbert Blands of the world. But, unlike the dealers, they seemed sincerely interested in confronting their own demons.

I became even more confident in this conclusion the next day, when I sat down with Everett C. Wilkie, Jr., a sardonic, cigarette-puffing consultant in rare books and manuscripts who had organized the workshop. "What surprised me the most," he told me, "was how cranky the law enforcement people were with the library community in general. They were saying, 'A, you won't prosecute; B, you won't put identification marks on your stuff; C, you don't take care of it; D, if we find it, you won't help us to get it back to you.' They were really very blunt about it."

"Did the librarians stick up for themselves?" I asked.

"No," he said with a glib smile. "It was all true."

Nonetheless, said Wilkie, "I don't think there was anyone in that room who actually wants their stuff stolen, and I think they have a pretty good idea how they would stop it if they only could. But a lot of it—security equipment, staff, you name it— comes down to money. The first thing you've got to do to affect your security program is to get your upper administration to buy into it. And if they don't buy into it, you've got problems."

In fact, I knew that some administrations were beginning to see the light—thanks, ironically, to Bland. His alleged thefts from the University of Florida, for example, served as a much-needed wake-up call to school officials. "Bland did several thousand dollars' worth of damage," said the librarian John E. Ingram, "but the ultimate effect of his 'work' is that we have better security for our stacks, we have better security for our reading room, we have surveillance, which we didn't really have before—and in the final analysis, we have a much more astute, perceptive staff working with the collection, which is probably the best benefit of all." Likewise, major reforms had been put into place at the University of Rochester library, which Bland is thought to have visited three times, once taking so much material that he left the floor snowy with paper shards. After purchasing a camera for the reading room, the rare books department sought the help of a nationally known security consultant in enacting additional measures—which were funded, appropriately enough, by insurance money from the Bland case. "The whole library has much better security, and the rare books department has vastly better security than when Gilbert Bland was here," reported the rare books librarian, Evelyn Walker.

Some observers, however, argued that even more fundamental reforms were necessary. Not the least—and certainly not the least restrained—was the irascible map mogul Graham Arader. "Some of these libraries now have hundreds of millions of dollars of books, and they expect to get security paying people who they get for thirty thousand dollars a year. They're going to have to start treating books like other objects worth as much money," he said. "They're going to have to segregate them and put them in rooms where they're virtually inaccessible. The books are going to have to be stored like gold bullion."

Librarians, he said, could learn a thing or two about security from their corporate counterparts: "The prop room at Disney—I guaran-goddamn-tee you that the curator of Disney knows where everything is and it's on inventory, and he's watching everything. That guy's on top of what he's doing, because if he wasn't, [Disney CEO Michael] Eisner would fire him. One of these librarians who are so critical of me wouldn't last a week there."

Never one to think small, Arader proposed nothing less than the complete elimination of most traditional rare books rooms, in favor of a few centralized and hypersecure research libraries. "There's no reason for any city—even New York—to have more than two major map collections," he said.

When I mentioned this concept to Wilkie, he found it impracticable, pointing out that the larger scale of such facilities might cause as many security problems as it solved. If it was difficult to keep tabs on someone like Bland in a small space, he said, imagine how hard it would be in a huge room filled with hundreds of researchers. Still, Wilkie did not think Arader was completely off base. He noted, for instance, that more and more research libraries are limiting access to serious scholars. To get in, patrons must provide—in advance—a precise description of their research and letters of recommendation. "They are just totally unapologetic about the fact that the general public isn't welcome," he said.

That idea, I told him, struck me as sad.

"It's sad, but it's not sad," he responded. "A lot of these places have stuff that just shouldn't be handled very much. I mean, you really should need to have a good reason to look at this stuff because it's got to last, well, basically forever."

It was hard to argue with that. The legacy of the Bland case, in fact, may be to help turn back the clock on our concept of libraries. In the mid-nineteenth century, when establishing his masterpiece of a research facility in Baltimore, George Peabody had insisted that, while it would contain "the best books on every subject," it would also be "for the free use of all persons who may desire to consult it." It was a progressive notion back then but one that seems to have failed the test of time. In the long run rare books rooms may look less like what Peabody envisioned and more like those of ancient times—repositories for sacred documents available to only a priestly caste, the "Learned Men of the Magic Library," as the Egyptians had called them. And while that system would be sure to have unfortunate consequences—isolating average people even further from their culture and their history—the current one may be even worse. As Wilkie put it: "Any halfway smart undergraduate student can pay his way through four years at a major university for the price of a razor blade."

T-MINUS FORTY SECONDS . . .

In June 1998, just a few days after my conversation with Wilkie, I returned to the Island of Lost Maps. In the more than a year that Gilbert Bland had been out of prison, FBI Special Agent Gray Hill had remained hard at work cleaning up the map thief's mess. Now, at long last, it looked as if Hill's exile was coming to an end.

The agent had just returned from the nation's capital, where, in addition to addressing the rare books librarians, he had met with an FBI technician to match one last set of maps with the books from which they had been taken. "This was my last run up to see the forensics expert," said an obviously weary Hill. "As far as I'm concerned, I'm done at this point."

Since the last time I saw Hill, two years earlier, he had managed to find homes for more than one hundred additional maps. It had been methodical and often frustrating work, but he could take heart in knowing that his efforts had not gone unappreciated. "One of the librarians came in with a real abrasiveness," he recalled. "But she went back with more maps than she had even known she was missing. At the end, she had tears in her eyes."

All told, he had been able to reunite nearly 180 of the roughly 250 wayward maps with their owners. Nonetheless, the Island of Lost Maps still had plenty of inhabitants, most of which were now scattered on a table in front of us at Hill's Charlottesville office. "I feel good about what I've done," he said, "but it does still halfway tick me off that some of them could possibly be matched up. . . . I've got history sitting here, and it should be returned to where it came from."

Did Gilbert Bland harbor the secret of where those remaining maps belonged? Hill found it unlikely. True, Bland had been less than honest with the FBI—failing to tell investigators, for instance, about his visits to libraries in Canada. But Hill believed simple forgetfulness probably also came into play. "When you've stolen from so many places," he said with a faint grin, "it's hard to remember where you got things."

And no matter what information Bland might be withholding, more maps could have been returned if only librarians had taken better care of their materials and kept better records, according to Hill. Fresh from dressing down librarians at the workshop in Washington, he was still full of venom. With some librarians, he said, the failure to take care of materials smacked of pure negligence. "It's like if you had a five-thousand-dollar bill in your wallet, and you said, 'I know I had one in there, but if I look it might be missing. So I just won't look.' "

If the libraries Bland had visited "spent a little more energy" searching for missing items, Hill believed he could get rid of even more of his maps. Still, he was haunted by the possibility that the remaining ones "belong to a library that we are not yet aware of."

In any event, it was no longer his concern. After two and a half long years on the case, he was ready to move on. It had been both an exasperating and an enlightening experience. "I have picked up a much greater appreciation for the art," he said. "The word *cartography* was not a normal part of my vocabulary before this case. So it has been an education, a broadening of the horizons."

"Are you going to miss having them around?" I asked.

He cast one last glance over the pile. "No," he said, looking genuinely relieved.

But, as often happens to those shipwrecked on islands, Agent Hill's dreams of rescue proved premature. When I called him many months later, the maps were still locked in his office, awaiting a permanent home. They would almost certainly wind up at the Library of Congress, Hill said. As usual, however, the federal bureaucracy was moving slowly, and final plans had not yet been completed.

In the meantime, Hill had managed to place a couple more maps not previously known to have been stolen. "Every once in a while somebody will be going through a book," he explained, "and all of a sudden they'll say, 'Hey, you know we're missing something out of here.' . . . It keeps coming in very slowly."

It would continue to come in slowly, this story. Or so I reflected as I stood on that rise, listening to the countdown and watching the waves roll in. The map thief's tale, I thought, might still be unfolding decades from now. I stared off into the lead gray sky. Somewhere beneath the distant clouds, unopened books sat on dusty shelves, crimes waiting to be discovered. And somewhere, too, beautiful maps hung on the walls of perfect homes, crimes waiting to be solved.

T-MINUS THIRTY SECONDS . . .

The last person I ever expected to hear from again was Gilbert Bland—and it's a good bet that the last person he ever planned on sharing his thoughts with was me. Yet, despite it all, there I was one day, furiously taking notes while he spoke about his life.

This final turn of events, like so many of the best discoveries, came out of the blue. It arrived in the form of a videocassette, provided by a source familiar with the case, who had offhandedly asked if I would be interested in watching it.

Somewhat less offhandedly I had said that sure, I might not mind at all. And so, within seconds, Bland appeared before me, neatly attired in jeans and a blue-on-blue-checked flannel shirt, a white T-shirt barely visible beneath his high-buttoned collar. For a moment I just stood there gaping, dumbfounded that years of waiting to hear him tell his story had suddenly ended with nothing more than the press of a PLAY button.

I had heard about this video before. It had been making the rounds among law enforcement types and librarians—shown, for instance, at that workshop on the case in Washington. Conducted by two campus police officers at the University of Delaware, the interview was filmed on March 27, 1997, near the end of Bland's incarceration. As it got under way the map thief sat at a table, sometimes crossing his arms or nervously pressing the fingertips of both hands against his reddish white sideburns, but more often resting his chin on one palm. He looked exhausted and sullen, at one point requesting to be placed in a cell away from other prisoners. "I'm under [psychiatric] medicine," he explained. "And sometimes when I've been on medication, people have beat me up before, and the thing is I literally can't defend myself. I'm not a violent person."

Still, this was not the timid Bland I had seen in court—nor, for that matter, the combative Bland I had heard over the phone. Instead, he seemed intelligent, polite, articulate, and, above all, as slippery as black ice—perhaps not unlike the Bland who had visited those libraries. Evasive about the details of his crimes, he often claimed amnesia:

Officer: And where are [the maps stolen from the university] at now?

Bland: I don't know.

Officer: You don't have any idea? Does the FBI have them?

Bland: The FBI might have them.

Officer: Did you sell any of the maps that you took from the University of Delaware's books?

Bland: I could have, but I couldn't be sure.

Officer: You couldn't be sure?

Bland: Right. . . .

Officer: Who would you have sold them to?

Bland: I—I don't remember that.

Officer: We're not asking for names. I mean, did you sell them to art dealers?

Bland: I went to map shows and sold maps at a map show. I don't know who I sold them to. It's been so long ago, and I've been through so much in the last year and a half, that I just can't remember.

At other points, however, his memory seemed to return with uncanny precision. He had no problem, for instance, in providing a detailed description of the room from which he had stolen maps. Nor had his methods of operation slipped his mind:

Officer: How did you get them out of the library?

Bland: I folded them up and put them inside my shirt.

Officer: Inside your shirt? Nobody [was] in there to stop
  you from doing it or to see you?

Bland: Well, when they left the room . . . I would just
  fold it up and put it in my shirt and walk out and
  take it with me. . . .

Officer: Put it in your shirt and then leave with it, huh?
  Didn't that destroy the value of the map by folding it
  like that?

Bland: No.

Officer: It didn't?

Bland: No, you'd get home and iron it out, and whatever creases were in it just came out.

Officer: How many other universities did you do this at?

Bland: Uh, a lot.

He was apologetic for his crimes, but the only explanation
he offered was the one given by his lawyers in court: "Business
was really bad and I was about to lose everything I had. And I
have a mental problem that was untreated at the time, and as a
result I came up with the crazy idea to do this. . . . I wish I was
in my right mind. I never would've done this."

The officers, to my frustration, were not particularly interested in his motivations. Their main concern was how future
Gilbert Blands could be stopped. His advice was as simple as it
was self-revealing: "If there would have been a [security] camera there I never would've went in, I never would've stayed
there, I never would've ordered any books . . ."

An invisible man hates cameras the way a vampire hates daylight. The most telling picture I ever saw of Bland shows no face. In that shot, taken outside a courthouse by a photographer for the Raleigh, North Carolina, *News & Observer,* the map thief stands with his cuffed hands held high, not only to obscure his eyes but to obliterate all of his features, as if he were trying by sheer will to make himself disappear. He had almost pulled it off: his crime spree left no film. But here at last he had been captured on video.

And yet, watching his image on that TV screen was strangely like seeing a satellite photograph of the Earth. On the one hand, it gave me a perspective that would otherwise have been impossible. I watched in fascination, for instance, as Bland slid his hand inside his shirt to demonstrate how he stole maps. I had imagined that moment a thousand times, but seeing it on tape gave me a real sense of witnessing the crime. On the other hand, this was a voyeurism of an oddly distant kind. It was as if I was viewing the Planet Bland from hundreds of miles in the air: I could make out the houses and buildings and factories— the facades and end results—but the life that hummed within them, the forces that had created them, remained hidden from view, a world only remotely sensed.

T-MINUS TWENTY SECONDS . . .

The breeze off the Pacific seemed to intensify, as if to keep pace with the collective sense of anticipation. Those of us gathered for the liftoff now squinted anxiously in the direction of the launchpad, knowing that we were about to see history. Not

only was the satellite itself a landmark piece of technology—
that very morning *The New York Times* had described it as "the
world's most powerful civilian spacecraft for observing the
Earth"—but its launch came during a revolutionary moment in
the history of cartography. As the science writer Stephen S.
Hall explained in *Mapping the Next Millennium:* "We find ourselves in the midst of what is arguably the greatest explosion in
mapping, and perhaps the greatest reconsideration of 'space'
(in every sense of that word), since an anonymous Babylonian
first attempted to organize human knowledge of the physical
world by drawing a map of the world on a clay tablet twenty-six
centuries ago."

As we head into the twenty-first century, the last great topographical mystery on Earth—the global seafloor—is finally surrendering its secrets. In 1995, for instance, scientists armed with
freshly declassified spy satellite data produced the first detailed
map of this vast terrain, 70 percent of the Earth's surface but
virtually uncharted until recent decades. As one researcher explained: "It's like being able to drain the oceans and look at the
Earth from space." The heavens, too, are being charted on
an almost unimaginable scale. The New Mexico–based Sloan
Digital Sky Survey—one of several ambitious space-mapping
ventures now under way worldwide—is using a high-tech telescope to chart one quarter of the sky, peering 1.5 billion light-
years not only into space but also back in time. By the time it's
complete in 2005, the survey will have mapped 100 million
galaxies, most of them now unlabeled and unstudied, along
with several hundred thousand quasars and tens of millions of

individual stars. The undertaking is the first attempt to digitize the universe—to put the heavens in a computer database available to all. "But it's just a first step," said Michael S. Turner, the project spokesman and chairman of the Astrophysics Department at the University of Chicago. "I think it is a very conservative prediction to say that by the end of this century, astronomers will have mapped the entire observable universe." No less staggering are the maps being made of microscopic worlds. As I write these words, scientists are in a frantic race to chart the human genome—the blueprint for each human being, made up of some 100,000 genes. All maps have consequences, but this one is certain to change the course of humanity. By allowing researchers to understand how the body works at its most fundamental level, the genome map could lead to the elimination of a dizzying array of diseases, from muscular dystrophy to cancer and diabetes. It may also result in the prolongation of life, even the retardation of the aging process— Ponce de León's Fountain of Youth discovered at last. And a leading genomist has declared that humankind is on the brink of doing what only God has done so far: create life-forms. Not cloned life-forms—entirely new life-forms, stitched together out of genetic scraps the way Dr. Frankenstein made his monster out of body parts. In the short run, such cut-and-paste organisms would be possible only on a microbial level—but someday the Earth may be prowled by complex beings every bit as "unnatural" as the creatures once found only on the edges of old maps and in the hinterlands of human thought.

Ah, but what of those hinterlands? With all the other stunning gains being made in mapping, will it also become possible to chart the complex terrain of the mind? A growing number of experts believe so. While some scientists study the genome in search of inherited causes for behavioral traits such as alcoholism, aggression, and risk taking—even criminality—others are mapping the brain itself. New imaging techniques allow researchers to look inside the living, working brain, thus "opening up the territory of the mind just as the first oceangoing ships once opened up the globe," in the words of the science writer Rita Carter, author of *Mapping the Mind*. Using state-of-the-art brain scans, scientists are able to pinpoint the exact locations of various brain components—meaning they can literally chart and observe the mechanics of our thoughts, moods, and memories.

These maps promise to inspire some bizarre journeys. The day may come when expectant parents can genetically alter their unborn children to make them less aggressive or impulsive, more cheerful and altruistic. The day, too, may come when all manner of problems, from mental illness and antisocial behavior to post-traumatic stress disorder, can be managed with psychoactive treatments so precise that "an individual's state of mind (and thus behavior) will be almost entirely malleable," according to Carter. The day may come, in short, when to understand the actions and motivations of another person, we must merely examine the peculiar geography of that individual's brain. Nonetheless, my own amateur experiments in the mapping of gray matter lead me to be skeptical. The physical brain might yield itself to this new kind of cartography, but my bet is that the mind—that strange borderland between inner life and outer experience, dreams and memory, body and soul—will prove as difficult to chart as the continent of Atlantis. I have come to believe that humans will always remain fundamentally inexplicable. Then again, there were those who used to say that about the Earth. And, as Carter observed: "These are the early days of mind exploration and the vision of the brain we have now is probably no more complete or accurate than a sixteenth-century map of the world."

T-MINUS TEN . . .

NINE . . .

EIGHT . . .

SEVEN . . .

SIX . . .

FIVE . . .

FOUR . . .

THREE . . .

TWO . . .

ONE . . .

IGNITION . . .

AND . . .

LIFTOFF.

It shot above the hills, a dazzling orange glow. As it rose, everything else seemed to go still; I would have believed the whole world was staring at the sky in wonder just then. It moved slowly and steadily away, a great distant fireball, and then it was gone, leaving behind a vast trail of smoke that snaked up to the heavens like some scribbled message, a cosmic scrawl I could not hope to decipher but felt I had been pondering for a very long time.

The satellite never reached orbit. Minutes after liftoff it went silent, disappeared. They never found it—not in space, not on land, not in the sea. It had simply vanished, swallowed by the great unknown.

Acknowledgments

IKE A MAP, A BOOK IS THE PRODUCT OF NOT one person but many. I am profoundly grateful to all those who opened their doors, lives, and hearts to me as I researched this project. The librarians Gary L. Menges, Cynthia Requardt, R. Russell Maylone, John E. Ingram, Evelyn Walker, Alice Schreyer, Brenda Peterson, and Jean Ashton, among others, were courageous and candid in discussing a very painful subject. The map dealer W. Graham Arader III gave me extraordinary amounts of time and access. Several others in his profession were also extremely forthcoming, especially Barry Lawrence Ruderman and the dealers I identified as Once Bitten and Twice Shy. A number of law enforcement officials, including Donald Pfouts, Thomas W. Durrer, and Clay Williams, were also vital to the making of this book. I want to give special thanks to Special Agent Gray Hill, as well as to the FBI offices in Richmond and Charlottesville, Virginia. In addition, I want to express my sincere appreciation to Jennifer Bryan, Vera Benson, Werner Muensterberger, Harriette Kaley, Hugh Kennedy, Don Etherington, John D. Bergen, Eileen E. Brady, Everett C. Wilkie, Jr., Heather Bland, Selby Kiffer, "Mr. Atlas," and all the others who were kind enough to be interviewed for the project.

This book would not have been possible without three people in particular. Jon Karp, my gifted editor at Random House, took a risk on an unproven author, then guided him through the publishing process with unfailing wisdom and patience. I also feel blessed to have worked with Sloan Harris, a literary agent of extraordinary skill, humor, and honesty. Finally, I owe an incalculable debt to the journalist Michael Paterniti, a driving force behind this project from start to finish. He was a superb critic and mentor—and an even better friend.

I am hugely grateful to Norman J. W. Thrower—a noted cartographic historian and author of *Maps and Civilization: Cartography in Culture and Society*—who read a draft of this text in an effort to ensure its factual accuracy. I was also lucky to get input from a number of other writers and friends. Kevin Davis was there on a daily basis for advice and encouragement, not to mention lunch at the Lincoln Grill. Sara Corbett inspired some breakthrough ideas early on, then helped guide the project through to completion. Bill Lychack, as always, made me dig deeper, think harder, write better. Elizabeth Lychack gave my copy a thorough scrubbing. Clay Harper offered both the pull-no-punches honesty of a trusted old friend and the shrewd perspective of a book industry insider. The awesome Tom Clynes and my talented screenwriting partner, David Freeman, also made invaluable suggestions about the text.

I consider myself blessed to have worked with production editorial guru Benjamin Dreyer and his superb staff: copy editor Susan Brown and proofreaders Evan Stone and Ruthie Epstein. I would also like to thank Amelia Zalcman, Deborah Foley, Andy Carpenter, Barbara Bachman, Richard Elman, Monica Gomez, and Janelle Duryea at Random House, as well as Teri Steinberg, Richard Abate, and Laura Paterson Davies at ICM.

Several editors at *Outside* magazine, including Hal Espen, Mark Bryant, Brad Wetzler, and Katie Arnold, worked on the story that led to this book. I'm especially grateful to Hampton Sides, who gave my raw article much-needed shape and focus.

Some pundits say writing can't be taught: they're wrong. I am eternally indebted to a number of marvelous teachers, both in the classroom and in the newsroom, who have challenged and inspired me over the years. Rita DuChateau, Bob Reid, Charles Sanders, Sheryl Larson, James Weinstein, Ray Elliott, Larry Doyle, Sharon Solwitz, Nicholas Delbanco, and Charles Baxter—thanks. You gave luster to my world as well as to my prose.

Many other people contributed, directly or indirectly, to *The Island of Lost Maps*. Will Tefft offered exceptional support and proposed marvelous schemes. Robert Karrow and the staff of the Newberry Library made me feel welcome at their wonderful cartographic collection. Richard Cohen kept me sane, not to mention out of debt. I also want to thank, in no particular order, Camille Altay and her wonderful clan, Gregg Chaney and Suellen Semekoski, Helena Kozik, Chris Rose, Chris Carr, Jim Beatty, F. J. Manasek, Lloyd and Marie Green, Shari Joffe and Andrew White, Harry Appelman and Mimi Brody, Jason Harper and Janet Siroto, Tom Kosinski, Alan Sanchez, Dolores Riccardo, Merla Mihalik, Wayne Sallee, Jackie Burford, Miles Burford, Tim Gould, Susan Condon, Dave Cullen, Maggie Garb, Cian Gallagher, John Hammond Moore, Elizabeth Schaaf at the Peabody Institute, Fred Musto at Yale, Linda Lidov at Space Imaging, Joseph H. Fitzgerald and Marcia J. Kanner at the Miami International Map Fair, Norman Strasma and Linda Mickle at the International Map Trade Association, George Combs at the Lloyd House, the members of my writers' group, the Cabin Thing crew, El Grupo del Hombres, the Downers Grove gang, *The Daily Illini* and its discontents, and the Tecalitlán Culinary Army.

My late father, Robert Harvey, gave me a love for both maps and words. This book is his as well as mine. I'm also grateful to my brother, Matthew, for his love, strength, biting humor, and free legal advice. And how does a son even begin to thank his mother? In this case, he says: *I appreciate the interview.* It was typically brave of Tinker Harvey to discuss, for public consumption, one of the darkest chapters of her life. She never ceases to amaze and inspire me.

Finally, to Rengin and Azize—thank you for more than I can express. Writing this book has been wonderful, but building a life with you is a greater joy and accomplishment by far.

Notes

Introduction: Strange Waters

xi   "HOUTMAN CORNELIUS" Carl Waldman and Alan Wexler, *Who Was Who in World Exploration* (New York: Facts on File, 1992), p. 327.

xii   *mappery* William Shakespeare, *Troilus and Cressida,* act I, sc. 3, line 205.

xiii   "black rock" See John Goss, *The Mapmaker's Art: An Illustrated History of Cartography* (Skokie, Ill.: Rand McNally, 1993), p. 95. See also Steven Frimmer, *Neverland: Fabled Places and Fabulous Voyages of History and Legend* (New York: Viking Press, 1976), p. 83.

xiv   "No foreign ship" George Masselman, *The Cradle of Colonialism* (New Haven and London: Yale University Press, 1963), p. 62.

xiv   the Portuguese quietly discovered Australia See William Eisler, *The Furthest Shore: Images of Terra Australis from the Middle Ages to Captain Cook* (Cambridge: Cambridge University Press, 1995), pp. 17–36.

xv Beach, Lucach, and Maletur See ibid., p. 37. See also Raymond H. Ramsay, *No Longer on the Map: Discovering Places That
Never Were* (New York: Viking Press, 1972), pp. 36–41.

xv "The route itself" Masselman, *Cradle of Colonialism*, pp. 62–63.

xvi "the vanguard of the age" Ibid., p. 87.

xvi "speculation in a totally modern fashion" Fernand Braudel,
The Wheels of Commerce, vol. 2: Civilization and Capitalism:
15th–18th Century, trans. Siân Reynolds (New York: Harper &
Row, 1982), p. 100.

xvii Secret Atlas See Lloyd A. Brown, *The Story of Maps* (Boston:
Little, Brown, 1949), p. 148.

xvii most profitable export See Allen M. Sievers, *The Mystical
World of Indonesia: Culture and Economic Development in Conflict*
(Baltimore: Johns Hopkins University Press, 1974), pp. 89–99.
See also Heinrich Eduard Jacob, *Coffee: The Epic of a Commod-
ity*, trans. Eden and Cedar Paul (New York: Viking Press, 1935),
pp. 107–121.

xvii *koffie . . . kopi* I could find no reference source containing the
exact etymology of the Malay-Indonesian word *kopi*. But Cor-
nell University's John U. Wolff, editor of *An Indonesian-English
Dictionary*, informed me that *kopi* was "most likely a loan
word" from the Dutch *koffie*. This view was generally supported by a number of other scholars I contacted.

xviii "TAMARAC, FLA." Anonymous author, Knight-Ridder / Tribune
story, "Police on the Trail of a Map Thief: Florida Antique
Shop Owner Is Suspected," *Chicago Tribune* (December 21,
1995): 14.

xix "Now when I was a little chap . . ." Joseph Conrad, *Heart of
Darkness*, ed. Stanley Appelbaum (1902; reprint, Mineola, N.Y.:
Dover Publications, 1990), p. 5.

xx   the bizarre case of Stephen Carrie Blumberg   See Nicholas A.
Basbanes's account in *A Gentle Madness: Bibliophiles, Bib-
liomanes, and the Eternal Passion for Books* (New York: Henry
Holt, 1995), pp. 465–519.

xxi   the flesh of Egyptian mummies   See Annick Le Guérer's
Scent: The Mysterious and Essential Powers of Smell, trans.
Richard Miller (New York: Turtle Bay Books, 1992), pp. 87–96.

xxi   "Alas, poor Egypt!"   Quoted in ibid., p. 90.

CHAPTER ONE: MR. PEABODY AND MR. NOBODY

3   "There is no other library"   Daniel Mark Epstein, "Mr.
Peabody and His Athenaeum," *New Criterion*, vol. 14, no. 2
(October 1995): 21–28. All quotations attributed to Epstein in
the chapter come from this article—as does some of the historical material, both here and in Chapter Four.

3   "a cathedral of books"   See *Guide to the Archives of the Peabody
Institute of the City of Baltimore: 1857–1977*, comp. Elizabeth
Schaaf (Baltimore: Archives of the Peabody Institute of Johns
Hopkins University, 1987), p. 17.

4   more than $7 million   See Elizabeth Schaaf, "George
Peabody: His Life and Legacy, 1795–1869," *Maryland Historical
Magazine*, vol. 90, no. 3 (Fall 1995): 269–285. See also Carl
Schoettler, "Banker Gave Baltimore a Musical Institute and the
Gift of Giving," *Baltimore Sun* (February 16, 1995): 1E.

4   "the most liberal philanthropist"   Quoted in Schaaf, "George
Peabody."

4   "Deprived as I was"   Quoted in Franklin Parker, *George
Peabody: A Biography*, rev. ed. (Nashville: Vanderbilt University
Press, 1995), p. 25.

5   "I hope may become useful"   George Peabody, "Founding Letter," in *Guide to the Archives*, p. 58.

5   "perhaps grander in its original design"   Parker, *George Peabody*, p. 91.

5   "for the free use of all persons"   Peabody, "Founding Letter," p. 59.

5   "the best works on every subject"   Ibid.

5   "to satisfy the researches"   Ibid.

6   "Taking advantage of the delay"   *Guide to the Archives*, pp. 15–17. Although she is listed as the compiler of this pamphlet, Schaaf informed me that she was, in fact, the author of the section quoted.

8   "should be guarded"   Peabody, "Founding Letter," p. 59.

9   a red notebook   A photocopy of this notebook was provided to me by a source who wished to remain anonymous.

9   "like a small candle"   *The Diario of Christopher Columbus's First Voyage to America, 1492–1493*, trans. Oliver Dunn and James E. Kelley, Jr. (Norman: University of Oklahoma Press, 1989), p. 59. The admiral's journal from the first voyage has been missing since 1554. We know its contents thanks to this abstract, made by Bartolomé de Las Casas in the early sixteenth century.

9   "Or was the mysterious light"   John Noble Wilford, *The Mysterious History of Columbus: An Exploration of the Man, the Myth, the Legacy* (New York: Alfred A. Knopf, 1991), p. 130.

14   "Great Washington"   Herman Melville, *Moby-Dick, or, The Whale* (1851; reprint, New York: Modern Library, 1992), p. 222.

CHAPTER TWO: IMAGINARY CREATURES

19   "Demons assaulted ships"   Quoted in Donald S. Johnson, *Phantom Islands of the Atlantic: The Legends of Seven Lands That Never Were*, rev. ed. (New York: Walker, 1996), pp. 28–43.

19   "one-eyed men"   *The Diario of Christopher Columbus's First Voyage to America, 1492–1493*, trans. Oliver Dunn and James E. Kelley, Jr. (Norman: University of Oklahoma Press, 1989), p. 133.

19   "were not as pretty"   Ibid., p. 321.

19   "back and breasts were like a woman's"   Henry Hudson, "A Second Voyage or Employment of Master Henry Hudson," in Donald S. Johnson, *Charting the Sea of Darkness: The Four Voyages of Henry Hudson* (New York: Kodansha International, 1995), p. 60.

20   "It is easy enough to move"   Steven Frimmer, *Neverland: Fabled Places and Fabulous Voyages of History and Legend* (New York: Viking Press, 1976), p. 18. For a more scholarly work on the same subject, see Percy G. Adams, *Travelers and Travel Liars: 1660–1800* (Berkeley and Los Angeles: University of California Press, 1962).

20   "It is a wonder"   Quoted in Tzvetan Todorov, *The Conquest of America*, trans. Richard Howard (New York: Harper & Row, 1984), p. 21. The passage is from Las Casas's *History of the Indies*, for which no complete English translation is available. I use translations from various authors.

21   "unlikely, even allowing for exaggeration"   Frances Wood, *Did Marco Polo Go to China?* (Boulder: Westview Press, 1996), p. 149.

21 hugely influential   See C.W.R.D. Moseley's introduction to the Penguin edition of *The Travels of Sir John Mandeville* (Harmondsworth, England: Penguin Books, 1983), pp. 9–39.

22 "good Christian men"   Ibid., p. 173.

22 "I, John Mandeville"   Ibid., p. 123.

22 "who live just on the smell"   Ibid., p. 137.

22 "as big as dogs"   Ibid., p. 183.

22 "a kind of fruit"   Ibid., p. 165.

22 "He was an unredeemable fraud"   Stephen Greenblatt, *Marvelous Possessions: The Wonder of the New World* (Chicago: University of Chicago Press, 1991), p. 31.

23 "The abundant identifying marks"   Ibid., pp. 33–34.

24 "I applied for a credit card"   Transcript from *The People of the State of California vs. Gilbert Anthony Bland, aka Jack Arnett, aka Jason Michael Pike,* Municipal Court of the San Diego Judicial District, October 3, 1973.

24 "The Clerk"   Ibid.

25 The defendant was born   Birth records on file with the Marion County, Ind., Health Department.

27 "It must show the area near the treasure"   Franklin W. Dixon, *The Clue in the Embers* (1955; reprint, New York: Grosset & Dunlap, 1972), p. 106.

27 "Wowee! What a treasure!"   Ibid., p. 162.

27 "These treasures are certainly government property!"   Ibid., p. 163.

28 "We don't expect a reward"   Ibid., p. 174.

28 "There is a disturbing darkness"   Frank McLynn, *Robert Louis Stevenson: A Biography* (New York: Random House, 1993), p. 199.

29 "The doctor opened the seals" Robert Louis Stevenson, *Treasure Island* (1883; reprint, Cleveland: World Publishing, 1946), p. 62.

29 "monstrous imposter" Ibid., p. 278.

30 "prodigious villain" Ibid.

30 "bland, polite, obsequious seaman" Ibid., p. 279.

30 "figure whose personality swings" Ian Bell, *Dreams of Exile: Robert Louis Stevenson, a Biography* (New York: Henry Holt, 1992), pp. 150–151.

30 "It was a strange collection" Stevenson, *Treasure Island*, p. 281.

31 "two old, dirty, and ragged charts" James Fenimore Cooper, *The Sea Lions, or, The Lost Sealers* (1849; reprint, New York: G. P. Putnam's Sons, 1896), p. 50.

31 "very considerable amount of treasure" Ibid., p. 35.

32 "no dangers, no toil" Ibid., p. 314.

32 "I'm afraid that" Ibid., p. 410.

32 "half-way belief" Ibid., p. 381.

32 "a little more than two thousand dollars" Ibid., p. 454.

32 "Seeing the impossibility of restoring the gold" Ibid.

33 "the greatest literary mystery" Paul Theroux, "Solving the Traven Mystery," *Sunday Times* of London (June 22, 1980): 44.

33 "Here was someone" Karl S. Guthke, *B. Traven: The Life Behind the Legends,* trans. Robert C. Sprung (Brooklyn: Lawrence Hill Books, 1991), p. 12.

33 "One of the maps" B. Traven, *The Treasure of the Sierra Madre* (1935; reprint, New York: Signet, 1968), p. 68.

34 "that eternal curse on gold" Ibid., p. 76.

37 Maps spoke to me Charles Baxter's superb essay "Talking Forks: Fiction and the Inner Life of Objects" helped me to clarify my thoughts on this subject. See Baxter, *Burning Down*

the House: Essays on Fiction (St. Paul, Minn.: Graywolf Press, 1997), pp. 79–108.

37   "It is almost as if one had to read"   Arthur H. Robinson and Barbara Bartz Petchenik, *The Nature of Maps: Essays Toward Understanding Maps and Mapping* (Chicago: University of Chicago Press, 1976), p. 45.

38   "infinite, eloquent suggestion"   Robert Louis Stevenson, "My First Book," in *The Lantern-Bearers and Other Essays,* ed. Jeremy Treglown (New York: Farrar, Straus and Giroux, 1988), p. 283. All further quotations from Stevenson in the chapter come from this short essay.

39   "napkin of the world"   See David Woodward, "Medieval Mappaemundi," in *The History of Cartography,* vol. 1: Cartography in Prehistoric, Ancient, and Medieval Europe and the Mediterranean, ed. J. B. Harley and David Woodward (Chicago: University of Chicago Press, 1987–), p. 287.

41   the various monstrous races   See chart in ibid., p. 331.

41   "Like the earth of a hundred years ago"   Aldous Huxley, *Heaven and Hell* (London: Chatto & Windus, 1956), p. 9.

41   "the antipodes of the mind"   Ibid., p. 16.

42   "strange psychological creatures"   Ibid., p. 11.

42   "an Old World of personal consciousness"   Ibid., p. 10.

42   "the mind's far continents"   Ibid., p. 84.

CHAPTER THREE: THE MAP MOGUL

51   "pitched fine art"   Hugh Kennedy, *Original Color* (New York: Nan A. Talese, 1996), p. 177.

55   "These Old Maps"   Karen Hube, "These Old Maps Offer You a New Way to Double Your Money," *Money,* vol. 26, no. 3 (March 1997): 172.

59   the Antiquarian Booksellers' Association of America
       drummed him   See Mark Singer's "Profiles: Wall Power," in
       New Yorker, vol. 63, no. 41 (November 30, 1987): 44–46ff. Some
       of the other information used in this chapter also comes from
       Singer's excellent article.

60   "I said, 'Graham, what are you doing?' "   Quoted in ibid.

61   reportedly sent a check for $8,000   See Associated Press story,
       "Rare Map of Houston, Missing Since '88, Is Returned," *Dallas
       Morning News* (June 4, 1996): 16D.

64   If you wanted to buy this volume in 1884   See chart in R. A.
       Skelton, *Maps: A Historical Survey of Their Study and Collecting* (Chi-
       cago: University of Chicago Press, 1972), p. 59. In addition to the
       prices mentioned here, the 1984 figure was supplied by Sotheby's.

68   "More than any one of the ancients"   Lloyd A. Brown, *The
       Story of Maps* (Boston: Little, Brown, 1949), p. 61.

69   "grinding persistence"   John Hale, *The Civilization of Europe
       in the Renaissance* (New York: Atheneum, 1994), pp. 193, 190.

69   "Please, if you love me"   Quoted in Nicholas A. Basbanes, *A
       Gentle Madness: Bibliophiles, Bibliomanes, and the Eternal Passion
       for Books* (New York: Henry Holt, 1995), p. 72.

70   "insatiable desire"   Ibid.

70   "rare, valuable, or merely strange objects"   Hale, *Civilization
       of Europe,* p. 530.

70   "caused an immediate and enormous stir"   Thomas Gold-
       stein, *Dawn of Modern Science: From the Ancient Greeks to the Re-
       naissance* (Boston: Houghton Mifflin, 1980), p. 22.

71   "Apart from the extravagant Bibles"   Lisa Jardine, *Worldly
       Goods: A New History of the Renaissance* (New York: Nan A.
       Talese, 1996), p. 205.

71   "The revival of Ptolemy"   Daniel J. Boorstin, *The Discoverers:*

A History of Man's Search to Know His World and Himself (New York: Random House, 1983), p. 152.

72   "toward the regions of India"   Passport issued by Spanish sovereigns, quoted in Samuel Eliot Morison, *The European Discovery of America: The Southern Voyages, A.D. 1492–1616* (New York: Oxford University Press, 1974), p. 43.

73   "were not housed according to their worth"   Quoted in John Addington Symonds, *Renaissance in Italy: The Revival of Learning,* vol. 2 (New York: Charles Scribner's Sons, 1907), p. 99.

73   "For him that steals"   Quoted in Alberto Manguel, *A History of Reading* (New York: Viking Press, 1996), p. 244.

74   Christie's conceded the volume had been stolen   See Susannah Herbert, "International: 1477 Ptolemy Atlas Stolen from Library," *Daily Telegraph* of London (November 7, 1997), as well as an unsigned Reuters story, "Stolen Rare Book by Ptolemy Recovered in London" (May 29, 1998).

76   nearly $800,000   This figure includes buyer's premiums and taxes.

77   computer financial crimes   See Douglas Pasternak and Bruce B. Auster, "Terrorism at the Touch of a Keyboard," *U.S. News & World Report,* vol. 125, no. 2 (July 13, 1998): 37.

CHAPTER FOUR: AN APPROACHING STORM

80   "The Spanish sailors"   Daniel J. Boorstin, *The Discoverers: A History of Man's Search to Know His World and Himself* (New York: Random House, 1983), p. 217.

82   "just wanted them"   Cynthia Requardt, text from briefing given to fellow rare books librarians during a panel on the Bland case, June 23, 1998.

82   Murders had risen nearly 9 percent   See Peter Hermann, "Violent Crime in Md. Rising," Baltimore *Sun* (December 30, 1995): 1B.

83   "We were advised"   Quoted in Frank D. Roylance and David Folkenflik, "Thief Cutting Rare Book at Peabody Was Let Go; FBI Seeks Man Linked Later to Similar Acts at Eight University Libraries," Baltimore *Sun* (December 14, 1995): 1A.

86   "Our goal"   Quoted in John Dorsey, "Auction of Peabody Books Draws Approval, Outrage," Baltimore *Sun* (May 28, 1989): 1F. The quotations from John Burgan, Regina Soria, and Arthur Gutman also come from this article.

90   "It put Baltimore on the world map"   Frank R. Shivers, Jr., "Visit Mount Vernon" brochure, sponsored by the Charles Street Association and Mount Vernon Cultural District.

90   "national treasure"   Brian Lewbart, spokesman for Downtown Partnership, quoted in Paul W. Valentine's "Washington Monument Reopened in Baltimore; Structure Has Been Closed Eight Years for Repair," *Washington Post* (December 5, 1992): C4.

91   upwards of $30,000   An exact price on the Mills atlas is difficult to pin down, since the book is so rare that it does not often change hands. This estimate was made by John Duncan, a retired history professor and owner of V. & J. Duncan Antique Maps and Prints in Savannah, Georgia.

93   "On December 7"   Posting on ExLibris, December 7, 1995.

Chapter Five: How to Make a Map, How to Take a Map

95   *"others have seen"*   Denis Wood with John Fels, *The Power of Maps* (New York: Guilford Press, 1992), p. 7.

95   "Progress in the science of cartography"   Lloyd A. Brown, *The Story of Maps* (Boston: Little, Brown, 1949), p. 18.

97   "world describers"   See Svetlana Alpers, "The Mapping Impulse in Dutch Art," in *Art and Cartography: Six Historical Essays,* ed. David Woodward (Chicago: University of Chicago Press, 1987), p. 59.

98   "maps enable us"   Quoted in ibid., p. 90.

98   copper plate for printing   Most of the material in this section is based on Coolie Verner's "Copperplate Printing," in *Five Centuries of Map Printing,* ed. David Woodward (Chicago: University of Chicago Press, 1975), pp. 51–75.

100   how long it took   See C. Koeman, *Joan Blaeu and His Grand Atlas: Introduction to the Facsimile Edition of Le Grand Atlas, 1663* (Amsterdam: Theatrum Orbis Terrarum, 1970), pp. 43–46.

100   "The planning involved"   Ibid., p. 43.

102   "The crossing of the border"   Avner Falk, "Border Symbolism," in *Maps from the Mind: Readings in Psychogeography,* ed. Howard F. Stein and William G. Niederland (Norman: University of Oklahoma Press, 1989), p. 145.

102   "The theological collection"   Michael H. Harris, *History of Libraries in the Western World,* 4th ed. (Lanham, Md.: Scarecrow Press, 1995), p. 8.

102   God would smite dead   2 Samuel 6:7.

103   "Some people seem to seek"   G. Raymond Babineau, "The Compulsive Border Crosser," *Psychiatry,* vol. 35 (August 1972): 281–290. Further quotations from Babineau also come from this article.

104   "Perhaps the most outstanding conclusion"   *The Warren Report: The Official Report on the Assassination of President John F.*

Kennedy, Associated Press, ed. (N.P.: Associated Press, 1964), pp. 160–161.

104 "Countless governments" Mark Monmonier, *Drawing the Line: Tales of Maps and Cartocontroversy* (New York: Henry Holt, 1995), p. 146.

CHAPTER SIX: THE INVISIBLE CRIME SPREE

107 he introduced the first modern ventilation system See James H. Bready, "Book and Authors," Baltimore *Sun* (July 17, 1949).

108 "If you get bitten by a flea" Quoted in Peter Young, "Lloyd to Assemble Historical Annapolis Data," Baltimore *Evening Sun* (November 30, 1960).

108 He delighted in recounting See Bready, "Books and Authors." The rough estimate of the number of books listed in Lloyd's bibliography is my own.

112 nineteen libraries In addition to the Peabody Library in Baltimore, the FBI reported that Bland stole materials from the following institutions: the American Antiquarian Society in Worcester, Massachusetts; the British Columbia Archives in Victoria; Brown University; Duke University; the Library of Virginia in Richmond; the New York State Library in Albany; Northwestern University; the University of British Columbia in Vancouver; the University of Chicago; the University of Delaware; the University of Florida; the University of North Carolina at Chapel Hill; the University of Rochester; the University of South Carolina; the University of Virginia; the University of Washington in Seattle; Washington University in St. Louis; and Wesleyan University in Middletown, Connecticut.

In addition, officials at the Newberry Library in Chicago told me that someone identifying himself as James Perry visited their reading rooms in 1994 but does not appear to have stolen anything—probably because the maps he examined had been stamped as property of the institution.

113   Learned Men of the Magic Library   See Michael H. Harris, *History of Libraries in the Western World,* 4th ed. (Lanham, Md.: Scarecrow Press, 1995), pp. 17–35. See also Alberto Manguel, *A History of Reading* (New York: Viking Press, 1996), pp. 187–199.

114   "war with the forces of oblivion"   Umberto Eco, *The Name of the Rose,* trans. William Weaver (New York: Harcourt Brace Jovanovich, 1983), p. 38.

114   "books are humanity in print"   Barbara W. Tuchman, "Excerpts of Barbara Tuchman's Lecture at Library of Congress," *Authors Guild Bulletin* (November–December 1979): 15–18.

125   returned by law enforcement officials   In addition to the Ogilby maps, two plates from a Mercator atlas were stolen from the University of Washington. Both were later recovered and returned by the FBI.

127   "poets and prose-writers"   Quoted in Luciano Canfora, *The Vanished Library,* trans. Martin Ryle (Berkeley and Los Angeles: University of California Press, 1989), p. 20.

128   "it is possible to sail"   Strabo, *The Geography of Strabo,* trans. Horace Leonard Jones, vol. 1 (Cambridge, Mass.: Harvard University Press, 1917), p. 433.

129   "Eratosthenes' measurement"   Norman J. W. Thrower, *Maps and Civilization: Cartography in Culture and Society,* 2d ed. (Chicago: University of Chicago Press, 1999), p. 21.

129   "distance ruled"   Hannah Arendt, *The Human Condition* (Chicago: University of Chicago Press, 1958), p. 250.

129 only 2,760 miles See chart in Samuel Eliot Morison, *Admiral of the Ocean Sea: A Life of Christopher Columbus* (Boston: Little, Brown, 1942), p. 68. Although Morison gives the figures in nautical miles, I have, for the sake of clarity, approximated them here in statute miles.

129 "had not the remotest idea" Samuel Eliot Morison, *The European Discovery of America: The Southern Voyages*, A.D. 1492–1616 (New York: Oxford University Press, 1974), p. 336.

129 "the shrinkage of space" Arendt, *Human Condition*, p. 250.

130 "will help to shrink the world" Frances Cairncross, *The Death of Distance: How the Communications Revolution Will Change Our Lives* (Boston: Harvard Business School Press, 1977), p. 279.

130 "In this modern age, very little remains" Quoted in Peter Whitfield, *New Found Lands: Maps in the History of Exploration* (New York: Routledge, 1998), p. 186.

131 "must thrill for the saddle" Theodore Roosevelt, *A Book-Lover's Holidays in the Open* (New York: Charles Scribner's Sons, 1916), p. vii.

CHAPTER SEVEN: A BRIEF HISTORY OF CARTOGRAPHIC CRIME

140 The man in the picture See John Goss, *The Mapmaker's Art: An Illustrated History of Cartography* (Skokie, Ill.: Rand McNally, 1993), pp. 141–148.

142 All cultures are thought to make maps See David Stea, James M. Blaut, and Jennifer Stephens, "Mapping as a Cultural Universal," in *The Construction of Cognitive Maps*, ed. Juval Portugali (Boston: Kluwer, 1996), pp. 1–16.

142 "In the Roman Empire" Daniel J. Boorstin, *The Discoverers: A*

History of Man's Search to Know His World and Himself (New York: Random House, 1983), p. 269.

142 locked in the innermost vaults   See Lloyd A. Brown, *The Story of Maps* (Boston: Little, Brown, 1949), pp. 8–9.

143 having failed to sell Portugal's King John II   In fact, the king may have been up to some thievery himself—with Columbus as his victim. Bartolomé de Las Casas wrote that "the King of Portugal wormed more and more information out of Christopher Columbus and [then] . . . he secretly equipped a caravel with Portuguese sailors and set it on the ocean to follow the route Columbus had charted for himself." A storm, however, forced the caravel back to Lisbon. Realizing he had "been the object of a double deal," Columbus "decided to leave Lisbon and come to Castile," wrote Las Casas. See Bartolomé de Las Casas, *History of the Indies,* trans. and ed. Andree Collard (New York: Harper & Row, 1971), p. 23.

143 "fearing the king would send"   Quoted in John Noble Wilford, *The Mysterious History of Columbus: An Exploration of the Man, the Myth, the Legacy* (New York: Alfred A. Knopf, 1991), p. 84.

143 "Bartholomeo prepared to join"   Lisa Jardine, *Worldly Goods: A New History of the Renaissance* (New York: Nan A. Talese, 1996), pp. 300–301.

145 the Italian secret agent   Ibid., pp. 107–108.

146 "brought with him a well-painted globe"   Quoted in Samuel Eliot Morison, *The European Discovery of America: The Southern Voyages,* A.D. *1492–1616* (New York: Oxford University Press, 1974), p. 319.

146 "In making the globe"   Jardine, *Worldly Goods,* p. 299.

146   Jorge Reinel   See Edouard Roditi's discussion of the Behaim-Reinel question in *Magellan of the Pacific* (London: Faber and Faber, 1972), pp. 103–111 and 129–136. See also Simon Berthon and Andrew Robinson, *The Shape of the World* (London: George Philip, 1991), p. 78.

147   "He knew where to sail"   Quoted in Morison, *European Discovery*, p. 381.

148   "The Spanish . . . kept their official charts"   Boorstin, *Discoverers*, pp. 267–268.

148   "master thief of the unknown world"   Quoted in John H. Parry, "Drake and the World Encompassed," in *Sir Francis Drake and the Famous Voyage, 1577–1580: Essays Commemorating the Quadricentennial of Drake's Circumnavigation of the Earth*, ed. Norman J. W. Thrower (Berkeley and Los Angeles: University of California Press, 1984), p. 2.

149   "prized these greatly"   Quoted in Alexander McKee, *The Queen's Corsair: Drake's Journey of Circumnavigation, 1577–1580* (New York: Stein & Day, 1978), p. 216.

149   "exactly what he required"   Ibid.

149   "Drake's smooth passage"   John Hampden, Introduction to *Francis Drake: Privateer*, ed. John Hampden (Tuscaloosa: University of Alabama Press, 1972), p. 16.

149   "In the sixteenth century"   Brown, *Story of Maps*, p. 9.

150   "a great Book full of Sea-Charts"   Quoted in *A Buccaneer's Atlas: Basil Ringrose's South Sea Waggoner*, ed. Derek Howse and Norman J. W. Thrower (Berkeley and Los Angeles: University of California Press, 1992), p. 22.

150   "The Spaniards cried"   Quoted in ibid., p. 22.

150   "royal influence"   Ibid., p. 1.

151   "the plans of some fortified places"   Quoted in Peter Barber, "Espionage!" in *Tales from the Map Room: Fact and Fiction About Maps and Their Makers*, ed. Peter Barber and Christopher Board (London: BBC Books, 1993), pp. 90–91.

151   the Battle of the Brandywine   See G.J.A. O'Toole, *Honorable Treachery: A History of U.S. Intelligence, Espionage, and Covert Action from the American Revolution to the CIA* (New York: Atlantic Monthly Press, 1991), p. 42.

151   "Spies directed by Washington"   J. B. Harley, "The Map User in the Revolution," in *Mapping the American Revolutionary War*, ed. J. B. Harley, Barbara Bartz Petchenik, and Lawrence W. Towner (Chicago: University of Chicago Press, 1978), p. 104.

151   "men were . . . prepared to risk their lives"   Ibid., p. 105.

151   "brought in with me"   Quoted in ibid., p. 103.

152   "knew no more about the [local] topography"   Quoted in Christopher Nelson, *Mapping the Civil War: Featuring Rare Maps from the Library of Congress* (Washington, D.C.: Starwood, 1992), p. 9.

152   "I *know* that the principal northern papers"   Quoted in O'Toole, *Honorable Treachery*, p. 132.

153   "There was no doubt"   Jay Robert Nash, *Spies: A Narrative Encyclopedia of Dirty Tricks and Double Dealing from Biblical Times to the Present* (New York: M. Evans, 1997), p. 251.

153   "Securing the blueprint"   Quoted in ibid., p. 54.

154   the largest and most spectacular escape   See John Hammond Moore's fine book on this episode, *The Faustball Tunnel: German POWs in America and Their Great Escape* (New York: Random House, 1978).

155   "stood traditional cartography on its ear"   Stephen S. Hall,

Mapping the Next Millennium: The Discovery of New Geographies (New York: Random House, 1992), p. 67.

157   no substitute for a good map   Some subsequent news reports suggested that the embassy bombing was no accident, after all. Quoting "senior U.S. and European military sources," the London *Observer* declared that the embassy was purposely targeted because it had been serving as a rebroadcast station for the Yugoslavian army. As one source at the U.S. National Imagery and Mapping Agency told the *Observer,* the "wrong map" story is "a damned lie." See John Sweeney, Jens Holsoe, and Ed Vulliamy, "Revealed: NATO Bombed Chinese Deliberately," London *Observer* (October 17, 1999): I. See also Joel Bleifuss, "A Tragic Mistake?," *In These Times,* vol. 24, no. I (December 12, 1999): 2–3.

157   a Michigan man named Bill Stewart   See Jack Lessenberry, "Making a Federal Case of It," *Detroit Metro Times* (August 9–15, 1995). A number of people protested Stewart's conviction, arguing that while the material he attempted to sell was technically restricted, it was neither secret nor particularly sensitive. As Lessenberry observed, *National Geographic* magazine had just published "even better maps of the same area."

157   a couple of priests   See unsigned article, "Thieves Steal Valuable Books from Yale Library," *Yale Alumni Magazine,* vol. 36, no. 8 (May 1973): 30. See also John Mongillo, Jr., and Jack Millea, "Two 'Priests' Are Indicted in Theft of Yale Volumes," *New Haven Register* (March 17, 1973): 1–2, as well as Dan Collins and John Mongillo, Jr., "Two Hundred Rare Volumes Missing at Yale," *New Haven Register* (March 18, 1973): 1–2A. I also consulted court records for this section.

158   "Avoid, as you would the plague"   St. Jerome, "Letter 52," *Select Letters of St. Jerome,* trans. F. A. Wright, eds. T. E. Page, E. Capps, and W.H.D. Rouse (New York: G. P. Putnam's Sons, 1933), p. 201.

158   unusual rogues' gallery   My list of modern-day cartographic criminals is not comprehensive, of course. Among the omissions are two notorious U.S. library crooks, Stephen Carrie Blumberg and James Shinn, neither of whom specialized in maps per se but both of whom had a fondness for travel literature. I've also excluded European thieves like Ian Hart, who during the early 1980s stole a fortune in old maps and atlases from the Bodleian Library at Oxford by hiding them in his trousers.

158   "was regarded with that special undergraduate awe"   Walt Philbin, "American Dream Now a Nightmare for Tulane Prof," New Orleans *States-Item* (January 13, 1979): A-6.

159   "I was there, I was tempted"   Ibid.

159   "I indeed ruined my life and career"   Quoted in unsigned story, "Tulane Prof Sentenced to One Year," New Orleans *States-Item* (January 8, 1979).

159   "the standard reference"   Unsigned, "Trade Reviews," *AB Bookman's Weekly,* vol. 85, no. 24 (June 11, 1990): 2524–2525.

159   "few great counterfeiters"   Lynn Glaser, *Counterfeiting in America: The History of an American Way to Wealth* (New York: Clarkson N. Potter, 1968), p. 118.

160   In July 1974 Glaser was arrested   See Richard Yurko, "Library Theft Disclosed; Prime Suspect Arraigned," *The Dartmouth* (July 9, 1974): I, 6. In preparing this section, I also consulted an unsigned Associated Press report, "Antique Document Dealer

Is Sentenced for Thefts of Rare Maps from 'U'," in the Min-
neapolis *Tribune* (November 25, 1982), as well as court documents.

160    $300,000 and $100,000   In May 1999, books containing the
1613 and 1632 maps were auctioned for $398,500 and $134,500,
respectively. Selby Kiffer of the rare books and manuscripts department at Sotheby's informed me that the individual Champlain maps accounted for the overwhelming part of each
book's value.

161   "For twenty-five years I have been handling"   Lynn Glaser,
America on Paper (Philadelphia: Associated Antiquaries, 1989),
p. 3.

161   wearing surgical gloves   See Beverly Goldberg, "Judge to Re-
consider Map Thief's Probation Sentence," *American Libraries*,
vol. 23, no. 6 (June 1992): 429–431.

161   "Mr. Straight"   See Joe Earle, "Ex-UGA Librarian Described
as 'Mr. Straight,' " *Atlanta Journal and Constitution* (January 21,
1987): B-1. I also consulted a number of other *Atlanta Journal
and Constitution* and *Athens Daily News/Banner-Herald* stories
for this section, as well as Nicholas A. Basbanes's account in *A
Gentle Madness: Bibliophiles, Bibliomanes, and the Eternal Passion
for Books* (New York: Henry Holt, 1995), pp. 488–490.

162   as much as $600,000   This estimate was provided by Selby
Kiffer at Sotheby's.

162   "a disgrace"   Quoted in Associated Press story, "Texas Legisla-
ture Considers King Holiday" (May 2, 1985). See also David Streitfeld, "Dealer Held in Library of Congress Theft," *Washington
Post* (March 13, 1992): F2; as well as Streitfeld, "Book Thief Sentenced to Six Months," *Washington Post* (October 1, 1992): C4.

163 "a rising star" Ric Kahn, "Two Faces of Serial Thief Bared in N.H.," *Boston Globe* (January 16, 1998): A1.

163 "He only feels comfortable" Defense attorney Stephen Jeffco, quoted in ibid. I also consulted a number of other *Boston Globe, Concord Monitor,* and Manchester *Union-Leader* stories for this section, as well as court and law-enforcement records.

165 "suspected of delivering weaponry" Randy Ellis and John Parker, "Man in Dutch Prison Not Tied to City Blast, Authorities Say," *Oklahoman* (December 30, 1995).

165 "I was involved in it" Quoted in Associated Press story, "American Held in Netherlands Denies Bombing Link," in *Oklahoman* (January 12, 1996).

165 "Thirty Questions About Oklahoma City" See Big Sky Patriot website, June 5, 1997.

167 Johnny Jenkins "Rare Book and Manuscript Thefts," *AB Bookman's Weekly,* vol. 69, no. 7 (February 15, 1982): 1224–1239.

168 "I suppose he was a man" Calvin Trillin, "American Chronicles: Knowing Johnny Jenkins," *New Yorker,* vol. 65, no. 37 (October 30, 1989): 79–97.

168 "[He and his assistant] have orders" Quoted in Berthon and Robinson, *Shape of the World,* p. 79.

172 "failed to mention" Katherine S. Van Eerde, *John Ogilby and the Taste of His Times* (Folkestone, England: Wm. Dawson & Sons, 1976), p. 108.

172 "made a special plea" Brown, *Story of Maps,* p. 169.

173 "made ungenerous use" Letter from Jefferson to Humboldt, December 6, 1813, in *The Journals of Zebulon Montgomery Pike: With Letters and Related Documents,* vol. 2, ed. Donald Jackson (Norman: University of Oklahoma Press, 1966), p. 387. Inter-

estingly, Jefferson made no such excuses for the British cartographer Aaron Arrowsmith, who apparently also borrowed
from Humboldt. "That . . . Arrowsmith should have stolen
your map of Mexico," Jefferson wrote, "was in the piratical
spirit of the country."

174   "Grand Peak"   Pike, *Journals,* vol. 1, p. 350.

174   "the highest altitude ever attained"   Douglas Botting, *Humboldt and the Cosmos* (New York: Harper & Row, 1973), p. 155.
Although he climbed to a record-breaking height of 18,893
feet above sea level, Humboldt stopped some 1,800 feet short
of Mount Chimborazo's summit.

174   "The study of maps"   Quoted in Helmut de Terra's *Humboldt: The Life and Times of Alexander von Humboldt, 1769–1859*
(New York: Alfred A. Knopf, 1955), p. 17.

174   "a truly magnificent cartographic achievement"   Carl I.
Wheat, *Mapping the Transmississippi West, 1540–1861,* vol. 1:
The Spanish Entrada to the Louisiana Purchase, 1540–1804
(San Francisco: Institute of Historical Cartography, 1957),
p. 132.

174   "a great variety of data"   Quoted in ibid., p. 134.

177   firsthand information gathered by French explorers   This is
the same Delisle map mentioned in Chapter Ten.

180   *"haunted by the feeling"*   Franz Kafka, *The Castle,* trans. Willa
and Edwin Muir (New York: Schocken Books, 1954), p. 54.

Chapter Eight: Pathfinding

183   "singularly unfavorable to travel"   John Charles Frémont, *Report of the Exploring Expedition to the Rocky Mountains* (1845;
reprint, Ann Arbor, Mich.: University Microfilms, 1966), p. 213.

184   "did little of importance"   Bernard DeVoto, *The Year of Decision: 1846* (Boston: Houghton Mifflin, 1942), p. 39.

184   "The map . . . radically and permanently altered"   Carl I. Wheat, *Mapping the Transmississippi West, 1540–1861*, vol. 2: From Lewis and Clark to Frémont, 1804–1845 (San Francisco: Institute of Historical Cartography, 1958), p. 199.

184   "fixing on a small sheet"   Quoted in Seymour I. Schwartz and Ralph E. Ehrenberg, *The Mapping of America* (New York: Harry N. Abrams, 1980), p. 262.

186   At 10:55 P.M.   Police records, Bayonne, N.J.

186   the boy's birth certificate   Birth records on file with the Marion County, Ind., Health Department.

187   "the allegations of the complaint"   Marion Superior Court records from April 14, 1954.

187   "was both verbally and physically abusive"   Paul R. Thomson, Jr., and James R. Creekmore, "Defendant's Sentencing Memorandum," *United States of America vs. Gilbert Joseph Bland*, U.S. District Court, Charlottesville, Va., October 7, 1996.

188   his personal effects   Police records, Bayonne, N.J.

191   "loftiest peak of the Rocky Mountains"   Frémont, *Report of the Expedition to the Rockies*, p. 70.

191   "stupid" and "foolhardy"   Charles Preuss, *Exploring with Frémont: The Private Diaries of Charles Preuss, Cartographer for John C. Frémont on His First, Second, and Fourth Expeditions to the Far West*, trans. and ed. Erwin G. and Elisabeth K. Gudde (Norman: University of Oklahoma Press, 1958), p. 55.

192   "dancing master"   John Moring, *Men with Sand: Great Explorers of the North American West* (Helena, Mont.: TwoDot, 1998), p. 166.

192   "occasional upholstering"   Andrew Rolle, *John Charles Frémont: Character as Destiny* (Norman: University of Oklahoma Press, 1991), p. 1.

192   "No one ever knew why"   Moring, *Men with Sand*, p. 166.

192   "psychiatric techniques"   Rolle, *John Charles Frémont*, p. xiv.

192   "fragmented sense of selfhood"   Ibid., p. 281.

192   "Because Frémont's formative years"   Ibid.

192   "In fact, even while on his expeditions"   Ibid., p. 278.

193   "reckless impetuosity"   Allan Nevins, *Frémont: The West's Greatest Adventurer*, vol. 1 (New York: Harper & Brothers, 1928), p. 114.

194   "To go back was impossible"   Frémont, *Report of the Expedition to the Rockies*, pp. 74–75.

195   "flushed with success, and familiar with the danger"   Ibid., p. 75.

196   "Bereft of two nurturing parents"   Rolle, *John Charles Frémont*, p. 281.

197   "habitual irregularity and incorrigible negligence"   Quoted in ibid., p. 9.

197   "mutiny, disobedience, and conduct prejudicial"   Quoted in Moring, *Men with Sand*, p. 179.

197   "of strange scenes and occurrences"   John Charles Frémont, *Narratives of Exploration and Adventure*, ed. Allan Nevins (New York: Longmans, Green, 1956), p. 29.

197   "There was a map of Vietnam"   Michael Herr, *Dispatches* (New York: Alfred A. Knopf, 1977), p. 3.

199   "has a pattern of problems"   Transcript of sentencing hearing in *United States of America vs. Gilbert Joseph Bland*, U.S. District Court, Charlottesville, Va., December 9, 1996.

201   massage parlor for American soldiers   See Frances FitzGerald, *Fire in the Lake: The Vietnamese and the Americans in Vietnam* (New York: Atlantic Monthly Press, 1972), p. 351.

204   "held its own dangers and terrors"   John D. Bergen, *Military Communications: A Test for Technology* (Washington, D.C.: Center of Military History, 1986), p. 340.

204   the invention of maps   See G. Malcolm Lewis, "The Origins of Cartography," in *The History of Cartography,* vol. I: Cartography in Prehistoric, Ancient, and Medieval Europe and the Mediterranean, ed. J. B. Harley and David Woodward (Chicago: University of Chicago Press, 1987), pp. 50–53.

206   "trying all of the apartment doors"   Police records, Ridgefield Park, N.J.

207   "a land rich in gold"   Quoted in Stephen Clissold, *The Seven Cities of Cíbola* (London: Eyre & Spottiswoode, 1961), pp. 101–102.

208   "It must exist"   Bernard DeVoto, *The Course of Empire* (Boston: Houghton Mifflin, 1952), p. 63.

208   "it had become . . . a mighty stream"   Carl I. Wheat, *Mapping the Transmississippi West, 1540–1861,* vol. 1: The Spanish Entrada to the Louisiana Purchase, 1540–1804 (San Francisco: Institute of Historical Cartography, 1957), pp. 140–141.

209   "the existence of a great river"   Frémont, *Report of the Expedition to the Rockies,* p. 196.

209   "with every stream . . . to see the great Buenaventura"   Ibid., p. 219.

209   "appallingly foolhardy"   Nevins, *Frémont,* p. 168.

211   "nervous disorder"   Jail docket, Bergen County Sheriff's Office, July 6, 1971.

211   "denie[d] illnesses"   Jail docket, Bergen County Sheriff's Office, January 21, 1971.

212   "going crazy"   Gilbert Bland, letter to Gov. William T. Cahill, September 29, 1972. Records of Gov. William T. Cahill, New Jersey State Archives.

212   a warrant for his arrest   Bench warrant issued in Sussex County, N.J., June 22, 1973.

213   "give consideration to retaining legal counsel"   Gov. William T. Cahill, letter to Gilbert Bland, October 5, 1972. Cahill mistakenly spelled the name *Blond*.

213   " 'snitching' as they call it"   Gilbert Bland, letter to U.S. District Judge Ben Krentzman, May 10, 1976.

214   "I have no intention"   Gilbert Bland, letter of unknown date to U.S. District Judge Ben Krentzman; received by Krentzman, April 6, 1977.

215   "Frémont's march south"   John Noble Wilford, *The Mapmakers* (New York: Alfred A. Knopf, 1981), p. 199.

215   "no hesitation in asserting"   *The Journals of Zebulon Montgomery Pike: With Letters and Related Documents,* vol. 2, ed. Donald Jackson (Norman: University of Oklahoma Press, 1966), pp. 26–27.

CHAPTER NINE: THE WATERS OF PARADISE

217   "a spring of running water"   Quoted in Samuel Eliot Morison, *The European Discovery of America: The Southern Voyages,* A.D. *1492–1616* (New York: Oxford University Press, 1974), p. 504.

217   "noble and beautiful well"   *The Travels of Sir John Mandeville,* trans. C.W.R.D. Moseley (Harmondsworth, England: Penguin Books, 1983), p. 123.

218   *el enflaquecimiento del sexo*   See Morison, *European Discovery of America,* p. 503.

218   lowest proportions of locally born citizens   In the 1990 U.S. Census, Florida ranked dead last for its percentage of residents born in-state. And, according to Census Bureau statistics, Florida was the tenth fastest-growing state in the country between 1990 and 1998.

219   "His interest in maps"   James R. Creekmore, letter to author, October 30, 1996. This letter included a "Statement Concerning Mr. Gilbert Bland," responding to a detailed list of questions I had sent to the map thief through his attorneys. Although the statement was only four paragraphs long—less than one full page—and contained almost no direct answers, it was the only response Bland would ever make to my inquiries about his life and motives.

219   owned by Karen Bland   Records of Maryland Department of Assessment and Taxation, Corporate Division.

219   "major customers"   Paul R. Thomson, Jr., and James R. Creekmore, "Defendant's Objections to Presentence Investigation Report," *United States of America vs. Gilbert Joseph Bland,* Charlottesville, Va., September 16, 1996.

220   "no longer . . . economically feasible"   Transcript of sentencing hearing in *United States of America vs. Gilbert Joseph Bland,* U.S. District Court, Charlottesville, Va., December 9, 1996.

221   "everyplace looks like noplace"   James Howard Kunstler, *The Geography of Nowhere: The Rise and Decline of America's Man-Made Landscape* (New York: Simon & Schuster, 1993), p. 131.

232   "For God doth know"   Genesis 3:5.

232   "eastward in Eden"   Genesis 2:8.

232   an orchard surrounded by a wall   See Jean Delumeau, *History of Paradise: The Garden of Eden in Myth and Tradition,* trans. Matthew O'Connell (New York: Continuum, 1995), p. 4.

233   "wall of fire"   Quoted in ibid., p. 44.

233   "great evidence of the earthly Paradise"   Christopher Columbus, "Narrative of the Third Voyage," in *The Four Voyages of Christopher Columbus,* trans. J. M. Cohen (New York: Penguin, 1969), pp. 220–222.

233   "the flood, and other accidents of time"   Walter Raleigh, *The History of the World,* book one (1614; reprint, London: printed for G. Conyers, et al., 1736), p. 23.

234   "shaped . . . when opened"   Quoted in Simon Berthon and Andrew Robinson, *The Shape of the World* (London: George Philip, 1991), pp. 57–58.

235   "See you later"   See Frank D. Roylance's account, "Fla. Man Is Sought in Book Cuttings: He and Wife Abruptly Close Map Shop," in *Baltimore Sun* (December 16, 1995): 1A.

236   declared Chapter Seven bankruptcy   Papers filed in U.S. Bankruptcy Court, Southern District of Florida, Fort Lauderdale Division, November 3, 1995.

CHAPTER TEN: THE JOY OF DISCOVERY

239   "I discovered"   Christopher Columbus, "The Barcelona Letter of 1493," trans. Lucia Graves, in Mauricio Obregón, ed., *The Columbus Papers: The Barcelona Letter of 1493, the Landfall Controversy, and the Indian Guides* (New York: Macmillan, 1991), pp. 65–69. All further quotations from the letter come from the Graves translation, with one exception: I use Felipe

Fernández-Armesto's choice of wording for the phrase "the conquest of what appears impossible."

241   *"He was charmed"*   Gianni Granzotto, *Christopher Columbus,* trans. Stephen Sartarelli (Garden City, N.Y.: Doubleday, 1985), p. 34.

244   OLD MAP POX   This poster was created by the map dealer F. J. Manasek.

252   "the first map of the whole world"   Peter Whitfield, *The Image of the World: Twenty Centuries of World Maps* (San Francisco: Pomegranate Artbooks, 1994), p. 50.

253   "chanced to notice a small copper globe"   Henry Stevens, *Recollections of Mr. James Lenox of New York and the Formation of His Library* (London: Henry Stevens & Son, 1886), p. 141.

254   "the final thrill"   Walter Benjamin, "Unpacking My Library: A Talk About Book Collecting," in *Illuminations,* trans. Harry Zohn, ed. Hannah Arendt (New York: Harcourt, Brace & World, 1968), p. 60.

255   "I have not a hair upon me"   Christopher Columbus, "Letter of Columbus to Their Majesties," in *Select Documents Illustrating the Four Voyages of Christopher Columbus,* trans. and ed. Cecil Jane (London: Hakluyt Society, 1933), pp. 108–110. The other Columbus quotations in this paragraph are from the same letter.

255   *"Almost anyone . . . would rest content"*   Felipe Fernández-Armesto, *Columbus* (New York: Oxford University Press, 1991), p. 192.

257   "search—successful or not"   Werner Muensterberger, *Collecting: An Unruly Passion* (Princeton, N.J.: Princeton University Press, 1994), p. 162.

258   "There is reason to believe"   Ibid., pp. 10, 13.

259   "The quest is never-ending"   Ibid., p. 162.

259   "an all-consuming passion"   Ibid., p. 6.

260   the notorious Don Vincente   See Nicholas A. Basbanes, *A Gentle Madness: Bibliophiles, Bibliomanes, and the Eternal Passion for Books* (New York: Henry Holt, 1995), pp. 33–34.

262   the story of the Unknown Pilot   See Samuel Eliot Morison's overview in *Admiral of the Ocean Sea: A Life of Christopher Columbus* (Boston: Little, Brown, 1942), pp. 61–63, as well as Gronzotto's account in *Christopher Columbus*, pp. 45–47.

262   "a protective figure"   Joseph Campbell, *The Hero with a Thousand Faces*, 2d ed. (Princeton, N.J.: Princeton University Press, 1968), pp. 69, 71.

263   "power-imbued fetish[es]"   Muensterberger, *Collecting*, p. 54.

263   "set [his] mind ablaze"   Quoted in Granzotto, *Christopher Columbus*, p. 57.

263   "still more inflamed"   Quoted in John Noble Wilford, *The Mysterious History of Columbus: An Exploration of the Man, the Myth, the Legacy* (New York: Alfred A. Knopf, 1991), p. 76.

263   "Some, to beautify their Halls"   Quoted in John Goss, *The Mapmaker's Art: An Illustrated History of Cartography* (Skokie, Ill.: Rand McNally, 1993), p. 344.

265   "As Freud has shown"   Campbell, *Hero with a Thousand Faces*, p. 51.

270   "*Something hidden. Go and find it*"   Rudyard Kipling, "The Explorer," in *Complete Verse* (London: Kyle Cathie, 1990), pp. 86–88.

CHAPTER ELEVEN: THE ISLAND OF LOST MAPS

273   El Wakwak   See Raymond H. Ramsay, *No Longer on the Map: Discovering Places That Never Were* (New York: Viking Press, 1972), p. 113.

273   "sirens abound"   Quoted in William G. Niederland's essay
        "The Pre-Renaissance Image of the World and the Discovery
        of America," in *Maps from the Mind: Readings in Psychogeogra-*
        phy, ed. Howard F. Stein and William G. Niederland (Norman:
        University of Oklahoma Press, 1989), p. 111.

274   "men who murdered their fathers"   Quoted in ibid., p. 111.

274   "produces all crops and all fruits"   Quoted in Jean Delumeau,
        History of Paradise: The Garden of Eden in Myth and Tradition,
        trans. Matthew O'Connell (New York: Continuum, 1995), p. 100.

274   "there are trees that yield birds"   Quoted in ibid., p. 103.

274   "have tails like animals"   Quoted in E. G. Ravenstein, *Martin*
        Behaim: His Life and His Globe (London: George Philip & Son,
        1908), p. 88.

274   "One of these islands [is] inhabited by men only"   Quoted in
        ibid., p. 105.

274   Drogeo   The Drogeo and Icaria legends stem from Nicolò
        Zeno's apocryphal sixteenth-century account of his ancestors'
        purported adventures. See Nicolò Zeno, *The Voyages of the*
        Venetian Brothers, Nicolò & Antonio Zeno, to the Northern Seas in
        the XIVth Century, ed. and trans. Richard Henry Major (Lon-
        don: Hakluyt Society, 1873), pp. 21–34. See also William H.
        Babcock, *Legendary Islands of the Atlantic: A Study in Medieval*
        Geography (New York: American Geographical Society, 1922),
        pp. 124–142, as well as Ramsay, *No Longer on the Map,* pp.
        53–76. Ramsay also covers the St. Brendan legend, pp. 77–85.

275   "full of men agrieving and lamenting"   Quoted in Howard
        Rollin Patch, *The Other World: According to the Descriptions in*
        Medieval Literature (Cambridge, Mass.: Harvard University
        Press, 1950), p. 35. In addition to Patch, information on Celtic
        island lore comes from Donald S. Johnson, *Phantom Islands of*

the Atlantic: The Legends of Seven Lands That Never Were, rev. ed. (New York: Walker, 1996), Ramsay, *No Longer on the Map,* and John Kirtland Wright, *The Geographical Lore of the Time of the Crusades: A Study in the History of Medieval Science and Tradition in Western Europe* (New York: American Geographical Society, 1925).

275 "a bird of monstrous size"   *Tales from the Thousand and One Nights,* trans. N. J. Dawood (New York: Penguin, 1973), p. 124.

275 Island of Jewels   See Joseph Campbell, *The Hero with a Thousand Faces,* 2d ed. (Princeton, N.J.: Princeton University Press, 1968), pp. 114–115.

275 "full of noises"   William Shakespeare, *The Tempest,* act III, sc. 2, lines 133–134.

275 the tale of Maushope   See Seon and Robert Manley's description in *Islands: Their Lives, Legends, and Lore* (Philadelphia: Chilton, 1970), pp. 18–21.

275 "where all the four seasons"   J. M. Barrie, *Peter Pan,* act II, sc. 1, lines 37–38.

275 "way west of Sumatra"   Dialogue from *King Kong,* screenplay by James Creelman and Ruth Rose, 1933.

276 "forested slopes were wreathed"   Michael Crichton, *Jurassic Park* (New York: Alfred A. Knopf, 1990), p. 79.

277 "misery acquaints a man"   Shakespeare, *Tempest,* act II, sc. 2, lines 40–41.

277 "a soul or a life-force"   Werner Muensterberger, *Collecting: An Unruly Passion* (Princeton, N.J.: Princeton University Press, 1994), p. 55.

277 "the relationship between collector and dealer"   Ibid., p. 159.

282 as much as half a million dollars   No official dollar estimate for the maps exists. This is a best-guess figure, based on my

conversations with several map experts and law enforcement officials familiar with the case.

282　"recovered, unharmed"　News release, U.S. Attorney's Office, Western District of Virginia, March 1, 1996.

285　"all possibility of deliverance"　Daniel Defoe, *Robinson Crusoe,* ed. Angus Ross (1719; reprint, Harmondsworth, England: Penguin, 1965), p. 112.

287　"wild ideas"　Ibid., p. 162. Further Defoe quotations in this chapter also come from the Penguin edition, pp. 162–165.

Chapter Twelve: Eldorado

289　Great Indian Trading Path　See Douglas L. Rights, "The Trading Path to the Indians," *North Carolina Historical Review,* vol. 8, no. 4 (October 1931): 403–426. See also Douglas Summers Brown's chapter on the path in *The Catawba Indians: The People of the River* (Columbia: University of South Carolina Press, 1966), pp. 69–100.

291　an Indian village　Some experts have argued that the forerunner of present-day Hillsborough is marked "Oenock" on the Ogilby-Moxon map. But R. P. Stephen Davis, Jr., a University of North Carolina research archaeologist who is excavating Indian settlements near downtown Hillsborough, told me that he believes the site is more likely to be a place Ogilby recorded as "Sabor."

291　"covetous and thievish"　John Lederer, "The First Expedition, From the head of the Pemaeoncock, alias York-River (due West) to the top of the Apalataean Mountains," in *The Discoveries of John Lederer,* ed. William P. Cumming (Charlottesville: University of Virginia Press, 1958), p. 27.

293   "the great and Golden Citie"   This phrase comes from the
       subtitle of Raleigh's book, *The Discoverie of the Large, Rich and
       Bewtiful Empyre of Guiana, with a relation of the great and Golden
       Citie of Manoa (which the Spanyards call El Dorado),* published in
       1596.

293   the first explorer known to have put Manoa   See Raymond
       H. Ramsay's discussion in *No Longer on the Map: Discovering
       Places That Never Were* (New York: Viking Press, 1972), pp.
       17–18.

294   "a man of many characters"   Robert Silverberg, *The Golden
       Dream: Seekers of El Dorado* (Athens: Ohio University Press,
       1996), p. 307.

294   "There are many possible readings"   Charles Nicholl, *The
       Creature in the Map: A Journey to El Dorado* (New York: William
       Morrow, 1995), p. 23.

294   "the graves have not beene opened"   Walter Raleigh, *The Dis-
       coverie of the Large, Rich and Bewtiful Empyre of Guiana,* ed. Neil
       L. Whitehead (Norman: University of Oklahoma Press, 1997),
       p. 196.

295   "the deare crossing in every path"   Ibid., p. 176.

297   80 percent in fifty years   See Mark Warhus's discussion in *An-
       other America: Native American Maps and the History of Our Land*
       (New York: St. Martin's Press, 1997), p. 80.

298   "Indigenous Americans communicated information"   Mark
       Monmonier, *Drawing the Line: Tales of Maps and Cartocontro-
       versy* (New York: Henry Holt, 1995), p. 107.

298   renaming perhaps half of the seven hundred thousand towns
       and cities   See Derek Nelson's discussion in *Off the Map: The
       Curious History of Place Names* (New York: Kodansha Interna-
       tional, 1997), p. 113.

300   "there is only the journey"   Nicholl, *Creature in the Map*, p. 11.

300   like so many dreamers, desperadoes, and idiots   Much of my background material for this paragraph comes from *The Search for El Dorado*, series ed. Dale M. Brown (Alexandria, Va.: Time-Life Books, 1994), pp. 7–34.

301   "The reports are false"   Quoted in Nicholl, *Creature in the Map*, p. 28.

301   "gallant knight"   Edgar Allan Poe, "Eldorado," in *Edgar Allan Poe: Sixty-seven Tales* (New York: Gramercy Books, 1990), p. 752.

Chapter Thirteen: Mr. Bland, I Presume

305   "I have taken a solemn, enduring oath"   Henry Morton Stanley, *How I Found Livingstone: Travels, Adventures, and Discoveries in Central Africa* (New York: Charles Scribner's Sons, 1913), pp. 308–309.

306   "fevers without number"   Ibid., p. 309.

307   "no theft nor sycophancy"   Letter quoted in Jean Delumeau, *History of Paradise: The Garden of Eden in Myth and Tradition*, trans. Matthew O'Connell (New York: Continuum, 1995), p. 76. This letter—written to the Byzantine emperor by someone claiming to be Prester John, around 1165—was widely circulated. "No one in the Middle Ages doubted its authenticity," wrote Delumeau.

307   "the Lost-Boy Complex"   See Eric Leed's chapter on the subject in *Shores of Discovery: How Expeditionaries Have Constructed the World* (New York: Basic Books, 1995), pp. 198–230.

307   more than twenty expeditions   It is interesting that the man who backed perhaps the most famous of these expeditions

was George Peabody, founder of that great library in Baltimore. According to Leed, the philanthropist underwrote Elisha Kent Kane's 1853 search for Franklin. A bay off the north of Greenland was later named Peabody Bay.

307   "The Franklin affair was the greatest disaster"   Peter Whitfield, *New Found Lands: Maps in the History of Exploration* (New York: Routledge, 1998), p. 181.

308   "I . . . begin to think myself somebody"   Quoted in John Bierman, *Dark Safari: The Life Behind the Legend of Henry Morton Stanley* (New York: Alfred A. Knopf, 1990), p. 118.

309   Dutch master Jan Vermeer   See James A. Welu, "Vermeer: His Cartographic Sources," *Art Bulletin,* vol. 57, no. 4 (December 1975): 529–547.

309   *"In thy face I see"*   William Shakespeare, *Henry VI, Part II,* act III, sc. 1, lines 202–203.

310   "I found myself gazing at him"   Stanley, *How I Found Livingstone,* p. 413.

310   "vent [his] joy"   Ibid., p. 411.

311   had trouble concentrating   Gilbert Bland, letter to U.S. District Court Judge James H. Michael, Jr., April 16, 1996.

312   "pattern of problems"   Transcript of sentencing hearing in *United States of America vs. Gilbert Joseph Bland,* U.S. District Court, Charlottesville, Va., December 9, 1996.

312   "The first thing I'd like to say"   Ibid.

313   "In the court's view"   Ibid.

313   "a persistent misunderstanding"   Order by Judge Michael, January 8, 1997.

314   "the penalty is not severe enough"   Quoted in Todd Nelson, "Judge Vetoes Plea Bargain in Map Case: The Plea Arrangement for a Man Who Admitted Taking Papers from UNC-CH

Is Termed Too Lenient," Raleigh, N.C., *News & Observer* (December 20, 1996): 1B.

322   "I think the biggest punishment"   Paul R. Thomson, Jr., in transcript of sentencing hearing in *United States of America vs. Gilbert Joseph Bland*, December 9, 1996.

322   "To discover is to draw the veil"   Mauricio Obregón, "Why Columbus?" in *The Columbus Papers: The Barcelona Letter of 1493, the Landfall Controversy, and the Indian Guides*, ed. Mauricio Obregón (New York: Macmillan, 1991), p. 3.

323   literally millions of people   See Adam Hochschild, *King Leopold's Ghost: A Story of Greed, Terror, and Heroism in Colonial Africa* (Boston: Houghton Mifflin, 1998), pp. 225–234. Hochschild estimates that through murder, starvation, exhaustion, exposure, disease, and declining birthrates, the population in the Congo Free State declined by 10 million as a result of Leopold's brutal policies.

323   "a genuine interest"   James R. Creekmore, letter to author, October 30, 1996.

325   "Nature conceives of innumerable things"   Quoted in Peter Whitfield, *The Image of the World: Twenty Centuries of World Maps* (San Francisco: Pomegranate Artbooks, 1994), p. 2.

EPILOGUE: LIFTING OFF

328   "I can see the whole state"   Quoted in John Noble Wilford, *The Mapmakers* (New York: Alfred A. Knopf, 1981), p. ix.

332   "The authorities never contacted me"   Although this source did not request anonymity—and although he was well aware

that I was a journalist working on the Bland story—I have chosen not to mention his name, since his comments did not
occur within the context of a formal interview.

341   "I'm under [psychiatric] medicine"   University of Delaware
videotape of Gilbert Bland, March 27, 1997.

344   The most telling picture I ever saw   See Corey Lowenstein's
photo accompanying Jay Price's story, "Quiet Appearance for
Map Thief," Raleigh, N.C., *News & Observer* (July 2, 1996): 1B.

345   "the world's most powerful civilian spacecraft"   William J.
Broad, "Private Spy in Space to Rival Military's," *New York
Times* (April 27, 1999): D1–2.

345   "We find ourselves in the midst"   Stephen S. Hall, *Mapping
the Next Millennium: The Discovery of New Geographies* (New
York: Random House, 1992), p. 6.

345   "It's like being able to drain"   The oceanographer David
Sandwell, quoted in Ken Miller, "Spy Data Gives First Clear
View of Sea Floor," Gannet News Service (October 23, 1995).
See also Earl Lane, "Bottom of Sea Viewed in Detail: Navy
Satellite Helps Map Oceans' Floors," *Newsday* (October 24,
1995): A17.

345   Sloan Digital Sky Survey   See Kelly Campbell, "What's Next:
A 3-D Map of 1 Billion Light Years," *Newsday* (September 29,
1998): C13; Charles W. Petit, "Mapping the Heavens," *U.S.
News & World Report,* vol. 124, no. 22 (June 22, 1998): 56; and
Alexandra Witze, "The Big Picture," *Dallas Morning News*
(April 27, 1998): 6D.

346   create life-forms   See Roger Highfield, "We Can Create
Life, Says Scientist," *Daily Telegraph* of London (January 25,
1999).

347   "opening up the territory of the mind"   Rita Carter, *Mapping the Mind* (Berkeley and Los Angeles: University of California Press, 1998), p. 6.

347   "an individual's state of mind"   Ibid., pp. 6–7.

348   "These are the early days"   Ibid., p. 8.

349   They never found it   Although investigators never located the satellite, they believe that they know what happened to it. In reviewing the mishap, a panel of experts concluded that, because of an electrical problem, the aerodynamic covering over the payload failed to come off properly. Because the covering did not fall away from the rocket, the satellite was probably dragged back down into the atmosphere, where it burned up. Another *Ikonos* satellite was launched—successfully—on September 24, 1999.

Index

Page numbers in italics refer to illustrations.

About the Author

MILES HARVEY is a correspondent
for *Outside* and a contributing
editor for *In These Times.*
He lives in Chicago with his wife
and daughter. He can be reached
on the Web at www.milesharvey.com.

025.8 HAR Harvey Mi
Harvey, Miles
island of lost maps, The : a true story of
cartographic crime

DATE DUE			
4/18/28			

2019